IT Revolution Press, LLC
25 NW 23rd Pl, Suite 6314
Portland, OR 97210

First Edition

Printed in the United States of America

10 9 8 7 6 5 4 3 2 1

Cover design by Strauber Design Studio

Cover illustration by eboy

Book design by Mammoth Collective

ISBN: 978-1942788003

Library of Congress Control Number: 2016951904

For information about special discounts for bulk purchases
or for information on booking authors for an event,
please visit ITRevolution.com.

THE DEVOPS HANDBOOK

TABLE OF CONTENTS

THE DEVOPS HANDBOOK

Aha!

The journey to complete *The DevOps Handbook* has been a long one—it started with weekly working Skype calls between the co-authors in February of 2011, with the vision of creating a prescriptive guide that would serve as a companion to the as-yet unfinished book *The Phoenix Project: A Novel About IT, DevOps, and Helping Your Business Win*.

More than five years later, with over two thousand hours of work, *The DevOps Handbook* is finally here. Completing this book has been an extremely long process, although one that has been highly rewarding and full of incredible learning, with a scope that is much broader than we originally envisioned. Throughout the project, all the co-authors shared a belief that DevOps is genuinely important, formed in a personal "aha" moment much earlier in each of our professional careers, which I suspect many of our readers will resonate with.

Gene Kim

I've had the privilege of studying high-performing technology organizations since 1999, and one of the earliest findings was that boundary-spanning between the different functional groups of IT Operations, Information Security, and Development was critical to success. But I still remember the first time I saw the magnitude of the downward spiral that would result when these functions worked toward opposing goals.

It was 2006, and I had the opportunity to spend a week with the group who managed the outsourced IT Operations of a large airline reservation service. They described the downstream consequences of their large, annual software releases: each release would cause immense chaos and disruption for the outsourcer, as well as customers; there would be SLA (service level agreement) penalties, because of the customer-impacting outages; there would be layoffs of the most talented and experienced staff, because of the resulting profit short-falls; there would be much unplanned work and firefighting so that the remaining staff couldn't work on the ever-growing service request backlogs coming from customers; the contract would be held together by the heroics of middle management; and everyone felt that the contract would be doomed to be put out for re-bid in three years.

The sense of hopelessness and futility that resulted created for me the beginnings of a moral crusade. Development seemed to always be viewed as strategic, but IT Operations was viewed as tactical, often delegated away or outsourced entirely, only to return in five years in worse shape than it was first handed over.

For many years, many of us knew that there must be a better way. I remember seeing the talks coming out of the 2009 Velocity Conference, describing amazing outcomes enabled by architecture, technical practices, and cultural norms that we now know as DevOps. I was so excited, because it clearly pointed to the better way that we had all been searching for. And helping spread that word was one of my personal motivations to co-author *The Phoenix Project*. You can imagine how incredibly rewarding it was to see the broader community react to that book, describing how it helped them achieve their own "aha" moments.

Jez Humble
My DevOps "aha" moment was at a start-up in 2000—my first job after graduating. For some time, I was one of two technical staff. I did everything: networking, programming, support, systems adminis-tration. We deployed software to production by FTP directly from our workstations.

Then in 2004 I got a job at ThoughtWorks, a consultancy where my first gig was working on a project involving about seventy people. I was on a team of eight engineers whose full-time job was to deploy our software into a production-like environment. In the beginning, it was really stressful. But over a few months we went from manual deployments that took two weeks to an automated deployment that took one hour, where we could roll forward and back in milliseconds using the blue-green deployment pattern during normal business hours.

That project inspired a lot of the ideas in both the *Continuous Delivery* (Addison-Wesley, 2000) book and this one. A lot of what drives me and others working in this space is the knowledge that, whatever your constraints, we can always do better, and the desire to help people on their journey.

Patrick Debois
For me, it was a collection of moments. In 2007 I was working on a data center migration project with some Agile teams. I was jealous that they had such high productivity—able to get so much done in so little time.

For my next assignment, I started experimenting with Kanban in Operations and saw how the dynamic of the team changed. Later, at the Agile Toronto 2008 conference I presented my IEEE paper on this, but I felt it didn't resonate widely in the Agile community. We started an Agile system administration group, but I overlooked the human side of things.

After seeing the 2009 Velocity Conference presentation "10 Deploys per Day" by John Allspaw and Paul Hammond, I was convinced others were thinking in a similar way. So I decided to organize the first DevOpsDays, accidently coining the term DevOps.

The energy at the event was unique and contagious. When people started to thank me because it changed their life for the better, I understood the impact. I haven't stopped promoting DevOps since.

John Willis
In 2008, I had just sold a consulting business that focused on large-scale, legacy IT operations practices around configuration management and monitoring (Tivoli) when I first met Luke Kanies (the founder of Puppet Labs). Luke was giving a presentation on Puppet at an O'Reilly open source conference on configuration management (CM).

At first I was just hanging out at the back of the room killing time and thinking, "What could this twenty-year-old tell me about configuration management?" After all, I had literally been working my entire life at some of the largest enterprises in the world, helping them architect CM and other operations management solutions. However, about five minutes into his session, I moved up to the first row and realized everything I had been doing for the last twenty years was wrong. Luke was describing what I now call second generation CM.

After his session I had an opportunity to sit down and have coffee with him. I was totally sold on what we now call infrastructure as code. However, while we met for coffee, Luke started going even further, explaining his ideas. He started telling me he believed that operations was going to have to start behaving like software developers. They were going to have to keep their configurations in source control and adopt CI/CD delivery patterns for their workflow. Being the old IT Operations person at the time, I think I replied to him with something like, "That idea is going to sink like Led Zeppelin with Ops folk." (I was clearly wrong.)

Then about a year later in 2009 at another O'Reilly conference, Velocity, I saw Andrew Clay Shafer give a presentation on Agile Infrastructure. In his presentation, Andrew showed this iconic picture of a wall between developers and operations with a metaphorical depiction of work being thrown over the wall. He coined this "the wall of confusion." The ideas he expressed in that presentation codified what Luke was trying to tell me a year earlier. That was the light bulb for me. Later that year, I was the only American invited to the original DevOpsDays in Ghent. By the time that event was over, this thing we call DevOps was clearly in my blood.

Clearly, the co-authors of this book all came to a similar epiphany, even if they came there from very different directions. But there is now an overwhelming weight of evidence that the problems described above happen almost everywhere, and that the solutions associated with DevOps are nearly universally applicable.

The goal of writing this book is to describe how to replicate the DevOps transformations we've been a part of or have observed, as well as dispel many of the myths of why DevOps won't work in certain situations. Below are some of the most common myths we hear about DevOps.

Myth—*DevOps is Only for Startups:* While DevOps practices have been pioneered by the web-scale, Internet "unicorn" companies such as Google, Amazon, Netflix, and Etsy, each of these organizations has, at some point in their history, risked going out of business because of the problems associated with more traditional "horse" organizations: highly dangerous code releases that were prone to catastrophic failure, inability to release features fast enough to beat the competition, compliance concerns, an inability to scale, high levels of distrust between Development and Operations, and so forth.

However, each of these organizations was able to transform their architecture, technical practices, and culture to create the amazing outcomes that we associate with DevOps. As Dr. Branden Williams, an information security executive, quipped, "Let there be no more talk of DevOps unicorns or horses but only thoroughbreds and horses heading to the glue factory."

Myth—*DevOps Replaces Agile*: DevOps principles and practices are compatible with Agile, with many observing that DevOps is a logical continuation of the Agile journey that started in 2001. Agile often serves as an effective enabler of DevOps, because of its focus on small teams continually delivering high quality code to customers.

Many DevOps practices emerge if we continue to manage our work beyond the goal of "potentially shippable code" at the end of each iteration, extending it to having our code always in a deployable state, with developers checking into trunk daily, and that we demonstrate our features in production-like environments.

Myth—*DevOps is incompatible with ITIL*: Many view DevOps as a backlash to ITIL or ITSM (IT Service Management), which was originally published in 1989. ITIL has broadly influenced multiple generations of Ops practitioners, including one of the co-authors, and is an ever-evolving library of practices intended to codify the processes and practices that underpin world-class IT Operations, spanning service strategy, design, and support.

DevOps practices can be made compatible with ITIL process. However, to support the shorter lead times and higher deployment frequencies associated with DevOps, many areas of the ITIL processes become fully automated, solving many problems associated with the configuration and release management processes (e.g., keeping the configuration management database and definitive software libraries up to date). And because DevOps requires fast detection and recovery when service incidents occur, the ITIL disciplines of service design, incident, and problem management remain as relevant as ever.

Myth—*DevOps is Incompatible with Information Security and Compliance*: The absence of traditional controls (e.g., segregation of duty, change approval processes, manual security reviews at the end of the project) may dismay information security and compliance professionals.

However, that doesn't mean that DevOps organizations don't have effective controls. Instead of security and compliance activities only being performed at the end of the project, controls are integrated into every stage of daily work in the software development life cycle, resulting in better quality, security, and compliance outcomes.

Myth—*DevOps Means Eliminating IT Operations, or "NoOps:"* Many misinterpret DevOps as the complete elimination of the IT Operations function. However, this is rarely the case. While the nature of IT Operations work may change, it remains as important as ever. IT Operations collaborates far earlier in the software life cycle with Development, who continues to work with IT Operations long after the code has been deployed into production.

Instead of IT Operations doing manual work that comes from work tickets, it enables developer productivity through APIs and self-serviced platforms that create environments, test and deploy code, monitor and display production telemetry, and so forth. By doing this, IT Operations become more like Development (as do QA and Infosec), engaged in product development, where the product is the platform that developers use to safely, quickly, and securely test, deploy, and run their IT services in production.

Myth—*DevOps is Just "Infrastructure as Code" or Automation:* While many of the DevOps patterns shown in this book require automation, DevOps also requires cultural norms and an architecture that allows for the shared goals to be achieved throughout the IT value stream. This goes far beyond just automation. As Christopher Little, a technology executive and one of the earliest chroniclers of DevOps, wrote, "DevOps isn't about automation, just as astronomy isn't about telescopes."

Myth—*DevOps is Only for Open Source Software:* Although many DevOps success stories take place in organizations using software such as the LAMP stack (Linux, Apache, MySQL, PHP), achieving DevOps outcomes is independent of the technology being used. Successes have been achieved with applications written in Microsoft.NET, COBOL, and mainframe assembly code, as well as with SAP and even embedded systems (e.g., HP LaserJet firmware).

SPREADING THE AHA! MOMENT

Each of the authors has been inspired by the amazing innovations happening in the DevOps community and the outcomes they are creating: they are creating safe systems of work, and enabling small teams to quickly and independently develop and validate code that can be safely deployed to customers. Given our belief that DevOps is a manifestation of creating dynamic, learning organizations that continually reinforce high-trust cultural norms, it is inevitable that these organizations will continue to innovate and win in the marketplace.

It is our sincere hope that *The DevOps Handbook* will serve as a valuable resource for many people in different ways: a guide for planning and executing DevOps transformations, a set of case studies to research and learn from, a chronicle of the history of DevOps, a means to create a coalition that spans Product Owners, Architecture, Development, QA, IT Operations, and Information Security to achieve common goals, a way to get the highest levels of leadership support for DevOps initiatives, as well as a moral imperative to change the way we manage technology organizations to enable better effectiveness and efficiency, as well as enabling a happier and more humane work environment, helping everyone become lifelong learners—this not only helps everyone achieve their highest goals as human beings, but also helps their organizations win.

Foreword
John Allspaw, CTO, Etsy
Brooklyn, NY, August 2016

In the past, many fields of engineering have experienced a sort of notable evolution, continually "leveling-up" its understanding of its own work. While there are university curriculums and professional support organizations situated within specific disciplines of engineering (civil, mechanical, electrical, nuclear, etc.), the fact is, modern society needs all forms of engineering to recognize the benefits of and work in a multidisciplinary way.

Think about the design of a high-performance vehicle. Where does the work of a mechanical engineer end and the work of an electrical engineer begin? Where (and how, and when) should someone with domain knowledge of aerodynamics (who certainly would have well-formed opinions on the shape, size, and placement of windows) collaborate with an expert in passenger ergonomics? What about the chemical influences of fuel mixture and oil on the materials of the engine and transmission over the lifetime of the vehicle? There are other questions we can ask about the design of an automobile, but the end result is the same: success in modern technical endeavors absolutely requires multiple perspectives and expertise to collaborate.

In order for a field or discipline to progress and mature, it needs to reach a point where it can thoughtfully reflect on its origins, seek out a diverse set of perspectives on those reflections, and place that synthesis into a context that is useful for how the community pictures the future.

This book represents such a synthesis and should be seen as a seminal collection of perspectives on the (I will argue, still emerging and quickly evolving) field of software engineering and operations.

No matter what industry you are in, or what product or service your organization provides, this way of thinking is paramount and necessary for survival for every business and technology leader.

Imagine a world where product owners, Development, QA, IT Operations, and Infosec work together, not only to help each other, but also to ensure that the overall organization succeeds. By working toward a common goal, they enable the fast flow of planned work into production (e.g., performing tens, hundreds, or even thousands of code deploys per day), while achieving world-class stability, reliability, availability, and security.

In this world, cross-functional teams rigorously test their hypotheses of which features will most delight users and advance the organizational goals. They care not just about implementing user features, but also actively ensure their work flows smoothly and frequently through the entire value stream without causing chaos and disruption to IT Operations or any other internal or external customer.

Simultaneously, QA, IT Operations, and Infosec are always working on ways to reduce friction for the team, creating the work systems that enable developers to be more productive and get better outcomes. By adding the expertise of QA, IT Operations, and Infosec into delivery teams and automated self-service tools and platforms, teams are able to use that expertise in their daily work without being dependent on other teams.

This enables organizations to create a safe system of work, where small teams are able to quickly and independently develop, test, and deploy code and value quickly, safely, securely, and reliably to customers. This allows organizations to maximize developer productivity, enable organizational learning, create high employee satisfaction, and win in the marketplace.

These are the outcomes that result from DevOps. For most of us, this is not the world we live in. More often than not, the system we work in is broken, resulting in extremely poor outcomes that fall well short of our true potential. In our world, Development and IT Operations are adversaries; testing and Infosec activities happen only at the end of a project, too late to correct any problems found; and almost any critical activity requires too much manual effort and too many handoffs, leaving us to always be waiting. Not only does this contribute to extremely long lead times to get anything done, but the quality of our work, especially production deployments, is also problematic and chaotic, resulting in negative impacts to our customers and our business.

As a result, we fall far short of our goals, and the whole organization is dissatisfied with the performance of IT, resulting in budget reductions and frustrated, unhappy employees who feel powerless to change the process and its outcomes.[†] The solution? We need to change how we work; DevOps shows us the best way forward.

To better understand the potential of the DevOps revolution, let us look at the Manufacturing Revolution of the 1980s. By adopting Lean principles and practices, manufacturing organizations dramatically improved plant productivity, customer lead times, product quality, and customer satisfaction, enabling them to win in the marketplace.

Before the revolution, average manufacturing plant order lead times were six weeks, with fewer than 70% of orders being shipped on time. By 2005, with the widespread implementation of Lean practices, average product lead times had dropped to less than three weeks, and more than 95% of orders were being shipped on time. Organizations that did not implement Lean practices lost market share, and many went out of business entirely.

Similarly, the bar has been raised for delivering technology products and services—what was good enough in previous decades is not good enough now. For each of the last four decades, the cost and time required to develop and deploy strategic business capabilities and features has dropped by orders of magnitude. During the 1970s and 1980s, most new features required one to five years to develop and deploy, often costing tens of millions of dollars.

By the 2000's, because of advances in technology and the adoption of Agile principles and practices, the time required to develop new functionality had

---

† This is just a small sample of the problems found in typical IT organizations.

dropped to weeks or months, but deploying into production would still require weeks or months, often with catastrophic outcomes.

And by 2010, with the introduction of DevOps and the neverending commoditization of hardware, software, and now the cloud, features (and even entire startup companies) could be created in weeks, quickly being deployed into production in just hours or minutes—for these organizations, deployment finally became routine and low risk. These organizations are able to perform experiments to test business ideas, discovering which ideas create the most value for customers and the organization as a whole, which are then further developed into features that can be rapidly and safely deployed into production.

Table 1. *The ever accelerating trend toward faster, cheaper, low-risk delivery of software*

	1970s–1980s	1990s	2000s–Present
Era	Mainframes	Client/Server	Commoditization and Cloud
Representative technology of era	COBOL, DB2 on MVS, etc.	C++, Oracle, Solaris, etc.	Java, MySQL, Red Hat, Ruby on Rails, PHP, etc.
Cycle time	1–5 years	3–12 months	2–12 weeks
Cost	$1M–$100M	$100k–$10M	$10k–$1M
At risk	The whole company	A product line or division	A product feature
Cost of failure	Bankruptcy, sell the company, massive layoffs	Revenue miss, CIO's job	Negligible

(Source: Adrian Cockcroft, "Velocity and Volume (or Speed Wins)," presentation at FlowCon, San Francisco, CA, November 2013.)

Today, organizations adopting DevOps principles and practices often deploy changes hundreds or even thousands of times per day. In an age where competitive advantage requires fast time to market and relentless experimentation, organizations that are unable to replicate these outcomes are destined to lose in the marketplace to more nimble competitors and could potentially go out of business entirely, much like the manufacturing organizations that did not adopt Lean principles.

These days, regardless of what industry we are competing in, the way we acquire customers and deliver value to them is dependent on the technology value stream. Put even more succinctly, as Jeffrey Immelt, CEO of General Electric, stated, "Every industry and company that is not bringing software to the core of their business will be disrupted." Or as Jeffrey Snover, Technical Fellow at Microsoft, said, "In previous economic eras, businesses created value by moving atoms. Now they create value by moving bits."

It's difficult to overstate the enormity of this problem—it affects every organization, independent of the industry we operate in, the size of our organization, whether we are profit or non-profit. Now more than ever, how technology work is managed and performed predicts whether our organizations will win in the marketplace, or even survive. In many cases, we will need to adopt principles and practices that look very different from those that have successfully guided us over the past decades. (See Appendix 1.)

Now that we have established the urgency of the problem that DevOps solves, let us take some time to explore in more detail the symptomatology of the problem, why it occurs, and why, without dramatic intervention, the problem worsens over time.

THE PROBLEM: SOMETHING IN YOUR ORGANIZATION MUST NEED IMPROVEMENT (OR YOU WOULDN'T BE READING THIS BOOK)

Most organizations are not able to deploy production changes in minutes or hours, instead requiring weeks or months. Nor are they able to deploy hundreds or thousands of changes into production per day; instead, they struggle to deploy monthly or even quarterly. Nor are production deployments routine, instead involving outages and chronic firefighting and heroics.

In an age where competitive advantage requires fast time to market, high service levels, and relentless experimentation, these organizations are at a significant competitive disadvantage. This is in large part due to their inability to resolve a core, chronic conflict within their technology organization.

THE CORE, CHRONIC CONFLICT
In almost every IT organization, there is an inherent conflict between Development and IT Operations which creates a downward spiral, resulting in

ever-slower time to market for new products and features, reduced quality, increased outages, and, worst of all, an ever-increasing amount of technical debt.

The term "technical debt" was first coined by Ward Cunningham. Analogous to financial debt, technical debt describes how decisions we make lead to problems that get increasingly more difficult to fix over time, continually reducing our available options in the future—even when taken on judiciously, we still incur interest.

One factor that contributes to this is the often competing goals of Development and IT Operations. IT organizations are responsible for many things. Among them are the two following goals, which must be pursued simultaneously:

- Respond to the rapidly changing competitive landscape

- Provide stable, reliable, and secure service to the customer

Frequently, Development will take responsibility for responding to changes in the market, deploying features and changes into production as quickly as possible. IT Operations will take responsibility for providing customers with IT service that is stable, reliable, and secure, making it difficult or even impossible for anyone to introduce production changes that could jeopardize production. Configured this way, Development and IT Operations have diametrically opposed goals and incentives.

Dr. Eliyahu M. Goldratt, one of the founders of the manufacturing management movement, called these types of configuration "the core, chronic conflict"— when organizational measurements and incentives across different silos prevent the achievement of global, organizational goals.[†]

This conflict creates a downward spiral so powerful it prevents the achievement of desired business outcomes, both inside and outside the IT organization. These chronic conflicts often put technology workers into situations that lead to poor software and service quality, and bad customer outcomes, as well as a daily need for workarounds, firefighting, and heroics, whether in Product

---

† In the manufacturing realm, a similar core, chronic conflict existed: the need to simultaneously ensure on-time shipments to customers and control costs. How this core, chronic conflict was broken is described in Appendix 2.

Management, Development, QA, IT Operations, or Information Security. (See Appendix 2.)

DOWNWARD SPIRAL IN THREE ACTS

The downward spiral in IT has three acts that are likely familiar to most IT practitioners.

The first act begins in IT Operations, where our goal is to keep applications and infrastructure running so that our organization can deliver value to customers. In our daily work, many of our problems are due to applications and infrastructure that are complex, poorly documented, and incredibly fragile. This is the technical debt and daily workarounds that we live with constantly, always promising that we'll fix the mess when we have a little more time. But that time never comes.

Alarmingly, our most fragile artifacts support either our most important revenue-generating systems or our most critical projects. In other words, the systems most prone to failure are also our most important and are at the epicenter of our most urgent changes. When these changes fail, they jeopardize our most important organizational promises, such as availability to customers, revenue goals, security of customer data, accurate financial reporting, and so forth.

The second act begins when somebody has to compensate for the latest broken promise—it could be a product manager promising a bigger, bolder feature to dazzle customers with or a business executive setting an even larger revenue target. Then, oblivious to what technology can or can't do, or what factors led to missing our earlier commitment, they commit the technology organization to deliver upon this new promise.

As a result, Development is tasked with another urgent project that inevitably requires solving new technical challenges and cutting corners to meet the promised release date, further adding to our technical debt—made, of course, with the promise that we'll fix any resulting problems when we have a little more time.

This sets the stage for the third and final act, where everything becomes just a little more difficult, bit by bit—everybody gets a little busier, work takes a little more time, communications become a little slower, and work queues get a little longer. Our work becomes more tightly coupled, smaller actions cause bigger failures, and we become more fearful and less tolerant of making changes. Work requires more communication, coordination, and approvals; teams must wait just a little longer for their dependent work to get done; and our quality keeps getting worse. The wheels begin grinding slower and require more effort to keep turning. (See Appendix 3.)

Although it's difficult to see in the moment, the downward spiral is obvious when one takes a step back. We notice that production code deployments are taking ever-longer to complete, moving from minutes to hours to days to weeks. And worse, the deployment outcomes have become even more problematic, that resulting in an ever-increasing number of customer-impacting outages that require more heroics and firefighting in Operations, further depriving them of their ability to pay down technical debt.

As a result, our product delivery cycles continue to move slower and slower, fewer projects are undertaken, and those that are, are less ambitious. Furthermore, the feedback on everyone's work becomes slower and weaker, especially the feedback signals from our customers. And, regardless of what we try, things seem to get worse—we are no longer able to respond quickly to our changing competitive landscape, nor are we able to provide stable, reliable service to our customers. As a result, we ultimately lose in the marketplace.

Time and time again, we learn that when IT fails, the entire organization fails. As Steven J. Spear noted in his book *The High-Velocity Edge*, whether the damages "unfold slowly like a wasting disease" or rapidly "like a fiery crash… the destruction can be just as complete."

WHY DOES THIS DOWNWARD SPIRAL HAPPEN EVERYWHERE?

For over a decade, the authors of this book have observed this destructive spiral occur in countless organizations of all types and sizes. We understand better than ever why this downward spiral occurs and why it requires DevOps principles to mitigate. First, as described earlier, every IT organization has two opposing goals, and second, every company is a technology company, whether they know it or not.

As Christopher Little, a software executive and one of the earliest chroniclers of DevOps, said, "Every company is a technology company, regardless of what business they think they're in. A bank is just an IT company with a banking license."[†]

---

† In 2013, the European bank HSBC employed more software developers than Google.

To convince ourselves that this is the case, consider that the vast majority of capital projects have some reliance upon IT. As the saying goes, "It is virtually impossible to make any business decision that doesn't result in at least one IT change."

In the business and finance context, projects are critical because they serve as the primary mechanism for change inside organizations. Projects are typically what management needs to approve, budget for, and be held accountable for; therefore, they are the mechanism that achieve the goals and aspirations of the organization, whether it is to grow or even shrink.[†]

Projects are typically funded through capital spending (i.e., factories, equipment, and major projects, and expenditures are capitalized when payback is expected to take years), of which 50% is now technology related. This is even true in "low tech" industry verticals with the lowest historical spending on technology, such as energy, metal, resource extraction, automotive, and construction. In other words, business leaders are far more reliant upon the effective management of IT in order to achieve their goals than they think.[‡]

THE COSTS: HUMAN AND ECONOMIC

When people are trapped in this downward spiral for years, especially those who are downstream of Development, they often feel stuck in a system that pre-ordains failure and leaves them powerless to change the outcomes. This powerlessness is often followed by burnout, with the associated feelings of fatigue, cynicism, and even hopelessness and despair.

Many psychologists assert that creating systems that cause feelings of powerlessness is one of the most damaging things we can do to fellow human beings—we deprive other people of their ability to control their own outcomes and even create a culture where people are afraid to do the right thing because of fear of punishment, failure, or jeopardizing their livelihood. This can create

---

† For now, let us suspend the discussion of whether software should be funded as a "project" or a "product." This is discussed later in the book.

‡ For instance, Dr. Vernon Richardson and his colleagues published this astonishing finding. They studied the 10-K SEC filings of 184 public corporations and divided them into three groups: A) firms with material weaknesses with IT-related deficiencies, B) firms with material weaknesses with no IT-related deficiencies, and C) "clean firms" with no material weaknesses. Firms in Group A saw eight times higher CEO turnover than Group C, and there was four times higher CFO turnover in Group A than in Group C. Clearly, IT may matter far more than we typically think.

the conditions of *learned helplessness*, where people become unwilling or unable to act in a way that avoids the same problem in the future.

For our employees, it means long hours, working on weekends, and a decreased quality of life, not just for the employee, but for everyone who depends on them, including family and friends. It is not surprising that when this occurs, we lose our best people (except for those that feel like they can't leave, because of a sense of duty or obligation).

In addition to the human suffering that comes with the current way of working, the opportunity cost of the value that we could be creating is staggering—the authors believe that we are missing out on approximately $2.6 trillion of value creation per year, which is, at the time of this writing, equivalent to the annual economic output of France, the sixth largest economy in the world.

Consider the following calculation—both IDC and Gartner estimated that in 2011, approximately 5% of the worldwide gross domestic product($3.1 trillion) was spent on IT (hardware, services, and telecom). If we estimate that 50% of that $3.1 trillion was spent on operating costs and maintaining existing systems, and that one-third of that 50% was spent on urgent and unplanned work or rework, approximately $520 billion was wasted.

If adopting DevOps could enable us, through better management and increased operational excellence, to halve that waste and redeploy that human potential into something that's five times the value (a modest proposal), we could create $2.6 trillion of value per year.

THE ETHICS OF DEVOPS: THERE IS A BETTER WAY

In the previous sections, we described the problems and the negative consequences of the status quo due to the core, chronic conflict, from the inability to achieve organizational goals, to the damage we inflict on fellow human beings. By solving these problems, DevOps astonishingly enables us to simultaneously improve organizational performance, achieve the goals of all the various functional technology roles (e.g., Development, QA, IT Operations, Infosec), and improve the human condition.

This exciting and rare combination may explain why DevOps has generated so much excitement and enthusiasm in so many in such a short time, including technology leaders, engineers, and much of the software ecosystem we reside in.

Ideally, small teams of developers independently implement their features, validate their correctness in production-like environments, and have their code deployed into production quickly, safely and securely. Code deployments are routine and predictable. Instead of starting deployments at midnight on Friday and spending all weekend working to complete them, deployments occur throughout the business day when everyone is already in the office and without our customers even noticing—except when they see new features and bug fixes that delight them. And, by deploying code in the middle of the workday, for the first time in decades IT Operations is working during normal business hours like everyone else.

By creating fast feedback loops at every step of the process, everyone can immediately see the effects of their actions. Whenever changes are committed into version control, fast automated tests are run in production-like environments, giving continual assurance that the code and environments operate as designed and are always in a secure and deployable state.

Automated testing helps developers discover their mistakes quickly (usually within minutes), which enables faster fixes as well as genuine learning—learning that is impossible when mistakes are discovered six months later during integration testing, when memories and the link between cause and effect have long faded. Instead of accruing technical debt, problems are fixed as they are found, mobilizing the entire organization if needed, because global goals outweigh local goals.

Pervasive production telemetry in both our code and production environments ensure that problems are detected and corrected quickly, confirming that everything is working as intended and customers are getting value from the software we create.

In this scenario, everyone feels productive—the architecture allows small teams to work safely and architecturally decoupled from the work of other teams who use self-service platforms that leverage the collective experience of Operations and Information Security. Instead of everyone waiting all the time, with large amounts of late, urgent rework, teams work independently and productively in small batches, quickly and frequently delivering new value to customers.

Even high-profile product and feature releases become routine by using dark launch techniques. Long before the launch date, we put all the required code for the feature into production, invisible to everyone except internal employees and small cohorts of real users, allowing us to test and evolve the feature until it achieves the desired business goal.

And, instead of firefighting for days or weeks to make the new functionality work, we merely change a feature toggle or configuration setting. This small change makes the new feature visible to ever-larger segments of customers, automatically rolling back if something goes wrong. As a result, our releases are controlled, predictable, reversible, and low stress.

It's not just feature releases that are calmer—all sorts of problems are being found and fixed early, when they are smaller, cheaper, and easier to correct. With every fix, we also generate organizational learnings, enabling us to prevent the problem from recurring and enabling us to detect and correct similar problems faster in the future.

Furthermore, everyone is constantly learning, fostering a hypothesis-driven culture where the scientific method is used to ensure nothing is taken for granted—we do nothing without measuring and treating product development and process improvement as experiments.

Because we value everyone's time, we don't spend years building features that our customers don't want, deploying code that doesn't work, or fixing something that isn't actually the cause of our problem.

Because we care about achieving goals, we create long-term teams that are responsible for meeting them. Instead of project teams where developers are reassigned and shuffled around after each release, never receiving feedback on their work, we keep teams intact so they can keep iterating and improving, using those learnings to better achieve their goals. This is equally true for the product teams who are solving problems for our external customers, as well as our internal platform teams who are helping other teams be more productive, safe, and secure.

Instead of a culture of fear, we have a high-trust, collaborative culture, where people are rewarded for taking risks. They are able to fearlessly talk about problems as opposed to hiding them or putting them on the backburner—after all, we must see problems in order to solve them.

And, because everyone fully owns the quality of their work, everyone builds automated testing into their daily work and uses peer reviews to gain confidence that problems are addressed long before they can impact a customer. These processes mitigate risk, as opposed to approvals from distant authorities, allowing us to deliver value quickly, reliably, and securely—even proving to skeptical auditors that we have an effective system of internal controls.

And when something does go wrong, we conduct *blameless post-mortems*, not to punish anyone, but to better understand what caused the accident and how to prevent it. This ritual reinforces our culture of learning. We also hold internal technology conferences to elevate our skills and ensure that everyone is always teaching and learning.

Because we care about quality, we even inject faults into our production environment so we can learn how our system fails in a planned manner. We conduct planned exercises to practice large-scale failures, randomly kill processes and compute servers in production, and inject network latencies and other nefarious acts to ensure we grow ever more resilient. By doing this, we enable better resilience, as well as organizational learning and improvement.

In this world, everyone has ownership in their work, regardless of their role in the technology organization They have confidence that their work matters and is meaningfully contributing to organizational goals, proven by their low-stress work environment and their organization's success in the marketplace. Their proof is that the organization is indeed winning in the marketplace.

THE BUSINESS VALUE OF DEVOPS

We have decisive evidence of the business value of DevOps. From 2013 through 2016, as part of Puppet Labs' *State Of DevOps Report,* to which authors Jez Humble and Gene Kim contributed, we collected data from over twenty-five thousand technology professionals, with the goal of better understanding the health and habits of organizations at all stages of DevOps adoption.

The first surprise this data revealed was how much high performing organizations using DevOps practices were outperforming their non–high performing peers in the following areas:

- Throughput metrics

- Code and change deployments (thirty times more frequent)

- Code and change deployment lead time (two hundred times faster)

- Reliability metrics

- Production deployments (sixty times higher change success rate)

- Mean time to restore service (168 times faster)

- Organizational performance metrics

- Productivity, market share, and profitability goals (two times more likely to exceed)

- Market capitalization growth (50% higher over three years)

In other words, high performers were both more agile and more reliable, providing empirical evidence that DevOps enables us to break the core, chronic conflict. High performers deployed code thirty times more frequently, and the time required to go from "code committed" to "successfully running in production" was two hundred times faster—high performers had lead times measured in minutes or hours, while low performers had lead times measured in weeks, months, or even quarters.

Furthermore, high performers were twice as likely to exceed profitability, market share, and productivity goals. And, for those organizations that provided a stock ticker symbol, we found that high performers had 50% higher market capitalization growth over three years. They also had higher employee job satisfaction, lower rates of employee burnout, and their employees were 2.2 times more likely to recommend their organization to friends as a great place to work.[†] High performers also had better information security outcomes. By integrating security objectives into all stages of the development and operations processes, they spent 50% less time remediating security issues.

DEVOPS HELPS SCALE DEVELOPER PRODUCTIVITY
When we increase the number of developers, individual developer productivity often significantly decreases due to communication, integration, and testing overhead. This is highlighted in the famous book by Frederick Brook, *The Mythical Man-Month*, where he explains that when projects are late, adding

---

† As measured by employee Net Promoter Score (eNPS). This is a significant finding, as research has shown that "companies with highly engaged workers grew revenues two and a half times as much as those with low engagement levels. And [publicly traded] stocks of companies with a high-trust work environment outperformed market indexes by a factor of three from 1997 through 2011."

more developers not only decreases individual developer productivity but also decreases overall productivity.

On the other hand, DevOps shows us that when we have the right architecture, the right technical practices, and the right cultural norms, small teams of developers are able to quickly, safely, and independently develop, integrate, test, and deploy changes into production. As Randy Shoup, formerly a director of engineering at Google, observed, large organizations using DevOps "have thousands of developers, but their architecture and practices enable small teams to still be incredibly productive, as if they were a startup."

The 2015 *State of DevOps Report* examined not only "deploys per day" but also "deploys per day per developer." We hypothesized that high performers would be able to scale their number of deployments as team sizes grew.

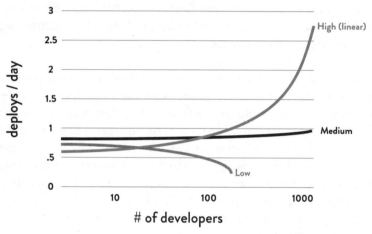

Figure 1. *Deployments/day vs. number of developers*
(Source: Puppet Labs, 2015 State Of DevOps Report.) [†]

Indeed, this is what we found. Figure 1 shows that in low performers, deploys per day per developer go down as team size increases, stays constant for medium performers, and increases linearly for high performers.

In other words, organizations adopting DevOps are able to linearly increase the number of deploys per day as they increase their number of developers, just as Google, Amazon, and Netflix have done. [‡]

---

† Only organizations that are deploying at least once per day are shown.

‡ Another more extreme example is Amazon. In 2011, Amazon was performing approximately seven thousand deploys per day. By 2015, they were performing 130,000 deploys per day.

THE UNIVERSALITY OF THE SOLUTION

One of the most influential books in the Lean manufacturing movement is *The Goal: A Process of Ongoing Improvement* written by Dr. Eliyahu M. Goldratt in 1984. It influenced an entire generation of professional plant managers around the world. It was a novel about a plant manager who had to fix his cost and product due date issues in ninety days, otherwise his plant would be shut down.

Later in his career, Dr. Goldratt described the letters he received in response to *The Goal*. These letters would typically read, "You have obviously been hiding in our factory, because you've described my life [as a plant manager] exactly…" Most importantly, these letters showed people were able to replicate the breakthroughs in performance that were described in the book in their own work environments.

The Phoenix Project: A Novel About IT, DevOps, and Helping Your Business Win, written by Gene Kim, Kevin Behr, and George Spafford in 2013, was closely modeled after *The Goal*. It is a novel that follows an IT leader who faces all the typical problems that are endemic in IT organizations: an over-budget, behind-schedule project that must get to market in order for the company to survive. He experiences catastrophic deployments; problems with availability, security, and compliance; and so forth. Ultimately, he and his team use DevOps principles and practices to overcome those challenges, helping their organization win in the marketplace. In addition, the novel shows how DevOps practices improved the workplace environment for the team, creating lower stress and higher satisfaction because of greater practitioner involvement throughout the process.

As with *The Goal*, there is tremendous evidence of the universality of the problems and solutions described in *The Phoenix Project*. Consider some of the statements found in the Amazon reviews: "I find myself relating to the characters in *The Phoenix Project*…I've probably met most of them over the course of my career," "If you have ever worked in any aspect of IT, DevOps, or Infosec you will definitely be able to relate to this book," or "There's not a character in *The Phoenix Project* that I don't identify with myself or someone I know in real life… not to mention the problems faced and overcome by those characters."

In the remainder of this book, we will describe how to replicate the transformation described in *The Phoenix Project*, as well provide many case studies of how other organizations have used DevOps principles and practices to replicate those outcomes.

THE DEVOPS HANDBOOK: AN ESSENTIAL GUIDE

The purpose of the *DevOps Handbook* is to give you the theory, principles, and practices you need to successfully start your DevOps initiative and achieve your desired outcomes. This guidance is based on decades of sound management theory, study of high performing technology organizations, work we have done helping organizations transform, and research that validates the effectiveness of the prescribed DevOps practices. As well as interviews with relevant subject matter experts and analyses of nearly one hundred case studies presented at the DevOps Enterprise Summit.

Broken into six parts, this book covers DevOps theories and principles using the Three Ways, a specific view of the underpinning theory originally introduced in *The Phoenix Project*. *The DevOps Handbook* is for everyone who performs or influences work in the technology value stream (which typically includes Product Management, Development, QA, IT Operations, and Information Security), as well as for business and marketing leadership, where most technology initiatives originate.

The reader is not expected to have extensive knowledge of any of these domains, or of DevOps, Agile, ITIL, Lean, or process improvement. Each of these topics is introduced and explained in the book as it becomes necessary.

Our intent is to create a working knowledge of the critical concepts in each of these domains, both to serve as a primer and to introduce the language necessary to help practitioners work with all their peers across the entire IT value stream, and to frame shared goals.

This book will be of value to business leaders and stakeholders who are increasingly reliant upon the technology organization for the achievement of their goals.

Furthermore, this book is intended for readers whose organizations might not be experiencing all the problems described in the book (e.g., long deployment lead times or painful deployments). Even readers in this fortunate position will benefit from understanding DevOps principles, especially those relating to shared goals, feedback, and continual learning.

In Part I, we present a brief history of DevOps and introduce the underpinning theory and key themes from relevant bodies of knowledge that span over decades. We then present the high level principles of the Three Ways: Flow, Feedback, and Continual Learning and Experimentaion.

Part II describes how and where to start, and presents concepts such as value streams, organizational design principles and patterns, organizational adoption patterns, and case studies.

Part III describes how to accelerate Flow by building the foundations of our deployment pipeline: enabling fast and effective automated testing, continuous integration, continuous delivery, and architecting for low-risk releases.

Part IV discusses how to accelerate and amplify Feedback by creating effective production telemetry to see and solve problems, better anticipate problems and achieve goals, enable feedback so that Dev and Ops can safely deploy changes, integrate A/B testing into our daily work, and create review and coordination processes to increase the quality of our work.

Part V describes how we accelerate Continual Learning by establishing a just culture, converting local discoveries into global improvements, and properly reserving time to create organizational learning and improvements.

Finally, in Part VI we describe how to properly integrate security and compliance into our daily work, by integrating preventative security controls into shared source code repositories and services, integrating security into our deployment pipeline, enhancing telemetry to better enable detection and recovery, protecting the deployment pipeline, and achieving change management objectives.

By codifying these practices, we hope to accelerate the adoption of DevOps practices, increase the success of DevOps initiatives, and lower the activation energy required for DevOps transformations.

PART I

The Three Ways

Part I
Introduction

In Part I of *The DevOps Handbook*, we will explore how the convergence of several important movements in management and technology set the stage for the DevOps movement. We describe value streams, how DevOps is the result of applying Lean principles to the technology value stream, and the Three Ways: Flow, Feedback, and Continual Learning and Experimentation.

Primary focuses within these chapters include:

- The principles of Flow, which accelerate the delivery of work from Development to Operations to our customers

- The principles of Feedback, which enable us to create ever safer systems of work

- The principles of Continual Learning and Experimentation foster a high-trust culture and a scientific approach to organizational improvement risk-taking as part of our daily work

A BRIEF HISTORY

DevOps and its resulting technical, architectural, and cultural practices represent a convergence of many philosophical and management movements. While many organizations have developed these principles independently, understanding that DevOps resulted from a broad stroke of movements, a phenomenon described by John Willis (one of the co-authors of this book) as the "convergence of DevOps," shows an amazing progression of thinking and improbable connections. There are decades of lessons learned from manufacturing, high reliability organization, high-trust management models, and others that have brought us to the DevOps practices we know today.

DevOps is the outcome of applying the most trusted principles from the domain of physical manufacturing and leadership to the IT value stream. DevOps relies on bodies of knowledge from Lean, Theory of Constraints, the Toyota Production System, resilience engineering, learning organizations, safety culture, human factors, and many others. Other valuable contexts that DevOps draws from include high-trust management cultures, servant leadership, and organizational change management. The result is world-class quality, reliability, stability, and security at ever lower cost and effort; and accelerated flow and reliability throughout the technology value stream, including Product Management, Development, QA, IT Operations, and Infosec.

While the foundation of DevOps can be seen as being derived from Lean, the Theory of Constraints, and the Toyota Kata movement, many also view DevOps as the logical continuation of the Agile software journey that began in 2001.

THE LEAN MOVEMENT

Techniques such as Value Stream Mapping, Kanban Boards, and Total Productive Maintenance were codified for the Toyota Production System in the 1980s. In 1997, the Lean Enterprise Institute started researching applications of Lean to other value streams, such as the service industry and healthcare.

Two of Lean's major tenets include the deeply held belief that *manufacturing lead time* required to convert raw materials into finished goods was the best predictor of quality, customer satisfaction, and employee happiness, and that one of the best predictors of short lead times was small batch sizes of work.

Lean principles focus on how to create value for the customer through systems thinking by creating constancy of purpose, embracing scientific thinking, creating flow and pull (versus push), assuring quality at the source, leading with humility, and respecting every individual.

THE AGILE MANIFESTO

The Agile Manifesto was created in 2001 by seventeen of the leading thinkers in software development. They wanted to create a lightweight set of values and principles against heavyweight software development processes such as waterfall development, and methodologies such as the Rational Unified Process.

One key principle was to "deliver working software frequently, from a couple of weeks to a couple of months, with a preference to the shorter timescale," emphasizing the desire for small batch sizes, incremental releases instead of large, waterfall releases. Other principles emphasized the need for small, self-motivated teams, working in a high-trust management model.

Agile is credited for dramatically increasing the productivity of many development organizations. And interestingly, many of the key moments in DevOps history also occurred within the Agile community or at Agile conferences, as described below.

AGILE INFRASTRUCTURE AND VELOCITY MOVEMENT

At the 2008 Agile conference in Toronto, Canada, Patrick Debois and Andrew Schafer held a "birds of a feather" session on applying Agile principles to infrastructure as opposed to application code. Although they were the only people who showed up, they rapidly gained a following of like-minded thinkers, including co-author John Willis.

Later, at the 2009 Velocity conference, John Allspaw and Paul Hammond gave the seminal "10 Deploys per Day: Dev and Ops Cooperation at Flickr" presentation, where they described how they created shared goals between Dev and Ops and used continuous integration practices to make deployment part of everyone's daily work. According to first hand accounts, everyone attending the presentation immediately knew they were in the presence of something profound and of historic significance.

Patrick Debois was not there, but was so excited by Allspaw and Hammond's idea that he created the first DevOpsDays in Ghent, Belgium, (where he lived) in 2009. There the term "DevOps" was coined.

THE CONTINUOUS DELIVERY MOVEMENT

Building upon the development discipline of continuous build, test, and integration, Jez Humble and David Farley extended the concept to *continuous delivery*, which defined the role of a "deployment pipeline" to ensure that code and infrastructure are always in a deployable state, and that all code checked in to trunk can be safely deployed into production. This idea was first presented at the 2006 Agile conference, and was also independently developed in 2009 by Tim Fitz in a blog post on his website titled "Continuous Deployment."[†]

TOYOTA KATA

In 2009, Mike Rother wrote *Toyota Kata: Managing People for Improvement, Adaptiveness and Superior Results,* which framed his twenty-year journey to understand and codify the Toyota Production System. He had been one of the graduate students who flew with GM executives to visit Toyota plants and helped develop the Lean toolkit, but he was puzzled when none of the companies adopting these practices replicated the level of performance observed at the Toyota plants.

He concluded that the Lean community missed the most important practice of all, which he called the *improvement kata.* He explains that every organization has work routines, and the improvement kata requires creating structure for the daily, habitual practice of improvement work, because daily practice is what improves outcomes. The constant cycle of establishing desired future states, setting weekly target outcomes, and the continual improvement of daily work is what guided improvement at Toyota.

The above describes the history of DevOps and relevant movements that it draws upon. Throughout the rest of Part I, we look at value streams, how Lean principles can be applied to the technology value stream, and the Three Ways of Flow, Feedback, and Continual Learning and Experimentation.

---

† DevOps also extends and builds upon the practices of *infrastructure as code*, which was pioneered by Dr. Mark Burgess, Luke Kanies, and Adam Jacob. In infrastructure as code, the work of Operations is automated and treated like application code, so that modern development practices can be applied to the entire development stream. This further enabled fast deployment flow, including continuous integration (pioneered by Grady Booch and integrated as one of the key 12 practices of Extreme Programming), continuous delivery (pioneered by Jez Humble and David Farley), and continuous deployment (pioneered by Etsy, Wealthfront, and Eric Ries's work at IMVU).

1 Agile, Continuous Delivery, and the Three Ways

In this chapter, an introduction to the underpinning theory of Lean Manufacturing is presented, as well as the Three Ways, the principles from which all of the observed DevOps behaviors can be derived.

Our focus here is primarily on theory and principles, describing many decades of lessons learned from manufacturing, high-reliability organizations, high-trust management models, and others, from which DevOps practices have been derived. The resulting concrete principles and patterns, and their practical application to the technology value stream, are presented in the remaining chapters of the book.

THE MANUFACTURING VALUE STREAM

One of the fundamental concepts in Lean is the *value stream*. We will define it first in the context of manufacturing and then extrapolate how it applies to DevOps and the technology value stream.

Karen Martin and Mike Osterling define value stream in their book *Value Stream Mapping: How to Visualize Work and Align Leadership for Organizational Transformation* as "the sequence of activities an organization undertakes to deliver upon a customer request," or "the sequence of activities required to design, produce, and deliver a good or service to a customer, including the dual flows of information and material."

In manufacturing operations, the value stream is often easy to see and observe: it starts when a customer order is received and the raw materials are released onto the plant floor. To enable fast and predictable lead times in any value stream, there is usually a relentless focus on creating a smooth and even flow of work, using techniques such as small batch sizes, reducing work in process

(WIP), preventing rework to ensure we don't pass defects to downstream work centers, and constantly optimizing our system toward our global goals.

THE TECHNOLOGY VALUE STREAM

The same principles and patterns that enable the fast flow of work in physical processes are equally applicable to technology work (and, for that matter, for all knowledge work). In DevOps, we typically define our technology value stream as the process required to convert a business hypothesis into a technology-enabled service that delivers value to the customer.

The input to our process is the formulation of a business objective, concept, idea, or hypothesis, and starts when we accept the work in Development, adding it to our committed backlog of work.

From there, Development teams that follow a typical Agile or iterative process will likely transform that idea into user stories and some sort of feature specification, which is then implemented in code into the application or service being built. The code is then checked in to the version control repository, where each change is integrated and tested with the rest of the software system.

Because value is created only when our services are running in production, we must ensure that we are not only delivering fast flow, but that our deployments can also be performed without causing chaos and disruptions such as service outages, service impairments, or security or compliance failures.

FOCUS ON DEPLOYMENT LEAD TIME

For the remainder of this book, our attention will be on deployment lead time, a subset of the value stream described above. This value stream begins when any engineer[†] in our value stream (which includes Development, QA, IT Operations, and Infosec) checks a change into version control and ends when that change is successfully running in production, providing value to the customer and generating useful feedback and telemetry.

The first phase of work that includes Design and Development is akin to Lean Product Development and is highly variable and highly uncertain, often requiring high degrees of creativity and work that may never be performed again, resulting in high variability of process times. In contrast, the second

---

† Going forward, *engineer* refers to anyone working in our value stream, not just developers.

phase of work, which includes Testing and Operations, is akin to Lean Manufacturing. It requires creativity and expertise, and strives to be predictable and mechanistic, with the goal of achieving work outputs with minimized variability (e.g., short and predictable lead times, near zero defects).

Instead of large batches of work being processed sequentially through the design/development value stream and then through the test/operations value stream (such as when we have a large batch waterfall process or long-lived feature branches), our goal is to have testing and operations happening simultaneously with design/development, enabling fast flow and high quality. This method succeeds when we work in small batches and build quality into every part of our value stream.[‡]

Defining Lead Time vs. Processing Time

In the Lean community, lead time is one of two measures commonly used to measure performance in value streams, with the other being processing time (sometimes known as touch time or task time).[§]

Whereas the lead time clock starts when the request is made and ends when it is fulfilled, the process time clock starts only when we begin work on the customer request—specifically, it omits the time that the work is in queue, waiting to be processed (figure 2).

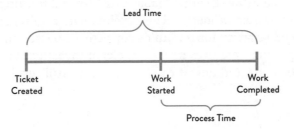

Figure 2. *Lead time vs. process time of a deployment operation*

Because lead time is what the customer experiences, we typically focus our process improvement attention there instead of on process time. However, the proportion of process time to lead time serves as an important measure

---

‡ In fact, with techniques such as test-driven development, testing occurs even before the first line of code is written.

§ In this book, the term *process time* will be favored for the same reason Karen Martin and Mike Osterling cite: "To minimize confusion, we avoid using the term cycle time as it has several definitions synonymous with processing time and pace or frequency of output, to name a few."

of efficiency—achieving fast flow and short lead times almost always requires reducing the time our work is waiting in queues.

The Common Scenario: Deployment Lead Times Requiring Months
In business as usual, we often find ourselves in situations where our deployment lead times require months. This is especially common in large, complex organizations that are working with tightly-coupled, monolithic applications, often with scarce integration test environments, long test and production environment lead times, high reliance on manual testing, and multiple required approval processes. When this occurs, our value stream may look like figure 3:

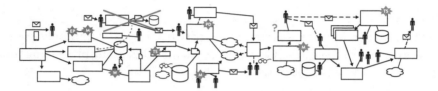

Figure 3: *A technology value stream with a deployment lead time of three months (Source: Damon Edwards, "DevOps Kaizen," 2015.)*

When we have long deployment lead times, heroics are required at almost every stage of the value stream. We may discover that nothing works at the end of the project when we merge all the development team's changes together, resulting in code that no longer builds correctly or passes any of our tests. Fixing each problem requires days or weeks of investigation to determine who broke the code and how it can be fixed, and still results in poor customer outcomes.

Our DevOps Ideal: Deployment Lead Times of Minutes
In the DevOps ideal, developers receive fast, constant feedback on their work, which enables them to quickly and independently implement, integrate, and validate their code, and have the code deployed into the production environment (either by deploying the code themselves or by others).

We achieve this by continually checking small code changes into our version control repository, performing automated and exploratory testing against it, and deploying it into production. This enables us to have a high degree of confidence that our changes will operate as designed in production and that any problems can be quickly detected and corrected.

This is most easily achieved when we have architecture that is modular, well encapsulated, and loosely-coupled so that small teams are able to work with high degrees of autonomy, with failures being small and contained, and without causing global disruptions.

In this scenario, our deployment lead time is measured in minutes, or, in the worst case, hours. Our resulting value stream map should look something like figure 4:

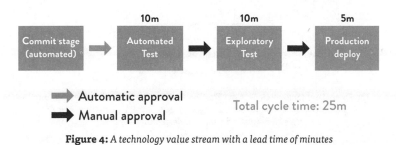

Figure 4: *A technology value stream with a lead time of minutes*

OBSERVING "%C/A" AS A MEASURE OF REWORK
In addition to lead times and process times, the third key metric in the technology value stream is percent complete and accurate (%C/A). This metric reflects the quality of the output of each step in our value stream. Karen Martin and Mike Osterling state that "the %C/A can be obtained by asking downstream customers what percentage of the time they receive work that is 'usable as is,' meaning that they can do their work without having to correct the information that was provided, add missing information that should have been supplied, or clarify information that should have and could have been clearer."

THE THREE WAYS: THE PRINCIPLES UNDERPINNING DEVOPS

The Phoenix Project presents the Three Ways as the set of underpinning principles from which all the observed DevOps behaviors and patterns are derived (figure 5).

The First Way enables fast left-to-right flow of work from Development to Operations to the customer. In order to maximize flow, we need to make work visible, reduce our batch sizes and intervals of work, build in quality by preventing defects from being passed to downstream work centers, and constantly optimize for the global goals.

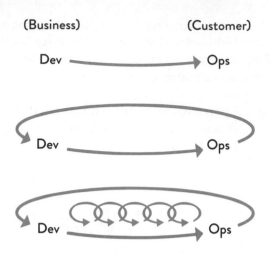

(Business)   (Customer)

Figure 5: *The Three Ways (Source: Gene Kim, "The Three Ways: The Principles Underpinning DevOps," IT Revolution Press blog, accessed August 9, 2016, http://itrevolution.com/ the-three-ways-principles-underpinning-devops/.)*

By speeding up flow through the technology value stream, we reduce the lead time required to fulfill internal or customer requests, especially the time required to deploy code into the production environment. By doing this, we increase the quality of work as well as our throughput, and boost our ability to out-experiment the competition.

The resulting practices include continuous build, integration, test, and deployment processes; creating environments on demand; limiting work in process (WIP); and building systems and organizations that are safe to change.

The Second Way enables the fast and constant flow of feedback from right to left at all stages of our value stream. It requires that we amplify feedback to prevent problems from happening again, or enable faster detection and recovery. By doing this, we create quality at the source and generate or embed knowledge where it is needed—this allows us to create ever-safer systems of work where problems are found and fixed long before a catastrophic failure occurs.

By seeing problems as they occur and swarming them until effective countermeasures are in place, we continually shorten and amplify our feedback loops, a core tenet of virtually all modern process improvement methodologies. This maximizes the opportunities for our organization to learn and improve.

The Third Way enables the creation of a generative, high-trust culture that supports a dynamic, disciplined, and scientific approach to experimentation and risk-taking, facilitating the creation of organizational learning, both from our successes and failures. Furthermore, by continually shortening and amplifying our feedback loops, we create ever-safer systems of work and are better able to take risks and perform experiments that help us learn faster than our competition and win in the marketplace.

As part of the Third Way, we also design our system of work so that we can multiply the effects of new knowledge, transforming local discoveries into global improvements. Regardless of where someone performs work, they do so with the cumulative and collective experience of everyone in the organization.

CONCLUSION

In this chapter, we described the concepts of value streams, lead time as one of the key measures of the effectiveness for both manufacturing and technology value streams, and the high-level concepts behind each of the Three Ways, the principles that underpin DevOps.

In the following chapters, the principles for each of the Three Ways are described in greater detail. The first of these principles is Flow, which is focused on how we create the fast flow of work in any value stream, whether it's in manufacturing or technology work. The practices that enable fast flow are described in Part III.

The First Way:
The Principles of Flow

In the technology value stream, work typically flows from Development to Operations, the functional areas between our business and our customers. The First Way requires the fast and smooth flow of work from Development to Operations, to deliver value to customers quickly. We optimize for this global goal instead of local goals, such as Development feature completion rates, test find/fix ratios, or Ops availability measures.

We increase flow by making work visible, by reducing batch sizes and intervals of work, and by building quality in, preventing defects from being passed to downstream work centers. By speeding up the flow through the technology value stream, we reduce the lead time required to fulfill internal and external customer requests, further increasing the quality of our work while making us more agile and able to out-experiment the competition.

Our goal is to decrease the amount of time required for changes to be deployed into production and to increase the reliability and quality of those services. Clues on how we do this in the technology value stream can be gleaned from how the Lean principles were applied to the manufacturing value stream.

MAKE OUR WORK VISIBLE

A significant difference between technology and manufacturing value streams is that our work is invisible. Unlike physical processes, in the technology value stream we cannot easily see where flow is being impeded or when work is piling up in front of constrained work centers. Transferring work between work centers is usually highly visible and slow because inventory must be physically moved.

However, in technology work the move can be done with a click of a button, such as by re-assigning a work ticket to another team. Because it is so easy, work can bounce between teams endlessly due to incomplete information, or work can be passed onto downstream work centers with problems that remain completely invisible until we are late delivering what we promised to the customer or our application fails in the production environment.

To help us see where work is flowing well and where work is queued or stalled, we need to make our work as visible as possible. One of the best methods of doing this is using visual work boards, such as kanban boards or sprint planning boards, where we can represent work on physical or electronic cards. Work originates on the left (often being pulled from a backlog), is pulled from work center to work center (represented in columns), and finishes when it reaches the right side of the board, usually in a column labeled "done" or "in production."

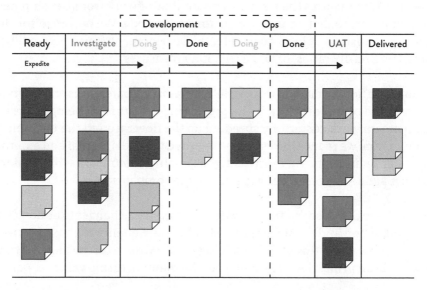

Figure 6: *An example kanban board, spanning Requirements, Dev, Test, Staging, and In Production (Source: David J. Andersen and Dominica DeGrandis, Kanban for ITOps, training materials for workshop, 2012.)*

Not only does our work become visible, we can also manage our work so that it flows from left to right as quickly as possible. Furthermore, we can measure lead time from when a card is placed on the board to when it is moved into the "Done" column.

Ideally, our kanban board will span the entire value stream, defining work as completed only when it reaches the right side of the board (figure 6). Work is not done when Development completes the implementation of a feature—

rather, it is only done when our application is running successfully in production, delivering value to the customer.

By putting all work for each work center in queues and making it visible, all stakeholders can more easily prioritize work in the context of global goals. Doing this enables each work center to single-task on the highest priority work until it is completed, increasing throughput.

LIMIT WORK IN PROCESS (WIP)

In manufacturing, daily work is typically dictated by a production schedule that is generated regularly (e.g., daily, weekly), establishing which jobs must be run based on customer orders, order due dates, parts available, and so forth.

In technology, our work is usually far more dynamic—this is especially the case in shared services, where teams must satisfy the demands of many different stakeholders. As a result, daily work becomes dominated by the priority *du jour*, often with requests for urgent work coming in through every communication mechanism possible, including ticketing systems, outage calls, emails, phone calls, chat rooms, and management escalations.

Disruptions in manufacturing are also highly visible and costly, often requiring breaking the current job and scrapping any incomplete work in process to start the new job. This high level of effort discourages frequent disruptions.

However, interrupting technology workers is easy, because the consequences are invisible to almost everyone, even though the negative impact to productivity may be far greater than in manufacturing. For instance, an engineer assigned to multiple projects must switch between tasks, incurring all the costs of having to re-establish context, as well as cognitive rules and goals.

Studies have shown that the time to complete even simple tasks, such as sorting geometric shapes, significantly degrades when multitasking. Of course, because our work in the technology value stream is far more cognitively complex than sorting geometric shapes, the effects of multitasking on process time is much worse.

We can limit multitasking when we use a kanban board to manage our work, such as by codifying and enforcing WIP (work in progress) limits for each column or work center that puts an upper limit on the number of cards that can be in a column.

For example, we may set a WIP limit of three cards for testing. When there are already three cards in the test lane, no new cards can be added to the lane unless a card is completed or removed from the "in work" column and put back into queue (i.e., putting the card back to the column to the left). Nothing can can be worked on until it is represented first in a work card, reinforcing that all work must be made visible.

Dominica DeGrandis, one of the leading experts on using kanbans in DevOps value streams, notes that "controlling queue size [WIP] is an extremely powerful management tool, as it is one of the few leading indicators of lead time—with most work items, we don't know how long it will take until it's actually completed."

Limiting WIP also makes it easier to see problems that prevent the completion of work.[†] For instance, when we limit WIP, we find that we may have nothing to do because we are waiting on someone else. Although it may be tempting to start new work (i.e., "It's better to be doing something than nothing"), a far better action would be to find out what is causing the delay and help fix that problem. Bad multitasking often occurs when people are assigned to multiple projects, resulting in many prioritization problems.

In other words, as David J. Andersen, author of *Kanban: Successful Evolutionary Change for Your Technology Business*, quipped, "Stop starting. Start finishing."

REDUCE BATCH SIZES

Another key component to creating smooth and fast flow is performing work in small batch sizes. Prior to the Lean manufacturing revolution, it was common practice to manufacture in large batch sizes (or lot sizes), especially for operations where job setup or switching between jobs was time-consuming or costly. For example, producing large car body panels requires setting large and heavy dies onto metal stamping machines, a process that could take days. When changeover cost is so expensive, we would often stamp as many panels at a time as possible, creating large batches in order to reduce the number of changeovers.

---

† Taiichi Ohno compared enforcing WIP limits to draining water from the river of inventory in order to reveal all the problems that obstruct fast flow.

However, large batch sizes result in skyrocketing levels of WIP and high levels of variability in flow that cascade through the entire manufacturing plant. The result is long lead times and poor quality—if a problem is found in one body panel, the entire batch has to be scrapped.

One of the key lessons in Lean is that in order to shrink lead times and increase quality, we must strive to continually shrink batch sizes. The theoretical lower limit for batch size is *single-piece flow*, where each operation is performed one unit at a time.[‡]

The dramatic differences between large and small batch sizes can be seen in the simple newsletter mailing simulation described in *Lean Thinking: Banish Waste and Create Wealth in Your Corporation* by James P. Womack and Daniel T. Jones.

Suppose in our own example we have ten brochures to send and mailing each brochure requires four steps: fold the paper, insert the paper into the envelope, seal the envelope, and stamp the envelope.

The large batch strategy (i.e., "mass production") would be to sequentially perform one operation on each of the ten brochures. In other words, we would first fold all ten sheets of paper, then insert each of them into envelopes, then seal all ten envelopes, and then stamp them.

On the other hand, in the small batch strategy (i.e., "single-piece flow"), all the steps required to complete each brochure are performed sequentially before starting on the next brochure. In other words, we fold one sheet of paper, insert it into the envelope, seal it, and stamp it—only then do we start the process over with the next sheet of paper.

The difference between using large and small batch sizes is dramatic (see figure 7). Suppose each of the four operations takes ten seconds for each of the ten envelopes. With the large batch size strategy, the first completed and stamped envelope is produced only after 310 seconds.

Worse, suppose we discover during the envelope sealing operation that we made an error in the first step of folding—in this case, the earliest we would discover the error is at two hundred seconds, and we have to refold and reinsert all ten brochures in our batch again.

---

‡ Also known as "batch size of one" or "1x1 flow," terms that refer to batch size and a WIP limit of one.

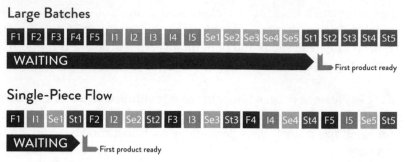

Figure 7: *Simulation of "envelope game" (fold, insert, seal, and stamp the envelope)*
(Source: Stefan Luyten, "Single Piece Flow: Why mass production isn't the most efficient way of doing 'stuff',"
Medium.com, August 8, 2014, https://medium.com/@stefanluyten/single-piece-flow-5d2c2bec845b#.9o7sn74ns.)

In contrast, in the small batch strategy the first completed stamped envelope is produced in only forty seconds, eight times faster than the large batch strategy. And, if we made an error in the first step, we only have to redo the one brochure in our batch. Small batch sizes result in less WIP, faster lead times, faster detection of errors, and less rework.

The negative outcomes associated with large batch sizes are just as relevant to the technology value stream as in manufacturing. Consider when we have an annual schedule for software releases, where an entire year's worth of code that Development has worked on is released to production deployment.

Like in manufacturing, this large batch release creates sudden, high levels of WIP and massive disruptions to all downstream work centers, resulting in poor flow and poor quality outcomes. This validates our common experience that the larger the change going into production, the more difficult the production errors are to diagnose and fix, and the longer they take to remediate.

In a post on *Startup Lessons Learned*, Eric Ries states, "The batch size is the unit at which work-products move between stages in a development [or DevOps] process. For software, the easiest batch to see is code. Every time an engineer checks in code, they are batching up a certain amount of work. There are many techniques for controlling these batches, ranging from the tiny batches needed for continuous deployment to more traditional branch-based development, where all of the code from multiple developers working for weeks or months is batched up and integrated together."

The equivalent to single piece flow in the technology value stream is realized with continuous deployment, where each change committed to version control is integrated, tested, and deployed into production. The practices that enable this are described in Part IV.

REDUCE THE NUMBER OF HANDOFFS

In the technology value stream, whenever we have long deployment lead times measured in months, it is often because there are hundreds (or even thousands) of operations required to move our code from version control into the production environment. To transmit code through the value stream requires multiple departments to work on a variety of tasks, including functional testing, integration testing, environment creation, server administration, storage administration, networking, load balancing, and information security.

Each time the work passes from team to team, we require all sorts of communication: requesting, specifying, signaling, coordinating, and often prioritizing, scheduling, deconflicting, testing, and verifying. This may require using different ticketing or project management systems; writing technical specification documents; communicating via meetings, emails, or phone calls; and using file system shares, FTP servers, and Wiki pages.

Each of these steps is a potential queue where work will wait when we rely on resources that are shared between different value streams (e.g., centralized operations). The lead times for these requests are often so long that there is constant escalation to have work performed within the needed timelines.

Even under the best circumstances, some knowledge is inevitably lost with each handoff. With enough handoffs, the work can completely lose the context of the problem being solved or the organizational goal being supported. For instance, a server administrator may see a newly created ticket requesting that user accounts be created, without knowing what application or service it's for, why it needs to be created, what all the dependencies are, or whether it's actually recurring work.

To mitigate these types of problems, we strive to reduce the number of handoffs, either by automating significant portions of the work or by reorganizing teams so they can deliver value to the customer themselves, instead of having to be constantly dependent on others. As a result, we increase flow by reducing the amount of time that our work spends waiting in queue, as well as the amount of non–value-added time. (See Appendix 4.)

CONTINUALLY IDENTIFY AND ELEVATE OUR CONSTRAINTS

To reduce lead times and increase throughput, we need to continually identify our system's constraints and improve its work capacity. In *Beyond the Goal*,

Dr. Goldratt states, "In any value stream, there is always a direction of flow, and there is always one and only constraint; any improvement not made at that constraint is an illusion." If we improve a work center that is positioned before the constraint, work will merely pile up at the bottleneck even faster, waiting for work to be performed by the bottlenecked work center.

On the other hand, if we improve a work center positioned *after* the bottleneck, it remains starved, waiting for work to clear the bottleneck. As a solution, Dr. Goldratt defined the "five focusing steps:"

- Identify the system's constraint.

- Decide how to exploit the system's constraint.

- Subordinate everything else to the above decisions.

- Elevate the system's constraint.

- If in the previous steps a constraint has been broken, go back to step one, but do not allow inertia to cause a system constraint.

In typical DevOps transformations, as we progress from deployment lead times measured in months or quarters to lead times measured in minutes, the constraint usually follows this progression:

- **Environment creation:** We cannot achieve deployments on-demand if we always have to wait weeks or months for production or test environments. The countermeasure is to create environments that are on demand and completely self-serviced, so that they are always available when we need them.

- **Code deployment:** We cannot achieve deployments on demand if each of our production code deployments take weeks or months to perform (i.e., each deployment requires 1,300 manual, error-prone steps, involving up to three hundred engineers). The countermeasure is to automate our deployments as much as possible, with the goal of being completely automated so they can be done self-service by any developer.

- **Test setup and run:** We cannot achieve deployments on demand if every code deployment requires two weeks to set up our test environments and data sets, and another four weeks to manually execute all our regression tests. The countermeasure is to automate our tests so we can execute deployments safely and to parallelize them so the test rate can keep up with our code development rate.

- **Overly tight architecture:** We cannot achieve deployments on demand if overly tight architecture means that every time we want to make a code change we have to send our engineers to scores of committee meetings in order to get permission to make our changes. Our countermeasure is to create more loosely coupled architecture so that changes can be made safely and with more autonomy, increasing developer productivity.

After all these constraints have been broken, our constraint will likely be Development or the product owners. Because our goal is to enable small teams of developers to independently develop, test, and deploy value to customers quickly and reliably, this is where we want our constraint to be. High performers, regardless of whether an engineer is in Development, QA, Ops, or Infosec, state that their goal is to help maximize developer productivity.

When the constraint is here, we are limited only by the number of good business hypotheses we create and our ability to develop the code necessary to test these hypotheses with real customers.

The progression of constraints listed above are generalizations of typical transformations—techniques to identify the constraint in actual value streams, such as through value stream mapping and measurements, are described later in this book.

ELIMINATE HARDSHIPS AND WASTE IN THE VALUE STREAM

Shigeo Shingo, one of the pioneers of the Toyota Production System, believed that waste constituted the largest threat to business viability—the commonly used definition in Lean is "the use of any material or resource beyond what the customer requires and is willing to pay for." He defined seven major types of manufacturing waste: inventory, overproduction, extra processing, transportation, waiting, motion, and defects.

More modern interpretations of Lean have noted that "eliminating waste" can have a demeaning and dehumanizing context; instead, the goal is reframed to reduce hardship and drudgery in our daily work through continual learning in order to achieve the organization's goals. For the remainder of this book, the term *waste* will imply this more modern definition, as it more closely matches the DevOps ideals and desired outcomes.

In the book *Implementing Lean Software Development: From Concept to Cash*, Mary and Tom Poppendieck describe waste and hardship in the software development stream as anything that causes delay for the customer, such as activities that can be bypassed without affecting the result.

The following categories of waste and hardship come from *Implementing Lean Software Development* unless otherwise noted:

- **Partially done work:** This includes any work in the value stream that has not been completed (e.g., requirement documents or change orders not yet reviewed) and work that is sitting in queue (e.g., waiting for QA review or server admin ticket). Partially done work becomes obsolete and loses value as time progresses.

- **Extra processes:** Any additional work that is being performed in a process that does not add value to the customer. This may include documentation not used in a downstream work center, or reviews or approvals that do not add value to the output. Extra processes add effort and increase lead times.

- **Extra features:** Features built into the service that are not needed by the organization or the customer (e.g., "gold plating"). Extra features add complexity and effort to testing and managing functionality.

- **Task switching:** When people are assigned to multiple projects and value streams, requiring them to context switch and manage dependencies between work, adding additional effort and time into the value stream.

- **Waiting:** Any delays between work requiring resources to wait until they can complete the current work. Delays increase cycle time and prevent the customer from getting value.

- **Motion:** The amount of effort to move information or materials from one work center to another. Motion waste can be created when people who need to communicate frequently are not colocated. Handoffs also create motion waste and often require additional communication to resolve ambiguities.

- **Defects:** Incorrect, missing, or unclear information, materials, or products create waste, as effort is needed to resolve these issues. The longer the time between defect creation and defect detection, the more difficult it is to resolve the defect.

- **Nonstandard or manual work:** Reliance on nonstandard or manual work from others, such as using non-rebuilding servers, test environments, and configurations. Ideally, any dependencies on Operations should be automated, self-serviced, and available on demand.

- **Heroics:** In order for an organization to achieve goals, individuals and teams are put in a position where they must perform unreasonable acts, which may even become a part of their daily work (e.g., nightly 2:00 a.m. problems in production, creating hundreds of work tickets as part of every software release).[†]

Our goal is to make these wastes and hardships—anywhere heroics become necessary—visible, and to systematically do what is needed to alleviate or eliminate these burdens and hardships to achieve our goal of fast flow.

CONCLUSION

Improving flow through the technology value stream is essential to achieving DevOps outcomes. We do this by making work visible, limiting WIP, reducing batch sizes and the number of handoffs, continually identifying and evaluating our constraints, and eliminating hardships in our daily work.

The specific practices that enable fast flow in the DevOps value stream are presented in Part IV. In the next chapter, we present The Second Way: The Principles of Feedback.

---

† Although heroics is not included in the Poppendieck categories of waste, it is included here because of how often it occurs, especially in Operation shared services.

3 The Second Way:
The Principles of Feedback

While the First Way describes the principles that enable the fast flow of work from left to right, the Second Way describes the principles that enable the reciprocal fast and constant feedback from right to left at all stages of the value stream. Our goal is to create an ever safer and more resilient system of work.

This is especially important when working in complex systems, when the earliest opportunity to detect and correct errors is typically when a catastrophic event is underway, such as a manufacturing worker being hurt on the job or a nuclear reactor meltdown in progress.

In technology, our work happens almost entirely within complex systems with a high risk of catastrophic consequences. As in manufacturing, we often discover problems only when large failures are underway, such as a massive production outage or a security breach resulting in the theft of customer data.

We make our system of work safer by creating fast, frequent, high quality information flow throughout our value stream and our organization, which includes feedback and feedforward loops. This allows us to detect and remediate problems while they are smaller, cheaper, and easier to fix; avert problems before they cause catastrophe; and create organizational learning that we integrate into future work. When failures and accidents occur, we treat them as opportunities for learning, as opposed to a cause for punishment and blame. To achieve all of the above, let us first explore the nature of complex systems and how they can be made safer.

WORKING SAFELY WITHIN COMPLEX SYSTEMS

One of the defining characteristics of a complex system is that it defies any single person's ability to see the system as a whole and understand how all the pieces fit together. Complex systems typically have a high degree of interconnectedness of tightly coupled components, and system-level behavior cannot be explained merely in terms of the behavior of the system components.

Dr. Charles Perrow studied the Three Mile Island crisis and observed that it was impossible for anyone to understand how the reactor would behave in all circumstances and how it might fail. When a problem was underway in one component, it was difficult to isolate from the other components, quickly flowing through the paths of least resistance in unpredictable ways.

Dr. Sidney Dekker, who also codified some of the key elements of safety culture, observed another characteristic of complex systems: doing the same thing twice will not predictably or necessarily lead to the same result. It is this characteristic that makes static checklists and best practices, while valuable, insufficient to prevent catastrophes from occurring. (See Appendix 5.)

Therefore, because failure is inherent and inevitable in complex systems, we must design a safe system of work, whether in manufacturing or technology, where we can perform work without fear, confident that any errors will be detected quickly, long before they cause catastrophic outcomes, such as worker injury, product defects, or negative customer impact.

After he decoded the causal mechanism behind the Toyota Product System as part of his doctoral thesis at Harvard Business School, Dr. Steven Spear stated that designing perfectly safe systems is likely beyond our abilities, but we can make it safer to work in complex systems when the four following conditions are met:[†]

- Complex work is managed so that problems in design and operations are revealed

- Problems are swarmed and solved, resulting in quick construction of new knowledge

- New local knowledge is exploited globally throughout the organization

- Leaders create other leaders who continually grow these types of capabilities

---

† Dr. Spear extended his work to explain the long-lasting successes of other organizations, such as the Toyota supplier network, Alcoa, and the US Navy's Nuclear Power Propulsion Program.

Each of these capabilities are required to work safely in a complex system. In the next sections, the first two capabilities and their importance are described, as well as how they have been created in other domains and what practices enable them in the technology value stream. (The third and fourth capabilities are described in chapter 4.)

SEE PROBLEMS AS THEY OCCUR

In a safe system of work, we must constantly test our design and operating assumptions. Our goal is to increase information flow in our system from as many areas as possible, sooner, faster, cheaper, and with as much clarity between cause and effect as possible. The more assumptions we can invalidate, the faster we can find and fix problems, increasing our resilience, agility, and ability to learn and innovate.

We do this by creating feedback and feedforward loops into our system of work. Dr. Peter Senge in his book *The Fifth Discipline: The Art & Practice of the Learning Organization* described feedback loops as a critical part of learning organizations and systems thinking. Feedback and feedforward loops cause components within a system to reinforce or counteract each other.

In manufacturing, the absence of effective feedback often contribute to major quality and safety problems. In one well-documented case at the General Motors Fremont manufacturing plant, there were no effective procedures in place to detect problems during the assembly process, nor were there explicit procedures on what to do when problems were found. As a result, there were instances of engines being put in backward, cars missing steering wheels or tires, and cars even having to be towed off the assembly line because they wouldn't start.

In contrast, in high performing manufacturing operations there is fast, frequent, and high quality information flow throughout the entire value stream—every work operation is measured and monitored, and any defects or significant deviations are quickly found and acted upon. These are the foundation of what enables quality, safety, and continual learning and improvement.

In the technology value stream, we often get poor outcomes because of the absence of fast feedback. For instance, in a waterfall software project, we may develop code for an entire year and get no feedback on quality until we begin the testing phase—or worse, when we release our software to customers.

When feedback is this delayed and infrequent, it is too slow to enable us to prevent undesirable outcomes.

In contrast, our goal is to create fast feedback and fastforward loops wherever work is performed, at all stages of the technology value stream, encompassing Product Management, Development, QA, Infosec, and Operations. This includes the creation of automated build, integration, and test processes, so that we can immediately detect when a change has been introduced that takes us out of a correctly functioning and deployable state.

We also create pervasive telemetry so we can see how all our system components are operating in the production environment, so that we can quickly detect when they are not operating as expected. Telemetry also allows us to measure whether we are achieving our intended goals and, ideally, is radiated to the entire value stream so we can see how our actions affect other portions of the system as a whole.

Feedback loops not only enable quick detection and recovery of problems, but they also inform us on how to prevent these problems from occurring again in the future. Doing this increases the quality and safety of our system of work, and creates organizational learning.

As Elisabeth Hendrickson, VP of Engineering at Pivotal Software, Inc. and author of *Explore It!: Reduce Risk and Increase Confidence with Exploratory Testing*, said, "When I headed up quality engineering, I described my job as 'creating feedback cycles.' Feedback is critical because it is what allows us to steer. We must constantly validate between customer needs, our intentions and our implementations. Testing is merely one sort of feedback."

SWARM AND SOLVE PROBLEMS TO BUILD NEW KNOWLEDGE

Obviously, it is not sufficient to merely detect when the unexpected occurs. When problems occur, we must swarm them, mobilizing whoever is required to solve the problem.

According to Dr. Spear, the goal of swarming is to contain problems before they have a chance to spread, and to diagnose and treat the problem so that it cannot recur. "In doing so," he says, "they build ever-deeper knowledge about how to manage the systems for doing our work, converting inevitable up-front ignorance into knowledge."

The paragon of this principle is the Toyota *Andon cord*. In a Toyota manufacturing plant, above every work center is a cord that every worker and manager is trained to pull when something goes wrong; for example, when a part is defective, when a required part is not available, or even when work takes longer than documented.[†]

When the Andon cord is pulled, the team leader is alerted and immediately works to resolve the problem. If the problem cannot be resolved within a specified time (e.g., fifty-five seconds), the production line is halted so that the entire organization can be mobilized to assist with problem resolution until a successful countermeasure has been developed.

Instead of working around the problem or scheduling a fix "when we have more time," we swarm to fix it immediately—this is nearly the opposite of the behavior at the GM Fremont plant described earlier. Swarming is necessary for the following reasons:

- It prevents the problem from progressing downstream, where the cost and effort to repair it increases exponentially and technical debt is allowed to accumulate.

- It prevents the work center from starting new work, which will likely introduce new errors into the system.

- If the problem is not addressed, the work center could potentially have the same problem in the next operation (e.g., fifty-five seconds later), requiring more fixes and work. (See Appendix 6.)

This practice of swarming seems contrary to common management practice, as we are deliberately allowing a local problem to disrupt operations globally. However, swarming enables learning. It prevents the loss of critical information due to fading memories or changing circumstances. This is especially critical in complex systems, where many problems occur because of some unexpected, idiosyncratic interaction of people, processes, products, places, and circumstances—as time passes, it becomes impossible to reconstruct exactly what was going on when the problem occurred.

As Dr. Spear notes, swarming is part of the "disciplined cycle of real-time problem recognition, diagnosis,…and treatment (countermeasures or corrective measures in manufacturing vernacular). It [is] the discipline of the

---

† In some of its plants, Toyota has moved to using an Andon button.

Shewhart cycle—plan, do, check, act—popularized by W. Edwards Deming, but accelerated to warp speed."

It is only through the swarming of ever smaller problems discovered ever earlier in the life cycle that we can deflect problems before a catastrophe occurs. In other words, when the nuclear reactor melts down, it is already too late to avert worst outcomes.

To enable fast feedback in the technology value stream, we must create the equivalent of an Andon cord and the related swarming response. This requires that we also create the culture that makes it safe, and even encouraged, to pull the Andon cord when something goes wrong, whether it is when a production incident occurs or when errors occur earlier in the value stream, such as when someone introduces a change that breaks our continuous build or test processes.

When conditions trigger an Andon cord pull, we swarm to solve the problem and prevent the introduction of new work until the issue has been resolved.[†] This provides fast feedback for everyone in the value stream (especially the person who caused the system to fail), enables us to quickly isolate and diagnose the problem, and prevents further complicating factors that can obscure cause and effect.

Preventing the introduction of new work enables continuous integration and deployment, which is single-piece flow in the technology value stream. All changes that pass our continuous build and integration tests are deployed into production, and any changes that cause any tests to fail trigger our Andon cord and are swarmed until resolved.

KEEP PUSHING QUALITY CLOSER TO THE SOURCE

We may inadvertently perpetuate unsafe systems of work due to the way we respond to accidents and incidents. In complex systems, adding more inspection steps and approval processes actually increases the likelihood of future failures. The effectiveness of approval processes decreases as we push decision-making further away from where the work is performed. Doing so not only lowers the quality of decisions but also increases our cycle time, thus decreasing

---

† Astonishingly, when the number of Andon cord pulls drop, plant managers will actually decrease the tolerances to get an increase in the number of Andon cord pulls in order to continue to enable more learnings and improvements and to detect ever-weaker failure signals.

the strength of the feedback between cause and effect, and reducing our ability to learn from successes and failures.[‡]

This can be seen even in smaller and less complex systems. When top-down, bureaucratic command and control systems become ineffective, it is usually because the variance between "who should do something" and "who is actually doing something" is too large, due to insufficient clarity and timeliness.

Examples of ineffective quality controls include:

- Requiring another team to complete tedious, error-prone, and manual tasks that could be easily automated and run as needed by the team who needs the work performed

- Requiring approvals from busy people who are distant from the work, forcing them to make decisions without an adequate knowledge of the work or the potential implications, or to merely rubber stamp their approvals

- Creating large volumes of documentation of questionable detail which become obsolete shortly after they are written

- Pushing large batches of work to teams and special committees for approval and processing and then waiting for responses

Instead, we need everyone in our value stream to find and fix problems in their area of control as part of our daily work. By doing this, we push quality and safety responsibilities and decision-making to where the work is performed, instead of relying on approvals from distant executives.

We use peer reviews of our proposed changes to gain whatever assurance is needed that our changes will operate as designed. We automate as much of the quality checking typically performed by a QA or Information Security department as possible. Instead of developers needing to request or schedule

---

‡ In the 1700s, the British government engaged in a spectacular example of top-down, bureaucratic command and control, which proved remarkably ineffective. At the time, Georgia was still a colony, and despite the fact that the British government was three thousand miles away and lacked firsthand knowledge of local land chemistry, rockiness, topography, accessibility to water, and other conditions, it tried to plan Georgia's entire agricultural economy. The results of the attempt were dismal and left Georgia with the lowest levels of prosperity and population in the thirteen colonies.

a test to be run, these tests can be performed on demand, enabling developers to quickly test their own code and even deploy those changes into production themselves.

By doing this, we truly make quality everyone's responsibility as opposed to it being the sole responsibility of a separate department. Information security is not just Information Security's job, just as availability isn't merely the job of Operations.

Having developers share responsibility for the quality of the systems they build not only improves outcomes but also accelerates learning. This is especially important for developers as they are typically the team that is furthest removed from the customer. As Gary Gruver observes, "It's impossible for a developer to learn anything when someone yells at them for something they broke six months ago—that's why we need to provide feedback to everyone as quickly as possible, in minutes, not months."

ENABLE OPTIMIZING FOR DOWNSTREAM WORK CENTERS

In the 1980s, Designing for Manufacturability principles sought to design parts and processes so that finished goods could be created with the lowest cost, highest quality, and fastest flow. Examples include designing parts that are wildly asymmetrical to prevent them from being put on backwards, and designing screw fasteners so that they are impossible to over-tighten.

This was a departure from how design was typically done, which focused on the external customers but overlooked internal stakeholders, such as the people performing the manufacturing.

Lean defines two types of customers that we must design for: the external customer (who most likely pays for the service we are delivering) and the internal customer (who receives and processes the work immediately after us). According to Lean, our most important customer is our next step downstream. Optimizing our work for them requires that we have empathy for their problems in order to better identify the design problems that prevent fast and smooth flow.

In the technology value stream, we optimize for downstream work centers by designing for operations, where operational non-functional requirements (e.g., architecture, performance, stability, testability, configurability, and security) are prioritized as highly as user features.

By doing this, we create quality at the source, likely resulting in a set of codified non-functional requirements that we can proactively integrate into every service we build.

CONCLUSION

Creating fast feedback is critical to achieving quality, reliability, and safety in the technology value stream. We do this by seeing problems as they occur, swarming and solving problems to build new knowledge, pushing quality closer to the source, and continually optimizing for downstream work centers.

The specific practices that enable fast flow in the DevOps value stream are presented in Part IV. In the next chapter, we present the Third Way, the Principles of Feedback

4

The Third Way:
The Principles of Continual Learning and Experimentation

While the First Way addresses work flow from left to right and the Second Way addresses the reciprocal fast and constant feedback from right to left, the Third Way focuses on creating a culture of continual learning and experimentation. These are the principles that enable constant creation of individual knowledge, which is then turned into team and organizational knowledge.

In manufacturing operations with systemic quality and safety problems, work is typically rigidly defined and enforced. For instance, in the GM Fremont plant described in the previous chapter, workers had little ability to integrate improvements and learnings into their daily work, with suggestions for improvement "apt to meet a brick wall of indifference."

In these environments, there is also often a culture of fear and low trust, where workers who make mistakes are punished, and those who make suggestions or point out problems are viewed as whistle-blowers and troublemakers. When this occurs, leadership is actively suppressing, even punishing, learning and improvement, perpetuating quality and safety problems.

In contrast, high-performing manufacturing operations require and actively promote learning—instead of work being rigidly defined, the system of work is dynamic, with line workers performing experiments in their daily work to generate new improvements, enabled by rigorous standardization of work procedures and documentation of the results.

In the technology value stream, our goal is to create a high-trust culture, reinforcing that we are all lifelong learners who must take risks in our daily work. By applying a scientific approach to both process improvement and product development, we learn from our successes and failures, identifying which ideas don't work and reinforcing those that do. Moreover, any local learnings are rapidly turned into global improvements, so that new techniques and practices can be used by the entire organization.

We reserve time for the improvement of daily work and to further accelerate and ensure learning. We consistently introduce stress into our systems to force continual improvement. We even simulate and inject failures in our production services under controlled conditions to increase our resilience.

By creating this continual and dynamic system of learning, we enable teams to rapidly and automatically adapt to an ever-changing environment, which ultimately helps us win in the marketplace.

ENABLING ORGANIZATIONAL LEARNING AND A SAFETY CULTURE

When we work within a complex system, by definition it is impossible for us to perfectly predict all the outcomes for any action we take. This is what contributes to unexpected, or even catastrophic, outcomes and accidents in our daily work, even when we take precautions and work carefully.

When these accidents affect our customers, we seek to understand why it happened. The root cause is often deemed to be human error, and the all too common management response is to "name, blame, and shame" the person who caused the problem.[†] And, either subtly or explicitly, management hints that the person guilty of committing the error will be punished. They then create more processes and approvals to prevent the error from happening again.

Dr. Sidney Dekker, who codified some of the key elements of safety culture and coined the term *just culture*, wrote, "Responses to incidents and accidents that are seen as unjust can impede safety investigations, promote fear rather than mindfulness in people who do safety-critical work, make organizations more bureaucratic rather than more careful, and cultivate professional secrecy, evasion, and self-protection."

These issues are especially problematic in the technology value stream—our work is almost always performed within a complex system, and how management chooses to react to failures and accidents leads to a culture of fear,

---

† The "name, blame, shame" pattern is part of the Bad Apple Theory criticized by Dr. Sydney Dekker and extensively discussed in his book *The Field Guide to Understanding Human Error*.

which then makes it unlikely that problems and failure signals are ever reported. The result is that problems remain hidden until a catastrophe occurs.

Dr. Ron Westrum was one of the first to observe the importance of organizational culture on safety and performance. He observed that in healthcare organizations, the presence of "generative" cultures was one of the top predictors of patient safety. Dr. Westrum defined three types of culture:

- Pathological organizations are characterized by large amounts of fear and threat. People often hoard information, withhold it for political reasons, or distort it to make themselves look better. Failure is often hidden.

- Bureaucratic organizations are characterized by rules and processes, often to help individual departments maintain their "turf." Failure is processed through a system of judgment, resulting in either punishment or justice and mercy.

- Generative organizations are characterized by actively seeking and sharing information to better enable the organization to achieve its mission. Responsibilities are shared throughout the value stream, and failure results in reflection and genuine inquiry.

Pathological	Bureaucratic	Generative
Information is hidden	Information may be ignored	Information is actively sought
Messengers are "shot"	Messengers are tolerated	Messengers are trained
Responsibilities are shirked	Responsibilities are compartmented	Responsibilities are shared
Bridging between teams is discouraged	Bridging between teams is allowed but discouraged	Bridging between teams is rewarded
Failure is covered up	Organizatoin is just and merciful	Failure causes inquiry
New ideas are crushed	New ideas create problems	New ideas are weclomed

Figure 8: *The Westrum organizational typology model: how organizations process information (Source: Ron Westrum, "A typology of organisation culture," BMJ Quality & Safety 13, no. 2 (2004), doi:10.1136/qshc.2003.009522.)*

Just as Dr. Westrum found in healthcare organizations, a high-trust, generative culture also predicted IT and organizational performance in technology value streams.

In the technology value stream, we establish the foundations of a generative culture by striving to create a safe system of work. When accidents and failures occur, instead of looking for human error, we look for how we can redesign the system to prevent the accident from happening again.

For instance, we may conduct a blameless post-mortem after every incident to gain the best understanding of how the accident occurred and agree upon what the best countermeasures are to improve the system, ideally preventing the problem from occurring again and enabling faster detection and recovery.

By doing this, we create organizational learning. As Bethany Macri, an engineer at Etsy who led the creation of the Morgue tool to help with recording of post-mortems, stated, "By removing blame, you remove fear; by removing fear, you enable honesty; and honesty enables prevention."

Dr. Spear observes that the result of removing blame and putting organizational learning in its place is that "organizations become ever more self-diagnosing and self-improving, skilled at detecting problems [and] solving them."

Many of these attributes were also described by Dr. Senge as attributes of learning organizations. In *The Fifth Discipline,* he wrote that these characteristics help customers, ensure quality, create competitive advantage and an energized and committed workforce, and uncover the truth.

INSTITUTIONALIZE THE IMPROVEMENT OF DAILY WORK

Teams are often not able or not willing to improve the processes they operate within. The result is not only that they continue to suffer from their current problems, but their suffering also grows worse over time. Mike Rother observed in *Toyota Kata* that in the absence of improvements, processes don't stay the same—due to chaos and entropy, processes actually degrade over time.

In the technology value stream, when we avoid fixing our problems, relying on daily workarounds, our problems and technical debt accumulates until all we are doing is performing workarounds, trying to avoid disaster, with no cycles leftover for doing productive work. This is why Mike Orzen, author of

Lean IT, observed, "Even more important than daily work is the improvement of daily work."

We improve daily work by explicitly reserving time to pay down technical debt, fix defects, and refactor and improve problematic areas of our code and environments—we do this by reserving cycles in each development interval, or by scheduling *kaizen blitzes*, which are periods when engineers self-organize into teams to work on fixing any problem they want.

The result of these practices is that everyone finds and fixes problems in their area of control, all the time, as part of their daily work. When we finally fix the daily problems that we've worked around for months (or years), we can eradicate from our system the less obvious problems. By detecting and responding to these ever-weaker failure signals, we fix problems when it is not only easier and cheaper but also when the consequences are smaller.

Consider the following example that improved workplace safety at Alcoa, an aluminum manufacturer with $7.8 billion in revenue in 1987. Aluminum manufacturing requires extremely high heat, high pressures, and corrosive chemicals. In 1987, Alcoa had a frightening safety record, with 2% of the ninety thousand employee workforce being injured each year—that's seven injuries per day. When Paul O'Neill started as CEO, his first goal was to have zero injuries to employees, contractors, and visitors.

O'Neill wanted to be notified within twenty-four hours of anyone being injured on the job—not to punish, but to ensure and promote that learnings were being generated and incorporated to create a safer workplace. Over the course of ten years, Alcoa reduced their injury rate by 95%.

The reduction in injury rates allowed Alcoa to focus on smaller problems and weaker failure signals—instead of notifying O'Neill only when injuries occurred, they started reporting any close calls as well.[†] By doing this, they improved workplace safety over the subsequent twenty years and have one of the most enviable safety records in the industry.

As Dr. Spear writes, "Alcoans gradually stopped working around the difficulties, inconveniences, and impediments they experienced. Coping, fire fighting, and making do were gradually replaced throughout the organization by a

---

† It is astonishing, instructional, and truly moving to see the level of conviction and passion that Paul O'Neill has about the moral responsibility leaders have to create workplace safety.

dynamic of identifying opportunities for process and product improvement. As those opportunities were identified and the problems were investigated, the pockets of ignorance that they reflected were converted into nuggets of knowledge." This helped give the company a greater competitive advantage in the market.

Similarly, in the technology value stream, as we make our system of work safer, we find and fix problems from ever weaker failure signals. For example, we may initially perform blameless post-mortems only for customer-impacting incidents. Over time, we may perform them for lesser team-impacting incidents and near misses as well.

TRANSFORM LOCAL DISCOVERIES INTO GLOBAL IMPROVEMENTS

When new learnings are discovered locally, there must also be some mechanism to enable the rest of the organization to use and benefit from that knowledge. In other words, when teams or individuals have experiences that create expertise, our goal is to convert that tacit knowledge (i.e., knowledge that is difficult to transfer to another person by means of writing it down or verbalizing) into explicit, codified knowledge, which becomes someone else's expertise through practice.

This ensures that when anyone else does similar work, they do so with the cumulative and collective experience of everyone in the organization who has ever done the same work. A remarkable example of turning local knowledge into global knowledge is the US Navy's Nuclear Power Propulsion Program (also known as "NR" for "Naval Reactors"), which has over 5,700 reactor-years of operation without a single reactor-related casualty or escape of radiation.

The NR is known for their intense commitment to scripted procedures and standardized work, and the need for incident reports for any departure from procedure or normal operations to accumulate learnings, no matter how minor the failure signal—they constantly update procedures and system designs based on these learnings.

The result is that when a new crew sets out to sea on their first deployment, they and their officers benefit from the collective knowledge of 5,700 accident-free reactor-years. Equally impressive is that their own experiences at sea will be added to this collective knowledge, helping future crews safely achieve their own missions.

In the technology value stream, we must create similar mechanisms to create global knowledge, such as making all our blameless post-mortem reports searchable by teams trying to solve similar problems, and by creating shared source code repositories that span the entire organization, where shared code, libraries, and configurations that embody the best collective knowledge of the entire organization can be easily utilized. All these mechanisms help convert individual expertise into artifacts that the rest of the organization can use.

INJECT RESILIENCE PATTERNS INTO OUR DAILY WORK

Lower performing manufacturing organizations buffer themselves from disruptions in many ways—in other words, they bulk up or add flab. For instance, to reduce the risk of a work center being idle (due to inventory arriving late, inventory that had to be scrapped, etc.), managers may choose to stockpile more inventory at each work center. However, that inventory buffer also increases WIP, which has all sorts of undesired outcomes, as previously discussed.

Similarly, to reduce the risk of a work center going down due to machinery failure, managers may increase capacity by buying more capital equipment, hiring more people, or even increasing floor space. All these options increase costs.

In contrast, high performers achieve the same results (or better) by improving daily operations, continually introducing tension to elevate performance, as well as engineering more resilience into their system.

Consider a typical experiment at one of Aisin Seiki Global's mattress factories, one of Toyota's top suppliers. Suppose they had two production lines, each capable of producing one hundred units per day. On slow days, they would send all production onto one line, experimenting with ways to increase capacity and identify vulnerabilities in their process, knowing that if overloading the line caused it to fail, they could send all production to the second line.

By relentless and constant experimentation in their daily work, they were able to continually increase capacity, often without adding any new equipment or hiring more people. The emergent pattern that results from these types of improvement rituals not only improves performance but also improves resilience, because the organization is always in a state of tension and change. This process of applying stress to increase resilience was named *antifragility* by author and risk analyst Nassim Nicholas Taleb.

In the technology value stream, we can introduce the same type of tension into our systems by seeking to always reduce deployment lead times, increase test coverage, decrease test execution times, and even by re-architecting if necessary to increase developer productivity or increase reliability.

We may also perform *game day* exercises, where we rehearse large scale failures, such as turning off entire data centers. Or we may inject ever-larger scale faults into the production environment (such as the famous Netflix "Chaos Monkey" which randomly kills processes and compute servers in production) to ensure that we're as resilient as we want to be.

LEADERS REINFORCE A LEARNING CULTURE

Traditionally, leaders were expected to be responsible for setting objectives, allocating resources for achieving those objectives, and establishing the right combination of incentives. Leaders also establish the emotional tone for the organizations they lead. In other words, leaders lead by "making all the right decisions."

However, there is significant evidence that shows greatness is not achieved by leaders making all the right decisions—instead, the leader's role is to create the conditions so their team can discover greatness in their daily work. In other words, creating greatness requires both leaders and workers, each of whom are mutually dependent upon each other.

Jim Womack, author of *Gemba Walks*, described the complementary working relationship and mutual respect that must occur between leaders and frontline workers. According to Womack, this relationship is necessary because neither can solve problems alone—leaders are not close enough to the work, which is required to solve any problem, and frontline workers do not have the broader organizational context or the authority to make changes outside of their area of work.[†]

---

† Leaders are responsible for the design and operation of processes at a higher level of aggregation where others have less perspective and authority.

Leaders must elevate the value of learning and disciplined problem solving. Mike Rother formalized these methods in what he calls the *coaching kata*. The result is one that mirrors the scientific method, where we explicitly state our True North goals, such as "sustain zero accidents" in the case of Alcoa, or "double throughput within a year" in the case of Aisin.

These strategic goals then inform the creation of iterative, shorter term goals, which are cascaded and then executed by establishing target conditions at the value stream or work center level (e.g., "reduce lead time by 10% within the next two weeks").

These target conditions frame the scientific experiment: we explicitly state the problem we are seeking to solve, our hypothesis of how our proposed countermeasure will solve it, our methods for testing that hypothesis, our interpretation of the results, and our use of learnings to inform the next iteration.

The leader helps coach the person conducting the experiment with questions that may include:

- What was your last step and what happened?

- What did you learn?

- What is your condition now?

- What is your next target condition?

- What obstacle are you working on now?

- What is your next step?

- What is your expected outcome?

- When can we check?

This problem-solving approach in which leaders help workers see and solve problems in their daily work is at the core of the Toyota Production System, of learning organizations, the Improvement Kata, and high-reliability organizations. Mike Rother observes that he sees Toyota "as an organization defined primarily by the unique behavior routines it continually teaches to all its members."

In the technology value stream, this scientific approach and iterative method guides all of our internal improvement processes, but also how we perform experiments to ensure that the products we build actually help our internal and external customers achieve their goals.

CONCLUSION

The principles of the Third Way address the need for valuing organizational learning, enabling high trust and boundary-spanning between functions, accepting that failures will always occur in complex systems, and making it acceptable to talk about problems so we can create a safe system of work. It also requires institutionalizing the improvement of daily work, converting local learnings into global learnings that can be used by the entire organization, as well as continually injecting tension into our daily work.

Although fostering a culture of continual learning and experimentation is the principle of the Third Way, it is also interwoven into the First and Second Ways. In other words, improving flow and feedback requires an iterative and scientific approach that includes framing of a target condition, stating a hypothesis of what will help us get there, designing and conducting experiments, and evaluating the results.

The results are not only better performance but also increased resilience, higher job satisfaction, and improved organization adaptability.

PART I CONCLUSION

In Part I of *The DevOps Handbook* we looked back at several movements in history that helped lead to the development of DevOps. We also looked at the three main principles that form the foundation for successful DevOps organizations: the principles of Flow, Feedback, and Continual Learning and Experimentation. In Part II, we will begin to look at how to start a DevOps movement in your organization.

PART II

Where to Start

Part II
Introduction

How do we decide where to start a DevOps transformation in our organization? Who needs to be involved? How should we organize our teams, protect their work capacity, and maximize their chances of succeess? These are the questions we aim to answer in Part II of *The DevOps Handbook*.

In the following chapters we will walk through the process of initiating a DevOps transformation. We begin by evaluating the value streams in our organization, locating a good place to start, and forming a strategy to create a dedicated transformation team with specific improvement goals and eventual expansion. For each value stream being transformed, we identify the work being performed and then look at organizational design strategies and organizational archetypes that best support the transformation goals.

Primary focuses in these chapters include:

- Selecting which value streams to start with

- Understanding the work being done in our candidate value streams

- Designing our organization and architecture with Conway's Law in mind

- Enabling market-oriented outcomes through more effective collaboration between functions throughout the value stream

- Protecting and enabling our teams

Beginning any transformation is full of uncertainty—we are charting a journey to an ideal end state, but where virtually all the intermediate steps are unknown. These next chapters are intended to provide a thought process to guide our decisions, provide actionable steps we can take, and illustrate case studies as examples.

5 Selecting Which Value Stream to Start With

Choosing a value stream for DevOps transformation deserves careful consideration. Not only does the value stream we choose dictate the difficulty of our transformation, but it also dictates who will be involved in the transformation. It will affect how we need to organize into teams and how we can best enable the teams and individuals in them.

Another challenge was noted by Michael Rembetsy, who helped lead the DevOps transformation as the Director of Operations at Etsy in 2009. He observed, "We must pick our transformation projects carefully—when we're in trouble, we don't get very many shots. Therefore, we must carefully pick and then protect those improvement projects that will most improve the state of our organization."

Let us examine how the Nordstrom team started their DevOps transformation initiative in 2013, which Courtney Kissler, their VP of E-Commerce and Store Technologies, described at the DevOps Enterprise Summit in 2014 and 2015.

Founded in 1901, Nordstrom is a leading fashion retailer that is focused on delivering the best possible shopping experience to their customers. In 2015, Nordstrom had annual revenue of $13.5 billion.

The stage for Nordstrom's DevOps journey was likely set in 2011 during one of their annual board of directors meetings. That year, one of the strategic topics discussed was the need for online revenue growth. They studied the plight of Blockbusters, Borders, and Barnes & Nobles, which demonstrated the dire consequences when traditional retailers were late creating competitive e-commerce capabilities—these organizations were clearly at risk of losing their position in the marketplace or even going out of business entirely.[†]

---

† These organizations were sometimes known as the "Killer B's that are Dying."

At that time, Courtney Kissler was the senior director of Systems Delivery and Selling Technology, responsible for a significant portion of the technology organization, including their in-store systems and online e-commerce site. As Kissler described, "In 2011, the Nordstrom technology organization was very much optimized for cost—we had outsourced many of our technology functions, we had an annual planning cycle with large batch, 'waterfall' software releases. Even though we had a 97% success rate of hitting our schedule, budget, and scope goals, we were ill-equipped to achieve what the five-year business strategy required from us, as Nordstrom started optimizing for speed instead of merely optimizing for cost."

Kissler and the Nordstrom technology management team had to decide where to start their initial transformation efforts. They didn't want to cause upheaval in the whole system. Instead, they wanted to focus on very specific areas of the business so that they could experiment and learn. Their goal was to demonstrate early wins, which would give everyone confidence that these improvements could be replicated in other areas of the organization. How exactly that would be achieved was still unknown.

They focused on three areas: the customer mobile application, their in-store restaurant systems, and their digital properties. Each of these areas had business goals that weren't being met; thus, they were more receptive to considering a different way of working. The stories of the first two are described below.

The Nordstrom mobile application had experienced an inauspicious start. As Kissler said, "Our customers were extremely frustrated with the product, and we had uniformly negative reviews when we launched it in the App Store. Worse, the existing structure and processes (aka "the system") had designed their processes so that they could only release updates twice per year." In other words, any fixes to the application would have to wait months to reach the customer.

Their first goal was to enable faster or on-demand releases, providing faster iteration and the ability to respond to customer feedback. They created a dedicated product team that was solely dedicated to supporting the mobile application, with the goal of enabling that team to be able to independently implement, test, and deliver value to the customer. By doing this, they would no longer have to depend on and coordinate with scores of other teams inside Nordstrom. Furthermore, they moved from planning once per year to a continuous planning process. The result was a single prioritized backlog of work for the mobile app based on customer need—gone were all the conflicting priorities when the team had to support multiple products.

Over the following year, they eliminated testing as a separate phase of work, instead integrating it into everyone's daily work.[†] They doubled the features being delivered per month and halved the number of defects—creating a successful outcome.

Their second area of focus was the systems supporting their in-store *Café Bistro* restaurants. Unlike the mobile app value stream where the business need was to reduce time to market and increase feature throughput, the business need here was to decrease cost and increase quality. In 2013, Nordstrom had completed eleven "restaurant re-concepts" which required changes to the in-store applications, causing a number of customer-impacting incidents. Disturbingly, they had planned forty-four more of these re-concepts for 2014—four times as many as in the previous year.

As Kissler stated, "One of our business leaders suggested that we triple our team size to handle these new demands, but I proposed that we had to stop throwing more bodies at the problem and instead improve the way we worked."

They were able to identify problematic areas, such as in their work intake and deployment processes, which is where they focused their improvement efforts. They were able to reduce code deployment lead times by 60% and reduce the number of production incidents 60% to 90%.

These successes gave the teams confidence that DevOps principles and practices were applicable to a wide variety of value streams. Kissler was promoted to VP of E-Commerce and Store Technologies in 2014.

In 2015, Kissler said that in order for the selling or customer-facing technology organization to enable the business to meet their goals, "...we needed to increase productivity in all our technology value streams, not just in a few. At the management level, we created an across-the-board mandate to reduce cycle times by 20% for all customer-facing services."

She continued, "This is an audacious challenge. We have many problems in our current state—process and cycle times are not consistently measured across teams, nor are they visible. Our first target condition requires us to help all our teams measure, make it visible, and perform experiments to start reducing their process times, iteration by iteration."

---

† The practice of relying on a stabilization phase or hardening phase at the end of a project often has very poor outcomes, because it means problems are not being found and fixed as part of daily work and are left unaddressed, potentially snowballing into larger issues.

Kissler concluded, "From a high level perspective, we believe that techniques such as value stream mapping, reducing our batch sizes toward single-piece flow, as well as using continuous delivery and microservices will get us to our desired state. However, while we are still learning, we are confident that we are heading in the right direction, and everyone knows that this effort has support from the highest levels of management."

In this chapter, various models are presented that will enable us to replicate the thought processes that the Nordstrom team used to decide which value streams to start with. We will evaluate our candidate value streams in many ways, including whether they are a *greenfield* or *brownfield* service, a *system of engagement* or a *system of record*. We will also estimate the risk/reward balance of transforming and assess the likely level of resistance we may get from the teams we would work with.

GREENFIELD VS. BROWNFIELD SERVICES

We often categorize our software services or products as either greenfield or brownfield. These terms were originally used for urban planning and building projects. Greenfield development is when we build on undeveloped land. Brownfield development is when we build on land that was previously used for industrial purposes, potentially contaminated with hazardous waste or pollution. In urban development, many factors can make greenfield projects simpler than brownfield projects—there are no existing structures that need to be demolished nor are there toxic materials that need to be removed.

In technology, a greenfield project is a new software project or initiative, likely in the early stages of planning or implementation, where we build our applications and infrastructure anew, with few constraints. Starting with a greenfield software project can be easier, especially if the project is already funded and a team is either being created or is already in place. Furthermore, because we are starting from scratch, we can worry less about existing code bases, processes, and teams.

Greenfield DevOps projects are often pilots to demonstrate feasibility of public or private clouds, piloting deployment automation, and similar tools. An example of a greenfield DevOps project is the Hosted LabVIEW product in 2009 at National Instruments, a thirty-year-old organization with five thousand employees and $1 billion in annual revenue. To bring this product to market quickly, a new team was created and allowed to operate outside of the existing IT processes and explore the use of public clouds. The initial team included an applications architect, a systems architect, two developers, a system automation developer, an operations lead, and two offshore operations staff. By using DevOps practices, they were able to deliver Hosted LabVIEW to market in half the time of their normal product introductions.

On the other end of the spectrum are brownfield DevOps projects, these are existing products or services that are already serving customers and have potentially been in operation for years or even decades. Brownfield projects often come with significant amounts of technical debt, such as having no test automation or running on unsupported platforms. In the Nordstrom example presented earlier in this chapter, both the in-store restaurant systems and e-commerce systems were brownfield projects.

Although many believe that DevOps is primarily for greenfield projects, DevOps has been used to successfully transform brownfield projects of all sorts. In fact, over 60% of the transformation stories shared at the DevOps Enterprise Summit in 2014 were for brownfield projects. In these cases, there was a large performance gap between what the customer needed and what the organization was currently delivering, and the DevOps transformations created tremendous business benefit.

Indeed, one of the findings in the 2015 *State of DevOps Report* validated that the age of the application was not a significant predictor of performance; instead, what predicted performance was whether the application was architected (or could be re-architected) for testability and deployability.

Teams supporting brownfield projects may be very receptive to experimenting with DevOps, particularly when there is a widespread belief that traditional methods are insufficient to achieve their goals—and especially if there is a strong sense of urgency around the need for improvement.[†]

When transforming brownfield projects, we may face significant impediments and problems, especially when no automated testing exists or when there is a tightly-coupled architecture that prevents small teams from developing, testing, and deploying code independently. How we overcome these issues are discussed throughout this book.

Examples of successful brownfield transformations include:

---

† That the services that have the largest potential business benefit are brownfield systems shouldn't be surprising. After all, these are the systems that are most relied upon and have the largest number of existing customers or highest amount of revenue depending upon them.

- **CSG (2013):** In 2013, CSG International had $747 million in revenue and over 3,500 employees, enabling over ninety thousand customer service agents to provide billing operations and customer care to over fifty million video, voice, and data customers, executing over six billion transactions, and printing and mailing over seventy million paper bill statements every month. Their initial scope of improvement was bill printing, one of their primary businesses, and involved a COBOL mainframe application and the twenty surrounding technology platforms. As part of their transformation, they started performing daily deployments into a production-like environment, and doubled the frequency of customer releases from twice annually to four times annually. As a result, they significantly increased the reliability of the application and reduced code deployment lead times from two weeks to less than one day.

- **Etsy (2009):** In 2009, Etsy had thirty-five employees and was generating $87 million in revenue, but after they "barely survived the holiday retail season," they started transforming virtually every aspect of how the organization worked, eventually turning the company into one of the most admired DevOps organizations and set the stage for a successful 2015 IPO.

CONSIDER BOTH SYSTEMS OF RECORD AND SYSTEMS OF ENGAGEMENT

The Gartner research firm has recently popularized the notion of *bimodal IT*, referring to the wide spectrum of services that typical enterprises support. Within bimodal IT there are *systems of record*, the ERP-like systems that run our business (e.g., MRP, HR, financial reporting systems), where the correctness of the transactions and data are paramount; and *systems of engagement*, which are customer-facing or employee-facing systems, such as e-commerce systems and productivity applications.

Systems of record typically have a slower pace of change and often have regulatory and compliance requirements (e.g., SOX). Gartner calls these types of systems "Type 1," where the organization focuses on "doing it right."

Systems of engagement typically have a much higher pace of change to support rapid feedback loops that enable them to conduct experimentation to discover how to best meet customer needs. Gartner calls these types of systems "Type 2," where the organization focuses on "doing it fast."

It may be convenient to divide up our systems into these categories; however, we know that the core, chronic conflict between "doing it right" and "doing it fast" can be broken with DevOps. The data from Puppet Labs' State of DevOps Reports—following the lessons of Lean manufacturing—shows that high performing organizations are able to simultaneously deliver higher levels of throughput and reliability.

Furthermore, because of how interdependent our systems are, our ability to make changes to any of these systems is limited by the system that is most difficult to safely change, which is almost always a system of record.

Scott Prugh, VP of Product Development at CSG, observed, "We've adopted a philosophy that rejects bi-modal IT, because every one of our customers deserve speed and quality. This means that we need technical excellence, whether the team is supporting a 30 year old mainframe application, a Java application, or a mobile application."

Consequently, when we improve brownfield systems, we should not only strive to reduce their complexity and improve their reliability and stability, we should also make them faster, safer, and easier to change. Even when new functionality is added just to greenfield systems of engagement, they often cause reliability problems in the brownfield systems of record they rely on. By making these downstream systems safer to change, we help the entire organization more quickly and safely achieve its goals.

START WITH THE MOST SYMPATHETIC AND INNOVATIVE GROUPS

Within every organization, there will be teams and individuals with a wide range of attitudes toward the adoption of new ideas. Geoffrey A. Moore first depicted this spectrum in the form of the technology adoption life cycle in *Crossing The Chasm*, where the chasm represents the classic difficulty of reaching groups beyond the *innovators* and *early adopters* (see figure 9).

In other words, new ideas are often quickly embraced by innovators and early adopters, while others with more conservative attitudes resist them (the *early majority, late majority,* and *laggards*). Our goal is to find those teams that already believe in the need for DevOps principles and practices, and who possess a desire and demonstrated ability to innovate and improve their own processes. Ideally, these groups will be enthusiastic supporters of the DevOps journey.

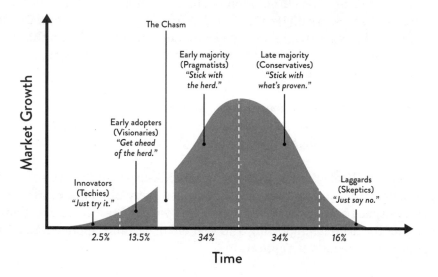

Figure 9: *The Technology Adoption Curve (Source: Moore and McKenna, Crossing The Chasm, 15.)*

Especially in the early stages, we will not spend much time trying to convert the more conservative groups. Instead, we will focus our energy on creating successes with less risk-averse groups and build out our base from there (a process that is discussed further in the next section). Even if we have the highest levels of executive sponsorship, we will avoid the *big bang approach* (i.e., starting everywhere all at once), choosing instead to focus our efforts in a few areas of the organization, ensuring that those initiatives are successful, and expanding from there.†

EXPANDING DEVOPS ACROSS OUR ORGANIZATION

Regardless of how we scope our initial effort, we must demonstrate early wins and broadcast our successes. We do this by breaking up our larger improvement

---

† Big bang, top-down transformations are possible, such as the Agile transformation at PayPal in 2012 that was led by their vice president of technology, Kirsten Wolberg. However, as with any sustainable and successful transformation, this required the highest level of management support and a relentless, sustained focus on driving the necessary outcomes.

goals into small, incremental steps. This not only creates our improvements faster, it also enables us to discover when we have made the wrong choice of value stream—by detecting our errors early, we can quickly back up and try again, making different decisions armed with our new learnings.

As we generate successes, we earn the right to expand the scope of our DevOps initiative. We want to follow a safe sequence that methodically grows our levels of credibility, influence, and support. The following list, adapted from a course taught by Dr. Roberto Fernandez, a William F. Pounds Professor in Management at MIT, describes the ideal phases used by change agents to build and expand their coalition and base of support:

1. **Find Innovators and Early Adopters:** In the beginning, we focus our efforts on teams who actually want to help—these are our kindred spirits and fellow travelers who are the first to volunteer to start the DevOps journey. In the ideal, these are also people who are respected and have a high degree of influence over the rest of the organization, giving our initiative more credibility.

2. **Build Critical Mass and Silent Majority:** In the next phase, we seek to expand DevOps practices to more teams and value streams with the goal of creating a stable base of support. By working with teams who are receptive to our ideas, even if they are not the most visible or influential groups, we expand our coalition who are generating more successes, creating a "bandwagon effect" that further increases our influence. We specifically bypass dangerous political battles that could jeopardize our initiative.

3. **Identify the Holdouts:** The "holdouts" are the high profile, influential detractors who are most likely to resist (and maybe even sabotage) our efforts. In general, we tackle this group only after we have achieved a silent majority, when we have established enough successes to successfully protect our initiative.

Expanding DevOps across an organization is no small task. It can create risk to individuals, departments, and the organization as a whole. But as Ron van Kemenade, CIO of ING, who helped transform the organization into one of the most admired technology organizations, said, "Leading change requires courage, especially in corporate environments where people are scared and fight you. But if you start small, you really have nothing to fear. Any leader needs to be brave enough to allocate teams to do some calculated risk-taking."

CONCLUSION

Peter Drucker, a leader in the development of management education, observed that "little fish learn to be big fish in little ponds." By choosing carefully where and how to start, we are able to experiment and learn in areas of our organization that create value without jeopardizing the rest of the organization. By doing this, we build our base of support, earn the right to expand the use of DevOps in our organization, and gain the recognition and gratitude of an ever-larger constituency.

Understanding the Work in Our Value Stream, Making it Visible, and Expanding it Across the Organization

Once we have identified a value stream to which we want to apply DevOps principles and patterns, our next step is to gain a sufficient understanding of how value is delivered to the customer: what work is performed and by whom, and what steps can we take to improve flow.

In the previous chapter, we learned about the DevOps transformation led by Courtney Kissler and the team at Nordstrom. Over the years, they have learned that one of the most efficient ways to start improving any value stream is to conduct a workshop with all the major stakeholders and perform a value stream mapping exercise—a process (described later in this chapter) designed to help capture all the steps required to create value.

Kissler's favorite example of the valuable and unexpected insights that can come from value stream mapping is when they tried to improve the long lead times associated with requests going through the Cosmetics Business Office application, a COBOL mainframe application that supported all the floor and department managers of their in-store beauty and cosmetic departments.

This application allowed department managers to register new salespeople for various product lines carried in their stores, so that they could track sales commissions, enable vendor rebates, and so forth.

Kissler explained:

> I knew this particular mainframe application well—earlier in my career, I supported this technology team, so I know firsthand that for nearly a decade, during each annual planning cycle, we would debate about how we needed to get this application off the mainframe. Of

course, like in most organizations, even when there was full management support, we never seemed to get around to migrating it.

My team wanted to conduct a value stream mapping exercise to determine whether the COBOL application really was the problem, or maybe there was a larger problem that we needed to address. They conducted a workshop that assembled everyone with any accountability for delivering value to our internal customers, including our business partners, the mainframe team, the shared service teams, and so forth.

What they discovered was that when department managers were submitting the 'product line assignment' request form, we were asking them for an employee number, which they didn't have—so they would either leave it blank or put in something like 'I don't know.' Worse, in order to fill out the form, department managers would have to inconveniently leave the store floor in order to use a PC in the back office. The end result was all this wasted time, with work bouncing back and forth in the process.

During the workshop, the participants conducted several experiments, including deleting the employee number field in the form and letting another department get that information in a downstream step. These experiments, conducted with the help of department managers, showed a four-day reduction in processing time. The team later replaced the PC application with an iPad application, which allowed managers to submit the necessary information without leaving the store floor, and the processing time was further reduced to seconds.

She said proudly, "With those amazing improvements, all the demands to get this application off the mainframe disappeared. Furthermore, other business leaders took notice and started coming to us with a whole list of further experiments they wanted to conduct with us in their own organizations. Everyone in the business and technology teams were excited by the outcome because they solved a real business problem, and, most importantly, they learned something in the process."

In the remainder of this chapter, we will go through the following steps: identifying all the teams required to create customer value, creating a value stream map to make visible all the required work, and using it to guide the teams in how to better and more quickly create value. By doing this, we can replicate the amazing outcomes described in this Nordstrom example.

IDENTIFYING THE TEAMS SUPPORTING OUR VALUE STREAM

As this Nordstrom example demonstrates, in value streams of any complexity, no one person knows all the work that must be performed in order to create value for the customer—especially since the required work must be performed by many different teams, often far removed from each other on the organization charts, geographically, or by incentives.

As a result, after we select a candidate application or service for our DevOps initiative, we must identify all the members of the value stream who are responsible for working together to create value for the customers being served. In general, this includes:

- **Product owner:** the internal voice of the business that defines the next set of functionality in the service

- **Development:** the team responsible for developing application functionality in the service

- **QA:** the team responsible for ensuring that feedback loops exist to ensure the service functions as desired

- **Operations:** the team often responsible for maintaining the production environment and helping ensure that required service levels are met

- **Infosec:** the team responsible for securing systems and data

- **Release managers:** the people responsible for managing and coordinating the production deployment and release processes

- **Technology executives or value stream manager:** in Lean literature, someone who is responsible for "ensuring that the value stream meets or exceeds the customer [and organizational] requirements for the overall value stream, from start to finish"

CREATE A VALUE STREAM MAP TO SEE THE WORK

After we identify our value stream members, our next step is to gain a concrete understanding of how work is performed, documented in the form of a value stream map. In our value stream, work likely begins with the product owner, in the form of a customer request or the formulation of a business hypothesis. Some time later, this work is accepted by Development, where features are implemented in code and checked in to our version control repository. Builds are then integrated, tested in a production-like environment, and finally deployed into production, where they (ideally) create value for our customer.

In many traditional organizations, this value stream will consist of hundreds, if not thousands, of steps, requiring work from hundreds of people. Because documenting any value stream map this complex likely requires multiple days, we may conduct a multi-day workshop, where we assemble all the key constituents and remove them from the distractions of their daily work.

Our goal is not to document every step and associated minutiae, but to sufficiently understand the areas in our value stream that are jeopardizing our goals of fast flow, short lead times, and reliable customer outcomes. Ideally, we have assembled those people with the authority to change their portion of the value stream.[†]

Damon Edwards, co-host of *DevOps Café* podcast, observed, "In my experience, these types of value stream mapping exercises are always an eye-opener. Often, it is the first time when people see how much work and heroics are required to deliver value to the customer. For Operations, it may be the first time that they see the consequences that result when developers don't have access to correctly configured environments, which contributes to even more crazy work during code deployments. For Development, it may be the first time they see all the heroics that are required by Test and Operations in order to deploy their code into production, long after they flag a feature as 'completed.'"

Using the full breadth of knowledge brought by the teams engaged in the value stream, we should focus our investigation and scrutiny on the following areas:

- Places where work must wait weeks or even months, such as getting production-like environments, change approval processes, or security review processes

- Places where significant rework is generated or received

[†] Which makes it all the more important that we limit the level of detail being collected—everyone's time is valuable and scarce.

Our first pass of documenting our value stream should only consist of high-level process blocks. Typically, even for complex value streams, groups can create a diagram with five to fifteen process blocks within a few hours. Each process block should include the lead time and process time for a work item to be processed, as well as the %C/A as measured by the downstream consumers of the output.[‡]

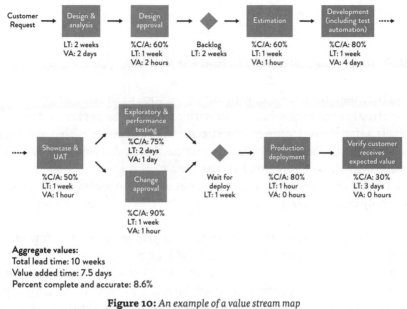

Figure 10: *An example of a value stream map (Source: Humble, Molesky, and O'Reilly, Lean Enterprise, 139.)*

We use the metrics from our value stream map to guide our improvement efforts. In the Nordstrom example, they focused on the low %C/A rates on the request form submitted by department managers due to the absence of employee numbers. In other cases, it may be long lead times or low %C/A rates when delivering correctly configured test environments to Development teams, or it might be the long lead times required to execute and pass regression testing before each software release.

Once we identify the metric we want to improve, we should perform the next level of observations and measurements to better understand the problem

---

‡ Conversely, there are many examples of using tools in a way that guarantees no behavior changes occur. For instance, an organization commits to an agile planning tool but then configures it for a waterfall process, which merely maintains status quo.

and then construct an idealized, future value stream map, which serves as a target condition to achieve by some date (e.g., usually three to twelve months).

Leadership helps define this future state and then guides and enables the team to brainstorm hypotheses and countermeasures to achieve the desired improvement to that state, perform experiments to test those hypotheses, and interpret the results to determine whether the hypotheses were correct. The teams keep repeating and iterating, using any new learnings to inform the next experiments.

CREATING A DEDICATED TRANSFORMATION TEAM

One of the inherent challenges with initiatives such as DevOps transformations is that they are inevitably in conflict with ongoing business operations. Part of this is a natural outcome of how successful businesses evolve. An organization that has been successful for any extended period of time (years, decades, or even centuries) has created mechanisms to perpetuate the practices that made them successful, such as product development, order administration, and supply chain operations.

Many techniques are used to perpetuate and protect how current processes operate, such as specialization, focus on efficiency and repeatability, bureaucracies that enforce approval processes, and controls to protect against variance. In particular, bureaucracies are incredibly resilient and are designed to survive adverse conditions—one can remove half the bureaucrats, and the process will still survive.

While this is good for preserving status quo, we often need to change how we work to adapt to changing conditions in the marketplace. Doing this requires disruption and innovation, which puts us at odds with groups who are currently responsible for daily operations and the internal bureaucracies, and who will almost always win.

In their book *The Other Side of Innovation: Solving the Execution Challenge,* Dr. Vijay Govindarajan and Dr. Chris Trimble, both faculty members of Dartmouth College's Tuck School of Business, described their studies of how disruptive innovation is achieved despite these powerful forces of daily operations. They documented how customer-driven auto insurance products were successfully developed and marketed at Allstate, how the profitable digital publishing business was created at the *Wall Street Journal*, the development of the breakthrough trail-running shoe at Timberland, and the development of the first electric car at BMW.

Based on their research, Dr. Govindarajan and Dr. Trimble assert that organizations need to create a dedicated transformation team that is able to operate outside of the rest of the organization that is responsible for daily operations (which they call the "dedicated team" and "performance engine" respectively).

First and foremost, we will hold this dedicated team accountable for achieving a clearly defined, measurable, system-level result (e.g., reduce the deployment lead time from "code committed into version control to successfully running in production" by 50%). In order to execute such an initiative, we do the following:

- Assign members of the dedicated team to be solely allocated to the DevOps transformation efforts (as opposed to "maintain all your current responsibilities, but spend 20% of your time on this new DevOps thing.").

- Select team members who are generalists, who have skills across a wide variety of domains.

- Select team members who have longstanding and mutually respectful relationships with the rest of the organization.

- Create a separate physical space for the dedicated team, if possible, to maximize communication flow within the team, and creating some isolation from the rest of the organization.

If possible, we will free the transformation team from many of the rules and policies that restrict the rest of the organization, as National Instruments did, described in the previous chapter. After all, established processes are a form of institutional memory—we need the dedicated team to create the new processes and learnings required to generate our desired outcomes, creating new institutional memory.

Creating a dedicated team is not only good for the team, but also good for the performance engine. By creating a separate team, we create the space for them to experiment with new practices, protecting the rest of the organization from the potential disruptions and distractions associated with it.

AGREE ON A SHARED GOAL

One of the most important parts of any improvement initiative is to define a measurable goal with a clearly defined deadline, between six months and two years in the future. It should require considerable effort but still be achievable. And achievement of the goal should create obvious value for the organization as a whole and to our customers.

These goals and the time frame should be agreed upon by the executives and known to everyone in the organization. We also want to limit the number of these types of initiatives going on simultaneously to prevent us from overly taxing the organizational change management capacity of leaders and the organization. Examples of improvement goals might include:

- Reduce the percentage of the budget spent on product support and unplanned work by 50%.

- Ensure lead time from code check-in to production release is one week or less for 95% of changes.

- Ensure releases can always be performed during normal business hours with zero downtime.

- Integrate all the required information security controls into the deployment pipeline to pass all required compliance requirements.

Once the high-level goal is made clear, teams should decide on a regular cadence to drive the improvement work. Like product development work, we want transformation work to be done in an iterative, incremental manner. A typical iteration will be in the range of two to four weeks. For each iteration, the teams should agree on a small set of goals that generate value and makes some progress toward the long-term goal. At the end of each iteration, teams should review their progress and set new goals for the next iteration.

KEEP OUR IMPROVEMENT PLANNING HORIZONS SHORT

In any DevOps transformation project, we need to keep our planning horizons short, just as if we were in a startup doing product or customer development. Our initiative should strive to generate measurable improvements or actionable data within weeks (or, in the worst case, months).

By keeping our planning horizons and iteration intervals short, we achieve the following:

- Flexibility and the ability to reprioritize and replan quickly

- Decrease the delay between work expended and improvement realized, which strengthens our feedback loop, making it more likely to reinforce desired behaviors—when improvement initiatives are successful, it encourages more investment

- Faster learning generated from the first iteration, meaning faster integration of our learnings into the next iteration

- Reduction in activation energy to get improvements

- Quicker realization of improvements that make meaningful differences in our daily work

- Less risk that our project is killed before we can generate any demonstrable outcomes

RESERVE 20% OF CYCLES FOR NON-FUNCTIONAL REQUIREMENTS AND REDUCING TECHNICAL DEBT

A problem common to any process improvement effort is how to properly prioritize it—after all, organizations that need it most are those that have the least amount of time to spend on improvement. This is especially true in technology organizations because of technical debt.

Organizations that struggle with financial debt only make interest payments and never reduce the loan principal, and may eventually find themselves in situations where they can no longer service the interest payments. Similarly, organizations that don't pay down technical debt can find themselves so burdened with daily workarounds for problems left unfixed that they can no longer complete any new work. In other words, they are now only making the interest payment on their technical debt.

We will actively manage this technical debt by ensuring that we invest at least 20% of all Development and Operations cycles on refactoring, investing in automation work and architecture and non-functional requirements (NFRs, sometimes referred to as the "ilities"), such as maintainability, manageability, scalability, reliability, testability, deployability, and security.

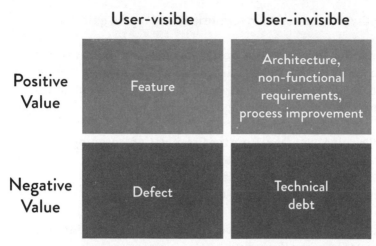

	User-visible	User-invisible
Positive Value	Feature	Architecture, non-functional requirements, process improvement
Negative Value	Defect	Technical debt

Figure 11: *Invest 20% of cycles on those that create positive, user-invisible value*
(Source: "Machine Learning and Technical Debt with D. Sculley," Software Engineering Daily podcast, November 17, 2015, http://softwareengineeringdaily.com/2015/11/17/ machine-learning-and-technical-debt-with-d-sculley/.)

After the near-death experience of eBay in the late 1990s, Marty Cagan, author of *Inspired: How To Create Products Customers Love,* the seminal book on product design and management, codified the following lesson:

> The deal [between product owners and] engineering goes like this: Product management takes 20% of the team's capacity right off the top and gives this to engineering to spend as they see fit. They might use it to rewrite, re-architect, or re-factor problematic parts of the code base...whatever they believe is necessary to avoid ever having to come to the team and say, 'we need to stop and rewrite [all our code].' If you're in really bad shape today, you might need to make this 30% or even more of the resources. However, I get nervous when I find teams that think they can get away with much less than 20%.

Cagan notes that when organizations do not pay their "20% tax," technical debt will increase to the point where an organization inevitably spends all of its cycles paying down technical debt. At some point, the services become so fragile that feature delivery grinds to a halt because all the engineers are working on reliability issues or working around problems.

By dedicating 20% of our cycles so that Dev and Ops can create lasting counter-measures to the problems we encounter in our daily work, we ensure that technical debt doesn't impede our ability to quickly and safely develop and operate our services in production. Elevating added pressure of technical debt from workers can also reduce levels of burnout.

Case Study
Operation InVersion at LinkedIn (2011)

LinkedIn's Operation InVersion presents an interesting case study that illustrates the need to pay down technical debt as a part of daily work. Six months after their successful IPO in 2011, LinkedIn continued to struggle with problematic deployments that became so painful that they launched Operation InVersion, where they stopped all feature development for two months in order to overhaul their computing environments, deployments, and architecture.

LinkedIn was created in 2003 to help users "connect to your network for better job opportunities." By the end of their first week of operation, they had 2,700 members. One year later, they had over one million members, and have grown exponentially since then. By November 2015, LinkedIn had over 350 million members, who generate tens of thousands of requests per second, resulting in millions of queries per second on the LinkedIn backend systems.

From the beginning, LinkedIn primarily ran on their homegrown Leo application, a monolithic Java application that served every page through servlets and managed JDBC connections to various backend Oracle databases. However, to keep up with growing traffic in their early years, two critical services were decoupled from Leo: the first handled queries around the member connection graph entirely in-memory, and the second was member search, which layered over the first.

By 2010, most new development was occurring in new services, with nearly one hundred services running outside of Leo. The problem was that Leo was only being deployed once every two weeks.

Josh Clemm, a senior engineering manager at LinkedIn, explained that by 2010, the company was having significant problems with Leo. Despite vertically scaling Leo by adding memory and CPUs, "Leo was often going down in production, it was difficult to troubleshoot and recover, and difficult to release new code....It was clear we needed to 'Kill Leo' and break it up into many small functional and stateless services."

In 2013, journalist Ashlee Vance of Bloomberg described how "when LinkedIn would try to add a bunch of new things at once, the site would crumble into a broken mess, requiring engineers to work long into the night and fix the problems." By Fall 2011, late nights were no longer a rite of passage or a bonding activity, because the problems had become intolerable. Some of LinkedIn's top engineers, including Kevin Scott, who had joined as the LinkedIn VP of Engineering three months before their initial public offering, decided to completely stop engineering work on new features and dedicate the whole department to fixing the site's core infrastructure. They called the effort Operation InVersion.

Scott launched Operation InVersion as a way to "inject the beginnings of a cultural manifesto into his team's engineering culture. There would be no new feature development until LinkedIn's computing architecture was re-vamped—it's what the business *and* his team needed."

Scott described one downside, "You go public, have all the world looking at you, and then we tell management that we're not going to deliver anything new while all of engineering works on this [InVersion] project for the next two months. It was a scary thing."

However, Vance described the massively positive results of Operation In-Version. "LinkedIn created a whole suite of software and tools to help it develop code for the site. Instead of waiting weeks for their new features to make their way onto LinkedIn's main site, engineers could develop a new service, have a series of automated systems examine the code for any bugs and issues the service might have interacting with existing features, and launch it right to the live LinkedIn site...LinkedIn's engineering corps [now] performs major upgrades to the site three times a day." By creating a safer system of work, the value they created included fewer late night cram sessions, with more time to develop new, innovative features.

As Josh Clemm described in his article on scaling at LinkedIn, "Scaling can be measured across many dimensions, including organizational.... [Operation InVersion] allowed the entire engineering organization to focus on improving tooling and deployment, infrastructure, and developer productivity. It was successful in enabling the engineering agility we need to build the scalable new products we have today....[In] 2010, we already had over 150 separate services. Today, we have over 750 services."

Kevin Scott stated, "Your job as an engineer and your purpose as a technology team is to help your company win. If you lead a team of engineers, it's better to take a CEO's perspective. Your job is to figure out what it is that your company, your business, your marketplace, your competitive environment needs. Apply that to your engineering team in order for your company to win."

By allowing LinkedIn to pay down nearly a decade of technical debt, Project InVersion enabled stability and safety, while setting the next stage of growth for the company. However, it required two months of total focus on non-functional requirements, at the expense of all the promised features made to the public markets during an IPO. By finding and fixing problems as part of our daily work, we manage our technical debt so that we avoid these "near death" experiences.

INCREASE THE VISIBILITY OF WORK

In order to be able to know if we are making progress toward our goal, it's essential that everyone in the organization knows the current state of work. There are many ways to make the current state visible, but what's most important is that the information we display is up to date, and that we constantly revise what we measure to make sure it's helping us understand progress toward our current target conditions.

The following section discusses patterns that can help create visibility and alignment across teams and functions.

USE TOOLS TO REINFORCE DESIRED BEHAVIOR

As Christopher Little, a software executive and one of the earliest chroniclers of DevOps, observed, "Anthropologists describe tools as a cultural artifact. Any discussion of culture after the invention of fire must also be about tools." Similarly, in the DevOps value stream, we use tools to reinforce our culture and accelerate desired behavior changes.

One goal is that our tooling reinforces that Development and Operations not only have shared goals, but have a common backlog of work, ideally stored in a common work system and using a shared vocabulary, so that work can be prioritized globally.

By doing this, Development and Operations may end up creating a shared work queue, instead of each silo using a different one (e.g., Development uses JIRA while Operations uses ServiceNow). A significant benefit of this is that when production incidents are shown in the same work systems as development work, it will be obvious when ongoing incidents should halt other work, especially when we have a kanban board.

Another benefit of having Development and Operations using a shared tool is a unified backlog, where everyone prioritizes improvement projects from a global perspective, selecting work that has the highest value to the organization or most reduces technical debt. As we identify technical debt, we add it to our prioritized backlog if we can't address it immediately. For issues that remain unaddressed, we can use our "20% time for non-functional requirements" to fix the top items from our backlog.

Other technologies that reinforce shared goals are chat rooms, such as IRC channels, HipChat, Campfire, Slack, Flowdock, and OpenFire. Chat rooms allow the fast sharing of information (as opposed to filling out forms that are processed through predefined workflows), the ability to invite other people as needed, and history logs that are automatically recorded for posterity and can be analyzed during post-mortem sessions.

An amazing dynamic is created when we have a mechanism that allows any team member to quickly help other team members, or even people outside their team—the time required to get information or needed work can go from days to minutes. In addition, because everything is being recorded, we may not need to ask someone else for help in the future—we simply search for it.

However, the rapid communication environment facilitated by chat rooms can also be a drawback. As Ryan Martens, the founder and CTO of Rally Software, observes, "In a chat room, if someone doesn't get an answer in a couple of minutes, it's totally accepted and expected that you can bug them again until they get what they need."

The expectations of immediate response can, of course, lead to undesired outcomes. A constant barrage of interruptions and questions can prevent people from getting necessary work done. As a result, teams may decide that certain types of requests should go through more structured and asynchronous tools.

CONCLUSION

In this chapter, we identified all the teams supporting our value stream and captured in a value stream map what work is required in order to deliver value to the customer. The value stream map provides the basis for understanding our current state, including our lead time and %C/A metrics for problematic areas, and informs how we set a future state.

This enables dedicated transformation teams to rapidly iterate and experiment to improve performance. We also make sure that we allocate a sufficient amount of time for improvement, fixing known problems and architectural issues, including our non-functional requirements. The case studies from Nordstrom and LinkedIn demonstrate how dramatic improvements can be made in lead times and quality when we find problems in our value stream and pay down technical debt.

7

How to Design Our Organization and Architecture with Conway's Law in Mind

In the previous chapters, we identified a value stream to start our DevOps transformation and established shared goals and practices to enable a dedicated transformation team to improve how we deliver value to the customer.

In this chapter, we will start thinking about how to organize ourselves to best achieve our value stream goals. After all, how we organize our teams affects how we perform our work. Dr. Melvin Conway performed a famous experiment in 1968 with a contract research organization that had eight people who were commissioned to produce a COBOL and an ALGOL compiler. He observed, "After some initial estimates of difficulty and time, five people were assigned to the COBOL job and three to the ALGOL job. The resulting COBOL compiler ran in five phases, the ALGOL compiler ran in three."

These observations led to what is now known as Conway's Law, which states that "organizations which design systems...are constrained to produce designs which are copies of the communication structures of these organizations.... The larger an organization is, the less flexibility it has and the more pronounced the phenomenon." Eric S. Raymond, author of the book *The Cathedral and the Bazaar: Musings on Linux and Open Source by an Accidental Revolutionary*, crafted a simplified (and now, more famous) version of Conway's Law in his Jargon File: "The organization of the software and the organization of the software team will be congruent; commonly stated as 'if you have four groups working on a compiler, you'll get a 4-pass compiler.'"

In other words, how we organize our teams has a powerful effect on the software we produce, as well as our resulting architectural and production outcomes. In order to get fast flow of work from Development into Operations, with high quality and great customer outcomes, we must organize our teams and our work so that Conway's Law works to our advantage. Done poorly, Conway's Law will prevent teams from working safely and independently; instead, they will be tightly coupled together, all waiting on each other for work to be done, with even small changes creating potentially global, catastrophic consequences.

An example of how Conway's Law can either impede or reinforce our goals can be seen in a technology that was developed at Etsy called Sprouter. Etsy's DevOps journey began in 2009, and is one of the most admired DevOps organizations, with 2014 revenue of nearly $200 million and a successful IPO in 2015.

Originally developed in 2007, Sprouter connected people, processes, and technology in ways that created many undesired outcomes. Sprouter, shorthand for "stored procedure router," was originally designed to help make life easier for the developers and database teams. As Ross Snyder, a senior engineer at Etsy, said during his presentation at Surge 2011, "Sprouter was designed to allow the Dev teams to write PHP code in the application, the DBAs to write SQL inside Postgres, with Sprouter helping them meet in the middle."

Sprouter resided between their front-end PHP application and the Postgres database, centralizing access to the database and hiding the database implementation from the application layer. The problem was that adding any changes to business logic resulted in significant friction between developers and the database teams. As Snyder observed, "For nearly any new site functionality, Sprouter required that the DBAs write a new stored procedure. As a result, every time developers wanted to add new functionality, they would need something from the DBAs, which often required them to wade through a ton of bureaucracy." In other words, developers creating new functionality had a dependency on the DBA team, which needed to be prioritized, communicated, and coordinated, resulting in work sitting in queues, meetings, longer lead times, and so forth. This is because Sprouter created a tight coupling between the development and database teams, preventing developers from being able to independently develop, test, and deploy their code into production.

Also, the database stored procedures were tightly coupled to Sprouter—any time a stored procedure was changed, it required changes to Sprouter too. The result was that Sprouter became an ever-larger single point of failure. Snyder explained that everything was so tightly coupled and required such a high level of synchronization as a result, that almost every deployment caused a mini-outage.

Both the problems associated with Sprouter and their eventual solution can be explained by Conway's Law. Etsy initially had two teams, the developers and the DBAs, who were each responsible for two layers of the service, the application logic layer and stored procedure layer. Two teams working on two layers, as Conway's Law predicts. Sprouter was intended to make life easier for both teams, but it didn't work as expected—when business rules changed, instead of changing only two layers, they now needed to make changes to three layers (in the application, in the stored procedures, and now in Sprouter). The resulting challenges of coordinating and prioritizing work across three teams significantly increased lead times and caused reliability problems.

In the spring of 2009, as part of what Snyder called "the great Etsy cultural transformation," Chad Dickerson joined as their new CTO. Dickerson put into motion many things, including a massive investment into site stability, having developers perform their own deployments into production, as well as beginning a two-year journey to eliminate Sprouter.

To do this, the team decided to move all the business logic from the database layer into the application layer, removing the need for Sprouter. They created a small team that wrote a PHP Object Relational Mapping (ORM) layer,[†] enabling the front-end developers to make calls directly to the database and reducing the number of teams required to change business logic from three teams down to one team.

As Snyder described, "We started using the ORM for any new areas of the site and migrated small parts of our site from Sprouter to the ORM over time. It took us two years to migrate the entire site off of Sprouter. And even though we all grumbled about Sprouter the entire time, it remained in production throughout."

By eliminating Sprouter, they also eliminated the problems associated with multiple teams needing to coordinate for business logic changes, decreased the number of handoffs, and significantly increased the speed and success of production deployments, improving site stability. Furthermore, because small teams could independently develop and deploy their code without requiring another team to make changes in other areas of the system, developer productivity increased.

---

† Among many things, an ORM abstracts a database, enabling developers to do queries and data manipulation as if they were merely another object in the programming language. Popular ORMs include Hibernate for Java, SQLAlchemy for Python, and ActiveRecord for Ruby on Rails.

Sprouter was finally removed from production and Etsy's version control repositories in early 2001. As Snyder said, "Wow, it felt good."[†]

As Snyder and Etsy experienced, how we design our organization dictates how work is performed, and, therefore, the outcomes we achieve. Throughout the rest of this chapter we will explore how Conway's Law can negatively impact the performance of our value stream, and, more importantly, how we organize our teams to use Conway's Law to our advantage.

ORGANIZATIONAL ARCHETYPES

In the field of decision sciences, there are three primary types of organizational structures that inform how we design our DevOps value streams with Conway's Law in mind: *functional*, *matrix*, and *market*. They are defined by Dr. Roberto Fernandez as follows:

- Functional-oriented organizations optimize for expertise, division of labor, or reducing cost. These organizations centralize expertise, which helps enable career growth and skill development, and often have tall hierarchical organizational structures. This has been the prevailing method of organization for Operations, (i.e., server admins, network admins, database admins, and so forth are all organized into separate groups).

- Matrix-oriented organizations attempt to combine functional and market orientation. However, as many who work in or manage matrix organizations observe, matrix organizations often result in complicated organizational structures, such as individual contributors reporting to two managers or more, and sometimes achieving neither of the goals of functional or market orientation.

- Market-oriented organizations optimize for responding quickly to customer needs. These organizations tend to be flat, composed of multiple, cross-functional disciplines (e.g., marketing, engineering, etc.), which often lead to potential redundancies across the organization. This is how many prominent organizations adopting DevOps operate—in extreme examples, such as at

---

† Sprouter was one of many technologies used in development and production that Etsy eliminated as part of their transformation.

Amazon or Netflix, each service team is simultaneously responsible for feature delivery and service support.[‡]

With these three categories of organizations in mind, let's explore further how an overly functional orientation, especially in Operations, can cause undesired outcomes in the technology value stream, as Conway's Law would predict.

PROBLEMS OFTEN CAUSED BY OVERLY FUNCTIONAL ORIENTATION ("OPTIMIZING FOR COST")

In traditional IT Operations organizations, we often use functional orientation to organize our teams by their specialties. We put the database administrators in one group, the network administrators in another, the server administrators in a third, and so forth. One of the most visible consequences of this is long lead times, especially for complex activities like large deployments where we must open up tickets with multiple groups and coordinate work handoffs, resulting in our work waiting in long queues at every step.

Compounding the issue, the person performing the work often has little visibility or understanding of how their work relates to any value stream goals (e.g., "I'm just configuring servers because someone told me to."). This places workers in a creativity and motivation vacuum.

The problem is exacerbated when each Operations functional area has to serve multiple value streams (i.e., multiple Development teams) who all compete for their scarce cycles. In order for Development teams to get their work done in a timely manner, we often have to escalate issues to a manager or director, and eventually to someone (usually an executive) who can finally prioritize the work against the global organizational goals instead of the functional silo goals. This decision must then get cascaded down into each of the functional areas to change the local priorities, and this, in turn, slows down other teams. When every team expedites their work, the net result is that every project ends up moving at the same slow crawl.

In addition to long queues and long lead times, this situation results in poor handoffs, large amounts of re-work, quality issues, bottlenecks, and delays.

---

‡ However, as will be explained later, equally prominent organizations such as Etsy and GitHub have functional orientation.

This gridlock impedes the achievement of important organizational goals, which often far outweigh the desire to reduce costs.[†]

Similarly, functional orientation can also be found with centralized QA and Infosec functions, which may have worked fine (or at least, well enough) when performing less frequent software releases. However, as we increase the number of Development teams and their deployment and release frequencies, most functionally-oriented organizations will have difficulty keeping up and delivering satisfactory outcomes, especially when their work is being performed manually. Now we'll study how market oriented organizations work.

ENABLE MARKET-ORIENTED TEAMS ("OPTIMIZING FOR SPEED")

Broadly speaking, to achieve DevOps outcomes, we need to reduce the effects of functional orientation ("optimizing for cost") and enable market orientation ("optimizing for speed") so we can have many small teams working safely and independently, quickly delivering value to the customer.

Taken to the extreme, market-oriented teams are responsible not only for feature development, but also for testing, securing, deploying, and supporting their service in production, from idea conception to retirement. These teams are designed to be cross-functional and independent—able to design and run user experiments, build and deliver new features, deploy and run their service in production, and fix any defects without manual dependencies on other teams, thus enabling them to move faster. This model has been adopted by Amazon and Netflix and is touted by Amazon as one of the primary reasons behind their ability to move fast even as they grow.

To achieve market orientation, we won't do a large, top-down reorganization, which often creates large amounts of disruption, fear, and paralysis. Instead, we will embed the functional engineers and skills (e.g., Ops, QA, Infosec) into each service team, or provide their capabilities to teams through automated

---

† Adrian Cockcroft remarked, "For companies who are now coming off of five-year IT outsourcing contracts, it's like they've been frozen in time, during one of the most disruptive times in technology." In other words, IT outsourcing is a tactic used to control costs through contractually-enforced stasis, with firm fixed prices that schedule annual cost reductions. However, it often results in organizations being unable to respond to changing business and technology needs.

self-service platforms that provide production-like environments, initiate automated tests, or perform deployments.

This enables each service team to independently deliver value to the customer without having to open tickets with other groups, such as IT Operations, QA, or Infosec.‡

MAKING FUNCTIONAL ORIENTATION WORK

Having just recommended market-orientated teams, it is worth pointing out that it is possible to create effective, high-velocity organizations with functional orientation. Cross-functional and market-oriented teams are one way to achieve fast flow and reliability, but they are not the only path. We can also achieve our desired DevOps outcomes through functional orientation, as long as everyone in the value stream views customer and organizational outcomes as a shared goal, regardless of where they reside in the organization.

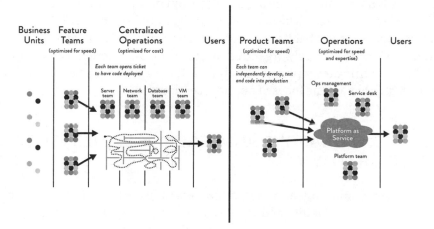

Figure 12: *Functional vs. market orientation*

Left: Functional orientation: all work flows through centralized IT Operations; Right: Market orientation: all product teams can deploy their loosely coupled components self-service into production. (Source: Humble, Molesky, and O'Reilly, Lean Enterprise, *Kindle edition, 4523 & 4592.)*

‡ For the remainder of this books, we will use *service teams* interchangeably with *feature teams, product teams, development teams,* and *delivery teams*. The intent is to specify the team primarily developing, testing, and securing the code so that value is delivered to the customer.

For example, high performance with a functional-oriented and centralized Operations group is possible, as long as service teams get what they need from Operations reliably and quickly (ideally on demand) and vice-versa. Many of the most admired DevOps organizations retain functional orientation of Operations, including Etsy, Google, and GitHub.

What these organizations have in common is a high-trust culture that enables all departments to work together effectively, where all work is transparently prioritized and there is sufficient slack in the system to allow high-priority work to be completed quickly. This is, in part, enabled by automated self-service platforms that build quality into the products everyone is building.

In the Lean manufacturing movement of the 1980s, many researchers were puzzled by Toyota's functional orientation, which was at odds with the best practice of having cross-functional, market-oriented teams. They were so puzzled it was called "the second Toyota paradox."

As Mike Rother wrote in *Toyota Kata*, "As tempting as it seems, one cannot reorganize your way to continuous improvement and adaptiveness. What is decisive is not the form of the organization, but how people act and react. The roots of Toyota's success lie not in its organizational structures, but in developing capability and habits in its people. It surprises many people, in fact, to find that Toyota is largely organized in a traditional, functional-department style." It is this development of habits and capabilities in people and the workforce that are the focus of our next sections.

TESTING, OPERATIONS, AND SECURITY AS EVERYONE'S JOB, EVERY DAY

In high-performing organizations, everyone within the team shares a common goal—quality, availability, and security aren't the responsibility of individual departments, but are a part of everyone's job, every day.

This means that the most urgent problem of the day may be working on or deploying a customer feature or fixing a Severity 1 production incident. Alternatively, the day may require reviewing a fellow engineer's change, applying emergency security patches to production servers, or making improvements so that fellow engineers are more productive.

Reflecting on shared goals between Development and Operations, Jody Mulkey, CTO at Ticketmaster, said, "For almost 25 years, I used an American football metaphor to describe Dev and Ops. You know, Ops is defense, who keeps the other team from scoring, and Dev is offense, trying to score goals. And one day, I realized how flawed this metaphor was, because they never all play on the field at the same time. They're not actually on the same team!"

He continued, "The analogy I use now is that Ops are the offensive linemen, and Dev are the 'skill' positions (like the quarterback and wide receivers) whose job it is to move the ball down the field—the job of Ops is to help make sure Dev has enough time to properly execute the plays."

A striking example of how shared pain can reinforce shared goals is when Facebook was undergoing enormous growth in 2009. They were experiencing significant problems related to code deployments—while not all issues caused customer-impacting issues, there was chronic firefighting and long hours. Pedro Canahuati, their director of production engineering, described a meeting full of Ops engineers where someone asked that all people not working on an incident close their laptops, and no one could.

One of the most significant things they did to help change the outcomes of deployments was to have all Facebook engineers, engineering managers, and architects rotate through on-call duty for the services they built. By doing this, everyone who worked on the service experienced visceral feedback on the upstream architectural and coding decisions they made, which made an enormous positive impact on the downstream outcomes.

ENABLE EVERY TEAM MEMBER TO BE A GENERALIST

In extreme cases of a functionally-oriented Operations organization, we have departments of specialists, such as network administrators, storage administrators, and so forth. When departments over-specialize, it causes *siloization*, which Dr. Spear describes as when departments "operate more like sovereign states." Any complex operational activity then requires multiple handoffs and queues between the different areas of the infrastructure, leading to longer lead times (e.g., because every network change must be made by someone in the networking department).

Because we rely upon an ever increasing number of technologies, we must have engineers who have specialized and achieved mastery in the technology areas we need. However, we don't want to create specialists who are "frozen in time," only understanding and able to contribute to that one area of the value stream.

One countermeasure is to enable and encourage every team member to be a generalist. We do this by providing opportunities for engineers to learn all the skills necessary to build and run the systems they are responsible for, and regularly rotating people through different roles. The term *full stack engineer* is now commonly used (sometimes as a rich source of parody) to describe generalists who are familiar—at least have a general level of understanding—with the entire application stack (e.g., application code, databases, operating systems, networking, cloud).

Table 2: *Specialists vs. Generalists vs. "E-shaped" Staff (experience, expertise, exploration, and execution)*

"I-shaped" (Specialists)	"T-shaped" (Generalists)	"E-shaped"
Deep expertise in one area	Deep expertise in one area	Deep expertise in a few areas
Very few skills or experience in other areas	Broad skills across many areas	Experience across many areas Proven execution skills Always innovating
Creates bottlenecks quickly	Can step up to remove bottlenecks	Almost limitless potential
Insensitive to downstream waste and impact	Sensitive to downstream waste and impact	
Prevents planning flexibility or absorption of variability	Helps make planning flexible and absorbs variability	

(Source: Scott Prugh, "Continuous Delivery," ScaledAgileFramework.com, February 14, 2013, http://scaledagileframework.com/continuous-delivery/.)

Scott Prugh writes that CSG International has undergone a transformation that brings most resources required to build and run the product onto one team, including analysis, architecture, development, test, and operations. "By cross-training and growing engineering skills, generalists can do orders of magnitude more work than their specialist counterparts, and it also improves our overall flow of work by removing queues and wait time." This approach is at odds with traditional hiring practices, but, as Prugh explains, it is well worth it. "Traditional managers will often object to hiring engineers with generalist skill sets, arguing that they are more expensive and that 'I can hire two server administrators for every multiskilled operations engineer.'" However, the business benefits of enabling faster flow are overwhelming. Furthermore, as Prugh notes, "[I]nvesting in cross training is the right thing for [employees'] career growth, and makes everyone's work more fun."

When we value people merely for their existing skills or performance in their current role rather than for their ability to acquire and deploy new skills, we (often inadvertently) reinforce what Dr. Carol Dweck describes as the *fixed mindset*, where people view their intelligence and abilities as static "givens" that can't be changed in meaningful ways.

Instead, we want to encourage learning, help people overcome learning anxiety, help ensure that people have relevant skills and a defined career road map, and so forth. By doing this, we help foster a *growth mindset* in our engineers—after all, a learning organization requires people who are willing to learn. By encouraging everyone to learn, as well as providing training and support, we create the most sustainable and least expensive way to create greatness in our teams—by investing in the development of the people we already have.

As Jason Cox, Director of Systems Engineering at Disney, described, "Inside of Operations, we had to change our hiring practices. We looked for people who had 'curiosity, courage, and candor,' who were not only capable of being generalists but also renegades...We want to promote positive disruption so our business doesn't get stuck and can move into the future." As we'll see in the next section, how we fund our teams also affects our outcomes.

FUND NOT PROJECTS, BUT SERVICES AND PRODUCTS

Another way to enable high-performing outcomes is to create stable service teams with ongoing funding to execute their own strategy and road map of initiatives. These teams have the dedicated engineers needed to deliver on concrete commitments made to internal and external customers, such as features, stories, and tasks.

Contrast this to the more traditional model where Development and Test teams are assigned to a "project" and then reassigned to another project as soon as the project is completed and funding runs out. This leads to all sorts of undesired outcomes, including developers being unable to see the long-term consequences of decisions they make (a form of feedback) and a funding model that only values and pays for the earliest stages of the software life cycle—which, tragically, is also the least expensive part for successful products or services.[†]

Our goal with a product-based funding model is to value the achievement of organizational and customer outcomes, such as revenue, customer lifetime value, or customer adoption rate, ideally with the minimum of output (e.g., amount of effort or time, lines of code). Contrast this to how projects are typically measured, such as whether it was completed within the promised budget, time, and scope.

DESIGN TEAM BOUNDARIES IN ACCORDANCE WITH CONWAY'S LAW

As organizations grow, one of the largest challenges is maintaining effective communication and coordination between people and teams. All too often, when people and teams reside on a different floor, in a different building, or in a different time zone, creating and maintaining a shared understanding and mutual trust becomes more difficult, impeding effective collaboration. Collaboration is also impeded when the primary communication mechanisms are work tickets and change requests, or worse, when teams are separated by contractual boundaries, such as when work is performed by an outsourced team.

As we saw in the Etsy Sprouter example at the beginning of this chapter, the way we organize teams can create poor outcomes, a side effect of Conway's Law. These include splitting teams by function (e.g., by putting developers and testers in different locations or by outsourcing testers entirely) or by architectural layer (e.g., application, database).

These configurations require significant communication and coordination between teams, but still results in a high amount of rework, disagreements over specifications, poor handoffs, and people sitting idle waiting for somebody else.

Ideally, our software architecture should enable small teams to be independently productive, sufficiently decoupled from each other so that work can be done without excessive or unnecessary communication and coordination.

---

† As John Lauderbach, currently VP of Information Technology at Roche Bros. Supermarkets, quipped, "Every new application is like a free puppy. It's not the upfront capital cost that kills you...It's the ongoing maintenance and support."

CREATE LOOSELY-COUPLED ARCHITECTURES TO ENABLE DEVELOPER PRODUCTIVITY AND SAFETY

When we have a tightly coupled architecture, small changes can result in large scale failures. As a result, anyone working in one part of the system must constantly coordinate with anyone else working in another part of the system they may affect, including navigating complex and bureaucratic change management processes.

Furthermore, to test that the entire system works together requires integrating changes with the changes from hundreds, or even thousands, of other developers, which may, in turn, have dependencies on tens, hundreds, or thousands of interconnected systems. Testing is done in scarce integration test environments, which often require weeks to obtain and configure. The result is not only long lead times for changes (typically measured in weeks or months) but also low developer productivity and poor deployment outcomes.

In contrast, when we have an architecture that enables small teams of developers to independently implement, test, and deploy code into production safely and quickly, we can increase and maintain developer productivity and improve deployment outcomes. These characteristics can be found in *service-oriented architectures* (SOAs) first described in the 1990s, in which services are independently testable and deployable. A key feature of SOAs is that they're composed of *loosely coupled* services with *bounded contexts*.‡

Having architecture that is loosely coupled means that services can update in production independently, without having to update other services. Services must be decoupled from other services and, just as important, from shared databases (although they can share a database *service*, provided they don't have any common schemas).

Bounded contexts are described in the book *Domain Driven Design* by Eric J. Evans. The idea is that developers should be able to understand and update the code of a service without knowing anything about the internals of its peer services. Services interact with their peers strictly through APIs and thus don't share data structures, database schemata, or other internal representations of objects. Bounded contexts ensure that services are compartmentalized and have well-defined interfaces, which also enables easier testing.

---

‡ These properties are also found in "microservices," which build upon the principles of SOA. One popular set of patterns for modern web architecture based on these principles is the "12-factor app."

Randy Shoup, former Engineering Director for Google App Engine, observed that "organizations with these types of service-oriented architectures, such as Google and Amazon, have incredible flexibility and scalability. These organizations have tens of thousands of developers where small teams can still be incredibly productive."

KEEP TEAM SIZES SMALL (THE "TWO-PIZZA TEAM" RULE)

Conway's Law helps us design our team boundaries in the context of desired communication patterns, but it also encourages us to keep our team sizes small, reducing the amount of inter-team communication and encouraging us to keep the scope of each team's domain small and bounded.

As part of its transformation initiative away from a monolithic code base in 2002, Amazon used the *two-pizza* rule to keep team sizes small—a team only as large as can be fed with two pizzas—usually about five to ten people.

This limit on size has four important effects:

1. It ensures the team has a clear, shared understanding of the system they are working on. As teams get larger, the amount of communication required for everybody to know what's going on scales in a combinatorial fashion.

2. It limits the growth rate of the product or service being worked on. By limiting the size of the team, we limit the rate at which their system can evolve. This also helps to ensure the team maintains a shared understanding of the system.

3. It decentralizes power and enables autonomy. Each two-pizza team (2PT) is as autonomous as possible. The team's lead, working with the executive team, decides on the key business metric that the team is responsible for, known as the fitness function, which becomes the overall evaluation criteria for the team's experiments. The team is then able to act autonomously to maximize that metric.[†]

4. Leading a 2PT is a way for employees to gain some leadership experience in an environment where failure does not have catastrophic consequences. An essential element of Amazon's strategy

---

† In the Netflix culture, one of the seven key values is "highly aligned, loosely coupled."

was the link between the organizational structure of a 2PT and the architectural approach of a service-oriented architecture.

Amazon CTO Werner Vogels explained the advantages of this structure to Larry Dignan of *Baseline* in 2005. Dignan writes:

> "Small teams are fast...and don't get bogged down in so-called administrivia....Each group assigned to a particular business is completely responsible for it....The team scopes the fix, designs it, builds it, implements it and monitors its ongoing use. This way, technology programmers and architects get direct feedback from the business people who use their code or applications—in regular meetings and informal conversations."

Another example of how architecture can profoundly improve productivity is the API Enablement program at Target, Inc.

Case Study
API Enablement at Target (2015)

Target is the sixth largest retailer in the US and spends over $1 billion on technology annually. Heather Mickman, a director of development for Target, described the beginnings of their DevOps journey: "In the bad old days, it used to take ten different teams to provision a server at Target, and when things broke, we tended to stop making changes to prevent further issues, which of course makes everything worse."

The hardships associated with getting environments and performing deployments created significant difficulties for development teams, as did getting access to data they needed. As Mickman described:

> The problem was that much of our core data, such as information on inventory, pricing, and stores, was locked up in legacy systems and mainframes. We often had multiple sources of truths of data, especially between e-commerce and our physical stores, which were owned by different teams, with different data structures and different priorities....The result was that if a new development team wanted to build something for our guests, it would take three to six months to build the integrations to get the data they needed. Worse, it would take another three to six months to do the manual

testing to make sure they didn't break anything critical, because of how many custom point-to-point integrations we had in a very tightly coupled system. Having to manage the interactions with the twenty to thirty different teams, along with all their dependencies, required lots of project managers, because of all the coordination and handoffs. It meant that development was spending all their time waiting in queues, instead of delivering results and getting stuff done.

This long lead time for retrieving and creating data in their systems of record was jeopardizing important business goals, such as integrating the supply chain operations of Target's physical stores and their e-commerce site, which now required getting inventory to stores and customer homes. This pushed the Target supply chain well beyond what it was designed for, which was merely to facilitate the movement of goods from vendors to distribution centers and stores.

In an attempt to solve the data problem, in 2012 Mickman led the API Enablement team to enable development teams to "deliver new capabilities in days instead of months." They wanted any engineering team inside of Target to be able to get and store the data they needed, such as information on their products or their stores, including operating hours, location, whether there was as Starbucks on-site, and so forth.

Time constraints played a large role in team selection. Mickman explained that:

> Because our team also needed to deliver capabilities in days, not months, I needed a team who could do the work, not give it to contractors—we wanted people with kickass engineering skills, not people who knew how to manage contracts. And to make sure our work wasn't sitting in queue, we needed to own the entire stack, which meant that we took over the Ops requirements as well....We brought in many new tools to support continuous integration and continuous delivery. And because we knew that if we succeeded, we would have to scale with extremely high growth, we brought in new tools such as the Cassandra database and Kafka message broker. When we asked for permission, we were told no, but we did it anyway, because we knew we needed it.

In the following two years, the API Enablement team enabled fifty-three new business capabilities, including Ship to Store and Gift Registry, as well as their integrations with Instacart and Pinterest. As Mickman described, "Working with Pinterest suddenly became very easy, because we just provided them our APIs."

In 2014, the API Enablement team served over 1.5 billion API calls per month. By 2015, this had grown to seventeen billion calls per month spanning ninety different APIs. To support this capability, they routinely performed eighty deployments per week.

These changes have created major business benefits for Target—digital sales increased 42% during the 2014 holiday season and increased another 32% in Q2. During the Black Friday weekend of 2015, over 280k in-store pickup orders were created. By 2015, their goal is to enable 450 of their 1,800 stores to be able to fulfill e-commerce orders, up from one hundred.

"The API Enablement team shows what a team of passionate change agents can do," Mickman says. "And it help set us up for the next stage, which is to expand DevOps across the entire technology organization."

CONCLUSION

Through the Etsy and Target case studies, we can see how architecture and organizational design can dramatically improve our outcomes. Done incorrectly, Conway's Law will ensure that the organization creates poor outcomes, preventing safety and agility. Done well, the organization enables developers to safely and independently develop, test, and deploy value to the customer.

8 How to Get Great Outcomes by Integrating Operations into the Daily Work of Development

Our goal is to enable market-oriented outcomes where many small teams can quickly and independently deliver value to the customer. This can be a challenge to achieve when Operations is centralized and functionally-oriented, having to serve the needs of many different development teams with potentially wildly different needs. The result can often be long lead times for needed Ops work, constant reprioritization and escalation, and poor deployment outcomes.

We can create more market-oriented outcomes by better integrating Ops capabilities into Dev teams, making both more efficient and productive. In this chapter, we'll explore many ways to achieve this, both at the organizational level and through daily rituals. By doing this, Ops can significantly improve the productivity of Dev teams throughout the entire organization, as well as enable better collaboration and organizational outcomes.

At Big Fish Games, which develops and supports hundreds of mobile and thousands of PC games and had more than $266 million in revenue in 2013, VP of IT Operations Paul Farrall was in charge of the centralized Operations organization. He was responsible for supporting many different business units that had a great deal of autonomy.

Each of these business units had dedicated development teams who often chose wildly different technologies. When these groups wanted to deploy new functionality, they would have to compete for a common pool of scarce Ops resources. Furthermore, everyone was struggling with unreliable Test and Integration environments, as well as extremely cumbersome release processes.

Farrall thought the best way to solve this problem was by embedding Ops expertise into Development teams. He observed, "When Dev teams had problems with testing or deployment, they needed more than just technology or environments. What they also needed was help and coaching. At first, we embedded Ops engineers and architects into each of the Dev teams, but there simply weren't enough Ops engineers to cover that many teams. We were able to help more teams with what we called an *Ops liaison* model and with fewer people."

Farrall defined two types of Ops liaisons: the business relationship manager and the dedicated release engineer. The business relationship managers worked with product management, line-of-business owners, project management, Dev management, and developers. They became intimately familiar with product group business drivers and product road maps, acted as advocates for product owners inside of Operations, and helped their product teams navigate the Operations landscape to prioritize and streamline work requests.

Similarly, the dedicated release engineer became intimately familiar with the product's Development and QA issues, and helped them get what they needed from the Ops organization to achieve their goals. They were familiar with the typical Dev and QA requests for Ops, and would often execute the needed work themselves. As needed, they would also pull in dedicated technical Ops engineers (e.g., DBAs, Infosec, storage engineers, network engineers), and help determine which self-service tools the entire Operations group should prioritize building.

By doing this, Farrall was able to help Dev teams across the organization become more productive and achieve their team goals. Furthermore, he helped the teams prioritize around his global Ops constraints, reducing the number of surprises discovered mid-project and ultimately increasing the overall project throughput.

Farrall notes that both working relationships with Operations and code release velocity were noticeably improved as a result of the changes. He concludes, "The Ops liaison model allowed us to embed IT Operations expertise into the Dev and Product teams without adding new headcount."

The DevOps transformation at Big Fish Games shows how a centralized Operations team was able to achieve the outcomes typically associated with market-oriented teams. We can employ the three following broad strategies:

- Create self-service capabilities to enable developers in the service teams to be productive.

- Embed Ops engineers into the service teams.

- Assign Ops liaisons to the service teams when embedding Ops is not possible.

Lastly, we describe how Ops engineers can integrate into the Dev team rituals used in their daily work, including daily standups, planning, and retrospectives.

CREATE SHARED SERVICES TO INCREASE DEVELOPER PRODUCTIVITY

One way to enable market-oriented outcomes is for Operations to create a set of centralized platforms and tooling services that any Dev team can use to become more productive, such as getting production-like environments, deployment pipelines, automated testing tools, production telemetry dashboards, and so forth.[†] By doing this, we enable Dev teams to spend more time building functionality for their customer, as opposed to obtaining all the infrastructure required to deliver and support that feature in production.

All the platforms and services we provide should (ideally) be automated and available on demand, without requiring a developer to open up a ticket and wait for someone to manually perform work. This ensures that Operations doesn't become a bottleneck for their customers (e.g., "We received your work request, and it will take six weeks to manually configure those test environments.").[‡]

By doing this, we enable the product teams to get what they need, when they need it, as well as reduce the need for communications and coordination. As Damon Edwards observed, "Without these self-service Operations platforms, the cloud is just Expensive Hosting 2.0."

In almost all cases, we will not mandate that internal teams use these platforms and services—these platform teams will have to win over and satisfy their

---

† The terms *platform*, *shared service*, and *toolchain* will be used interchangeably in this book.

‡ Ernest Mueller observed, "At Bazaarvoice, the agreement was that these platform teams that make tools accept requirements, but not work from other teams."

internal customers, sometimes even competing with external vendors. By creating this effective internal marketplace of capabilities, we help ensure that the platforms and services we create are the easiest and most appealing choice available (the path of least resistance).

For instance, we may create a platform that provides a shared version control repository with pre-blessed security libraries, a deployment pipeline that automatically runs code quality and security scanning tools, which deploys our applications into *known, good environments* that already have production monitoring tools installed on them. Ideally, we make life so much easier for Dev teams that they will overwhelmingly decide that using our platform is the easiest, safest, and most secure means to get their applications into production.

We build into these platforms the cumulative and collective experience of everyone in the organization, including QA, Operations, and Infosec, which helps to create an ever safer system of work. This increases developer productivity and makes it easy for product teams to leverage common processes, such as performing automated testing and satisfying security and compliance requirements.

Creating and maintaining these platforms and tools is real product development—the customers of our platform aren't our external customer but our internal Dev teams. Like creating any great product, creating great platforms that everyone loves doesn't happen by accident. An internal platform team with poor customer focus will likely create tools that everyone will hate and quickly abandon for other alternatives, whether for another internal platform team or an external vendor.

Dianne Marsh, Director of Engineering Tools at Netflix, states that her team's charter is to "support our engineering teams' innovation and velocity. We don't build, bake, or deploy anything for these teams, nor do we manage their configurations. Instead, we build tools to enable self-service. It's okay for people to be dependent on our tools, but it's important that they don't become dependent on us."

Often, these platform teams provide other services to help their customers learn their technology, migrate off of other technologies, and even provide coaching and consulting to help elevate the state of the practice inside the organization. These shared services also facilitate standardization, which enable engineers to quickly become productive, even if they switch between teams. For instance, if every product team chooses a different toolchain, engineers may have to learn an entirely new set of technologies to do their work, putting the team goals ahead of the global goals.

In organizations where teams can only use approved tools, we can start by removing this requirement for a few teams, such as the transformation team, so that we can experiment and discover what capabilities make those teams more productive.

Internal shared services teams should continually look for internal toolchains that are widely being adopted in the organization, deciding which ones make sense to be supported centrally and made available to everyone. In general, taking something that's already working somewhere and expanding its usage is far more likely to succeed than building these capabilities from scratch.[†]

EMBED OPS ENGINEERS INTO OUR SERVICE TEAMS

Another way we can enable more market-oriented outcomes is by enabling product teams to become more self-sufficient by embedding Operations engineers within them, thus reducing their reliance on centralized Operations. These product teams may also be completely responsible for service delivery and service support.

By embedding Operations engineers into the Dev teams, their priorities are driven almost entirely by the goals of the product teams they are embedded in—as opposed to Ops focusing inwardly on solving their own problems. As a result, Ops engineers become more closely connected to their internal and external customers. Furthermore, the product teams often have the budget to fund the hiring of these Ops engineers, although interviewing and hiring decisions will likely still be done from the centralized Operations group, to ensure consistency and quality of staff.

Jason Cox said, "In many parts of Disney we have embedded Ops (system engineers) inside the product teams in our business units, along with inside Development, Test, and even Information Security. It has totally changed the dynamics of how we work. As Operations Engineers, we create the tools and capabilities that transform the way people work, and even the way they think. In traditional Ops, we merely drove the train that someone else built. But in

---

† After all, designing a system upfront for re-use is a common and expensive failure mode of many enterprise architectures.

modern Operations Engineering, we not only help build the train, but also the bridges that the trains roll on."

For new large Development projects, we may initially embed Ops engineers into those teams. Their work may include helping decide what to build and how to build it, influencing the product architecture, helping influence internal and external technology choices, helping create new capabilities in our internal platforms, and maybe even generating new operational capabilities. After the product is released to production, embedded Ops engineers may help with the production responsibilities of the Dev team.

They will take part in all of the Dev team rituals, such as planning meetings, daily standups, and demonstrations where the team shows off new features and decides which ones to ship. As the need for Ops knowledge and capabilities decreases, Ops engineers may transition to different projects or engagements, following the general pattern that the composition within product teams changes throughout its life cycle.

This paradigm has another important advantage: pairing Dev and Ops engineers together is an extremely efficient way to cross-train operations knowledge and expertise into a service team. It can also have the powerful benefit of transforming operations knowledge into automated code that can be far more reliable and widely reused.

ASSIGN AN OPS LIAISON TO EACH SERVICE TEAM

For a variety of reasons, such as cost and scarcity, we may be unable to embed Ops engineers into every product team. However, we can get many of the same benefits by assigning a designated liaison for each product team.

At Etsy, this model is called "designated Ops." Their centralized Operations group continues to manage all the environments—not just production environments but also pre-production environments—to help ensure they remain consistent. The designated Ops engineer is responsible for understanding:

- What the new product functionality is and why we're building it

- How it works as it pertains to operability, scalability, and observability (diagramming is strongly encouraged)

- How to monitor and collect metrics to ensure the progress, success, or failure of the functionality

- Any departures from previous architectures and patterns, and the justifications for them

- Any extra needs for infrastructure and how usage will affect infrastructure capacity

- Feature launch plans

Furthermore, just like in the embedded Ops model, this liaison attends the team standups, integrating their needs into the Operations road map and performing any needed tasks. We rely on these liaisons to escalate any resource contention or prioritization issue. By doing this, we identify any resource or time conflicts that should be evaluated and prioritized in the context of wider organizational goals.

Assigning Ops liaisons allows us to support more product teams than the embedded Ops model. Our goal is to ensure that Ops is not a constraint for the product teams. If we find that Ops liaisons are stretched too thin, preventing the product teams from achieving their goals, then we will likely need to either reduce the number of teams each liaison supports or temporarily embed an Ops engineer into specific teams.

INTEGRATE OPS INTO DEV RITUALS

When Ops engineers are embedded or assigned as liaisons into our product teams, we can integrate them into our Dev team rituals. In this section, our goal is to help Ops engineers and other non-developers better understand the existing Development culture and proactively integrate them into all aspects of planning and daily work. As a result, Operations is better able to plan and radiate any needed knowledge into the product teams, influencing work long before it gets into production. The following sections describe some of the standard rituals used by Development teams using agile methods and how we would integrate Ops engineers into them. By no means are agile practices a prerequisite for this step—as Ops engineers, our goal is to discover what rituals the product teams follow, integrate into them, and add value to them.[†]

---

† However, if we discover that the entire Development organization merely sits at their desks all day without ever talking to each other, we may have to find a different way to engage them, such as buying them lunch, starting a book club, taking turns doing "lunch and learn" presentations, or having conversations to discover what everyone's biggest problems are, so that we can figure out how we can make their lives better.

As Ernest Mueller observed, "I believe DevOps works a lot better if Operations teams adopt the same agile rituals that Dev teams have used—we've had fantastic successes solving many problems associated with Ops pain points, as well as integrating better with Dev teams."

INVITE OPS TO OUR DEV STANDUPS

One of the Dev rituals popularized by Scrum is the daily standup, a quick meeting where everyone on the team gets together and presents to each other three things: what was done yesterday, what is going to be done today, and what is preventing you from getting your work done.[†]

The purpose of this ceremony is to radiate information throughout the team and to understand the work that is being done and is going to be done. By having team members present this information to each other, we learn about any tasks that are experiencing roadblocks and discover ways to help each other move our work toward completion. Furthermore, by having managers present, we can quickly resolve prioritization and resource conflicts.

A common problem is that this information is compartmentalized within the Development team. By having Ops engineers attend, Operations can gain an awareness of the Development team's activities, enabling better planning and preparation—for instance, if we discover that the product team is planning a big feature rollout in two weeks, we can ensure that the right people and resources are available to support the rollout. Alternatively, we may highlight areas where closer interaction or more preparation is needed (e.g., creating more monitoring checks or automation scripts). By doing this, we create the conditions where Operations can help solve our current team problems (e.g., improving performance by tuning the database, instead of optimizing code) or future problems before they turn into a crisis (e.g., creating more integration test environments to enable performance testing).

INVITE OPS TO OUR DEV RETROSPECTIVES

Another widespread agile ritual is the retrospective. At the end of each development interval, the team discusses what was successful, what could be improved, and how to incorporate the successes and improvements in future iterations or projects. The team comes up with ideas to make things better

---

† Scrum is an agile development methodology, described as "a flexible, holistic product development strategy where a development team works as a unit to reach a common goal." It was first fully described by Ken Schwaber and Mike Beedle in the book *Agile Software Development with Scrum*. In this book, we use the term "agile development" or "iterative development" to encompass the various techniques used by special methodologies such as Agile and Scrum.

and reviews experiments from the previous iteration. This is one of the primary mechanisms where organizational learning and the development of counter-measures occurs, with resulting work implemented immediately or added to the team's backlog.

Having Ops engineers attend our project team retrospectives means they can also benefit from any new learnings. Furthermore, when there is a deployment or release in that interval, Operations should present the outcomes and any resulting learnings, creating feedback into the product team. By doing this, we can improve how future work is planned and performed, improving our outcomes. Examples of feedback that Operations can bring to a retrospective include:

- "Two weeks ago, we found a monitoring blind-spot and agreed on how to fix it. It worked. We had an incident last Tuesday, and we were able to quickly detect and correct it before any customers were impacted."

- "Last week's deployment was one of the most difficult and lengthy we've had in over a year. Here are some ideas on how it can be improved."

- "The promotion campaign we did last week was far more difficult than we thought it would be, and we should probably not make an offer like that again. Here are some ideas on other offers we can make to achieve our goals."

- "During the last deployment, the biggest problem we had was our firewall rules are now thousands of lines long, making it extremely difficult and risky to change. We need to re-architect how we prevent unauthorized network traffic."

Feedback from Operations helps our product teams better see and understand the downstream impact of decisions they make. When there are negative outcomes, we can make the changes necessary to prevent them in the future. Operations feedback will also likely identify more problems and defects that should be fixed—it may even uncover larger architectural issues that need to be addressed.

The additional work identified during project team retrospectives falls into the broad category of improvement work, such as fixing defects, refactoring, and automating manual work. Product managers and project managers may want to defer or deprioritize improvement work in favor of customer features.

However, we must remind everyone that improvement of daily work is more important than daily work itself, and that all teams must have dedicated capacity for this (e.g., reserving 20% of all cycles for improvement work, scheduling one day per week or one week per month, etc.). Without doing this, the productivity of the team will almost certainly grind to a halt under the weight of its own technical and process debt.

MAKE RELEVANT OPS WORK VISIBLE ON SHARED KANBAN BOARDS

Often, Development teams will make their work visible on a project board or kanban board. It's far less common, however, for work boards to show the relevant Operations work that must be performed in order for the application to run successfully in production, where customer value is actually created. As a result, we are not aware of necessary Operations work until it becomes an urgent crisis, jeopardizing deadlines or creating a production outage.

Because Operations is part of the product value stream, we should put the Operations work that is relevant to product delivery on the shared kanban board. This enables us to more clearly see all the work required to move our code into production, as well as keep track of all Operations work required to support the product. Furthermore, it enables us to see where Ops work is blocked and where work needs escalation, highlighting areas where we may need improvement.

Kanban boards are an ideal tool to create visibility, and visibility is a key component in properly recognizing and integrating Ops work into all the relevant value streams. When we do this well, we achieve market-oriented outcomes, regardless of how we've drawn our organization charts.

CONCLUSION

Throughout this chapter, we explored ways to integrate Operations into the daily work of Development, and looked at how to make our work more visible to Operations. To accomplish this, we explored three broad strategies, including creating self-service capabilities to enable developers in service teams to be productive, embedding Ops engineers into the service teams, and assigning Ops liaisons to the service teams when embedding Ops engineers was not possible. Lastly, we described how Ops engineers can integrate with the Dev team through inclusion in their daily work, including daily standups, planning, and retrospectives.

PART II CONCLUSION

In Part II: *Where to Start*, we explored a variety of ways to think about DevOps transformations, including how to choose where to start, relevant aspects of architecture and organizational design, and how to organize our teams. We also explored how to integrate Ops into all aspects of Dev planning and daily work.

In Part III: The First Way, *The Technical Practices of Flow*, we will now start to explore how to implement the specific technical practices to realize the principles of flow, which enable the fast flow of work from Development to Operations without causing chaos and disruption downstream.

PART III

The First Way
The Technical Practices of Flow

Part III
Introduction

In Part III, our goal is to create the technical practices and architecture required to enable and sustain the fast flow of work from Development into Operations without causing chaos and disruption to the production environment or our customers. This means we need to reduce the risk associated with deploying and releasing changes into production. We will do this by implementing a set of technical practices known as *continuous delivery*.

Continuous delivery includes creating the foundations of our automated deployment pipeline, ensuring that we have automated tests that constantly validate that we are in a deployable state, having developers integrate their code into trunk daily, and architecting our environments and code to enable low-risk releases. Primary focuses within these chapters include:

- Creating the foundation of our deployment pipeline

- Enabling fast and reliable automated testing

- Enabling and practicing continuous integration and testing

- Automating, enabling, and architecting for low-risk releases

Implementing these practices reduces the lead time to get production-like environments, enables continuous testing that gives everyone fast feedback on their work, enables small teams to safely and independently develop, test, and deploy their code into production, and makes production deployments and releases a routine part of daily work.

Furthermore, integrating the objectives of QA and Operations into everyone's daily work reduces firefighting, hardship, and toil, while making people more productive and increasing joy in the work we do. We not only improve outcomes, but our organization is better able to win in the marketplace.

Create the Foundations of
Our Deployment Pipeline

In order to create fast and reliable flow from Dev to Ops, we must ensure that we always use production-like environments at every stage of the value stream. Furthermore, these environments must be created in an automated manner, ideally on demand from scripts and configuration information stored in version control, and entirely self-serviced, without any manual work required from Operations. Our goal is to ensure that we can re-create the entire production environment based on what's in version control.

All too often, the only time we discover how our applications perform in anything resembling a production-like environment is during production deployment—far too late to correct problems without the customer being adversely impacted. An illustrative example of the spectrum of problems that can be caused by inconsistently built applications and environments is the Enterprise Data Warehouse program led by Em Campbell-Pretty at a large Australian telecommunications company in 2009. Campbell-Pretty became the general manager and business sponsor for this $200 million program, inheriting responsibility for all the strategic objectives that relied upon this platform.

In her presentation at the 2014 DevOps Enterprise Summit, Campbell-Pretty explained, "At the time, there were ten streams of work in progress, all using waterfall processes, and all ten streams were significantly behind schedule. Only one of the ten streams had successfully reached User Acceptance Testing [UAT] on schedule, and it took another six months for that stream to complete UAT, with the resulting capability falling well short of business expectations. This under-performance was the main catalyst for the department's Agile transformation."

However, after using Agile for nearly a year, they experienced only small improvements, still falling short of their needed business outcomes. Campbell-Pretty held a program-wide retrospective and asked, "After reflecting on all our experiences over the last release, what are things we could do that would double our productivity?"

Throughout the project, there was grumbling about the "lack of business engagement." However, during the retrospective, "improve availability of environments" was at the top of the list. In hindsight, it was obvious—Development teams needed provisioned environments in order to begin work, and were often waiting up to eight weeks.

They created a new integration and build team that was responsible for "building quality into our processes, instead of trying to inspect quality after the fact." It was initially comprised of database administrators (DBAs) and automation specialists tasked with automating their environment creation process. The team quickly made a surprising discovery: only 50% of the source code in their development and test environments matched what was running in production.

Campbell-Pretty observed, "Suddenly, we understood why we encountered so many defects each time we deployed our code into new environments. In each environment, we kept fixing forward, but the changes we made were not being put back into version control."

The team carefully reverse-engineered all the changes that had been made to the different environments and put them all into version control. They also automated their environment creation process so they could repeatedly and correctly spin up environments.

Campbell-Pretty described the results, noting that "the time it took to get a correct environment went from eight weeks to one day. This was one of the key adjustments that allowed us to hit our objectives concerning our lead time, the cost to deliver, and the number of escaped defects that made it into production."

Campbell-Pretty's story shows the variety of problems that can be traced back to inconsistently constructed environments and changes not being systematically put back into version control.

Throughout the remainder of this chapter, we will discuss how to build the mechanisms that will enable us to create environments on demand, expand the use of version control to everyone in the value stream, make infrastructure easier to rebuild than to repair, and ensure that developers run their code in production-like environments along every stage of the software development life cycle.

ENABLE ON DEMAND CREATION OF DEV, TEST, AND PRODUCTION ENVIRONMENTS

As seen in the enterprise data warehouse example above, one of the major contributing causes of chaotic, disruptive, and sometimes even catastrophic software releases, is the first time we ever get to see how our application behaves in a production-like environment with realistic load and production data sets is during the release.[†] In many cases, development teams may have requested test environments in the early stages of the project.

However, when there are long lead times required for Operations to deliver test environments, teams may not receive them soon enough to perform adequate testing. Worse, test environments are often mis-configured or are so different from our production environments that we still end up with large production problems despite having performed pre-deployment testing.

In this step, we want developers to run production-like environments on their own workstations, created on demand and self-serviced. By doing this, developers can run and test their code in production-like environments as part of their daily work, providing early and constant feedback on the quality their work.

Instead of merely documenting the specifications of the production environment in a document or on a wiki page, we create a common build mechanism that creates all of our environments, such as for development, test, and production. By doing this, anyone can get production-like environments in minutes, without opening up a ticket, let alone having to wait weeks.[‡]

[†] In this context, environment is defined as everything in the application stack except for the application, including the databases, operating systems, networking, virtualization, and all associated configurations.

[‡] Most developers want to test their code, and they have often gone to extreme lengths to obtain test environments to do so. Developers have been known to reuse old test environments from previous projects (often years old) or ask someone who has a reputation of being able to find one—they just won't ask where it came from, because, invariably, someone somewhere is now missing a server.

To do this requires defining and automating the creation of our known, good environments, which are stable, secure, and in a risk-reduced state, embodying the collective knowledge of the organization. All our requirements are embedded, not in documents or as knowledge in someone's head, but codified in our automated environment build process.

Instead of Operations manually building and configuring the environment, we can use automation for any or all of the following:

- Copying a virtualized environment (e.g., a VMware image, running a Vagrant script, booting an Amazon Machine Image file in EC2)

- Building an automated environment creation process that starts from "bare metal" (e.g., PXE install from a baseline image)

- Using "infrastructure as code" configuration management tools (e.g., Puppet, Chef, Ansible, Salt, CFEngine, etc.)

- Using automated operating system configuration tools (e.g., Solaris Jumpstart, Red Hat Kickstart, Debian preseed)

- Assembling an environment from a set of virtual images or containers (e.g., Vagrant, Docker)

- Spinning up a new environment in a public cloud (e.g., Amazon Web Services, Google App Engine, Microsoft Azure), private cloud, or other PaaS (platform as a service, such as OpenStack or Cloud Foundry, etc.).

Because we've carefully defined all aspects of the environment ahead of time, we are not only able to create new environments quickly, but also ensure that these environments will be stable, reliable, consistent, and secure. This benefits everyone.

Operations benefits from this capability, to create new environments quickly, because automation of the environment creation process enforces consistency and reduces tedious, error-prone manual work. Furthermore, Development benefits by being able to reproduce all the necessary parts of the production environment to build, run, and test their code on their workstations. By doing this, we enable developers to find and fix many problems, even at the earliest stages of the project, as opposed to during integration testing or worse, in production.

By providing developers an environment they fully control, we enable them to quickly reproduce, diagnose, and fix defects, safely isolated from production services and other shared resources. They can also experiment with changes to the environments, as well as to the infrastructure code that creates it (e.g., configuration management scripts), further creating shared knowledge between Development and Operations.[†]

CREATE OUR SINGLE REPOSITORY OF TRUTH FOR THE ENTIRE SYSTEM

In the previous step, we enabled the on demand creation of the development, test, and production environments. Now we must ensure that all parts of our software system.

For decades, comprehensive use of version control has increasingly become a mandatory practice of individual developers and development teams.[‡] A version control system records changes to files or sets of files stored within the system. This can be source code, assets, or other documents that may be part of a software development project. We make changes in groups called commits or revisions. Each revision, along with metadata such as who made the change and when, is stored within the system in one way or another, allowing us to commit, compare, merge, and restore past revisions to objects to the repository. It also minimizes risks by establishing a way to revert objects in production to previous versions. (In this book, the following terms will be used interchangeably: checked in to version control, committed into version control, code commit, change commit, commit.)

When developers put all their application source files and configurations in version control, it becomes the single repository of truth that contains the precise intended state of the system. However, because delivering value to the customer requires both our code and the environments they run in, we need our environments in version control as well. In other words, version control is for everyone in our value stream, including QA, Operations, Infosec,

---

† Ideally, we should be finding errors before integration testing when is too late in the testing cycle to create fast feedback for developers. If we are unable to do so, we likely have an architectural issue that needs to be addressed. Designing our systems for testability, to include the ability to discover most defects using a non-integrated virtual environment on a development workstation, is a key part of creating an architecture that supports fast flow and feedback.

‡ The first version control system was likely UPDATE on the CDC6600 (1969). Later came SCCS (1972), CMS on VMS (1978), RCS (1982), and so forth.

as well as developers. By putting all production artifacts into version control, our version control repository enables us to repeatedly and reliably reproduce all components of our working software system—this includes our applications and production environment, as well as all of our pre-production environments.

To ensure that we can restore production service repeatedly and predictably (and, ideally, quickly) even when catastrophic events occur, we must check in the following assets to our shared version control repository:

- All application code and dependencies (e.g., libraries, static content, etc.)

- Any script used to create database schemas, application reference data, etc.

- All the environment creation tools and artifacts described in the previous step (e.g., VMware or AMI images, Puppet or Chef recipes, etc.)

- Any file used to create containers (e.g., Docker or Rocket definition or composition files)

- All supporting automated tests and any manual test scripts

- Any script that supports code packaging, deployment, database migration, and environment provisioning

- All project artifacts (e.g., requirements documentation, deployment procedures, release notes, etc.)

- All cloud configuration files (e.g., AWS Cloudformation templates, Microsoft Azure Stack DSC files, OpenStack HEAT)

- Any other script or configuration information required to create infrastructure that supports multiple services (e.g., enterprise service buses, database management systems, DNS zone files, configuration rules for firewalls, and other networking devices).[†]

---

† One may observe that version control fulfills some of the ITIL constructs of the Definitive Media Library (DML) and Configuration Management Database (CMDB), inventorying everything required to re-create the production environment.

We may have multiple repositories for different types of objects and services, where they are labelled and tagged alongside our source code. For instance, we may store large virtual machine images, ISO files, compiled binaries, and so forth in artifact repositories (e.g., Nexus, Artifactory). Alternatively, we may put them in blob stores (e.g., Amazon S3 buckets) or put Docker images into Docker registries, and so forth.

It is not sufficient to merely be able to re-create any previous state of the production environment; we must also be able to re-create the entire pre-production and build processes as well. Consequently, we need to put into version control everything relied upon by our build processes, including our tools (e.g., compilers, testing tools) and the environments they depend upon.[‡]

In Puppet Labs' 2014 *State of DevOps Report*, the use of version control by Ops was the highest predictor of both IT performance and organizational performance. In fact, whether Ops used version control was a higher predictor for both IT performance and organizational performance than whether Dev used version control.

The findings from Puppet Labs' 2014 *State of DevOps Report* underscores the critical role version control plays in the software development process. We now know when all application and environment changes are recorded in version control, it enables us to not only quickly see all changes that might have contributed to a problem, but also provides the means to roll back to a previous known, running state, allowing us to more quickly recover from failures.

But why does using version control for our environments predict IT and organizational performance better than using version control for our code?

Because in almost all cases, there are orders of magnitude more configurable settings in our environment than in our code. Consequently, it is the environment that needs to be in version control the most.[§]

[‡] In future steps, we will also check in to version control all the supporting infrastructure we build, such as the automated test suites and our continuous integration and deployment pipeline infrastructure.

[§] Anyone who has done a code migration for an ERP system (e.g., SAP, Oracle Financials, etc.) may recognize the following situation: When a code migration fails, it is rarely due to a coding error. Instead, it's far more likely that the migration failed due to some difference in the environments, such as between Development and QA or QA and Production.

Version control also provides a means of communication for everyone working in the value stream—having Development, QA, Infosec, and Operations able to see each other's changes helps reduce surprises, creates visibility into each other's work, and helps build and reinforce trust. (See Appendix 7.)

MAKE INFRASTRUCTURE EASIER TO REBUILD THAN TO REPAIR

When we can quickly rebuild and re-create our applications and environments on demand, we can also quickly rebuild them instead of repairing them when things go wrong. Although this is something that almost all large-scale web operations do (i.e., more than one thousand servers), we should also adopt this practice even if we have only one server in production.

Bill Baker, a distinguished engineer at Microsoft, quipped that we used to treat servers like pets: "You name them and when they get sick, you nurse them back to health. [Now] servers are [treated] like cattle. You number them and when they get sick, you shoot them."

By having repeatable environment creation systems, we are able to easily increase capacity by adding more servers into rotation (i.e., horizontal scaling). We also avoid the disaster that inevitably results when we must restore service after a catastrophic failure of irreproducible infrastructure, created through years of undocumented and manual production changes.

To ensure consistency of our environments, whenever we make production changes (configuration changes, patching, upgrading, etc.), those changes need to be replicated everywhere in our production and pre-production environments, as well as in any newly created environments.

Instead of manually logging into servers and making changes, we must make changes in a way that ensures all changes are replicated everywhere automatically and that all our changes are put into version control.

We can rely on our automated configuration systems to ensure consistency (e.g., Puppet, Chef, Ansible, Salt, Bosh, etc.), or we can create new virtual machines or containers from our automated build mechanism and deploy them into production, destroying the old ones or taking them out of rotation.[†]

---

† At Netflix, the average age of Netflix AWS instance is twenty-four days, with 60% being less than one week old.

The latter pattern is what has become known as *immutable infrastructure*, where manual changes to the production environment are no longer allowed—the only way production changes can be made is to put the changes into version control and re-create the code and environments from scratch. By doing this, no variance is able to creep into production.

To prevent uncontrolled configuration variances, we may disable remote logins to production servers[‡] or routinely kill and replace production instances, ensuring that manually-applied production changes are removed. This action motivates everyone to put their changes in the correct way through version control. By applying such measures, we are systematically reducing the ways our infrastructure can drift from our known, good states (e.g., configuration drift, fragile artifacts, works of art, snowflakes, and so forth).

Also, we must keep our pre-production environments up to date—specifically, we need developers to stay running on our most current environment. Developers will often want to keep running on older environments because they fear environment updates may break existing functionality. However, we want to update them frequently so we can find problems at the earliest part of the life cycle.[§]

MODIFY OUR DEFINITION OF DEVELOPMENT "DONE" TO INCLUDE RUNNING IN PRODUCTION-LIKE ENVIRONMENTS

Now that our environments can be created on demand and everything is checked in to version control, our goal is to ensure that these environments are being used in the daily work of Development. We need to verify that our application runs as expected in a production-like environment long before the end of the project or before our first production deployment.

Most modern software development methodologies prescribe short and iterative development intervals, as opposed to the big bang approach (e.g., the waterfall `model). In general, the longer the interval between deployment, the worse the outcomes. For example, in the Scrum methodology a *sprint* is a time-boxed development interval (typically one month or less) within which

---

‡ Or allow it only in emergencies, ensuring that a copy of the console log is automatically emailed to the operations team.

§ The entire application stack and environment can be bundled into containers, which can enable unprecedented simplicity and speed across the entire deployment pipeline.

we are required to be done, widely defined as when we have "working and potentially shippable code."

Our goal is to ensure that Development and QA are routinely integrating the code with production-like environments at increasingly frequent intervals throughout the project.[†] We do this by expanding the definition of "done" beyond just correct code functionality (addition in bold text): at the end of each development interval, we have integrated, tested, working and potentially shippable code, **demonstrated in a production-like environment.**

In other words, we will only accept development work as done when it can be successfully built, deployed, and confirmed that it runs as expected in a production-like environment, instead of merely when a developer believes it to be done—ideally, it runs under a production-like load with a production-like dataset, long before the end of a sprint. This prevents situations where a feature is called done merely because a developer can run it successfully on their laptop but nowhere else.

By having developers write, test, and run their own code in a production-like environment, the majority of the work to successfully integrate our code and environments happens during our daily work, instead of at the end of the release. By the end of our first interval, our application can be demonstrated to run correctly in a production-like environment, with the code and environment having been integrated together many times over, ideally with all the steps automated (no manual tinkering required).

Better yet, by the end of the project, we will have successfully deployed and run our code in production-like environments hundreds or even thousands of times, giving us confidence that most of our production deployment problems have been found and fixed.

Ideally, we use the same tools, such as monitoring, logging, and deployment, in our pre-production environments as we do in production. By doing this, we have familiarity and experience that will help us smoothly deploy and run, as well as diagnose and fix, our service when it is in production.

---

† The term *integration* has many slightly different usages in Development and Operations. In Development, integration typically refers to code integration, which is the integration of multiple code branches into trunk in version control. In continuous delivery and DevOps, *integration testing* refers to the testing of the application in a production-like environment or integrated test environment.

By enabling Development and Operations to gain a shared mastery of how the code and environment interact, and practicing deployments early and often, we significantly reduce the deployment risks that are associated with production code releases. This also allows us to eliminate an entire class of operational and security defects and architectural problems that are usually caught too late in the project to fix.

CONCLUSION

The fast flow of work from Development to Operations requires that anyone can get production-like environments on demand. By allowing developers to use production-like environments even at the earliest stages of a software project, we significantly reduce the risk of production problems later. This is one of many practices that demonstrate how Operations can make developers far more productive. We enforce the practice of developers running their code in production-like environments by incorporating it into the definition of "done."

Furthermore, by putting all production artifacts into version control, we have a "single source of truth" that allows us to re-create the entire production environment in a quick, repeatable, and documented way, using the same development practices for Operations work as we do for Development work. And by making production infrastructure easier to rebuild than to repair, we make resolving problems easier and faster, as well as making it easier to expand capacity.

Having these practices in place sets the stage for enabling comprehensive test automation, which is explored in the next chapter.

10 Enable Fast and Reliable Automated Testing

At this point, Development and QA are using production-like environments in their daily work, and we are successfully integrating and running our code into a production-like environment for every feature that is accepted, with all changes checked in to version control. However, we are likely to get undesired outcomes if we find and fix errors in a separate test phase, executed by a separate QA department only after all development has been completed. And, if testing is only performed a few times a year, developers learn about their mistakes months after they introduced the change that caused the error. By then, the link between cause and effect has likely faded, solving the problem requires firefighting and archaeology, and, worst of all, our ability to learn from the mistake and integrate it into our future work is significantly diminished.

Automated testing addresses another significant and unsettling problem. Gary Gruver observes that "without automated testing, the more code we write, the more time and money is required to test our code—in most cases, this is a totally unscalable business model for any technology organization."

Although Google now undoubtedly exemplifies a culture that values automated testing at scale, this wasn't always the case. In 2005, when Mike Bland joined the organization, deploying to Google.com was often extremely problematic, especially for the Google Web Server (GWS) team.

As Bland explains, "The GWS team had gotten into a position in the mid 2000s where it was extremely difficult to make changes to the web server, a C++ application that handled all requests to Google's home page and many other Google web pages. As important and prominent as Google.com was, being on the GWS team was not a glamorous assignment—it was often the dumping ground for all the different teams who were creating various search functionality, all of whom were developing code independently of each other. They had problems such as builds and tests taking too long, code being put into production without being tested, and teams checking in large, infrequent changes that conflicted with those from other teams."

The consequences of this were large—search results could have errors or become unacceptably slow, affecting thousands of search queries on Google.com. The potential result was not only loss of revenue, but customer trust.

Bland describes how it affected developers deploying changes, "Fear became the mind-killer. Fear stopped new team members from changing things because they didn't understand the system. But fear also stopped experienced people from changing things because they understood it all too well."[†] Bland was part of the group that was determined to solve this problem.

GWS team lead Bharat Mediratta believed automated testing would help. As Bland describes, "They created a hard line: no changes would be accepted into GWS without accompanying automated tests. They set up a continuous build and religiously kept it passing. They set up test coverage monitoring and ensured that their level of test coverage went up over time. They wrote up policy and testing guides, and insisted that contributors both inside and outside the team follow them."

The results were startling. As Bland notes, "GWS quickly became one of the most productive teams in the company, integrating large numbers of changes from different teams every week while maintaining a rapid release schedule. New team members were able to make productive contributions to this complex system quickly, thanks to good test coverage and code health. Ultimately, their radical policy enabled the Google.com home page to quickly expand its capabilities and thrive in an amazingly fast-moving and competitive technology landscape."

But GWS was still a relatively small team in a large and growing company. The team wanted to expand these practices across the entire organization. Thus, the Testing Grouplet was born, an informal group of engineers who wanted

---

† Bland described that at Google, one of the consequences of having so many talented developers was that it created "imposter syndrome," a term coined by psychologists to informally describe people who are unable to internalize their accomplishments. Wikipedia states that "despite external evidence of their competence, those exhibiting the syndrome remain convinced that they are frauds and do not deserve the success they have achieved. Proof of success is dismissed as luck, timing, or as a result of deceiving others into thinking they are more intelligent and competent than they believe themselves to be."

to elevate automated testing practices across the entire organization. Over the next five years, they helped replicate this culture of automated testing across all of Google.[‡]

Now when any Google developer commits code, it is automatically run against a suite of hundreds of thousands of automated tests. If the code passes, it is automatically merged into trunk, ready to be deployed into production. Many Google properties build hourly or daily, then pick which builds to release; others adopt a continuous "Push on Green" delivery philosophy.

The stakes are higher than ever—a single code deployment error at Google can take down every property, all at the same time (such as a global infrastructure change or when a defect is introduced into a core library that every property depends upon).

Eran Messeri, an engineer in the Google Developer Infrastructure group, notes, "Large failures happen occasionally. You'll get a ton of instant messages and engineers knocking on your door. [When the deployment pipeline is broken,] we need to fix it right away, because developers can no longer commit code. Consequently, we want to make it very easy to roll back."

What enables this system to work at Google is engineering professionalism and a high-trust culture that assumes everyone wants to do a good job, as well as the ability to detect and correct issues quickly. Messeri explains, "There are no hard policies at Google, such as, 'If you break production for more than ten projects, you have an SLA to fix the issue within ten minutes.' Instead, there is mutual respect between teams and an implicit agreement that everyone does whatever it takes to keep the deployment pipeline running. We all know that one day, I'll break your project by accident; the next day, you may break mine."

What Mike Bland and the Testing Grouplet team achieved has made Google one of the most productive technology organizations in the world. By 2013, automated testing and continuous integration at Google enabled over four thousand small teams to work together and stay productive, all simultaneously developing, integrating, testing, and deploying their code into production. All their code is in a single, shared repository, made up of billions of files, all

---

‡ They created training programs, pushed the famous *Testing on the Toilet* newsletter (which they posted in the bathrooms), the Test Certified roadmap and certification program, and led multiple "fix-it" days (i.e., improvement blitzes), which helped teams improve their automated testing processes so they could replicate the amazing outcomes that the GWS team was able to achieve.

being continuously built and integrated, with 50% of their code being changed each month. Some other impressive statistics on their performance include:

- 40,000 code commits/day

- 50,000 builds/day (on weekdays, this may exceed 90,000)

- 120,000 automated test suites

- 75 million test cases run daily

- 100+ engineers working on the test engineering, continuous integration, and release engineering tooling to increase developer productivity (making up 0.5% of the R&D workforce)

In the remainder of this chapter, we will go through the continuous integration practices required to replicate these outcomes.

CONTINUOUSLY BUILD, TEST, AND INTEGRATE OUR CODE AND ENVIRONMENTS

Our goal is to build quality into our product, even at the earliest stages, by having developers build automated tests as part of their daily work. This creates a fast feedback loop that helps developers find problems early and fix them quickly, when there are the fewest constraints (e.g., time, resources).

In this step, we create automated test suites that increase the frequency of integration and testing of our code and our environments from periodic to continuous. We do this by building our deployment pipeline, which will perform integration of our code and environments and trigger a series of tests every time a new change is put into version control.† (See figure 13.)

The deployment pipeline, first defined by Jez Humble and David Farley in their book *Continuous Delivery: Reliable Software Releases Through Build, Test,*

---

† In Development, *continuous integration* often refers to the continuous integration of multiple code branches into trunk and ensuring that it passes unit tests. However, in the context of continuous delivery and DevOps, continuous integration also mandates running on production-like environments and passing acceptance and integration tests. Jez Humble and David Farley disambiguate these by calling the latter CI+. In this book, *continuous integration* will always refer to CI+ practices.

and Deployment Automation, ensures that all code checked in to version control is automatically built and tested in a production-like environment. By doing this, we find any build, test, or integration errors as soon as a change is introduced, enabling us to fix them immediately. Done correctly, this allows us to always be assured that we are in a deployable and shippable state.

To achieve this, we must create automated build and test processes that run in dedicated environments. This is critical for the following reasons:

- Our build and test process can run all the time, independent of the work habits of individual engineers.

- A segregated build and test process ensures that we understand all the dependencies required to build, package, run, and test our code (i.e., removing the "it worked on the developer's laptop, but it broke in production" problem).

- We can package our application to enable the repeatable installation of code and configurations into an environment (e.g., on Linux RPM, yum, npm; on Windows, OneGet; alternatively framework-specific packaging systems can be used, such as EAR and WAR files for Java, gems for Ruby, etc.).

- Instead of putting our code in packages, we may choose to package our applications into deployable containers (e.g., Docker, Rkt, LXD, AMIs).

- Environments can be made more production-like in a way that is consistent and repeatable (e.g., compilers are removed from the environment, debugging flags are turned off, etc.)

Our deployment pipeline validates after every change that our code successfully integrates into a production-like environment. It becomes the platform through which testers request and certify builds during acceptance testing and usability testing, and it will run automated performance and security validations.

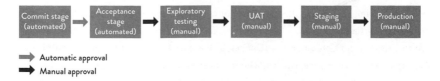

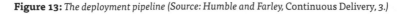
Automatic approval
Manual approval

Figure 13: *The deployment pipeline (Source: Humble and Farley,* Continuous Delivery, *3.)*

Furthermore, it will be used to self-service builds to UAT (user acceptance testing), integration testing, and security testing environments. In future steps, as we evolve the deployment pipeline, it will also be used to manage all activities required to take our changes from version control to deployment.

A variety of tools have been designed to provide deployment pipeline functionality, many of them open source (e.g., Jenkins, ThoughtWorks Go, Concourse, Bamboo, Microsoft Team Foundation Server, TeamCity, Gitlab CI, as well as cloud-based solutions such as Travis CI and Snap).[†]

We begin the deployment pipeline by running the commit stage, which builds and packages the software, runs automated unity tests, and performs additional validation such as static code analysis, duplication and test coverage analysis, and checking style.[‡] If successful, this triggers the acceptance stage, which automatically deploys the packages created in the commit stage into a production-like environment and runs the automated acceptance tests.

Once changes are accepted into version control, we want to package our code only once, so that the same packages are used to deploy code throughout our entire deployment pipeline. By doing this, code will be deployed into our integrated test and staging environments in the same way that it is deployed into production. This reduces variances that can avoid downstream errors that are difficult to diagnose (e.g., using different compilers, compiler flags, library versions, or configurations).[§]

The goal of the deployment pipeline is to provide everyone in the value stream, especially developers, the fastest possible feedback that a change has taken

---

† If we create containers in our deployment pipeline and have an architecture such as microservices, we can enable each developer to build immutable artifacts where developers assemble and run all the service components in an environment identical to production on their workstation. This enables developers to build and run more tests on their workstation instead of on testing servers, giving us even faster feedback on their work.

‡ We may even require that these tools are run before changes are accepted into version control (e.g., get pre-commit hooks). We may also run these tools within the developer *integrated development environment* (IDE; where the developer edits, compiles, and runs code), which creates an even faster feedback loop.

§ We can also use containers, such as Docker, as the packaging mechanism. Containers enable the capability to write once, run anywhere. These containers are created as part of our build process and can be quickly deployed and run in any environment. Because the same container is run in every environment, we help enforce the consistency of all our build artifacts.

us out of a deployable state. This could be a change to our code, to any of our environments, to our automated tests, or even to the deployment pipeline infrastructure (e.g., a Jenkins configuration setting).

As a result, our deployment pipeline infrastructure becomes as foundational for our development processes as our version control infrastructure. Our deployment pipeline also stores the history of each code build, including information about which tests were performed on which build, which builds have been deployed to which environment, and what the test results were. In combination with the information in our version control history, we can quickly determine what caused our deployment pipeline to break and, likely, how to fix the error.

This information also helps us fulfill evidence requirements for audit and compliance purposes, with evidence being automatically generated as part of daily work.

Now that we have a working deployment pipeline infrastructure, we must create our *continuous integration* practices, which require three capabilities:

- A comprehensive and reliable set of automated tests that validate we are in a deployable state.

- A culture that "stops the entire production line" when our validation tests fail.

- Developers working in small batches on trunk rather than long-lived feature branches.

In the next section, we describe why fast and reliable automated testing is needed and how to build it.

BUILD A FAST AND RELIABLE AUTOMATED VALIDATION TEST SUITE

In the previous step, we started to create the automated testing infrastructure that validates that we have a *green build* (i.e., whatever is in version control is in a buildable and deployable state). To underscore why we need to perform this integration and testing step continuously, consider what happens when we only perform this operation periodically, such as during a nightly build process.

Suppose we have a team of ten developers, with everyone checking their code into version control daily, and a developer introduces a change that breaks our nightly build and test job. In this scenario, when we discover the next day that we no longer have a green build, it will take minutes, or more likely hours, for our development team to figure out which change caused the problem, who introduced it, and how to fix it.

Worse, suppose the problem wasn't caused by a code change, but was due to a test environment issue (e.g., an incorrect configuration setting somewhere). The development team may believe that they fixed the problem because all the unit tests pass, only to discover that the tests will still fail later that night.

Further complicating the issue, ten more changes will have been checked in to version control by the team that day. Each of these changes has the potential to introduce more errors that could break our automated tests, further increasing the difficulty of successfully diagnosing and fixing the problem.

In short, slow and periodic feedback kills. Especially for larger development teams. The problem becomes even more daunting when we have tens, hundreds, or even thousands of other developers checking their changes into version control each day. The result is that our builds and automated tests are frequently broken, and developers even stop checking their changes into version control ("Why bother, since the builds and tests are always broken?"). Instead they wait to integrate their code at the end of the project, resulting in all the undesired outcomes of large batch size, big bang integrations, and production deployments.[†]

To prevent this scenario, we need fast automated tests that run within our build and test environments whenever a new change is introduced into version control. In this way we can find and fix any problems immediately, as the Google Web Server example demonstrated. By doing this, we ensure our batches remains small, and, at any given point in time, we remain in a deployable state.

In general, automated tests fall into one of the following categories, from fastest to slowest:

- **Unit tests**: These typically test a single method, class, or function in isolation, providing assurance to the developer that their code

---

† It is exactly this problem that led to the development of continuous integration practices.

operates as designed. For many reasons, including the need to keep our tests fast and stateless, unit tests often "stub out" databases and other external dependencies (e.g., functions are modified to return static, predefined values, instead of calling the real database).[‡]

- **Acceptance tests**: These typically test the application as a whole to provide assurance that a higher level of functionality operates as designed (e.g., the business acceptance criteria for a user story, the correctness of an API), and that regression errors have not been introduced (i.e., we broke functionality that was previously operating correctly). Humble and Farley define the difference between unit and acceptance testing as, "The aim of a unit test is to show that a single part of the application does what the programmer intends it to....The objective of acceptance tests is to prove that our application does what the customer meant it to, not that it works the way its programmers think it should." After a build passes our unit tests, our deployment pipeline runs it against our acceptance tests. Any build that passes our acceptance tests is then typically made available for manual testing (e.g., exploratory testing, UI testing, etc.), as well as for integration testing.

- **Integration tests**: Integration tests are where we ensure that our application correctly interacts with other production applications and services, as opposed to calling stubbed out interfaces. As Humble and Farley observe, "much of the work in the SIT environment involves deploying new versions of each of the applications until they all cooperate. In this situation the smoke test is usually a fully fledged set of acceptance tests that run against the whole application." Integration tests are performed on builds that have passed our unit and acceptance tests. Because integration tests are often brittle, we want to minimize the number of integration tests and find as many of our defects as possible during unit and acceptance testing. The ability to use virtual or simulated versions of remote services when running acceptance tests becomes an essential architectural requirement.

---

‡ There is a broad category of architectural and testing techniques used to handle the problems of tests requiring input from external integration points, including "stubs," "mocks," "service virtualization," and so forth. This becomes even more important for acceptance and integration testing, which place far more reliance on external states.

When facing deadline pressures, developers may stop creating unit tests as part of their daily work, regardless of how we've defined 'done.' To detect this, we may choose to measure and make visible our test coverage (as a function of number of classes, lines of code, permutations, etc.), maybe even failing our validation test suite when it drops below a certain level (e.g., when less than 80% of our classes have unit tests).[†]

Martin Fowler observes that, in general, "a ten-minute build [and test process] is perfectly within reason...[We first] do the compilation and run tests that are more localized unit tests with the database completely stubbed out. Such tests can run very fast, keeping within the ten minute guideline. However any bugs that involve larger scale interactions, particularly those involving the real database, won't be found. The second stage build runs a different suite of tests [acceptance tests] that do hit the real database and involve more end-to-end behavior. This suite may take a couple of hours to run."

CATCH ERRORS AS EARLY IN OUR AUTOMATED TESTING AS POSSIBLE
A specific design goal of our automated test suite is to find errors as early in the testing as possible. This is why we run faster-running automated tests (e.g., unit tests) before slower-running automated tests (e.g., acceptance and integration tests), which are both run before any manual testing.

Another corollary of this principle is that any errors should be found with the fastest category of testing possible. If most of our errors are found in our acceptance and integration tests, the feedback we provide to developers is orders of magnitude slower than with unit tests—and integration testing requires using scarce and complex integration test environments, which can only be used by one team at a time, further delaying feedback.

Furthermore, not only are errors detected during integration testing difficult and time-consuming for developers to reproduce, even validating that it has been fixed is difficult (i.e., a developer creates a fix but then needs to wait four hours to learn whether the integration tests now pass).

Therefore, whenever we find an error with an acceptance or integration test, we should create a unit test that could find the error faster, earlier, and cheaper. Martin Fowler described the notion of the "ideal testing pyramid," where we are able to catch most of our errors using our unit tests. (See figure 14.) In

---

† We should do this only when our teams already value automated testing—this type of metric is easily gamed by developers and managers.

contrast, in many testing programs the inverse is true, where most of the investment is in manual and integration testing.

Ideal vs. Non-Ideal Testing Pyramids

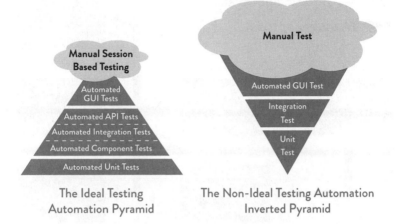

Figure 14: *The ideal and non-ideal automated testing pyramids (Source: Martin Fowler, "TestPyramid.")*

If we find that unit or acceptance tests are too difficult and expensive to write and maintain, it's likely that we have an architecture that is too tightly coupled, where strong separation between our module boundaries no longer exist (or maybe never existed). In this case, we will need to create a more loosely-coupled system so modules can be independently tested without integration environments. Acceptance test suites for even the most complex applications that run in minutes are possible.

ENSURE TESTS RUN QUICKLY (IN PARALLEL, IF NECESSARY)
Because we want our tests to run quickly, we need to design our tests to run in parallel, potentially across many different servers. We may also want to run different categories of tests in parallel. For example, when a build passes our acceptance tests, we may run our performance testing in parallel with our security testing, as shown in figure 15. We may or may not allow manual exploratory testing until the build has passed all our automated tests—which enables faster feedback, but may also allow manual testing on builds that will eventually fail.

We make any build that passes all our automated tests available to use for exploratory testing, as well as for other forms of manual or resource-intensive testing (such as performance testing). We want to do all such testing as frequently as possible and practical, either continually or on a schedule.

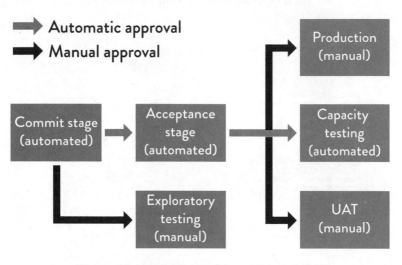

Figure 15: *Running automated and manual tests in parallel*
(Source: Humble and Farley, Continuous Delivery, *Kindle edition, location 3868.)*

Any tester (which includes all our developers) should use the latest build that has passed all the automated tests, as opposed to waiting for developers to flag a specific build as ready to test. By doing this, we ensure that testing happens as early in the process as possible.

WRITE OUR AUTOMATED TESTS BEFORE WE WRITE THE CODE ("TEST DRIVEN DEVELOPMENT")

One of the most effective ways to ensure we have reliable automated testing, is to write those tests as part of our daily work, using techniques such as *test-driven development* (TDD) and *acceptance test-driven development* (ATDD). This is when we begin every change to the system by first writing an automated test that validates the expected behavior *fails*, and then we write the code to make the tests pass.

This technique was developed by Kent Beck in the late 1990s as part of Extreme Programming, and has the following three steps:

1. Ensure the tests fail. "Write a test for the next bit of functionality you want to add." Check in.

2. Ensure the tests pass. "Write the functional code until the test passes."Check in.

3. "Refactor both new and old code to make it well structured."Ensure the tests pass. Check in again.

These automated test suites are checked in to version control alongside our code, which provides a living, up-to-date specification of the system. Developers wishing to understand how to use the system can look at this test suite to find working examples of how to use the system's API.[†]

AUTOMATE AS MANY OF OUR MANUAL TESTS AS POSSIBLE

Our goal is to find as many code errors through our automated test suites, reducing our reliance on manual testing. In her 2013 presentation at Flowcon titled "On the Care and Feeding of Feedback Cycles," Elisabeth Hendrickson observed, "Although testing can be automated, creating quality cannot. To have humans executing tests that should be automated is a waste of human potential."

By doing this, we enable all our testers (which, of course, includes developers) work on high-value activities that cannot be automated, such as exploratory testing or improving the test process itself.

However, merely automating all our manual tests may create undesired outcomes—we do not want automated tests that are unreliable or generate false positives (i.e., tests that should have passed because the code is functionally correct but failed due to problems such as slow performance, causing timeouts, uncontrolled starting state, or unintended state due to using database stubs or shared test environments).

Unreliable tests that generate false positives create significant problems—they waste valuable time (e.g., forcing developers to re-run the test to determine whether there is actually a problem), increase the overall effort of running and interpreting our test results, and often result in stressed developers ignoring test results entirely or turning off the automated tests in favor of focusing on creating code.

---

† Nachi Nagappan, E. Michael Maximilien, and Laurie Williams (from Microsoft Research, IBM Almaden Labs, and North Carolina State University, respectively) conducted a study that showed teams using TDD produced code 60%–90% better in terms of defect density than non-TDD teams, while taking only 15%–35% longer.

The result is always the same: we detect the problems later, the problems are more difficult to fix, and our customers have worse outcomes, which in turn creates stress across the value stream.

To mitigate of this, a small number of reliable, automated tests are almost always preferable over a large number of manual or unreliable automated tests. Therefore, we focus on automating only the tests that genuinely validate the business goals we are trying to achieve. If abandoning a test results in production defects, we should add it back to our manual test suite, with the ideal of eventually automating it.

As Gary Gruver, formerly VP of Quality Engineering, Release Engineering and Operations for Macys.com, described observes, "For a large retailer e-commerce site, we went from running 1,300 manual tests that we ran every ten days to running only ten automated tests upon every code commit—it's far better to run a few tests that we trust than to run tests that aren't reliable. Over time, we grew this test suite to having hundreds of thousands of automated tests."

In other words, we start with a small number of reliable automated tests and add to them over time, creating an ever-increasing level of assurance that we will quickly detect any changes to the system that take us out of a deployable state.

INTEGRATE PERFORMANCE TESTING INTO OUR TEST SUITE
All too often, we discover that our application performs poorly during integration testing or after it has been deployed to production. Performance problems are often difficult to detect, such as when things slow down over time, going unnoticed until it is too late (e.g., database queries without an index). And many problems are difficult to solve, especially when they are caused by architectural decisions we made or unforeseen limitations of our networking, database, storage, or other systems.

Our goal is to write and run automated performance tests that validate our performance across the entire application stack (code, database, storage, network, virtualization, etc.) as part of the deployment pipeline, so we detect problems early, when the fixes are cheapest and fastest.

By understanding how our application and environments behave under a production-like load, we can do a far better job at capacity planning, as well as detecting conditions such as:

- When our database query times grow non-linearly (e.g., we forget to turn on database indexing, and page load goes from one hundred minutes to thirty seconds).

- When a code change causes the number of database calls, storage use, or network traffic to increase ten-fold.

When we have acceptance tests that are able to be run in parallel, we can use them as the basis of our performance tests. For instance, suppose we run an e-commerce site and have identified "search" and "checkout" as two high-value operations that must perform well under load. To test this, we may run thousands of parallel search acceptance tests simultaneously with thousands of parallel checkout tests.

Due to the large amount of compute and I/O that is required to run performance tests, creating a performance testing environment can easily be more complex than creating the production environment for the application itself. Because of this, we may build our performance testing environment at the start of any project and ensure that we dedicate whatever resources are required to build it early and correctly.

To find performance problems early, we should log performance results and evaluate each performance run against previous results. For instance, we might fail the performance tests if performance deviates more than 2% from the previous run.

INTEGRATE NON-FUNCTIONAL REQUIREMENTS TESTING INTO OUR TEST SUITE

In addition to testing that our code functions as designed and it performs under production-like loads, we also want to validate every other attribute of the system we care about. These are often called non-functional requirements, which include availability, scalability, capacity, security, and so forth.

Many of these requirements are fulfilled by the correct configuration of our environments, so we must also build automated tests to validate that our environments have been built and configured properly. For example, we want to enforce the consistency and correctness of the following, which many non-functional requirements rely upon (e.g., security, performance, availability):

- Supporting applications, databases, libraries, etc.

- Language interpreters, compilers, etc.

- Operating systems (e.g., audit logging enabled, etc.)

- All dependencies

When we use infrastructure as code configuration management tools (e.g., Puppet, Chef, Ansible, Salt, Bosh), we can use the same testing frameworks that we use to test our code to also test that our environments are configured and operating correctly (e.g., encoding environment tests into cucumber or gherkin tests).

Furthermore, similar to how we run analysis tools on our application in our deployment pipeline (e.g., static code analysis, test coverage analysis), we should run tools that analyze the code that constructs our environments (e.g., Foodcritic for Chef, puppet-lint for Puppet). We should also run any security hardening checks as part of our automated tests to ensure that everything is configured securely and correctly (e.g., server-spec).

At any point in time, our automated tests can validate that we have a green build and that we are in a deployable state. Now, we must create an Andon cord so that when someone breaks the deployment pipeline, we take all necessary steps to get back into a green build state.

PULL OUR ANDON CORD WHEN THE DEPLOYMENT PIPELINE BREAKS

When we have a green build in our deployment pipeline, we have a high degree of confidence that our code and environment will operate as designed when we deploy our changes into production.

In order to keep our deployment pipeline in a green state, we will create a virtual Andon Cord, similar to the physical one in the Toyota Production System. Whenever someone introduces a change that causes our build or automated tests to fail, no new work is allowed to enter the system until the problem is fixed. And if someone needs help to resolve the problem, they can bring in whatever help they need, as in the Google example at the beginning of this chapter.

When our deployment pipeline is broken, at a minimum, we notify the entire team of the failure, so anyone can either fix the problem or roll-back the commit. We may even configure the version control system to prevent further code commits until the first stage (i.e., builds and unit tests) of the deployment pipeline is back in a green state. If the problem was due to an automated test generating a false positive error, the offending test should either be rewritten or removed.[†] Every member of the team should be empowered to roll back the commit to get back into a green state.

Randy Shoup, former engineering director for Google App Engine, wrote about the importance of bringing the deployment back into a green state. "We prioritize the team goals over individual goals—whenever we help someone move their work forward, we help the entire team. This applies whether we're helping someone fix the build or an automated test, or even performing a code review for them. And of course, we know that they'll do the same for us, when we need help. This system worked without a lot of formality or policy—everyone knew that our job was not just 'write code,' but it was to 'run a service.' This is why we prioritized all quality issues, especially those related to reliability and scaling, at the highest level, treating them as a Priority 0 'show-stopper' problems. From a systems perspective, these practices keep us from slipping backwards."

When later stages of the deployment pipeline fail, such as acceptance tests or performance tests, instead of stopping all new work, we will have developers and testers on-call who are responsible for fixing these problems immediately. They should also create new tests that run at an earlier stage in the deployment pipeline to catch any future regressions. For example, if we discover a defect in our acceptance tests, we should write a unit test to catch the problem. Similarly, if we discover a defect in exploratory testing, we should write a unit or acceptance test.

To increase the visibility of automated test failures, we should create highly visible indicators so that the entire team can see when our build or automated tests are failing. Many teams have created highly visible build lights that get mounted on a wall, indicating the current build status, or other fun ways of telling the team the build is broken, including lava lamps, playing a voice sample or song, klaxons, traffic lights, and so forth.

In many ways, this step is more challenging than creating our builds and test servers—those were purely technical activities, whereas this step requires changing human behavior and incentives. However, continuous integration

---

† If the process for rolling back the code is not well-known, a potential countermeasure is to schedule a *pair programmed rollback*, so that it can be better documented.

and continuous delivery require these changes, as we explore in the next section.

WHY WE NEED TO PULL THE ANDON CORD

The consequence of not pulling the Andon cord and immediately fixing any deployment pipeline issues results in the all too familiar problem where it becomes ever more difficult to bring our applications and environment back into a deployable state. Consider the following situation:

- Someone checks in code that breaks the build or our automated tests, but no one fixes it.

- Someone else checks in another change onto the broken build, which also doesn't pass our automated tests—but no one sees the failing test results which would have enabled us to see the new defect, let alone fix it.

- Our existing tests don't run reliably, so we are very unlikely to build new tests. (Why bother? We can't even get the current tests to run.)

When this happens, our deployments to any environment become as unreliable as when we had no automated tests or were using a waterfall method, where the majority of our problems are being discovered in production. The inevitable outcome of this vicious cycle is that we end up where we started, with an unpredictable "stabilization phase" that takes weeks or months where our whole team is plunged into crisis, trying to get all our tests to pass, taking shortcuts because of deadline pressures, and adding to our technical debt.[†]

CONCLUSION

In this chapter, we have created a comprehensive set of automated tests to confirm that we have a green build that is still in a passing and deployable state. We have organized our test suites and testing activities into a deployment pipeline. We have also created the cultural norm of doing whatever it takes

---

† This is sometimes called the *water-Scrum-fall anti-pattern*, which refers to when an organization claims to be using Agile-like practices, but, in reality, all testing and defect fixing are performed at the end of the project.

to get back into a green build state if someone introduces a change that breaks any of our automated tests.

By doing this, we set the stage for implementing continuous integration, which allows many small teams to independently and safely develop, test, and deploy code into production, delivering value to customers.

11 Enable and Practice Continuous Integration

In the previous chapter, we created the automated testing practices to ensure that developers get fast feedback on the quality of their work. This becomes even more important as we increase the number of developers and the number of branches they work on in version control.

The ability to "branch" in version control systems was created primarily to enable developers to work on different parts of the software system in parallel, without the risk of individual developers checking in changes that could destabilize or introduce errors into trunk (sometimes also called master or mainline).[†]

However, the longer developers are allowed to work in their branches in isolation, the more difficult it becomes to integrate and merge everyone's changes back into trunk. In fact, integrating those changes becomes exponentially more difficult as we increase the number of branches and the number of changes in each code branch.

Integration problems result in a significant amount of rework to get back into a deployable state, including conflicting changes that must be manually merged or merges that break our automated or manual tests, usually requiring multiple developers to successfully resolve. And because integration has traditionally been done at the end of the project, when it takes far longer then planned, we are often forced to cut corners to make the release date.

This causes another downward spiral: when merging code is painful, we tend to do it less often, making future merges even worse. Continuous integration

---

† Branching in version control has been used in many ways, but is typically used to divide work between team members by release, promotion, task, component, technology platforms, and so forth.

was designed to solve this problem by making merging into trunk a part of everyone's daily work.

The surprising breadth of problems that continuous integration solves, as well as the solutions themselves, are exemplified in Gary Gruver's experience as the director of engineering for HP's LaserJet Firmware division, which builds the firmware that runs all their scanners, printers, and multifunction devices.

The team consisted of four hundred developers distributed across the US, Brazil, and India. Despite the size of their team, they were moving far too slowly. For years, they were unable to deliver new features as quickly as the business needed.

Gruver described the problem thus, "Marketing would come to us with a million ideas to dazzle our customer, and we'd just tell them, 'Out of your list, pick the two things you'd like to get in the next six to twelve months.'"

They were only completing two firmware releases per year, with the majority of their time spent porting code to support new products. Gruver estimated that only 5% of their time was spent creating new features—the rest of the time was spent on non-productive work associated with their technical debt, such as managing multiple code branches and manual testing, as shown below:

- 20% on detailed planning (Their poor throughput and high lead times were misattributed to faulty estimation, and so, hoping to get a better answer, they were asked to estimate the work in greater detail.)

- 25% spent porting code, all maintained on separate code branches

- 10% spent integrating their code between developer branches

- 15% spent completing manual testing

Gruver and his team created a goal of increasing the time spent on innovation and new functionality by a factor of ten. The team hoped this goal could be achieved through:

- Continuous integration and trunk-based development

- Significant investment in test automation

- Creation of a hardware simulator so tests could be run on a virtual platform

- The reproduction of test failures on developer workstations

- A new architecture to support running all printers off a common build and release

Before this, each product line would require a new code branch, with each model having a unique firmware build with capabilities defined at compile time.[†] The new architecture would have all developers working in a common code base, with a single firmware release supporting all LaserJet models built off of trunk, with printer capabilities being established at runtime in an XML configuration file.

Four years later, they had one codebase supporting all twenty-four HP LaserJet product lines being developed on trunk. Gruver admits trunk-based development requires a big mindset shift. Engineers thought trunk-based development would never work, but once they started, they couldn't imagine ever going back. Over the years we've had several engineers leave HP, and they would call me to tell me about how backward development was in their new companies, pointing out how difficult it is to be effective and release good code when there is no feedback that continuous integration gives them.

However, trunk-based development required them to build more effective automated testing. Gruver observed, "Without automated testing, continuous integration is the fastest way to get a big pile of junk that never compiles or runs correctly." In the beginning, a full manual testing cycle required six weeks.

In order to have all firmware builds automatically tested, they invested heavily in their printer simulators and created a testing farm in six weeks—within a few years two thousand printer simulators ran on six racks of servers that would load the firmware builds from their deployment pipeline. Their continuous integration (CI) system ran their entire set of automated unit, acceptance, and integration tests on builds from trunk, just as described in the

---

† Compile flags (#define and #ifdef) were used to enable/disable code execution for presence of copiers, paper size supported, and so on.

previous chapter. Furthermore, they created a culture that halted all work anytime a developer broke the deployment pipeline, ensuring that developers quickly brought the system back into a green state.

Automated testing created fast feedback that enabled developers to quickly confirm that their committed code actually worked. Unit tests would run on their workstations in minutes, three levels of automated testing would run on every commit as well as every two and four hours. The final full regression testing would run every twenty-four hours. During this process, they:

- Reduced the build to one build per day, eventually doing ten to fifteen builds per day

- Went from around twenty commits per day performed by a "build boss" to over one hundred commits per day performed by individual developers

- Enabled developers to change or add 75k–100k lines of code each day

- Reduced regression test times from six weeks to one day

This level of productivity could never have been supported prior to adopting continuous integration, when merely creating a green build required days of heroics. The resulting business benefits were astonishing:

- Time spent on driving innovation and writing new features increased from 5% of developer time to 40%.

- Overall development costs were reduced by approximately 40%.

- Programs under development were increased by about 140%.

- Development costs per program were decreased by 78%.

What Gruver's experience shows is that, after comprehensive use of version control, continuous integration is one of the most critical practices that enable the fast flow of work in our value stream, enabling many development teams to independently develop, test, and deliver value. Nevertheless, continuous integration remains a controversial practice. The remainder of this chapter describes the practices required to implement continuous integration, as well as how to overcome common objections.

SMALL BATCH DEVELOPMENT AND WHAT HAPPENS WHEN WE COMMIT CODE TO TRUNK INFREQUENTLY

As described in the previous chapters, whenever changes are introduced into version control that cause our deployment pipeline to fail, we quickly swarm the problem to fix it, bringing our deployment pipeline back into a green state. However, significant problems result when developers work in long-lived private branches (also known as "feature branches"), only merging back into trunk sporadically, resulting in a large batch size of changes. As described in the HP LaserJet example, what results is significant chaos and rework in order to get their code into a releasable state.

Jeff Atwood, founder of the Stack Overflow site and author of the *Coding Horror* blog, observes that while there are many branching strategies, they can all be put on the following spectrum:

- **Optimize for individual productivity:** Every single person on the project works in their own private branch. Everyone works independently, and nobody can disrupt anyone else's work; however, merging becomes a nightmare. Collaboration becomes almost comically difficult—every person's work has to be painstakingly merged with everyone else's work to see even the smallest part of the complete system.

- **Optimize for team productivity:** Everyone works in the same common area. There are no branches, just a long, unbroken straight line of development. There's nothing to understand, so commits are simple, but each commit can break the entire project and bring all progress to a screeching halt.

Atwood's observation is absolutely correct—stated more precisely, the required effort to successfully merge branches back together increases exponentially as the number of branches increase. The problem lies not only in the rework this "merge hell" creates, but also in the delayed feedback we receive from our deployment pipeline. For instance, instead of performance testing against a fully integrated system happening continuously, it will likely happen only at the end of our process.

Furthermore, as we increase the rate of code production as we add more developers, we increase the probability that any given change will impact someone else and increase the number of developers who will be impacted when someone breaks the deployment pipeline.

Here is one last troubling side-effect of large batch size merges: when merging is difficult, we become less able and motivated to improve and refactor our code, because refactorings are more likely to cause rework for everyone else. When this happens, we are more reluctant to modify code that has dependencies throughout the codebase, which is (tragically) where we may have the highest payoffs.

This is how Ward Cunningham, developer of the first wiki, first described technical debt: when we do not aggressively refactor our codebase, it becomes more difficult to make changes and to maintain over time, slowing down the rate at which we can add new features. Solving this problem was one of the primary reasons behind the creation of continuous integration and trunk-based development practices, to optimize for team productivity over individual productivity.

ADOPT TRUNK-BASED DEVELOPMENT PRACTICES

Our countermeasure to large batch size merges is to institute continuous integration and trunk-based development practices, where all developers check in their code to trunk at least once per day. Checking code in this frequently reduces our batch size to the work performed by our entire developer team in a single day. The more frequently developers check in their code to trunk, the smaller the batch size and the closer we are to the theoretical ideal of single-piece flow.

Frequent code commits to trunk means we can run all automated tests on our software system as a whole and receive alerts when a change breaks some other part of the application or interferes with the work of another developer. And because we can detect merge problems when they are small, we can correct them faster.

We may even configure our deployment pipeline to reject any commits (e.g., code or environment changes) that take us out of a deployable state. This method is called *gated commits*, where the deployment pipeline first confirms that the submitted change will successfully merge, build as expected, and pass all the automated tests before actually being merged into trunk. If not, the developer will be notified, allowing corrections to be made without impacting anyone else in the value stream.

The discipline of daily code commits also forces us to break our work down into smaller chunks while still keeping trunk in a working, releasable state.

And version control becomes an integral mechanism of how the team communicates with each other—everyone has a better shared understanding of the system, is aware of the state of the deployment pipeline, and can help each other when it breaks. As a result, we achieve higher quality and faster deployment lead times.

Having these practices in place, we can now again modify our definition of "done" (addition in bold text): "At the end of each development interval, we must have integrated, tested, working, and potentially shippable code, demonstrated in a production-like environment, **created from trunk using a one-click process, and validated with automated tests.**"

Adhering to this revised definition of done helps us further ensure the ongoing testability and deployability of the code we're producing. By keeping our code in a deployable state, we are able to eliminate the common practice of having a separate test and stabilization phase at the end of the project.

Case Study
Continuous Integration at Bazaarvoice (2012)

Ernest Mueller, who helped engineer the DevOps transformation at National Instruments, later helped transform the development and release processes at Bazaarvoice in 2012. Bazaarvoice supplies customer generated content (e.g., reviews, ratings) for thousands of retailers, such as Best Buy, Nike, and Walmart.

At that time, Bazaarvoice had $120 million in revenue and was preparing for an IPO.[†] The business was primarily driven by the Bazaarvoice Conversations application, a monolithic Java application comprised of nearly five million lines of code dating back to 2006, spanning fifteen thousand files. The service ran on 1,200 servers across four data centers and multiple cloud service providers.

Partially as a result of switching to an Agile development process and to two-week development intervals, there was a tremendous desire to increase release frequency from their current ten-week production release schedule. They had also started to decouple parts of their monolithic application, breaking it down into microservices.

---

† The production release was delayed due to their (successful) IPO.

Their first attempt at a two-week release schedule was in January of 2012. Mueller observed, "It didn't go well. It caused massive chaos, with forty-four production incidents filed by our customers. The major reaction from management was basically 'Let's not ever do that again.'"

Mueller took over the release processes shortly afterward, with the goal of doing bi-weekly releases without causing customer downtime. The business objectives for releasing more frequently included enabling faster A/B testing (described in upcoming chapters) and increasing the flow of features into production. Mueller identified three core problems:

- Lack of test automation made any level of testing during the two-week intervals inadequate to prevent large-scale failures.

- The version control branching strategy allowed developers to check in new code right up to the production release.

- The teams running microservices were also performing independent releases, which were often causing issues during the monolith release or vice versa.

Mueller concluded that the monolithic Conversations application deployment process needed to be stabilized, which required continuous integration. In the six weeks that followed, developers stopped doing feature work to focus instead on writing automated testing suites, including unit tests in JUnit, regression tests in Selenium, and getting a deployment pipeline running in TeamCity. "By running these tests all the time, we felt like we could make changes with some level of safety. And most importantly, we could immediately find when someone broke something, as opposed to discovering it only after it's in production."

They also changed to a trunk/branch release model, where every two weeks they created a new dedicated release branch, with no new commits allowed to that branch unless there was an emergency—all changes would be worked through a sign-off process, either per-ticket or per-team through their internal wiki. That branch would go through a QA process, which would then be promoted into production.

The improvements to predictability and quality of the releases were startling:

- January 2012 release: forty-four customer incidents (continuous integration effort begins)

- March 6, 2012 release: five days late, five customer incidents

- March 22, 2012 release: on time, one customer incident

- April 5, 2012 release: on time, zero customer incidents

Mueller further described how successful this effort was:

> We had such success with releases every two weeks, we went to weekly releases, which required almost no changes from the engineering teams. Because releases became so routine, it was as simple as doubling the number of releases on the calendar and releasing when the calendar told us to. Seriously, it was almost a non-event. The majority of changes required were in our customer service and marketing teams, who had to change their processes, such as changing the schedule of their weekly customer emails to make sure customers knew that feature changes were coming. After that, we started working toward our next goals, which eventually led to speeding up our testing times from three plus hours to less than an hour, reducing the number of environments from four to three (Dev, Test, Production, eliminating Staging), and moving to a full continuous delivery model where we enable fast, one-click deployments.

CONCLUSION

Trunk-based development is likely the most controversial practice discussed in this book. Many engineers will not believe that it's possible, even those that prefer working uninterrupted on a private branch without having to deal with other developers. However, the data from Puppet Labs' 2015 *State of DevOps Report* is clear: trunk-based development predicts higher throughput and better stability, and even higher job satisfaction and lower rates of burnout.

While convincing developers may be difficult at first, once they see the extraordinary benefits, they will likely become lifetime converts, as the HP LaserJet and Bazaarvoice examples illustrate. Continuous integration practices set the stage for the next step, which is automating the deployment process and enabling low-risk releases.

Automate and Enable Low-Risk Releases

Chuck Rossi is the director of release engineering at Facebook. One of his responsibilities is overseeing the daily code push. In 2012, Rossi described their process as follows: "Starting around 1 p.m., I switch over to 'operations mode' and work with my team to get ready to launch the changes that are going out to Facebook.com that day. This is the more stressful part of the job and really relies heavily on my team's judgment and past experience. We work to make sure that everyone who has changes going out is accounted for and is actively testing and supporting their changes."

Just prior to the production push, all developers with changes going out must be present and check in on their IRC chat channel—any developers not present have their changes automatically removed from the deployment package. Rossi continued, "If everything looks good and our test dashboards and canary tests† are green, we push the big red button and the entire Facebook.com server fleet gets the new code delivered. Within twenty minutes, thousands and thousands of machines are up on new code with no visible impact to the people using the site."‡

Later that year, Rossi doubled their software release frequency to twice daily. He explained that the second code push gave engineers not on the US West Coast the ability to "move and ship as quickly as any other engineer in the company," and also gave everyone a second opportunity each day to ship code and launch features.

---

† A canary release test is when software is deployed to a small group of production servers to make sure nothing terrible happens to them with live customer traffic.

‡ The Facebook frontend codebase is primarily written in PHP. In 2010, to increase site performance, the PHP code was converted into C++ by their internally developed HipHop compiler, which was then compiled into a 1.5 GB executable. This file was then copied onto production servers using BitTorrent, enabling the copy operation to be completed in fifteen minutes.

Number of developers pushing code by week

Figure 16: *Number of developers deploying per week at Facebook*
(Source: Chuck Rossi, "Ship early and ship twice as often.")

Kent Beck, the creator of the Extreme Programming methodology, one of the leading proponents of Test Driven Development, and technical coach at Facebook, further comments on the their code release strategy in an article posted on his Facebook page: "Chuck Rossi made the observation that there seem to be a fixed number of changes Facebook can handle in one deployment. If we want more changes, we need more deployments. This has led to a steady increase in deployment pace over the past five years, from weekly to daily to thrice daily deployments of our PHP code and from six to four to two week cycles for deploying our mobile apps. This improvement has been driven primarily by the release engineering team."

By using continuous integration and making code deployment a low-risk process, Facebook has enabled code deployment to be a part of everyone's daily work and sustain developer productivity. This requires that code deployment be automated, repeatable, and predictable. In the practices described in the book so far, even though our code and environments have been tested together, most likely we are not deploying to production very often because deployments are manual, time-consuming, painful, tedious, and error-prone, and they often involve an inconvenient and unreliable handoff between Development and Operations.

And because it is painful, we tend to do it less and less frequently, resulting in another self-reinforcing downward spiral. By deferring production deployments, we accumulate ever-larger differences between the code to be deployed and what's running in production, increasing the deployment batch size. As deployment batch size grows, so does the risk of unexpected outcomes associated with the change, as well as the difficulty fixing them.

In this chapter, we reduce the friction associated with production deployments, ensuring that they can be performed frequently and easily, either by Operations or Development. We do this by extending our deployment pipeline.

Instead, of merely continually integrating our code in a production-like environment, we will enable the promotion into production of any build that passes our automated test and validation process, either on demand (i.e., at the push of a button) or automatically (i.e., any build that passes all the tests is automatically deployed).

Because of the number of practices presented, extensive footnotes are provided with numerous examples and additional information, without interrupting the presentation of concepts in the chapter.

AUTOMATE OUR DEPLOYMENT PROCESS

Achieving outcomes like those at Facebook requires that we have an automated mechanism that deploys our code into production. Especially if we have a deployment process that has existed for years, we need to fully document the steps in the deployment process, such as in a value stream mapping exercise, which we can assemble in a workshop or document incrementally (e.g., in a wiki).

Once we have the process documented, our goal is to simplify and automate as many of the manual steps as possible, such as:

- Packaging code in ways suitable for deployment

- Creating pre-configured virtual machine images or containers

- Automating the deployment and configuration of middleware

- Copying packages or files onto production servers

- Restarting servers, applications, or services

- Generating configuration files from templates

- Running automated smoke tests to make sure the system is working and correctly configured

- Running testing procedures

- Scripting and automating database migrations

Where possible, we will re-architect to remove steps, particularly those that take a long time to complete. We also want to not only reduce our lead times but also the number of handoffs as much as possible in order to reduce errors and loss of knowledge.

Having developers focus on automating and optimizing the deployment process can lead to significant improvements in deployment flow, such as ensuring that small application configuration changes no longer need new deployments or new environments.

However, this requires that Development works closely with Operations to ensure that all the tools and processes we co-create can be used downstream, as opposed to alienating Operations or reinventing the wheel.

Many tools that provide continuous integration and testing also support the ability to extend the deployment pipeline so that validated builds can be promoted into production, typically after the production acceptance tests are performed (e.g., the Jenkins Build Pipeline plugin, ThoughtWorks Go.cd and Snap CI, Microsoft Visual Studio Team Services, and Pivotal Concourse).

The requirements for our deployment pipeline include:

- **Deploying the same way to every environment:** By using the same deployment mechanism for every environment (e.g., development, test, and production), our production deployments are likely to be far more successful, since we know that it has been successfully performed many times already earlier in the pipeline.

- **Smoke testing our deployments:** During the deployment process, we should test that we can connect to any supporting systems (e.g., databases, message buses, external services) and run a single test transaction through the system to ensure that our system is performing as designed. If any of these tests fail, we should fail the deployment.

- **Ensure we maintain consistent environments:** In previous steps, we created a single-step environment build process so that the development, test, and production environments had a common build mechanism. We must continually ensure that these environments remain synchronized.

Of course, when any problems occur during deployment, we pull the Andon cord and swarm the problem until the problem is resolved, just as we do when our deployment pipeline fails in any of the earlier steps.

Case Study
Daily Deployments at CSG International (2013)

CSG International runs one of the largest bill printing operations in the US. Scott Prugh, their chief architect and VP of Development, in an effort to improve the predictability and reliability of their software releases, doubled their release frequency from two per year to four per year (halving their deployment interval from twenty-eight weeks to fourteen weeks).

Although the Development teams were using continuous integration to deploy their code into test environments daily, the production releases were being performed by the Operations team. Prugh observed, "It was as if we had a 'practice team' that practiced daily (or even more frequently) in low-risk test environments, perfecting their processes and tools. But our production 'game team' got very few attempts to practice, only twice per year. Worse, they were practicing in the high-risk production environments, which were often very different than the pre-production environments with different constraints—the development environments were missing many production assets such as security, firewalls, load balancers, and a SAN."

To solve this problem, they created a Shared Operations Team (SOT) that was responsible for managing all the environments (development, test, production) performing daily deployments into those development and test environments, as well as doing production deployments and releases every fourteen weeks. Because the SOT was doing deployments every day, any problems they encountered that were left unfixed would simply occur again the next day. This created tremendous motivation to automate tedious or error-prone manual steps and to fix any issues that could potentially happen again. Because the deployments were performed nearly one hundred times before the production release, most problems were found and fixed long before then.

Doing this revealed problems that were previously only experienced by the Ops team, which were then problems for the entire value stream to solve. The daily deployments enabled daily feedback on which practices worked and which didn't.

They also focused on making all their environments look as similar as possible, including the restricted security access rights and load balancers. Prugh writes, "We made non-production environments as similar to production as possible, and we sought to emulate production constraints in as many ways as possible. Early exposure to production-class environments altered the designs of the architecture to make them friendlier in these constrained or different environments. Everyone gets smarter from this approach."

Prugh also observes:

"We have experienced many cases where changes to database schemas are either 1) handed off to a DBA team for them to 'go and figure it out' or 2) automated tests that run on unrealistically small data sets (i.e., "100's of MB vs. 100's of GBs"), which led to production failures. In our old way of working, this would become a late-night blame game between teams trying to unwind the mess. We created a development and deployment process that removed the need for handoffs to DBAs by cross-training developers, automating schema changes, and executing them daily. We created realistic load testing against sanitized customer data, ideally running migrations every day. By doing this, we run our service hundreds of times with realistic scenarios before seeing actual production traffic."[†]

Their results were astonishing. By doing daily deployments and doubling the frequency of production releases, the number of production incidents went down by 91%, MTTR went down by 80%, and the deployment lead time required for the service to run in production in a "fully hands-off state" went from fourteen days to one day.

Prugh reported that deployments became so routine that the Ops team was playing video games by the end of the first day. In addition to deployments going more smoothly for Dev and Ops, in 50% of the cases the customer received the value in half the time, underscoring how more frequent deployments can be good for Development, QA, Operations, and the customer.

---

† In their experiments, they found that SOT teams were successful, regardless of whether they were managed by Development or Operations, as long as the teams were staffed with the right people and were dedicated to SOT success.

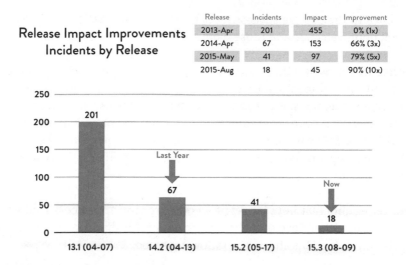

Release Impact Improvements
Incidents by Release

Release	Incidents	Impact	Improvement
2013-Apr	201	455	0% (1x)
2014-Apr	67	153	66% (3x)
2015-May	41	97	79% (5x)
2015-Aug	18	45	90% (10x)

Figure 17: *Daily deployments and increasing release frequency resulted in decrease in # of production incidents and MTTR (Source: "DOES15 - Scott Prugh & Erica Morrison - Conway & Taylor Meet the Strangler (v2.0)," YouTube video, 29:39, posted by DevOps Enterprise Summit, November 5, 2015, https:// www.youtube.com/watch?v=tKdIHCLoDUg.)*

ENABLE AUTOMATED SELF-SERVICE DEPLOYMENTS

Consider the following quote from Tim Tischler, Director of Operations Automation at Nike, Inc., that describes the common experience of a generation of developers: "As a developer, there has never been a more satisfying point in my career than when I wrote the code, when I pushed the button to deploy it, when I could see the production metrics confirm that it actually worked in production, and when I could fix it myself if it didn't."

Developers' ability to self-deploy code into production, to quickly see happy customers when their feature works, and to quickly fix any issues without having to open up a ticket with Operations has diminished over the last decade—in part as a result of a need for control and oversight, perhaps driven by security and compliance requirements.

The resulting common practice is for Operations to perform code deployments, because separation of duties is a widely accepted practice to reduce the risk of production outages and fraud. However, to achieve DevOps outcomes, our goal is to shift our reliance to other control mechanisms that can mitigate these risks equally or even more effectively, such as through automated testing, automated deployment, and peer review of changes.

The Puppet Labs' 2013 *State of DevOps Report*, which surveyed over four thousand technology professionals, found that there was no statistically significant difference in the change success rates between organizations where Development deployed code and those where Operations deployed code.

In other words, when there are shared goals that span Development and Operations, and there is transparency, responsibility, and accountability for deployment outcomes, it doesn't matter who performs the deployment. In fact, we may even have other roles, such as testers or project managers, able to deploy to certain environments so they can get their own work done quickly, such as setting up demonstrations of specific features in test or UAT environments.

To better enable fast flow, we want a code promotion process that can be performed by either Development or Operations, ideally without any manual steps or handoffs. This affects the following steps:

- **Build:** Our deployment pipeline must create packages from version control that can be deployed to any environment, including production.

- **Test:** Anyone should be able to run any or all of our automated test suite on their workstation or on our test systems.

- **Deploy:** Anybody should be able to deploy these packages to any environment where they have access, executed by running scripts that are also checked in to version control.

These are the practices that enable deployments to be performed successfully, regardless of who is performing the deployment.

INTEGRATE CODE DEPLOYMENT INTO THE DEPLOYMENT PIPELINE
Once the code deployment process is automated, we can make it part of the deployment pipeline. Consequently, our deployment automation must provide the following capabilities:

- Ensure that packages created during the continuous integration process are suitable for deployment into production

- Show the readiness of production environments at a glance

- Provide a push-button, self-service method for any suitable version of the packaged code to be deployed into production

- Record automatically, for auditing and compliance purposes, which commands were run on which machines when, who authorized it, and what the output was

- Run a smoke test to ensure the system is operating correctly and the configuration settings, including items such as database connection strings, are correct

- Provide fast feedback for the deployer so they can quickly determine whether their deployment was successful (e.g., did the deployment succeed, is the application performing as expected in production, etc.)

Our goal is ensure that deployments are fast—we don't want to have to wait hours to determine whether our code deployment succeeded or failed and then need hours to deploy any needed code fixes. Now that we have technologies such as containers, it is possible to complete even the most complex deployments in seconds or minutes. In Puppet Labs' 2014 *State of DevOps Report*, the data showed that high performers had deployment lead times measured in minutes or hours, while the lowest performers had deployment lead times measured in months.

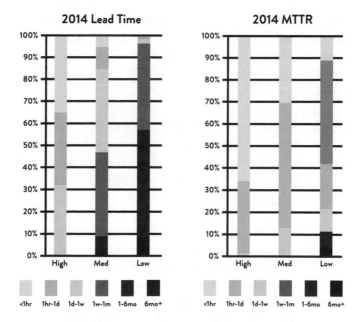

Figure 18: *High performers had much faster deployment lead times and much faster time to restore production service after incidents (Source: Puppet Labs, 2014 State of DevOps Report.)*

By building this capability, we now have a "deploy code" button that allows us to safely and quickly promote changes to our code and our environments into production through our deployment pipeline.

Case Study
Etsy—Self-Service Developer Deployment, an Example of Continuous Deployment (2014)

Unlike at Facebook where deployments are managed by release engineers, at Etsy deployments are performed by anyone who wants to perform a deployment, such as Development, Operations, or Infosec. The deployment process at Etsy has become so safe and routine that new engineers will perform a production deployment on their first day at work—as have Etsy board members and even dogs!

As Noah Sussman, a test architect at Etsy, wrote, "By the time 8am rolls around on a normal business day, 15 or so people and dogs are starting to queue up, all of them expecting to collectively deploy up to 25 changesets before the day is done."

Engineers who want to deploy their code first go to a chat room, where engineers add themselves to the deploy queue, see the deployment activity in progress, see who else is in the queue, broadcast their activities, and get help from other engineers when they need it. When it's an engineer's turn to deploy, they are notified in the chat room.

The goal at Etsy has been to make it easy and safe to deploy into production with the fewest number of steps and the least amount of ceremony. Likely before the developer even checks in code, they will run on their workstation all 4,500 unit tests, which takes less than one minute. All calls to external systems, such as databases, have been stubbed out.

After they check their changes in to trunk in version control, over seven thousand automated trunk tests are instantly run on their continuous integration (CI) servers. Sussman writes, "Through trial-and-error, we've settled on about 11 minutes as the longest that the automated tests can run during a push. That leaves time to re-run the tests once during a deployment [if someone breaks something and needs to fix it], without going too far past the 20 minute time limit."

If all the tests were run sequentially, Sussman states that "the 7,000 trunk tests would take about half an hour to execute. So we split these tests up into subsets, and distribute those onto the 10 machines in our Jenkins [CI] cluster....Splitting up our test suite and running many tests in parallel, gives us the desired 11 minute runtime."

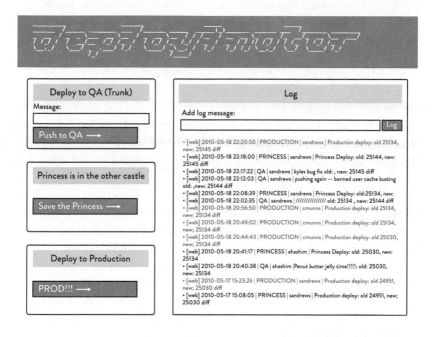

Figure 19: *The Deployinator console at Etsy (Source: Erik Kastner, "Quantum of Deployment," CodeasCraft. com, May 20, 2010, https://codeascraft.com/2010/05/20/quantum-of-deployment/.)*

The next tests to run are the *smoke tests*, which are system level tests that run cURL to execute PHPUnit test cases. Following these tests, the functional tests are run, which execute end-to-end GUI-driven tests on a live server—this server is either their QA environment or staging environment (nicknamed "Princess"), which is actually a production server that has been taken out of rotation, ensuring that it exactly matches the production environment.

Once it is an engineer's turn to deploy, Erik Kastner writes, "you go to Deployinator [an internally developed tool, see figure 19] and push the button to get it on QA. From there it visits Princess....Then, when it's ready to go live, you hit the "Prod" button and soon your code is live, and everyone in IRC [chat channel] knows who pushed what code, complete with a link to the diff. For anyone not on IRC, there's the email that everyone gets with the same information."

In 2009, the deployment process at Etsy was a cause of stress and fear. By 2011, it had become a routine operation, happening twenty-five to fifty times per day, helping engineers get their code quickly into production, delivering value to their customers.

DECOUPLE DEPLOYMENTS FROM RELEASES

In the traditional launch of a software project, releases are driven by our marketing launch date. On the prior evening, we deploy our completed software (or as close to complete as we could get) into production. The next morning, we announce our new capabilities to the world, start taking orders, deliver the new functionality to customer, etc.

However, all too often things don't go according to plan. We may experience production loads that we never tested or designed for, causing our service to fail spectacularly, both for our customers and our organization. Worse, restoring service may require a painful rollback process or an equally risky *fix forward* operation, where we make changes directly in production, this can all be a truly miserable experience for workers. When everything is finally working, everyone breathes a sigh of relief, grateful that production deployments and releases don't happen more often.

Of course, we know that we need to be deploying more frequently to achieve our desired outcome of smooth and fast flow, not less frequently. To enable this, we need to decouple our production deployments from our feature releases. In practice, the terms *deployment* and *release* are often used interchangeably. However, they are two distinct actions that serve two very different purposes:

- Deployment is the installation of a specified version of software to a given environment (e.g., deploying code into an integration test environment or deploying code into production). Specifically, a deployment may or may not be associated with a release of a feature to customers.

- Release is when we make a feature (or set of features) available to all our customers or a segment of customers (e.g., we enable the feature to be used by 5% of our customer base). Our code and environments should be architected in such a way that the release of functionality does not require changing our application code.[†]

In other words, when we conflate deployment and release, it makes it difficult to create accountability for successful outcomes—decoupling these two activities allows us to empower Development and Operations to be responsible for the success of fast and frequent deployments, while enabling product owners to be responsible for the successful business outcomes of the release (i.e., was building and launching the feature worth our time).

The practices described so far in this book ensure that we are doing fast and frequent production deployments throughout feature development, with the goal of reducing the risk and impact of deployment errors. The remaining risk is release risk, which is whether the features we put into production achieve the desired customer and business outcomes.

If we have extremely long deployment lead times, this dictates how frequently we can release new features to the marketplace. However, as we become able to deploy on demand, how quickly we expose new functionality to customers becomes a business and marketing decision, not a technical decision. There are two broad categories of release patterns we can use:

- **Environment-based release patterns:** This is where we have two or more environments that we deploy into, but only one environment is receiving live customer traffic (e.g., by configuring our load balancers). New code is deployed into a non-live environment, and the release is performed moving traffic to this environment. These are extremely powerful patterns, because they typically require little or no change to our applications. These patterns include *blue-green deployments*, *canary releases*, and *cluster immune systems*, all of which will be discussed shortly.

- **Application-based release patterns:** This is where we modify our application so that we can selectively release and expose specific application functionality by small configuration changes. For instance, we can implement feature flags that progressively expose new functionality in production to the development team, all internal employees, 1% of our customers, or, when we are

---

† Operation Desert Shield may serve as an effective metaphor. Starting on August 7, 1990, thousands of men and materials were safely deployed over four months into the production theater, culminating in a single, multi-disciplinary, highly coordinated release.

confident that the release will operate as designed, our entire customer base. As discussed earlier, this enables a technique called dark launching, where we stage all the functionality to be launched in production and test it with production traffic before our release. For instance, we may invisibly test our new functionality with production traffic for weeks before our launch in order to expose problems so that they can be fixed before our actual launch.

ENVIRONMENT-BASED RELEASE PATTERNS

Decoupling deployments from our releases dramatically changes how we work. We no longer have to perform deployments in the middle of the night or on weekends to lower the risk of negatively impacting customers. Instead, we can do deployments during typical business hours, enabling Ops to finally have normal working hours, just like everyone else.

This section focuses on environment-based release patterns, which require no changes to application code. We do this by having multiple environments to deploy into, but only one of them receives live customer traffic. By doing this, we can significantly decrease the risk associated with production releases and reduce the deployment lead time.

The Blue-Green Deployment Pattern

The simplest of the three patterns is called blue-green deployment. In this pattern, we have two production environments: blue and green. At any time, only one of these is serving customer traffic—in figure 20, the green environment is live.

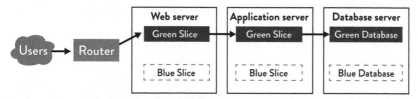

Figure 20: *Blue-green deployment patterns (Source: Humble and North,* Continuous Delivery, *261.)*

To release a new version of our service, we deploy to the inactive environment where we can perform our testing without interrupting the user experience. When we are confident that everything is functioning as designed, we execute our release by directing traffic to the blue environment. Thus, blue becomes live and green becomes staging. Roll back is performed by sending customer traffic back to the green environment.[†]

The blue-green deployment pattern is simple, and it is extremely easy to retrofit onto existing systems. It also has incredible benefits, such as enabling the team to perform deployments during normal business hours and conduct simple changeovers (e.g., changing a router setting, changing a symlink) during off-peak times. This alone can dramatically improve the work conditions for the team performing the deployment.

Dealing with Database Changes

Having two versions of our application in production creates problems when they depend upon a common database—when the deployment requires database schema changes or adding, modifying, or deleting tables or columns, the database cannot support both versions of our application. There are two general approaches to solving this problem:

- **Create two databases (i.e., a blue and green database):** Each version—blue (old) and green (new)—of the application has its own database. During the release, we put the blue database into read-only mode, perform a backup of it, restore onto the green database, and finally switch traffic to the green environment. The problem with this pattern is that if we need to roll back to the blue version, we can potentially lose transactions if we don't manually migrate them from the green version first.

- **Decouple database changes from application changes:** Instead of supporting two databases, we decouple the release of database changes from the release of application changes by doing two things: First, we make only additive changes to our database, we

---

† Other ways that we can implement the blue-green pattern include setting up multiple Apache/ NGINX web servers to listen on different physical or virtual interfaces; employing multiple virtual roots on Windows IIS servers bound to different ports; using different directories for every version of the system, with a symbolic link determining which one is live (e.g., as Capistrano does for Ruby on Rails); running multiple versions of services or middleware concurrently, with each listening on different ports; using two different data centers and switching traffic between the data centers, instead of using them merely as hot- or warm-spares for disaster recovery purposes (incidentally, by routinely using both environments, we are continually ensuring that our disaster recovery process works as designed); or using different availability zones in the cloud.

never mutate existing database objects, and second, we make no assumptions in our application about which database version will be in production. This is very different than how we've been traditionally trained to think about databases, where we avoid duplicating data. The process of Decoupling database changes from application changes was used by IMVU (among others) around 2009, enabling them to do fifty deployments per day, some of which required database changes.[†]

Case Study
Dixons Retail—Blue-Green Deployment for Point-Of-Sale System (2008)

Dan North and Dave Farley, co-authors of *Continuous Delivery*, were working on a project for Dixons Retail, a large British retailer involving thousands of point-of-sale (POS) systems that resided in hundreds of retail stores and operating under a number of different customer brands.

Although blue-green deployments are mostly associated with online web services, North and Farley used this pattern to significantly reduce the risk and changeover times for POS upgrades.

Traditionally, upgrading POS systems are a big bang, waterfall project: the POS clients and the centralized server are upgraded at the same time, which requires extensive downtime (often an entire weekend), as well as significant network bandwidth to push out the new client software to all the retail stores. When things don't go entirely according to plan, it can be incredibly disruptive to store operations.

For this upgrade, there was not enough network bandwidth to upgrade all the POS systems simultaneously, which made the traditional strategy impossible. To solve this problem, they used the blue-green strategy and created

---

† This pattern is also commonly referred to as the expand/contract pattern, which Timothy Fitz described when he said, "We do not change (mutate) database objects, such as columns or tables. Instead, we first expand, by adding new objects, then, later, contract by removing the old ones." Furthermore, increasingly, there are technologies that enable virtualization, versioning, labeling, and roll back of databases, such as Redgate, Delphix, DBMaestro, and Datical, as well as open source tools, such as DBDeploy, that make database changes dramatically safer and faster.

two production versions of the centralized server software, enabling them to simultaneously support the old and new versions of the POS clients.

After they did this, weeks before the planned POS upgrade, they started sending out new versions of client POS software installers to the retail stores over the slow network links, deploying the new software onto the POS systems in an inactive state. Meanwhile, the old version kept running as normal.

When all the POS clients had everything staged for the upgrade (the upgraded client and server had tested together successfully, and new client software had been deployed to all clients), the store managers were empowered to decide when to release the new version.

Depending on their business needs, some managers wanted to use the new features immediately and released right away, while others wanted to wait. In either case, whether releasing features immediately or waiting, it was significantly better for the managers than having the centralized IT department choose for them when the release would occur.

The result was a significantly smoother and faster release, higher satisfaction from the store managers, and far less disruption to store operations. Furthermore, this application of blue-green deployments to thick-client PC applications demonstrates how DevOps patterns can be universally applied to different technologies, often in very surprising ways but with the same fantastic outcomes.

The Canary and Cluster Immune System Release Patterns

The blue-green release pattern is easy to implement and can dramatically increase the safety of software releases. There are variants of this pattern that can further improve safety and deployment lead times using automation, but with the potential trade-off of additional complexity.

The canary release pattern automates the release process of promoting to successively larger and more critical environments as we confirm that the code is operating as designed.

The term *canary release* comes from the tradition of coal miners bringing caged canaries into mines to provide early detection of toxic levels of carbon monoxide. If there was too much gas in the cave, it would kill the canaries before it killed the miners, alerting them to evacuate.

In this pattern, when we perform a release, we monitor how the software in each environment is performing. When something appears to be going wrong, we roll back; otherwise, we deploy to the next environment.[†]

Figure 21 shows the groups of environments Facebook created to support this release pattern:

- **A1 group:** Production servers that only serve internal employees

- **A2 group:** Production servers that only serve a small percentage of customers and are deployed when certain acceptance criteria have been met (either automated or manual)

- **A3 group:** The rest of the production servers, which are deployed after the software running in the A2 cluster meets certain acceptance criteria

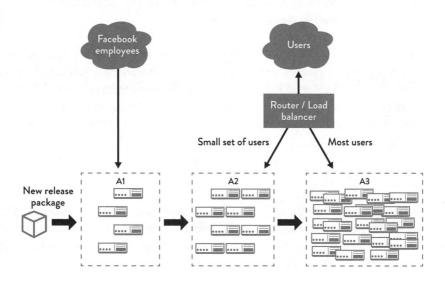

Figure 21: *The canary release pattern (Source: Humble and Farley,* Continuous Delivery, *263.)*

---

† Note that canary releases require having multiple versions of our software running in production simultaneously. However, because each additional version we have in production creates additional complexity to manage, we should keep the number of versions to a minimum. This may require the use of the expand/contract database pattern described earlier.

The cluster immune system expands upon the canary release pattern by linking our production monitoring system with our release process and by automating the roll back of code when the user-facing performance of the production system deviates outside of a predefined expected range, such as when the conversion rates for new users drops below our historical norms of 15%–20%.

There are two significant benefits to this type of safeguard. First, we protect against defects that are hard to find through automated tests, such as a web page change that renders some critical page element invisible (e.g., CSS change). Second, we reduce the time required to detect and respond to the degraded performance created by our change.[‡]

APPLICATION-BASED PATTERNS TO ENABLE SAFER RELEASES

In the previous section, we created environment-based patterns that allowed us to decouple our deployments from our releases by using multiple environments and by switching between which environment was live, which can be entirely implemented at the infrastructure level.

In this section, we describe application-based release patterns that we can implement in our code, allowing even greater flexibility in how we safely release new features to our customer, often on a per-feature basis. Because application-based release patterns are implemented in the application, these require involvement from Development.

Implement Feature Toggles

The primary way we enable application-based release patterns is by implementing feature toggles, which provide us with the mechanism to selectively enable and disable features without requiring a production code deployment. Feature toggles can also control which features are visible and available to specific user segments (e.g., internal employees, segments of customers).

Feature toggles are usually implemented by wrapping application logic or UI elements with a conditional statement, where the feature is enabled or disabled based on a configuration setting stored somewhere. This can be as simple as an application configuration file (e.g., configuration files in JSON, XML), or

---

‡ The cluster immune system was first documented by Eric Ries while working at IMVU. This functionality is also supported by Etsy in their Feature API library, as well as by Netflix.

it might be through a directory service or even a web service specifically designed to manage feature toggling.[†]

Feature toggles also enable us to do the following:

- **Roll back easily:** Features that create problems or interruptions in production can be quickly and safely disabled by merely changing the feature toggle setting. This is especially valuable when deployments are infrequent—switching off one particular stakeholder's features is usually much easier than rolling back an entire release.

- **Gracefully degrade performance:** When our service experiences extremely high loads that would normally require us to increase capacity or, worse, risk having our service fail in production, we can use feature toggles to reduce the quality of service. In other words, we can increase the number of users we serve by reducing the level of functionality delivered (e.g., reduce the number of customers who can access a certain feature, disable CPU-intensive features such as recommendations, etc.).

- **Increase our resilience through a service-oriented architecture:** If we have a feature that relies on another service that isn't complete yet, we can still deploy our feature into production but hide it behind a feature toggle. When that service finally becomes available, we can toggle the feature on. Similarly, when a service we rely upon fails, we can turn off the feature to prevent calls to the downstream service while keeping the rest of the application running.

To ensure that we find errors in features wrapped in feature toggles, our automated acceptance tests should run with all feature toggles on. (We should also test that our feature toggling functionality works correctly too!)

---

† One sophisticated example of such a service is Facebook's Gatekeeper, an internally developed service that dynamically selects which features are visible to specific users based on demographic information such as location, browser type, and user profile data (age, gender, etc.). For instance, a particular feature could be configured so that it is only accessible by internal employees, 10% of their user base, or only users between the ages of twenty-five and thirty-five. Other examples include the Etsy Feature API and the Netflix Archaius library.

Feature toggles enable the decoupling of code deployments and feature releases, later in the book we use feature toggles to enable hypothesis-driven development and A/B testing, furthering our ability to achieve our desired business outcomes.

Perform Dark Launches

Feature toggles allow us to deploy features into production without making them accessible to users, enabling a technique known as *dark launching*. This is where we deploy all the functionality into production and then perform testing of that functionality while it is still invisible to customers. For large or risky changes, we often do this for weeks before the production launch, enabling us to safely test with the anticipated production-like loads.

For instance, suppose we dark launch a new feature that poses significant release risk, such as new search features, account creation processes, or new database queries. After all the code is in production, keeping the new feature disabled, we may modify user session code to make calls to new functions—instead of displaying the results to the user, we simply log or discard the results.

For example, we may have 1% of our online users make invisible calls to a new feature scheduled to be launched to see how our new feature behaves under load. After we find and fix any problems, we progressively increase the simulated load by increasing the frequency and number of users exercising the new functionality. By doing this, we are able to safely simulate production-like loads, giving us confidence that our service will perform as it needs to.

Furthermore, when we launch a feature, we can progressively roll out the feature to small segments of customers, halting the release if any problems are found. That way, we minimize the number of customers who are given a feature only to have it taken away because we find a defect or are unable to maintain the required performance.

In 2009, when John Allspaw was VP of Operations at Flickr, he wrote to the Yahoo! executive management team about their dark launch process, saying that it "increases *everyone's* confidence almost to the point of apathy, as far as fear of load-related issues are concerned. I have no idea how many code deploys there were made to production on any given day in the past 5 years...because for the most part I don't care, because those changes made in production have such a low chance of causing issues. When they have caused issues, everyone on the Flickr staff can find on a webpage *when* the change was made, *who* made the change, and exactly (line-by-line) *what* the change was."[†]

Later, when we have built adequate production telemetry in our application and environments, we can also enable faster feedback cycles to validate our business assumptions and outcomes immediately after we deploy the feature into production.

By doing this, we no longer wait until a big bang release to test whether customers want to use the functionality we build. Instead, by the time we announce and release our big feature, we have already tested our business hypotheses and run countless experiments to continually refine our product with real customers, which helps us validate that the features will achieve the desired customer outcomes.

Case Study
Dark Launch of Facebook Chat (2008)

For nearly a decade, Facebook has been one of the most widely visited Internet sites, as measured by pages viewed and unique site users. In 2008, it had over seventy million daily active users, which created a challenge for the team that was developing the new Facebook Chat functionality.[‡]

Eugene Letuchy, an engineer on the Chat team, wrote about how the number of concurrent users presented a huge software engineering challenge: "The most resource-intensive operation performed in a chat system is not sending messages. It is rather keeping each online user aware of the online-idle-offline states of their friends, so that conversations can begin."

Implementing this computationally-intensive feature was one of the largest technical undertakings ever at Facebook and took almost a year to complete.[§] Part of the complexity of the project was due to the wide variety of tech-

---

† Similarly, as Chuck Rossi, Director of Release Engineering at Facebook, described, "All the code supporting every feature we're planning to launch over the next six months has already been deployed onto our production servers. All we need to do is turn it on."

‡ By 2015, Facebook had over one billion active users, growing 17% over the previous year.

§ This problem has a worst-case computational characteristic of $O(n^3)$. In other words, the compute time increases exponentially as the function of the number of online users, the size of their friend lists, and the frequency of online/offline state change.

nologies needed to achieve the desired performance, including C++, JavaScript, and PHP, as well as their first use of Erlang in their back-end infrastructure.

Throughout the course of the year-long endeavor, the Chat team checked their code in to version control, where it would be deployed into production at least once per day. At first, the Chat functionality was visible only to the Chat team. Later, it was made visible to all internal employees, but it was completely hidden from external Facebook users through Gatekeeper, the Facebook feature toggling service.

As part of their dark launch process, every Facebook user session, which runs JavaScript in the user browser, had a test harness loaded into it—the chat UI elements were hidden, but the browser client would send invisible test chat messages to the back-end chat service that was already in production, enabling them to simulate production-like loads throughout the entire project, allowing them to find and fix performance problems long before the customer release.

By doing this, every Facebook user was part of a massive load testing program, which enabled the team to gain confidence that their systems could handle realistic production-like loads. The Chat release and launch required only two steps: modifying the Gatekeeper configuration setting to make the Chat feature visible to some portion of external users, and having Facebook users load new JavaScript code that rendered the Chat UI and disabled the invisible test harness. If something went wrong, the two steps would be reversed. When the launch day of Facebook Chat arrived, it was surprisingly successful and uneventful, seeming to scale effortlessly from zero to seventy million users overnight. During the release, they incrementally enabled the chat functionality to ever-larger segments of the customer population—first to all internal Facebook employees, then to 1% of the customer population, then to 5%, and so forth. As Letuchy wrote, "The secret for going from zero to seventy million users overnight is to avoid doing it all in one fell swoop."

SURVEY OF CONTINUOUS DELIVERY AND CONTINUOUS DEPLOYMENT IN PRACTICE

In *Continuous Delivery,* Jez Humble and David Farley define the term *continuous delivery.* The term *continuous deployment* was first mentioned by Tim Fitz in his blog post "Continuous Deployment at IMVU: Doing the impossible fifty times a day." However, in 2015, during the construction of *The DevOps Handbook,* Jez Humble commented, "In the last five years, there has been confusion around the terms continuous delivery versus continuous deployment—and, indeed, my own thinking and definitions have changed since we wrote the book. Every organization should create their variations, based on what they need. The key thing we should care about is not the form, but the outcomes: deployments should be low-risk, push-button events we can perform on demand."

His updated definitions of continuous delivery and continuous deployment are as follows:

> When all developers are working in small batches on trunk, or everyone is working off trunk in short-lived feature branches that get merged to trunk regularly, and when trunk is always kept in a releasable state, and when we can release on demand at the push of a button during normal business hours, we are doing continuous delivery. Developers get fast feedback when they introduce any regression errors, which include defects, performance issues, security issues, usability issues, etc. When these issues are found, they are fixed immediately so that trunk is always deployable.

> In addition to the above, when we are deploying good builds into production on a regular basis through self-service (being deployed by Dev or by Ops)—which typically means that we are deploying to production at least once per day per developer, or perhaps even automatically deploying every change a developer commits—this is when we are engaging in continuous deployment.

Defined this way, continuous delivery is the prerequisite for continuous deployment—just as continuous integration is a prerequisite for continuous delivery. Continuous deployment is likely applicable in the context of web services that are delivered online. However, continuous delivery is applicable in almost every context where we desire deployments and releases that have high quality, fast lead times and have highly predictable, low-risk outcomes, including for embedded systems, COTS products, and mobile apps.

At Amazon and Google, most teams practice continuous delivery, although some perform continuous deployment— thus, there is considerable variation between teams in how frequently they deploy code and how deployments are performed. Teams are empowered to choose how to deploy based on the risks they are managing. For example, the Google App Engine team often deploys once per day, while the Google Search property deploys several times per week.

Similarly, most of the cases studies presented in this book are also continuous delivery, such as the embedded software running on HP LaserJet printers, the CSG bill printing operations running on twenty technology platforms including a COBOL mainframe application, Facebook, and Etsy. These same patterns can be used for software that runs on mobile phones, ground control stations that control satellites, and so forth.

CONCLUSION

As the Facebook, Etsy, and CSG examples have shown, releases and deployments do not have to be high-risk, high-drama affairs that require tens or hundreds of engineers to work around the clock to complete. Instead, they can be made entirely routine and a part of everyone's daily work.

By doing this, we can reduce our deployment lead times from months to minutes, allowing our organizations to quickly deliver value to our customer without causing chaos and disruption. Furthermore, by having Dev and Ops work together, we can finally make Operations work humane.

13 Architect for Low-Risk Releases

Almost every well-known DevOps exemplar has had near-death experiences due to architectural problems, such as in the stories presented about LinkedIn, Google, eBay, Amazon, and Etsy. In each case, they were able to successfully migrate to a more suitable architecture that addressed their current problems and organizational needs.

This is the principle of evolutionary architecture—Jez Humble observes that architecture of "any successful product or organization will necessarily evolve over its life cycle." Before his tenure at Google, Randy Shoup served as chief engineer and distinguished architect at eBay from 2004 to 2011. He observes that "both eBay and Google are each on their fifth entire rewrite of their architecture from top to bottom."

He reflects, "Looking back with 20/20 hindsight, some technology [and architectural choices] look prescient and others look shortsighted. Each decision most likely best served the organizational goals at the time. If we had tried to implement the 1995 equivalent of micro-services out of the gate, we would have likely failed, collapsing under our own weight and probably taking the entire company with us."[†]

The challenge is how to keep migrating from the architecture we have to the architecture we need. In the case of eBay, when they needed to re-architect, they would first do a small pilot project to prove to themselves that they understood the problem well enough to even undertake the effort. For instance, when Shoup's team was planning on moving certain portions of the site to full-stack Java in 2006, they looked for the area that would get them the biggest bang for their buck by sorting the site pages by revenue produced. They chose

---

† eBay's architecture went through the following phases: Perl and files (v1, 1995), C++ and Oracle (v2, 1997), XSL and Java (v3, 2002), full-stack Java (v4, 2007), Polyglot microservices (2013+).

the highest revenue areas, stopping when there was not enough of a business return to justify the effort.

What Shoup's team did at eBay is a textbook example of evolutionary design, using a technique called the *strangler application* pattern—instead of "ripping out and replacing" old services with architectures that no longer support our organizational goals, we put the existing functionality behind an API and avoid making further changes to it. All new functionality is then implemented in the new services that use the new desired architecture, making calls to the old system when necessary.

The strangler application pattern is especially useful for helping migrate portions of a monolithic application or tightly coupled services to one that is more loosely coupled. All too often, we find ourselves working within an architecture that has become too tightly-coupled and too interconnected, often having been created years (or decades) ago.

The consequences of overly tight architectures are easy to spot: every time we attempt to commit code in to trunk or release code in to production, we risk creating global failures (e.g., we break everyone else's tests and function-ality, or the entire site goes down). To avoid this, every small change requires enormous amounts of communication and coordination over days or weeks, as well as approvals from any group that could potentially be affected. Deployments become problematic as well—the number of changes that are batched together for each deployment grows, further complicating the integration and test effort, and increasing the already high likelihood of something going wrong.

Even deploying small changes may require coordinating with hundreds (or even thousands) of other developers, with any one of them able to create a catastrophic failure, potentially requiring weeks to find and fix the problem. (This results in another symptom: "My developers spend only 15% of their time coding—the rest of their time is spent in meetings.")

These all contribute to an extremely unsafe system of work, where small changes have seemingly unknowable and catastrophic consequences. It also often contributes to a fear of integrating and deploying our code, and the self-reinforcing downward spiral of deploying less frequently.

From an enterprise architecture perspective, this downward spiral is the consequence of the Second Law of Architectural Thermodynamics, especially in large, complex organizations. Charles Betz, author of *Architecture and*

Patterns for IT Service Management, Resource Planning, and Governance: Making Shoes for the Cobbler's Children, observes, "[IT project owners] are not held accountable for their contributions to overall system entropy." In other words, reducing our overall complexity and increasing the productivity of all our development teams is rarely the goal of an individual project.

In this chapter, we will describe steps we can take to reverse the downward spiral, review the major architectural archetypes, examine the attributes of architectures that enable developer productivity, testability, deployability, and safety, as well as evaluate strategies that allow us to safely migrate from whatever current architecture we have to one that better enables the achievement of our organizational goals.

AN ARCHITECTURE THAT ENABLES PRODUCTIVITY, TESTABILITY, AND SAFETY

In contrast to a tightly-coupled architecture that can impede everyone's productivity and ability to safely make changes, a loosely-coupled architecture with well-defined interfaces that enforce how modules connect with each other promotes productivity and safety. It enables small, productive, two-pizza teams that are able to make small changes that can be safely and independently deployed. And because each service also has a well-defined API, it enables easier testing of services and the creation of contracts and SLAs between teams.

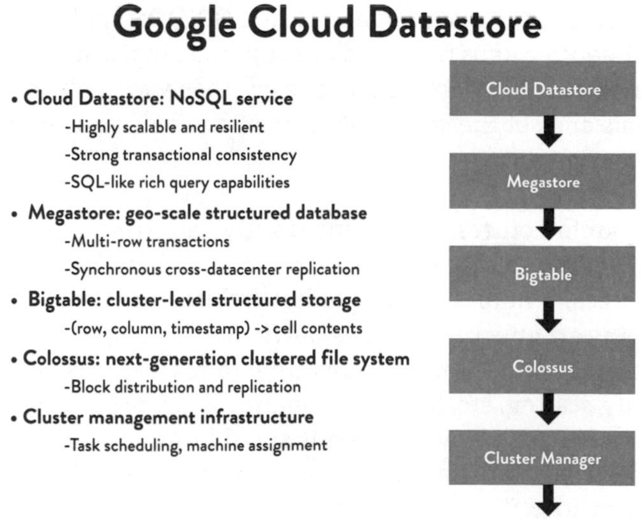

Google Cloud Datastore

- **Cloud Datastore: NoSQL service**
  - Highly scalable and resilient
  - Strong transactional consistency
  - SQL-like rich query capabilities
- **Megastore: geo-scale structured database**
  - Multi-row transactions
  - Synchronous cross-datacenter replication
- **Bigtable: cluster-level structured storage**
  - (row, column, timestamp) -> cell contents
- **Colossus: next-generation clustered file system**
  - Block distribution and replication
- **Cluster management infrastructure**
  - Task scheduling, machine assignment

Cloud Datastore → Megastore → Bigtable → Colossus → Cluster Manager

Figure 22: *Google cloud datastore (Source: Shoup, "From the Monolith to Micro-services.")*

As Randy Shoup describes, "This type of architecture has served Google extremely well—for a service like Gmail, there's five or six other layers of services underneath it, each very focused on a very specific function. Each service is supported by a small team, who builds it and runs their functionality, with each group potentially making different technology choices. Another example is the Google Cloud Datastore service, which is one of the largest NoSQL services in the world—and yet it is supported by a team of only about eight people, largely because it is based on layers upon layers of dependable services built upon each other."

This kind of service-oriented architecture allows small teams to work on smaller and simpler units of development that each team can deploy independently, quickly, and safely. Shoup notes, "Organizations with these types of architectures, such as Google and Amazon, show how it can impact organizational structures, [creating] flexibility and scalability. These are both organizations with tens of thousands of developers, where small teams can still be incredibly productive."

ARCHITECTURAL ARCHETYPES: MONOLITHS VS. MICROSERVICES

At some point in their history, most DevOps organizations were hobbled by tightly-coupled, monolithic architectures that—while extremely successful at helping them achieve product/market fit—put them at risk of organizational failure once they had to operate at scale (e.g., eBay's monolithic C++ application in 2001, Amazon's monolithic OBIDOS application in 2001, Twitter's monolithic Rails front-end in 2009, and LinkedIn's monolithic Leo application in 2011). In each of these cases, they were able to re-architect their systems and set the stage not only to survive, but also to thrive and win in the marketplace.

Monolithic architectures are not inherently bad—in fact, they are often the best choice for an organization early in a product life cycle. As Randy Shoup observes, "There is no one perfect architecture for all products and all scales. Any architecture meets a particular set of goals or range of requirements and constraints, such as time to market, ease of developing functionality, scaling, etc. The functionality of any product or service will almost certainly evolve over time—it should not be surprising that our architectural needs will change as well. What works at scale 1x rarely works at scale 10x or 100x."

Table 3: *Architectural archetypes*

	Pros	Cons
Monolithic v1 (All functionality in one application)	• Simple at first • Low inter-process latencies • Single codebase, one deployment unit • Resource-efficient at small scales	• Coordination overhead increases as team grows • Poor enforcement of modularity • Poor scaling • All-or-nothing deploy (downtime, failures) • Long build times
Monolithic v2 (Sets of monolithic tiers: "front end presentation," "application server," "database layer")	• Simple at first • Join queries are easy • Single schema, deployment • Resource-efficient at small scales	• Tendency for increased coupling over time • Poor scaling and redundancy (all or nothing, vertical only) • Difficult to tune properly • All-or-nothing schema management
Microservice (Modular, independent, graph relationship vs. tiers, isolated persistence)	• Each unit is simple • Independent scaling and performance • Independent testing and deployment • Can optimally tune performance (caching, replication, etc.)	• Many cooperating units • Many small repos • Requires more sophisticated tooling and dependency management • Network latencies

(Source: Shoup, "From the Monolith to Micro-services.")

The major architectural archetypes are shown in table 3, each row indicates a different evolutionary need for an organization, with each column giving the pros and cons of each of the different archetypes. As the table shows, a monolithic architecture that supports a startup (e.g., rapid prototyping of new features, and potential pivots or large changes in strategies) is very different from an architecture that needs hundreds of teams of developers, each of whom must be able to independently deliver value to the customer. By supporting evolutionary architectures, we can ensure that our architecture always serves the current needs of the organization.

One of the most studied architecture transformations occurred at Amazon. In an interview with ACM Turing Award-winner and Microsoft Technical Fellow Jim Gray, Amazon CTO Werner Vogels explains that Amazon.com started in 1996 as a "monolithic application, running on a web server, talking to a database on the back end. This application, dubbed Obidos, evolved to hold all the business logic, all the display logic, and all the functionality that Amazon eventually became famous for: similarities, recommendations, Listmania, reviews, etc."

As time went by, Obidos grew too tangled, with complex sharing relationships meaning individual pieces could not be scaled as needed. Vogels tells Gray that this meant "many things that you would like to see happening in a good software environment couldn't be done anymore; there were many complex pieces of software combined into a single system. It couldn't evolve anymore."

Describing the thought process behind the new desired architecture, he tells Gray, "We went through a period of serious introspection and concluded that a service-oriented architecture would give us the level of isolation that would allow us to build many software components rapidly and independently."

Vogels notes, "The big architectural change that Amazon went through in the past five years [from 2001–2005] was to move from a two-tier monolith to a fully-distributed, decentralized, services platform serving many different applications. A lot of innovation was necessary to make this happen, as we were one of the first to take this approach." The lessons from Vogel's experience at Amazon that are important to our understanding of architecture shifts include the following:

- **Lesson 1:** When applied rigorously, strict service orientation is an excellent technique to achieve isolation; you achieve a level of ownership and control that was not seen before.

- **Lesson 2:** Prohibiting direct database access by clients makes performing scaling and reliability improvements to your service state possible without involving your clients.

- **Lesson 3:** Development and operational process greatly benefits from switching to service-orientation. The services model has been a key enabler in creating teams that can innovate quickly with a strong customer focus. Each service has a team associated with it, and that team is completely responsible for the service—from scoping out the functionality to architecting, building, and operating it.

The extent to which applying these lessons enhances developer productivity and reliability is breathtaking. In 2011, Amazon was performing approximately fifteen thousands deployments per day. By 2015, they were performing nearly 136,000 deployments per day.

USE THE STRANGLER APPLICATION PATTERN TO SAFELY EVOLVE OUR ENTERPRISE ARCHITECTURE

The term *strangler application* was coined by Martin Fowler in 2004 after he was inspired by seeing massive strangler vines during a trip to Australia, writing, "They seed in the upper branches of a fig tree and gradually work their way down the tree until they root in the soil. Over many years they grow into fantastic and beautiful shapes, meanwhile strangling and killing the tree that was their host."

If we have determined that our current architecture is too tightly coupled, we can start safely decoupling parts of the functionality from our existing architecture. By doing this, we enable teams supporting the decoupled functionality to independently develop, test, and deploy their code into production with autonomy and safety, and reduce architectural entropy.

As described earlier, the strangler application pattern involves placing existing functionality behind an API, where it remains unchanged, and implementing new functionality using our desired architecture, making calls to the old system when necessary. When we implement strangler applications, we seek to access all services through versioned APIs, also called *versioned services* or *immutable services*.

Versioned APIs enable us to modify the service without impacting the callers, which allows the system to be more loosely coupled—if we need to modify the arguments, we create a new API version and migrate teams who depend on our service to the new version. After all, we are not achieving our re-architecting goals if we allow our new strangler application to get tightly-coupled into other services (e.g., connecting directly to another service's database).

If the services we call do not have cleanly-defined APIs, we should build them or at least hide the complexity of communicating with such systems within a client library that has a cleanly defined API.

By repeatedly decoupling functionality from our existing tightly-coupled system, we move our work into a safe and vibrant ecosystem where developers can be far more productive resulting in the legacy application shrinking in functionality. It might even disappear entirely as all the needed functionality migrates to our new architecture.

By creating strangler applications, we avoid merely reproducing existing functionality in some new architecture or technology—often, our business processes are far more complex than necessary due to the idiosyncrasies of the existing systems, which we will end up replicating. (By researching the user, we can often re-engineer the process so that we can design a far simpler and more streamlined means to achieving the business goal.)[†]

An observation from Martin Fowler underscores this risk, "Much of my career has involved rewrites of critical systems. You would think such a thing is easy—just make the new one do what the old one did. Yet they are always much more complex than they seem, and overflowing with risk. The big cut-over date looms, and the pressure is on. While new features (there are always new features) are liked, old stuff has to remain. Even old bugs often need to be added to the rewritten system."

As with any transformation, we seek to create quick wins and deliver early incremental value before continuing to iterate. Up-front analysis helps us identify the smallest possible piece of work that will usefully achieve a business outcome using the new architecture.

Case Study
Strangler Pattern at Blackboard Learn (2011)

Blackboard Inc. is one of the pioneers of providing technology for educational institutions, with annual revenue of approximately $650 million in 2011. At that time, the development team for their flagship Learn product, packaged

---

† The strangler application pattern involves incrementally replacing a whole system, usually a legacy system, with a completely new one. Conversely, *branching by abstraction*, a term coined by Paul Hammant, is a technique where we create an abstraction layer between the areas that we are changing. This enables evolutionary design of the application architecture while allowing everybody to work off trunk/master and practice continuous integration.

software that was installed and run on-premise at their customer sites, was living with the daily consequences of a legacy J2EE codebase that went back to 1997. As David Ashman, their chief architect, observes, "we still have fragments of Perl code still embedded throughout our codebase."

In 2010, Ashman was focused on the complexity and growing lead times associated with the old system, observing that "our build, integration, and testing processes kept getting more and more complex and error prone. And the larger the product got, the longer our lead times and the worse the outcomes for our customers. To even get feedback from our integration process would require twenty-four to thirty-six hours."

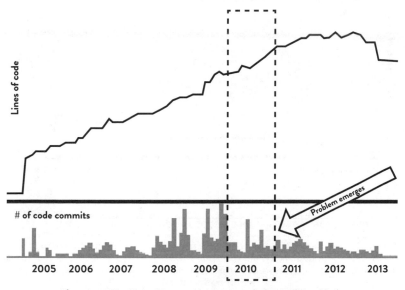

Figure 23: *Blackboard Learn code repository: before Building Blocks*
(Source: "DOES14 - David Ashman - Blackboard Learn - Keep Your Head in the Clouds," YouTube video, 30:43, posted by DevOps Enterprise Summit 2014, October 28, 2014, https://www.youtube.com/watch?v=SSmixnMpsI4.)

How this started to impact developer productivity was made visible to Ashman in graphs generated from their source code repository going all the way back to 2005.

In figure 24, the top graph represents the number of lines of code in the monolithic Blackboard Learn code repository; the bottom graph represents the number of code commits. The problem that became evident to Ashman was that the number of code commits started to decrease, objectively showing the increasing difficulty of introducing code changes, while the number of lines of code continued to increase. Ashman noted, "To me, it said we needed to do something, otherwise the problems would keep getting worse, with no end in sight."

As a result, in 2012 Ashman focused on implementing a code re-architecturing project that used the strangler pattern. The team accomplished this by creating what they internally called *Building Blocks*, which allowed developers to work in separate modules that were decoupled from the monolithic codebase and accessed through fixed APIs. This enabled them to work with far more autonomy, without having to constantly communicate and coordinate with other development teams.

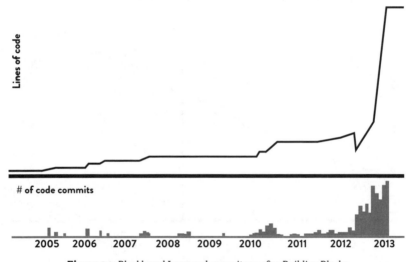

Figure 24: *Blackboard Learn code repository: after Building Blocks*
(Source: "DOES14 - David Ashman - Blackboard Learn - Keep Your Head in the Clouds." YouTube video, 30:43, posted by DevOps Enterprise Summit 2014, October 28, 2014, https://www.youtube.com/watch?v=SSmixnMpsI4.)

When Building Blocks were made available to developers, the size of the monolith source code repository began to decrease (as measured by number of lines of code). Ashman explained that this was because developers were moving their code into the Building Block modules source code repository. "In fact," Ashman reported, "every developer given a choice would work in the Building Block codebase, where they could work with more autonomy and freedom and safety."

The graph above shows the connection between the exponential growth in the number of lines of code and the exponential growth of the number of code commits for the Building Blocks code repositories. The new Building Blocks codebase allowed developers to be more productive, and they made the work safer because mistakes resulted in small, local failures instead of major catastrophes that impacted the global system.

Ashman concluded, "Having developers work in the Building Blocks architecture made for impressive improvements in code modularity, allowing them to work with more independence and freedom. In combination with the updates to our build process, they also got faster, better feedback on their work, which meant better quality. "

CONCLUSION

To a large extent, the architecture that our services operate within dictates how we test and deploy our code. This was validated in Puppet Labs' 2015 *State of DevOps Report*, showing that architecture is one of the top predictors of the productivity of the engineers that work within it and of how changes can be quickly and safely made.

Because we are often stuck with architectures that were optimized for a different set of organizational goals, or for an era long-passed, we must be able to safely migrate from one architecture to another. The case studies presented in this chapter, as well as the Amazon case study previously presented, describe techniques like the strangler pattern that can help us migrate between architectures incrementally, enabling us to adapt to the needs of the organization.

PART III CONCLUSION

Within the previous chapters of Part III, we have implemented the architecture and technical practices that enable the fast flow of work from Dev to Ops, so that value can be quickly and safely delivered to customers.

In Part IV: The Second Way, *The Technical Practices of Feedback*, we will create the architecture and mechanisms to enable the reciprocal fast flow of feedback from right to left, to find and fix problems faster, radiate feedback, and ensure better outcomes from our work. This enables our organization to further increase the rate at which it can adapt.

PART IV

The Second Way
The Technical Practices of Feedback

In Part III, we described the architecture and technical practices required to create fast flow from Development into Operations. Now in Part IV, we describe how to implement the technical practices of the Second Way, which are required to create fast and continuous feedback from Operations to Development.

By doing this, we shorten and amplify feedback loops so that we can see problems as they occur and radiate this information to everyone in the value stream. This allows us to quickly find and fix problems earlier in the software development life cycle, ideally long before they cause a catastrophic failure.

Furthermore, we will create a system of work where knowledge acquired downstream in Operations is integrated into the upstream work of Development and Product Management. This allows us to quickly create improvements and learnings, whether it's from a production issue, a deployment issue, early indicators of problems, or our customer usage patterns.

Additionally, we will create a process that allows everyone to get feedback on their work, makes information visible to enable learning, and enables us to rapidly test product hypotheses, helping us determine if the features we are building are helping us achieve our organizational goals.

We will also demonstrate how to create telemetry from our build, test, and deploy processes, as well as from user behavior, production issues and outages, audit issues, and security breaches. By amplifying signals as part of our daily work, we make it possible to see and solve problems as they occur, and we grow safe systems of work that allow us to confidently make changes and run product experiments, knowing we can quickly detect and remediate failures. We will do all of this by exploring the following:

- Creating telemetry to enable seeing and solving problems

- Using our telemetry to better anticipate problems and achieve goals

- Integrating user research and feedback into the work of product teams

- Enabling feedback so Dev and Ops can safely perform deployments

- Enabling feedback to increase the quality of our work through peer reviews and pair programming

The patterns in this chapter help reinforce the common goals of Product Management, Development, QA, Operations, and Infosec, and encourage them to share in the responsibility of ensuring that services run smoothly in production and collaborate on the improvement of the system as a whole. Where possible, we want to link cause to effect. The more assumptions we can invalidate, the faster we can discover and fix problems, but also the greater our ability to learn and innovate.

Throughout the following chapters, we will implement feedback loops, enabling everyone to work together toward shared goals, to see problems as they occur, enable quick detection and recovery, and ensure that features not only operate as designed in production, but also achieve organizational goals and support organizational learning.

14 Create Telemetry to Enable Seeing and Solving Problems

A fact of life in Operations is that things go wrong—small changes may result in many unexpected outcomes, including outages and global failures that impact all our customers. This is the reality of operating complex systems; no single person can see the whole system and understand how all the pieces fit together.

When production outages and other problems occur in our daily work, we don't often have the information we need to solve the problem. For example, during an outage we may not be able to determine whether the issue is due to a failure in our application (e.g., defect in the code), in our environment (e.g., a networking problem, server configuration problem), or something entirely external to us (e.g., a massive denial of service attack).

In Operations, we may deal with this problem with the following rule of thumb: When something goes wrong in production, we just reboot the server. If that doesn't work, reboot the server next to it. If that doesn't work, reboot all the servers. If that doesn't work, blame the developers, they're always causing outages.

In contrast, the Microsoft Operations Framework (MOF) study in 2001 found that organizations with the highest service levels rebooted their servers twenty times less frequently than average and had five times fewer "blue screens of death." In other words, they found that the best-performing organizations were much better at diagnosing and fixing service incidents, in what Kevin Behr, Gene Kim, and George Spafford called a "culture of causality" in *The Visible Ops Handbook*. High performers used a disciplined approach to solving problems, using production telemetry to understand possible contributing factors to focus their problem solving, as opposed to lower performers who would blindly reboot servers.

To enable this disciplined problem-solving behavior, we need to design our systems so that they are continually creating *telemetry*, widely defined as "an automated communications process by which measurements and other data are collected at remote points and are subsequently transmitted to receiving equipment for monitoring." Our goal is to create telemetry within our applications and environments, both in our production and pre-production environments as well as in our deployment pipeline.

Michael Rembetsy and Patrick McDonnell described how production monitoring was a critical part of Etsy's DevOps transformation that started in 2009. This was because they were standardizing and transitioning their entire technology stack to the LAMP stack (Linux, Apache, MySQL, and PHP), abandoning a myriad of different technologies being used in production that were increasingly difficult to support.

At the 2012 Velocity Conference, McDonnell described how much risk this created, "We were changing some of our most critical infrastructure, which, ideally, customers would never notice. However, they'd definitely notice if we screwed something up. We needed more metrics to give us confidence that we weren't actually breaking things while we were doing these big changes, both for our engineering teams and for team members in the non-technical areas, such as marketing."

McDonnell explained further, "We started collecting all our server information in a tool called Ganglia, displaying all the information into Graphite, an open source tool we invested heavily into. We started aggregating metrics together, everything from business metrics to deployments. This is when we modified Graphite with what we called 'our unparalleled and unmatched vertical line technology' that overlaid onto every metric graph when deployments happened. By doing this, we could more quickly see any unintended deployment side effects. We even started putting TV screens all around the office so that everyone could see how our services were performing."

By enabling developers to add telemetry to their features as part of their daily work, they created enough telemetry to help make deployments safe. By 2011, Etsy was tracking over two hundred thousand production metrics at every layer of the application stack (e.g., application features, application health, database, operating system, storage, networking, security, etc.) with the top thirty most important business metrics prominently displayed on their "deploy dashboard." By 2014, they were tracking over eight hundred thousand metrics, showing their relentless goal of instrumenting everything and making it easy for engineers to do so.

As Ian Malpass, an engineer at Etsy, quipped, "If Engineering at Etsy has a religion, it's the Church of Graphs. If it moves, we track it. Sometimes we'll draw a graph of something that isn't moving yet, just in case it decides to make a run for it....Tracking everything is key to moving fast, but the only way to do it is to make tracking anything easy....We enable engineers to track what they need to track, at the drop of a hat, without requiring time-sucking configuration changes or complicated processes."

One of the findings of the 2015 *State of DevOps Report* was that high performers could resolve production incidents 168 times faster than their peers, with the median high performer having a MTTR measured in minutes, while the median low performer had an MTTR measured in days. The top two technical practices that enabled fast MTTR were the use of version control by Operations and having telemetry and proactive monitoring in the production environment.

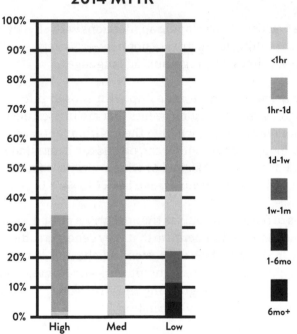

Figure 25: *Incident resolution time for high, medium, and low performers (Source: Puppet Labs, 2014 State of DevOps Report.)*

As was created at Etsy, our goal in this chapter is to ensure that we always have enough telemetry so that we can confirm that our services are correctly operating in production. And when problems do occur, make it possible to quickly determine what is going wrong and make informed decisions on how best to fix it, ideally long before customers are impacted. Furthermore, telemetry is what enables us to assemble our best understanding of reality and detect when our understanding of reality is incorrect.

CREATE OUR CENTRALIZED TELEMETRY INFRASTRUCTURE

Operational monitoring and logging is by no means new—multiple generations of Operations engineers have used and customized monitoring frameworks (e.g., HP OpenView, IBM Tivoli, and BMC Patrol/BladeLogic) to ensure the health of production systems. Data was typically collected through agents that ran on servers or through agent-less monitoring (e.g., SNMP traps or polling based monitors). There was often a graphical user interface (GUI) front end, and back-end reporting was often augmented through tools such as Crystal Reports.

Similarly, the practices of developing applications with effective logging and managing the resulting telemetry are not new—a variety of mature logging libraries exist for almost all programming languages.

However, for decades we have ended up with silos of information, where Development only creates logging events that are interesting to developers, and Operations only monitors whether the environments are up or down. As a result, when inopportune events occur, no one can determine why the entire system is not operating as designed or which specific component is failing, impeding our ability to bring our system back to a working state.

In order for us to see all problems as they occur, we must design and develop our applications and environments so that they generate sufficient telemetry, allowing us to understand how our system is behaving as a whole. When all levels of our application stack have monitoring and logging, we enable other important capabilities, such as graphing and visualizing our metrics, anomaly detection, proactive alerting and escalation, etc.

In *The Art of Monitoring*, James Turnbull describes a modern monitoring architecture, which has been developed and used by Operations engineers at web-scale companies (e.g., Google, Amazon, Facebook). The architecture often consisted of open source tools, such as Nagios and Zenoss, that were customized and deployed at a scale that was difficult to accomplish with licensed commercial software at the time. This architecture has the following components:

- **Data collection at the business logic, application, and environments layer:** In each of these layers, we are creating telemetry in the form of events, logs, and metrics. Logs may be stored in application-specific files on each server (e.g., /var/log/httpd-error.log), but preferably we want all our logs sent to a common service that enables easy centralization, rotation, and deletion. This is provided by most operating systems, such as syslog for Linux, the Event Log for Windows, etc. Furthermore, we gather metrics at all layers of the application stack to better understand how our system is behaving. At the operating system level, we can collect metrics such as CPU, memory, disk, or network usage over time using tools like collectd, Ganglia, etc. Other tools that collect performance information include AppDynamics, New Relic, and Pingdom.

- **An event router responsible for storing our events and metrics:** This capability potentially enables visualization, trending, alerting, anomaly detection, and so forth. By collecting, storing, and aggregating all our telemetry, we better enable further analysis and health checks. This is also where we store configurations related to our services (and their supporting applications and environments) and is likely where we do threshold-based alerting and health checks.[†]

Once we have centralized our logs, we can transform them into metrics by counting them in the event router—for example, a log event such as "child pid 14024 exit signal Segmentation fault" can be counted and summarized as a single segfault metric across our entire production infrastructure.

By transforming logs into metrics, we can now perform statistical operations on them, such as using anomaly detection to find outliers and variances even earlier in the problem cycle. For instance, we might configure our alerting to notify us if we went from "ten segfaults last week" to "thousands of segfaults in the last hour," prompting us to investigate further.

In addition to collecting telemetry from our production services and environments, we must also collect telemetry from our deployment pipeline when important events occur, such as when our automated tests pass or fail and when we perform deployments to any environment. We should also collect

---

† Example tools include Sensu, Nagios, Zappix, LogsStash, Splunk, Sumo Logic, Datadog, and Riemann.

telemetry on how long it takes us to execute our builds and tests. By doing this, we can detect conditions that could indicate problems, such as if the performance test or our build takes twice as long as normal, allowing us to find and fix errors before they go into production.

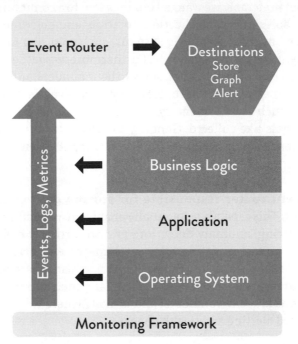

Figure 26: *Monitoring framework (Source: Turnbull,* The Art of Monitoring, *Kindle edition, chap. 2.)*

Furthermore, we should ensure that it is easy to enter and retrieve information from our telemetry infrastructure. Preferably, everything should be done through self-service APIs, as opposed to requiring people to open up tickets and wait to get reports.

Ideally, we will create telemetry that tells us exactly when anything of interest happens, as well as where and how. Our telemetry should also be suitable for manual and automated analysis and should be able to be analyzed without having the application that produced the logs on hand. As Adrian Cockcroft pointed out, "Monitoring is so important that our monitoring systems need to be more available and scalable than the systems being monitored."

From here on, the term *telemetry* will be used interchangeably with *metrics*, which includes all event logging and metrics created by our services at all levels of our application stack and generated from all our production and pre-production environments, as well as from our deployment pipeline.

CREATE APPLICATION LOGGING TELEMETRY THAT HELPS PRODUCTION

Now that we have a centralized telemetry infrastructure, we must ensure that the applications we build and operate are creating sufficient telemetry. We do this by having Dev and Ops engineers create production telemetry as part of their daily work, both for new and existing services.

Scott Prugh, chief architect and vice president of Development at CSG, said, "Every time NASA launches a rocket, it has millions of automated sensors reporting the status of every component of this valuable asset. And yet, we often don't take the same care with software—we found that creating application and infrastructure telemetry to be one of the highest return investments we've made. In 2014, we created over one billion telemetry events per day, with over one hundred thousand code locations instrumented."

In the applications we create and operate, every feature should be instrumented—if it was important enough for an engineer to implement, it is certainly important enough to generate enough production telemetry so that we can confirm that it is operating as designed and that the desired outcomes are being achieved.[†]

Every member of our value stream will use telemetry in a variety of ways. For example, developers may temporarily create more telemetry in their application to better diagnose problems on their workstation, while Ops engineers may use telemetry to diagnose a production problem. In addition, Infosec and auditors may review the telemetry to confirm the effectiveness of a required control, and a product manager may use them to track business outcomes, feature usage, or conversion rates.

To support these various usage models, we have different logging levels, some of which may also trigger alerts, such as the following:

- **DEBUG level:** Information at this level is about anything that happens in the program, most often used during debugging. Often, debug logs are disabled in production but temporarily enabled during troubleshooting.

---

† A variety of application logging libraries exist that make it easy for developers to create useful telemetry, and we should choose one that allows us to send all our application logs to the centralized logging infrastructure that we created in the previous section. Popular examples include rrd4j and log4j for Java, and log4r and ruby-cabin for Ruby.

- **INFO level:** Information at this level consists of actions that are user-driven or system specific (e.g., "beginning credit card transaction").

- **WARN level:** Information at this level tells us of conditions that could potentially become an error (e.g., a database call taking longer than some predefined time). These will likely initiate an alert and troubleshooting, while other logging messages may help us better understand what led to this condition.

- **ERROR level:** Information at this level focuses on error conditions (e.g., API call failures, internal error conditions).

- **FATAL level:** Information at this level tells us when we must terminate (e.g., a network daemon can't bind a network socket).

Choosing the right logging level is important. Dan North, a former Thought-Works consultant who was involved in several projects in which the core continuous delivery concepts took shape, observes, "When deciding whether a message should be ERROR or WARN, imagine being woken up at 4 a.m. Low printer toner is not an ERROR."

To help ensure that we have information relevant to the reliable and secure operations of our service, we should ensure that all potentially significant application events generate logging entries, including those provided on this list assembled by Anton A. Chuvakin, a research VP at Gartner's GTP Security and Risk Management group:

- Authentication/authorization decisions (including logoff)

- System and data access

- System and application changes (especially privileged changes)

- Data changes, such as adding, editing, or deleting data

- Invalid input (possible malicious injection, threats, etc.)

- Resources (RAM, disk, CPU, bandwidth, or any other resource that has hard or soft limits)

- Health and availability

- Startups and shutdowns

- Faults and errors

- Circuit breaker trips

- Delays

- Backup success/failure

To make it easier to interpret and give meaning to all these log entries, we should (ideally) create logging hierarchical categories, such as for non-functional attributes (e.g., performance, security) and for attributes related to features (e.g., search, ranking).

USE TELEMETRY TO GUIDE PROBLEM SOLVING

As described in the beginning of this chapter, high performers use a disciplined approach to solving problems. This is in contrast to the more common practice of using rumor and hearsay, which can lead to the unfortunate metric of *mean time until declared innocent*—how quickly can we convince everyone else that we didn't cause the outage.

When there is a culture of blame around outages and problems, groups may avoid documenting changes and displaying telemetry where everyone can see them to avoid being blamed for outages.

Other negative outcomes due to lack of public telemetry include a highly charged political atmosphere, the need to deflect accusations, and, worse, the inability to create institutional knowledge around how the incidents occurred and the learnings needed to prevent these errors from happening again in the future.[†]

In contrast, telemetry enables us to use the scientific method to formulate hypotheses about what is causing a particular problem and what is required to solve it. Examples of questions we can answer during problem resolution include:

---

† In 2004, Gene Kim, Kevin Behr and George Spafford described this as a symptom of lacking a "culture of causality," noting that high-performing organizations recognize that 80% of all outages are caused by change and 80% of MTTR is spent trying to determine what changed.

- What evidence do we have from our monitoring that a problem is actually occurring?

- What are the relevant events and changes in our applications and environments that could have contributed to the problem?

- What hypotheses can we formulate to confirm the link between the proposed causes and effects?

- How can we prove which of these hypotheses are correct and successfully effect a fix?

The value of fact-based problem solving lies not only in significantly faster MTTR (and better customer outcomes), but also in its reinforcement of the perception of a win/win relationship between Development and Operations.

ENABLE CREATION OF PRODUCTION METRICS AS PART OF DAILY WORK

To enable everyone to be able to find and fix problems in their daily work, we need to enable everyone to create metrics in their daily work that can be easily created, displayed, and analyzed. To do this, we must create the infrastructure and libraries necessary to make it as easy as possible for anyone in Development or Operations to create telemetry for any functionality they build. In the ideal, it should be as easy as writing one line of code to create a new metric that shows up in a common dashboard where everyone in the value stream can see it.

This was the philosophy that guided the development of one of the most widely used metrics libraries, called StatsD, which was created and open-sourced at Etsy. As John Allspaw described, "We designed StatsD to prevent any developer from saying, 'It's too much of a hassle to instrument my code.' Now they can do it with one line of code. It was important to us that for a developer, adding production telemetry didn't feel as difficult as doing a database schema change."

StatsD can generate timers and counters with one line of code (in Ruby, Perl, Python, Java, and other languages) and is often used in conjunction with Graphite or Grafana, which renders metric events into graphs and dashboards.

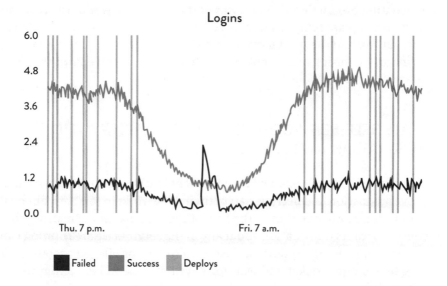

Figure 27: *One line of code to generate telemetry using StatsD and Graphite at Etsy (Source: Ian Malpass, "Measure Anything, Measure Everything.")*

Figure 27 above shows an example of how a single line of code creates a user login event (in this case, one line of PHP code: "StatsD::increment("login. successes")). The resulting graph shows the number of successful and failed logins per minute, and overlaid on the graph are vertical lines that represent a production deployment.

When we generate graphs of our telemetry, we will also overlay onto them when production changes occur, because we know that the significant majority of production issues are caused by production changes, which include code deployments. This is part of what allows us to have a high rate of change, while still preserving a safe system of work.

Alternative libraries to StatsD that allow developers to generate production telemetry can be easily aggregated and analyzed include JMX and codahale metrics. Other tools that create metrics invaluable for problem solving include New Relic, AppDynamics, and Dynatrace. Tools such as munin and collectd can be used to create similar functionality.†

---

† A whole other set of tools to aid in monitoring, aggregation, and collection include Splunk, Zabbix, Sumo Logic, DataDog, as well as Nagios, Cacti, Sensu, RRDTool, Netflix Atlas, Riemann, and others. Analysts often call this broad category of tools "application performance monitors."

By generating production telemetry as part of our daily work, we create an ever-improving capability to not only see problems as they occur, but also to design our work so that problems in design and operations can be revealed, allowing an increasing number of metrics to be tracked, as we saw in the Etsy case study.

CREATE SELF-SERVICE ACCESS TO TELEMETRY AND INFORMATION RADIATORS

In the previous steps, we enabled Development and Operations to create and improve production telemetry as part of their daily work. In this step, our goal is to radiate this information to the rest of the organization, ensuring that anyone who wants information about any of the services we are running can get it without needing production system access or privileged accounts, or having to open up a ticket and wait for days for someone to configure the graph for them.

By making telemetry fast, easy to get, and sufficiently centralized, everyone in the value stream can share a common view of reality. Typically, this means that production metrics will be radiated on web pages generated by a centralized server, such as Graphite or any of the other technologies described in the previous section.

We want our production telemetry to be highly visible, which means putting it in central areas where Development and Operations work, thus allowing everyone who is interested to see how our services are performing. At a minimum, this includes everyone in our value stream, such as Development, Operations, Product Management, and Infosec.

This is often referred to as an *information radiator*, defined by the Agile Alliance as "the generic term for any of a number of handwritten, drawn, printed, or electronic displays which a team places in a highly visible location, so that all team members as well as passers-by can see the latest information at a glance: count of automated tests, velocity, incident reports, continuous integration status, and so on. This idea originated as part of the Toyota Production System."

By putting information radiators in highly visible places, we promote responsibility among team members, actively demonstrating the following values:

- The team has nothing to hide from its visitors (customers, stakeholders, etc.)

- The team has nothing to hide from itself: it acknowledges and confronts problems

Now that we possess the infrastructure to create and radiate production telemetry to the entire organization, we may also choose to broadcast this information to our internal customers and even to our external customers. For example, we might do this by creating publicly-viewable service status pages so that customers can learn how the services they depend upon are performing.

Although there may be some resistance to providing this amount of transparency, Ernest Mueller describes the value of doing so:

> One of the first actions I take when starting in an organization is to use information radiators to communicate issues and detail the changes we are making—this is usually extremely well-received by our business units, who were often left in the dark before. And for Development and Operations groups who must work together to deliver a service to others, we need that constant communication, information, and feedback.

We may even extend this transparency further—instead of trying to keep customer-impacting problems a secret, we can broadcast this information to our external customers. This demonstrates that we value transparency, thereby helping to build and earn customers' trust.[†] (See Appendix 10.)

Case Study
Creating Self-Service Metrics at LinkedIn (2011)

As described in Part III, LinkedIn was created in 2003 to help users connect "to your network for better job opportunities." By November 2015, LinkedIn had over 350 million members generating tens of thousands of requests per second, resulting in millions of queries per second on the LinkedIn backend systems.

Prachi Gupta, Director of Engineering at LinkedIn, wrote in 2011 about the importance of production telemetry: "At LinkedIn, we emphasize

---

† Creating a simple dashboard should be part of creating any new product or service—automated tests should confirm that both the service and dashboard are working correctly, helping both our customers and our ability to safely deploy code.

making sure the site is up and our members have access to complete site functionality at all times. Fulfilling this commitment requires that we detect and respond to failures and bottlenecks as they start happening. That's why we use these time-series graphs for site monitoring to detect and react to incidents within minutes...This monitoring technique has proven to be a great tool for engineers. It lets us move fast and buys us time to detect, triage, and fix problems."

However in 2010, even though there was an incredibly large volume of telemetry being generated, it was extremely difficult for engineers to get access to the data, let alone analyze it. Thus began Eric Wong's summer intern project at LinkedIn, which turned into the production telemetry initiative that created InGraphs.

Wong wrote, "To get something as simple as CPU usage of all the hosts running a particular service, you would need to file a ticket and someone would spend 30 minutes putting it [a report] together."

At the time, LinkedIn was using Zenoss to collect metrics, but as Wong explains, "Getting data from Zenoss required digging through a slow web interface, so I wrote some python scripts to help streamline the process. While there was still manual intervention in setting up metric collection, I was able to cut down the time spent navigating Zenoss' interface."

Over the course of the summer, he continued to add functionality to In-Graphs so that engineers could see exactly what they wanted to see, adding the ability to make calculations across multiple datasets, view week-over-week trending to compare historical performance, and even define custom dashboards to pick exactly which metrics would be displayed on a single page.

In writing about the outcomes of adding functionality to InGraphs and the value of this capability, Gupta notes, "The effectiveness of our monitoring system was highlighted in an instant where our InGraphs monitoring functionality tied to a major web-mail provider started trending downwards and the provider realized they had a problem in their system only after we reached out to them!"

What started off as a summer internship project is now one of the most visible parts of LinkedIn operations. InGraphs has been so successful that the real-time graphs are featured prominently in the company's engineering offices where visitors can't fail to see them.

FIND AND FILL ANY TELEMETRY GAPS

We have now created the infrastructure necessary to quickly create production telemetry throughout our entire application stack and radiate it throughout our organization.

In this step, we will identify any gaps in our telemetry that impede our ability to quickly detect and resolve incidents—this is especially relevant if Dev and Ops currently have little (or no) telemetry. We will use this data later to better anticipate problems, as well as to enable everyone to gather the information they need to make better decisions to achieve organizational goals.

Achieving this requires that we create enough telemetry at all levels of the application stack for all our environments, as well as for the deployment pipelines that support them. We need metrics from the following levels:

- **Business level:** Examples include the number of sales transactions, revenue of sales transactions, user signups, churn rate, A/B testing results, etc.

- **Application level:** Examples include transaction times, user response times, application faults, etc.

- **Infrastructure level (e.g., database, operating system, networking, storage):** Examples include web server traffic, CPU load, disk usage, etc.

- **Client software level (e.g., JavaScript on the client browser, mobile application):** Examples include application errors and crashes, user measured transaction times, etc.

- **Deployment pipeline level:** Examples include build pipeline status (e.g., red or green for our various automated test suites), change deployment lead times, deployment frequencies, test environment promotions, and environment status.

By having telemetry coverage in all of these areas, we will be able to see the health of everything that our service relies upon, using data and facts instead of rumors, finger-pointing, blame, and so forth.

Further, we better enable detection of security-relevant events by monitoring any application and infrastructure faults (e.g., abnormal program terminations, application errors and exceptions, and server and storage errors). Not only does this telemetry better inform Development and Operations when our services are crashing, but these errors are often indicators that a security vulnerability is being actively exploited.

By detecting and correcting problems earlier, we can fix them while they are small and easy to fix, with fewer customers impacted. Furthermore, after every production incident, we should identify any missing telemetry that could have enabled faster detection and recovery; or, better yet, we can identify these gaps during feature development in our peer review process.

APPLICATION AND BUSINESS METRICS

At the application level, our goal is to ensure that we are generating telemetry not only around application health (e.g., memory usage, transaction counts, etc.), but also to measure to what extent we are achieving our organizational goals (e.g., number of new users, user login events, user session lengths, percent of users active, how often certain features are being used, and so forth).

For example, if we have a service that is supporting e-commerce, we want to ensure that we have telemetry around all of the user events that lead up to a successful transaction that generates revenue. We can then instrument all the user actions that are required for our desired customer outcomes.

These metrics will vary according to different domains and organizational goals. For instance, for e-commerce sites, we may want to maximize the time spent on the site; however, for search engines, we may want to reduce the time spent on the site, since long sessions may indicate that users are having difficulty finding what they're looking for.

In general, business metrics will be part of a *customer acquisition funnel*, which is the theoretical steps a potential customer will take to make a purchase. For instance, in an e-commerce site, the measurable journey events include total time on site, product link clicks, shopping cart adds, and completed orders.

Ed Blankenship, Senior Product Manager for Microsoft Visual Studio Team Services, describes, "Often, feature teams will define their goals in an acquisition funnel, with the goal of their feature being used in every customer's daily work. Sometimes they're informally described as 'tire kickers,' 'active users,' 'engaged users,' and 'deeply engaged users,' with telemetry supporting each stage."

Our goal is to have every business metric be *actionable*—these top metrics should help inform how to change our product and be amenable to experimentation and A/B testing. When metrics aren't actionable, they are likely vanity metrics that provide little useful information—these we want to store, but likely not display, let alone alert on.

Ideally, anyone viewing our information radiators will be able to make sense of the information we are showing in the context of desired organizational outcomes, such as goals around revenue, user attainment, conversion rates, etc. We should define and link each metric to a business outcome metric at the earliest stages of feature definition and development, and measure the outcomes after we deploy them in production. Furthermore, doing this helps product owners describe the business context of each feature for everyone in the value stream.

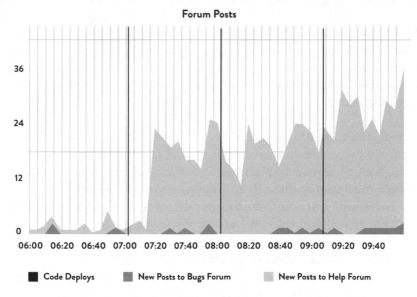

Figure 28: *Amount of user excitement of new features in user forum posts after deployments (Source: Mike Brittain, "Tracking Every Release," CodeasCraft.com, December 8, 2010, https://codeascraft.com/2010/12/08/track-every-release/.)*

Further business context can be created by being aware of and visually displaying time periods relevant to high-level business planning and operations, such as high transaction periods associated with peak holiday selling seasons, end-of-quarter financial close periods, or scheduled compliance audits. This information may be used as a reminder to avoid scheduling risky changes when availability is critical or avoid certain activities when audits are in progress.

By radiating how customers interact with what we build in the context of our goals, we enable fast feedback to feature teams so they can see whether the capabilities we are building are actually being used and to what extent they are achieving business goals. As a result, we reinforce the cultural expectations that instrumenting and analyzing customer usage is also a part of our daily work, so we better understand how our work contributes to our organizational goals.

INFRASTRUCTURE METRICS

Just as we did for application metrics, our goal for production and non-production infrastructure is to ensure that we are generating enough telemetry so that if a problem occurs in any environment, we can quickly determine whether infrastructure is a contributing cause of the problem. Furthermore, we must be able to pinpoint exactly what in the infrastructure is contributing to the problem (e.g., database, operating system, storage, networking, etc.).

We want to make as much infrastructure telemetry visible as possible, across all the technology stakeholders, ideally organized by service or application. In other words, when something goes wrong with something in our environment, we need to know exactly what applications and services could be or are being affected.[†]

In decades past, creating links between a service and the production infrastructure it depended on was often a manual effort (such as ITIL CMDBs or creating configuration definitions inside alerting tools in tools such as Nagios). However, increasingly these links are now registered automatically within our services, which are then dynamically discovered and used in production through tools such as Zookeeper, Etcd, Consul, etc.

These tools enable services to register themselves, storing information that other services need to interact with it (e.g., IP address, port numbers, URIs). This solves the manual nature of the ITIL CMDB and is absolutely necessary when services are made up of hundreds (or thousands or even millions) of nodes, each with dynamically assigned IP addresses.[‡]

Regardless of how simple or complex our services are, graphing our business metrics alongside our application and infrastructure metrics allow us to detect

---

† Exactly as an ITIL Configuration Management Database (CMDB) would prescribe.

‡ Consul may be of specific interest, as it creates an abstraction layer that easily enables service mapping, monitoring, locks, and key-value configuration stores, as well as host clustering and failure detection.

when things go wrong. For instance, we may see that new customer signups drop to 20% of daily norms, and then immediately also see that all our database queries are taking five times longer than normal, enabling us to focus our problem solving.

Furthermore, business metrics create context for our infrastructure metrics, enabling Development and Operations to better work together toward common goals. As Jody Mulkey, CTO of Ticketmaster/LiveNation, observes, "Instead of measuring Operations against the amount of downtime, I find it's much better to measure both Dev and Ops against the real business consequences of downtime: how much revenue should we have attained, but didn't."[§]

Note that in addition to monitoring our production services, we also need telemetry for those services in our pre-production environments (e.g., development, test, staging, etc.). Doing this enables us to find and fix issues before they go into production, such as detecting when we have ever-increasing database insert times due to a missing table index.

OVERLAYING OTHER RELEVANT INFORMATION ONTO OUR METRICS

Even after we have created our deployment pipeline that allows us to make small and frequent production changes, changes still inherently create risk. Operational side-effects are not just outages, but also significant disruptions and deviations from standard operations.

To make changes visible, we make work visible by overlaying all production deployment activities on our graphs. For instance, for a service that handles a large number of inbound transactions, production changes can result in a significant *settling period*, where performance degrades substantially as all cache lookups miss.

To better understand and preserve quality of service, we want to understand how quickly performance returns to normal, and if necessary, take steps to improve performance.

Similarly, we want to overlay other useful operational activities, such as when the service is under maintenance or being backed up, in places where we may want to display or suppress alerts.

---

§ This could be the cost of production downtime or the costs associated with a late feature. In product development terms, the second metric is known as *cost of delay*, and is key to making effective prioritization decisions.

CONCLUSION

The improvements enabled by production telemetry from Etsy and LinkedIn show us how critical it is to see problems as they occur, so we can search out the cause and quickly remedy the situation. By having all elements of our service emitting telemetry that can be analyzed, whether it is in our application, database, or in our environment, and making that telemetry widely available, we can find and fix problems long before they cause something catastrophic, ideally long before a customer even notices that something is wrong. The result is not only happier customers, but, by reducing the amount of firefighting and crises when things go wrong, we have a happier and more productive workplace with less stress and lower levels of burnouts.

15 Analyze Telemetry to Better Anticipate Problems and Achieve Goals

As we saw in the previous chapter, we need sufficient production telemetry in our applications and infrastructure to see and solve problems as they occur. In this chapter, we will create tools that allow us to discover variances and ever-weaker failure signals hidden in our production telemetry so we can avert catastrophic failures. Numerous statistical techniques will be presented, along with case studies demonstrating their use.

A great example of analyzing telemetry to proactively find and fix problems before customers are impacted can be seen at Netflix, a global provider of streaming films and television series. Netflix had revenue of $6.2 billion from seventy-five million subscribers in 2015. One of their goals is to provide the best experience to those watching videos online around the world, which requires a robust, scalable, and resilient delivery infrastructure. Roy Rapoport describes one of the challenges of managing the Netflix cloud-based video delivery service: "Given a herd of cattle that should all look and act the same, which cattle look different from the rest? Or more concretely, if we have a thousand-node stateless compute cluster, all running the same software and subject to the same approximate traffic load, our challenge is to find any nodes that don't look like the rest of the nodes."

One of the statistical techniques that the team used at Netflix in 2012 was *outlier detection,* defined by Victoria J. Hodge and Jim Austin of the University of York as detecting "abnormal running conditions from which significant performance degradation may well result, such as an aircraft engine rotation defect or a flow problem in a pipeline."

Rapoport explains that Netflix "used outlier detection in a very simple way, which was to first compute what was the 'current normal' right now, given population of nodes in a compute cluster. And then we identified which nodes didn't fit that pattern, and removed those nodes from production."

Rapoport continues, "We can automatically flag misbehaving nodes without having to actually define what the 'proper' behavior is in any way. And since we're engineered to run resiliently in the cloud, we don't tell anyone in Operations to do something—instead, we just kill the sick or misbehaving compute node, and then log it or notify the engineers in whatever form they want."

By implementing the Server Outlier Detection process, Rapoport states, Netflix has "massively reduced the effort of finding sick servers, and, more importantly, massively reduced the time require Rapoport states d to fix them, resulting in improved service quality. The benefit of using these techniques to preserve employee sanity, work/life balance, and service quality cannot be overstated." The work done at Netflix highlights one very specific way we can use telemetry to mitigate problems before they impact our customer.

Throughout this chapter we will explore many statistical and visualization techniques (including outlier detection) that we can use to analyze our telemetry to better anticipate problems. This enables us to solve problems faster, cheaper, and earlier than ever, before our customer or anyone in our organization is impacted; furthermore, we will also create more context for our data to help us make better decisions and achieve our organizational goals.

USE MEANS AND STANDARD DEVIATIONS TO DETECT POTENTIAL PROBLEMS

One of the simplest statistical techniques that we can use to analyze a production metric is computing its *mean* (or average) and *standard deviations*. By doing this, we can create a filter that detects when this metric is significantly different from its norm, and even configure our alerting so that we can take corrective action (e.g., notify on-call production staff at 2 a.m. to investigate when database queries are significantly slower than average).

When critical production services have problems, waking people at 2 a.m. may be the right thing to do. However, when we create alerts that are not actionable or are false-positives, we've unnecessarily woken up people in the middle of the night. As John Vincent, an early leader in the DevOps movement, observed, "Alert fatigue is the single biggest problem we have right now...We need to be more intelligent about our alerts or we'll all go insane."

We create better alerts by increasing the signal-to-noise ratio, focusing on the variances or outliers that matter. Suppose we are analyzing the number of unauthorized login attempts per day. Our collected data has a Gaussian distribution (i.e., normal or bell curve distribution) that matches the graph in the figure 29. The vertical line in the middle of the bell curve is the mean, and the first, second, and third standard deviations indicated by the other vertical lines contain 68%, 95%, and 99.7% of the data, respectively.

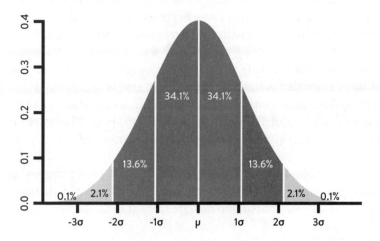

Figure 29: *Standard deviations (σ) & mean (μ) with Gaussian distribution (Source: Wikipedia's "Normal Distribution" entry, https://en.wikipedia.org/wiki/Normal_distribution.)*

A common use of standard deviations is to periodically inspect the data set for a metric and alert if it has significantly varied from the mean. For instance, we may set an alert for when the number of unauthorized login attempts per day is three standard deviations greater than the mean. Provided that this data set has Gaussian distribution, we would expect that only 0.3% of the data points would trigger the alert.

Even this simple type of statistical analysis is valuable, because no one had to define a static threshold value, something which is infeasible if we are tracking thousands or hundreds of thousands of production metrics.

For the remainder of this book, we will use the terms *telemetry, metric,* and *data sets* interchangeably—in other words, a *metric* (e.g., "page load times") will map to a *data set* (e.g., 2 ms, 8 ms, 11 ms, etc.), the term used by statisticians to describe a matrix of data points where each column represents a variable of which statistical operations are performed.

INSTRUMENT AND ALERT ON UNDESIRED OUTCOMES

Tom Limoncelli, co-author of *The Practice of Cloud System Administration: Designing and Operating Large Distributed Systems* and a former Site Reliability Engineer at Google, relates the following story on monitoring: "When people ask me for recommendations on what to monitor, I joke that in an ideal world, we would delete all the alerts we currently have in our monitoring system. Then, after each user-visible outage, we'd ask what indicators would have predicted that outage and then add those to our monitoring system, alerting as needed. Repeat. Now we only have alerts that prevent outages, as opposed to being bombarded by alerts after an outage already occurred."

In this step, we will replicate the outcomes of such an exercise. One of the easiest ways to do this is to analyze our most severe incidents in the recent past (e.g., 30 days) and create a list of telemetry that could have enabled earlier and faster detection and diagnosis of the problem, as well as easier and faster confirmation that an effective fix had been implemented.

For instance, if we had an issue where our NGINX web server stopped responding to requests, we would look at the leading indicators that could have warned us earlier that we were starting to deviate from standard operations, such as:

- **Application level:** increasing web page load times, etc.

- **OS level:** server free memory running low, disk space running low, etc.

- **Database level:** database transaction times taking longer than normal, etc.

- **Network level:** number of functioning servers behind the load balancer dropping, etc.

Each of these metrics is a potential precursor to a production incident. For each, we would configure our alerting systems to notify them when they deviate sufficiently from the mean, so that we can take corrective action.

By repeating this process on ever-weaker failure signals, we find problems ever earlier in the life cycle, resulting in fewer customer impacting incidents and near misses. In other words, we are preventing problems as well as enabling quicker detection and correction.

PROBLEMS THAT ARISE WHEN OUR TELEMETRY DATA HAS NON-GAUSSIAN DISTRIBUTION

Using means and standard deviations to detect variance can be extremely useful. However, using these techniques on many of the telemetry data sets that we use in Operations will not generate the desired results. As Dr. Toufic Boubez observes, "Not only will we get wakeup calls at 2 a.m., we'll get them at 2:37 a.m., 4:13 a.m., 5:17 a.m. This happens when the underlying data that we're monitoring doesn't have a Gaussian distribution."

In other words, when the distribution of the data set does not have the Gaussian bell curve described earlier, the properties associated with standard deviations do not apply. For example, consider the scenario in which we are monitoring the number of file downloads per minute from our website. We want to detect periods when we have unusually high numbers of downloads, such as when our download rate is greater than three standard deviations from our average, so that we can proactively add more capacity.

Figure 30 shows our number of simultaneous downloads per minute over time, with a bar overlaid on top. When the bar is black, the number of downloads within a given period (sometimes called a "sliding window") is at least three standard deviations from the average. Otherwise, it is gray.

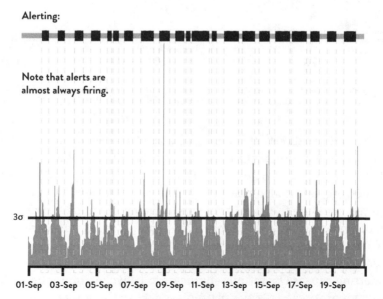

Figure 30: *Downloads per minute: over-alerting when using "3 standard deviation" rule (Source: Dr. Toufic Boubez, "Simple math for anomaly detection.")*

The obvious problem that the graph shows is that we are alerting almost all of the time. This is because in almost any given period of time, we have instances when the download count exceeds our three standard deviation threshold.

To confirm this, when we create a histogram (see figure 31) that shows the frequency of downloads per minute, we can see that it does not have the classic, symmetrical bell curve shape. Instead, it is obvious that the distribution is skewed toward the lower end, showing that the majority of the time we have very few downloads per minute but that download counts frequently spike three standard deviations higher.

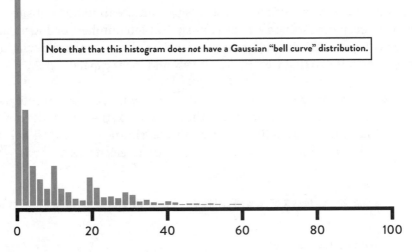

Figure 31: *Downloads per minute: histogram of data showing non-Gaussian distribution (Source: Dr. Toufic Boubez, "Simple math for anomaly detection.")*

Many production data sets are non-Gaussian distribution. Dr. Nicole Forsgren explains, "In Operations, many of our data sets have what we call 'chi squared' distribution. Using standard deviations for this data not only results in over- or under-alerting, but it also results in nonsensical results." She continues, "When you compute the number of simultaneous downloads that are three standard deviations below the mean, you end up with a negative number, which obviously doesn't make sense."

Over-alerting causes Operations engineers to be woken up in the middle of the night for protracted periods of time, even when there are few actions that they can appropriately take. The problem associated with under-alerting is just as significant. For instance, suppose we are monitoring the number of completed transactions, and the completed transaction count drops by 50% in the middle of the day due to a software component failure. If this is still within three standard deviations of the mean, no alert will be generated, meaning that our customers will discover the problem before we do, at which point the problem may be much more difficult to solve.

Fortunately, there are techniques we can use to detect anomalies in even non-Gaussian data sets, which are described next.

Case Study
Auto-Scaling Capacity at Netflix (2012)

Another tool developed at Netflix to increase service quality, Scryer, addresses some of the shortcomings of Amazon Auto Scaling (AAS), which dynamically increases and decreases AWS compute server counts based on workload data. Scryer works by predicting what customer demands will be based on historical usage patterns and provisions the necessary capacity.

Scryer addressed three problems with AAS. The first was dealing with rapid spikes in demand. Because AWS instance startup times can be ten to forty-five minutes, additional compute capacity was often delivered too late to deal with spikes in demand. The second problem was that after outages, the rapid decrease in customer demand led to AAS removing too much compute capacity to handle future incoming demand. The third problem was that AAS didn't factor in known usage traffic patterns when scheduling compute capacity.

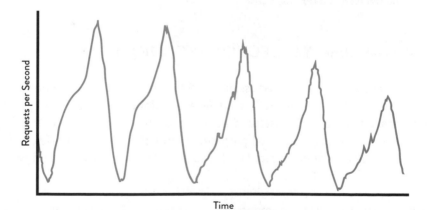

Figure 32: *Netflix customer viewing demand for five days (Source: Daniel Jacobson, Danny Yuan, and Neeraj Joshi, "Scryer: Netflix's Predictive Auto Scaling Engine," The Netflix Tech Blog, November 5, 2013, http://techblog.netflix.com/2013/11/scryer-netflixs-predictive-auto-scaling.html.)*

Netflix took advantage of the fact that their consumer viewing patterns were surprisingly consistent and predictable, despite not having Gaussian distributions. Below is a chart reflecting customer requests per second throughout the work week, showing regular and consistent customer viewing patterns Monday through Friday.

Scryer uses a combination of outlier detections to throw out spurious data points and then uses techniques such as Fast Fourier Transform (FFT) and linear regression to smooth the data while preserving legitimate traffic spikes that recur in their data. The result is that Netflix can forecast traffic demand with surprising accuracy.

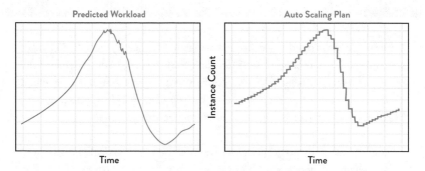

Figure 33: *Netflix Scryer forecasting customer traffic and the resulting AWS schedule of compute resources (Source: Jacobson, Yuan, Joshi, "Scryer: Netflix's Predictive Auto Scaling Engine.")*

Only months after first using Scryer in production, Netflix significantly improved their customer viewing experience, improved service availability, and reduced Amazon EC2 costs.

USING ANOMALY DETECTION TECHNIQUES

When our data does not have Gaussian distribution, we can still find noteworthy variances using a variety of methods. These techniques are broadly categorized as *anomaly detection,* often defined as "the search for items or events which do not conform to an expected pattern." Some of these capabilities can be found inside our monitoring tools, while others may require help from people with statistical skills.

Tarun Reddy, VP of Development and Operations at Rally Software, actively advocates this active collaboration between Operations and statistics, observing, "To better enable service quality, we put all our production metrics into

Tableau, a statistical analysis software package. We even have an Ops engineer trained in statistics who writes R code (another statistical package)—this engineer has her own backlog, filled with requests from other teams inside the company who want to find variance ever earlier, before it causes an even larger variance that could affect our customers."

One of the statistical techniques we can use is called *smoothing*, which is especially suitable if our data is a time series, meaning each data point has a time stamp (e.g., download events, completed transaction events, etc.). Smoothing often involves using moving averages (or rolling averages), which transform our data by averaging each point with all the other data within our sliding window. This has the effect of smoothing out short-term fluctuations and highlighting longer-term trends or cycles.[†]

An example of this smoothing effect is shown in the figure 34. The black line represents the raw data, while the blue line indicates the thirty day moving average (i.e., the average of the trailing thirty days).[‡]

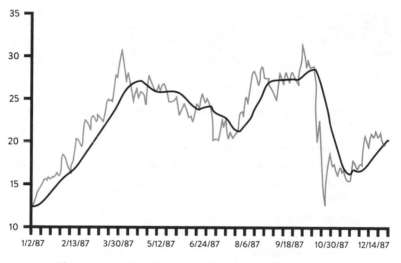

Figure 34: *Autodesk share price and thirty day moving average filter* (Source: Jacobson, Yuan, Joshi, "Scryer: Netflix's Predictive Auto Scaling Engine.")

---

† Smoothing and other statistical techniques are also used to manipulate graphic and audio files. For instance, image smoothing (or blurring) as each pixel is replaced by the average of all its neighbors.

‡ Other examples of smoothing filters include weighted moving averages or exponential smoothing (which linearly or exponentially weight more recent data points over older data points, respectively), and so forth.

More exotic filtering techniques exist, such as Fast Fourier Transforms, which has been widely used in image processing, and the Kolmogorov-Smirnov test (found in Graphite and Grafana), which is often used to find similarities or differences in periodic/seasonal metric data.

We can expect that a large percentage of telemetry concerning user data will have periodic/seasonal similarities—web traffic, retail transactions, movie watching, and many other user behaviors have very regular and surprisingly predictable daily, weekly, and yearly patterns. This enables us to be able to detect situations that vary from historical norms, such as when our order transaction rate on a Tuesday afternoon drops to 50% of our weekly norms.

Because of the usefulness of these techniques in forecasting, we may be able to find people in the Marketing or Business Intelligence departments with the knowledge and skills necessary to analyze this data. We may want to seek these people out and explore working together to identify shared problems and use improved anomaly detection and incident prediction to solve them.[†]

Case Study
Advanced Anomaly Detection (2014)

At Monitorama in 2014, Dr. Toufic Boubez described the power of using anomaly detection techniques, specifically highlighting the effectiveness of the Komogorov-Smirnov test, a technique that is often used in statistics to determine whether two data sets differ significantly and is found in the popular Graphite and Grafana tool. The purpose of presenting this case study here is not as a tutorial, but to demonstrate how a class of statistical techniques can be used in our work, as well as how it's likely being used in our organizations in completely different applications.

Figure 35 shows the number of transactions per minute at an e-commerce site. Note the weekly periodicity of the graph, with transaction volume

---

† Tools we can using to solve these types of problems include Microsoft Excel (which remains one of the easiest and fastest ways to manipulate data for one-time purposes), as well as statistical packages such as SPSS, SAS, and the open source R project, now one of the most widely used statistical packages. Many other tools have been created, including several that Etsy has open-sourced, such as Oculus, which finds graphs with similar shapes that may indicate correlation; Opsweekly, which tracks alert volumes and frequencies; and Skyline, which attempts to identify anomalous behavior in system and application graphs.

dropping on the weekends. By visual inspection, we can see that something peculiar seems to happen on the fourth week when normal transaction volume doesn't return to normal levels on Monday. This suggests an event we should investigate.

Alerting:

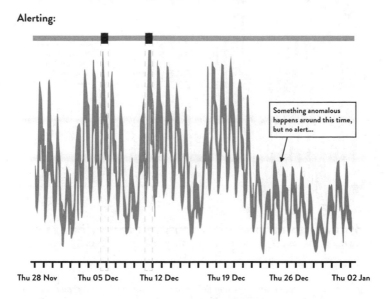

Figure 35: *Transaction volume: under-alerting using "3 standard deviation" rule (Source: Dr. Toufic Boubez, "Simple math for anomaly detection.")*

Using the three standard deviation rule would only alert us twice, missing the critical Monday dropoff in transaction volume. Ideally, we would also want to be alerted that the data has drifted from our expected Monday pattern.

"Even saying 'Kolmogorov-Smirnov' is a great way to impress everyone," Dr. Boubez jokes. "But what Ops engineers should tell statisticians is that these types of *non-parametric* techniques are great for Operations data, because it makes no assumptions about normality or any other probability distribution, which is crucial for us to understand what's going on in our very complex systems. These techniques compare two probability distributions, allowing us to compare periodic or seasonal data, which helps us find variances in data that varies from day to day or week to week."

Figure 36, on the following page, shows is the same data set with the K-S filter applied, with the third area highlighting the anomalous Monday where transaction volume didn't return to normal levels. This would have alerted us of a problem in our system that would have been virtually impossible to detect using visual inspection or using standard deviations. In this scenario, this early detection could prevent a customer impacting event, as well as better enable us to achieve our organizational goals.

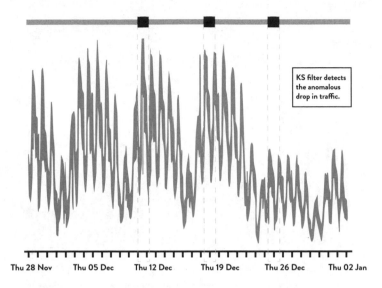

KS filter detects the anomalous drop in traffic.

Thu 28 Nov   Thu 05 Dec   Thu 12 Dec   Thu 19 Dec   Thu 26 Dec   Thu 02 Jan

Figure 36: *Transaction volume: using Kolmogorov-Smirnov test to alert on anomalies*
(Source: Dr. Toufic Boubez, "Simple math for anomaly detection.")

CONCLUSION

In this chapter, we explored several different statistical techniques that can be used to analyze our production telemetry so we can find and fix problems earlier than ever, often when they are still small and long before they cause catastrophic outcomes. This enables us to find ever-weaker failure signals that we can then act upon, creating an ever safer system of work, as well as increasing our ability to achieve our goals.

Specific case studies were presented, including how Netflix used these techniques to proactively remove compute servers from production and auto-scale their compute infrastructure. We also discussed how to use a moving average and the Kolmogorov-Smirnov filter, both of which can be found in popular telemetry graphing tools.

In the next chapter, we will describe how to integrate production telemetry into the daily work of Development in order to make deployments safer and improve the system as a whole.

16 Enable Feedback So Development and Operations Can Safely Deploy Code

In 2006, Nick Galbreath was VP of Engineering at Right Media, responsible for both the Development and Operations departments for an online advertising platform that displayed and served over ten billion impressions daily.

Galbreath described the competitive landscape they operated in:

> In our business, ad inventory levels were extremely dynamic, so we needed to respond to market conditions within minutes. This meant that Development had to be able to quickly make code changes and get them into production as soon as possible, otherwise we would lose to faster competitors. We found that having a separate group for testing, and even deployment, was simply too slow. We had to integrate all these functions into one group, with shared responsibilities and goals. Believe it or not, our biggest challenge was getting developers to overcome their fear of deploying their own code!

There is an interesting irony here: Dev often complains about Ops being afraid to deploy code. But in this case, when given the power to deploy their own code, developers became just as afraid to perform code deployments.

The fear of deploying code that was shared by both Dev and Ops at Right Media is not unusual. However, Galbreath observed that providing faster and more frequent feedback to engineers performing deployments (whether Dev or Ops), as well as reducing the batch size of their work, created safety and then confidence.

After observing many teams go through this transformation, Galbreath describes their progression as follows:

We start with no one in Dev or Ops being willing to push the "deploy code" button that we've built that automates the entire code deployment process, because of the paralyzing fear of being the first person to potentially bring all of the production systems down. Eventually, when someone is brave enough to volunteer to push their code into production, inevitably, due to incorrect assumptions or production subtleties that weren't fully appreciated, the first production deployment doesn't go smoothly—and because we don't have enough production telemetry, we only find out about the problems when customers tell us.

To fix the problem, our team urgently fixes the code and pushes it into production, but this time with more production telemetry added to our applications and environment. This way, we can actually confirm that our fix restored service correctly, and we'll be able to detect this type of problem before a customer tells us next time.

Later, more developers start to push their own code into production. And because we're working in a complex system, we'll still probably break something in production, but this time we'll be able to quickly see what functionality broke, and quickly decide whether to roll back or fix-forward, resolving the problem. This is a huge victory for the entire team and everyone celebrates— we're now on a roll.

However, the team wants to improve the outcomes of their deployments, so developers proactively get more peer reviews of their code changes (described in chapter 18), and everyone helps each other write better automated tests so we can find errors before deployment. And because everyone now knows that the smaller our production changes, the fewer problems we will have, developers start checking ever-smaller increments of code more frequently into the deployment pipeline, ensuring that their change is working successfully in production before moving to their next change.

We are now deploying code more frequently than ever, and service stability is better than ever too. We have re-discovered that the secret to smooth and continuous flow is making small, frequent changes that anyone can inspect and easily understand.

Galbreath observes that the above progression benefits everyone, including Development, Operations, and Infosec. "As the person who is also responsible for security, it's reassuring to know that we can deploy fixes into production quickly, because changes are going into production throughout the entire day. Furthermore, it always amazes me how interested every engineer becomes in security when you find problems in their code that they are responsible for and that they can quickly fix themselves."

The Right Media story shows that it is not enough to merely automate the deployment process—we must also integrate the monitoring of production telemetry into our deployment work, as well as establish the cultural norms that everyone is equally responsible for the health of the entire value stream.

In this chapter, we create the feedback mechanisms that enable us to improve the health of the value stream at every stage of the service life cycle, from product design through development and deployment and into operation and eventually retirement. By doing this, we ensure that our services are "production ready," even at the earliest stages of the project, as well as integrating the learnings from each release and production problem into our future work, resulting in better safety and productivity for everyone.

USE TELEMETRY TO MAKE DEPLOYMENTS SAFER

In this step, we ensure that we are actively monitoring our production telemetry when anyone performs a production deployment, as was illustrated in the Right Media story. This allows whoever is doing the deployment, be it Dev or Ops, to quickly determine whether features are operating as designed after the new release is running in production. After all, we should never consider our code deployment or production change to be done until it is operating as designed in the production environment.

We do this by actively monitoring the metrics associated with our feature during our deployment to ensure we haven't inadvertently broken our service—or worse, that we broke another service. If our change breaks or impairs any functionality, we quickly work to restore service, bringing in whoever else is required to diagnose and fix the issue.[†]

As described in Part III, our goal is to catch errors in our deployment pipeline before they get into production. However, there will still be errors that we don't detect, and we rely on production telemetry to quickly restore service. We may choose to turn off broken features with feature toggles (which is often

---

[†] By doing this, along with the required architecture, we "optimize for MTTR, instead of MTBF," a popular DevOps maxim to describe our desire to optimize for recovering from failures quickly, as opposed to attempting to prevent failures.

the easiest and least risky option since it involves no deployments to production), or *fix forward* (i.e., make code changes to fix the defect, which are then pushed into production through the deployment pipeline), or *roll back* (e.g., switch back to the previous release by using feature toggles or by taking broken servers out of rotation using the blue-green or canary release patterns, etc.)

Although fixing forward can often be dangerous, it can be extremely safe when we have automated testing and fast deployment processes, and sufficient telemetry that allows us to quickly confirm whether everything is functioning correctly in production.

Figure 37 shows a deployment of PHP code change at Etsy that generated a spike in PHP runtime warnings—in this case, the developer quickly noticed the problem within minutes, and generated a fix and deployed it into production, resolving the issue in less than ten minutes.

Because production deployments are one of the top causes of production issues, each deployment and change event is overlaid onto our metric graphs to ensure that everyone in the value stream is aware of relevant activity, enabling better communication and coordination, as well as faster detection and recovery.

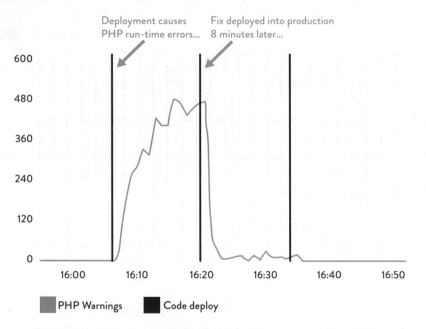

Figure 37: *Deployment to Etsy.com causes PHP run-time warnings and is quickly fixed (Source: Mike Brittain, "Tracking Every Release.")*

DEV SHARES PAGER ROTATION DUTIES WITH OPS

Even when our production deployments and releases go flawlessly, in any complex service we will still have unexpected problems, such as incidents and outages that happen at inopportune times (every night at 2 a.m.). Left unfixed, these can cause recurring problems and suffering for Ops engineers downstream, especially when these problems are not made visible to the upstream engineers responsible for creating the problem.

Even if the problem results in a defect being assigned to the feature team, it may be prioritized below the delivery of new features. The problem may keep recurring for weeks, months, or even years, causing continual chaos and disruption in Operations. This is an example of how upstream work centers can locally optimize for themselves but actually degrade performance for the entire value stream.

To prevent this from happening, we will have everyone in the value stream share the downstream responsibilities of handling operational incidents. We can do this by putting developers, development managers, and architects on pager rotation, just as Pedro Canahuati, Facebook Director of Production Engineering, did in 2009. This ensures everyone in the value stream gets visceral feedback on any upstream architectural and coding decisions they make.

By doing this, Operations doesn't struggle, isolated and alone with code-related production issues; instead, everyone is helping find the proper balance between fixing production defects and developing new functionality, regardless of where we reside in the value stream. As Patrick Lightbody, SVP of Product Management at New Relic, observed in 2011, "We found that when we woke up developers at 2 a.m., defects were fixed faster than ever."

One side effect of this practice is that it helps Development management see that business goals are not achieved simply because features have been marked as "done." Instead, the feature is only done when it is performing as designed in production, without causing excessive escalations or unplanned work for either Development or Operations.[†]

This practice is equally applicable for market-oriented teams, responsible for both developing the feature and running it in production, and for functionally-

---

† ITIL defines warranty as when a service can run in production reliably without intervention for a predefined period of time (e.g., two weeks). This definition of warranty should ideally be integrated into our collective definition of "done."

oriented teams. As Arup Chakrabarti, Operations Engineering Manager at PagerDuty, observed during a 2014 presentation, "It's becoming less and less common for companies to have dedicated on-call teams; instead, everyone who touches production code and environments is expected to be reachable in the event of downtime."

Regardless of how we've organized our teams, the underlying principles remain the same: when developers get feedback on how their applications perform in production, which includes fixing it when it breaks, they become closer to the customer, this creates a buy-in that everyone in the value stream benefits from.

HAVE DEVELOPERS FOLLOW WORK DOWNSTREAM

One of the most powerful techniques in interaction and user experience design (UX) is contextual inquiry. This is when the product team watches a customer use the application in their natural environment, often working at their desk. Doing so often uncovers startling ways that customers struggle with the application, such as requiring scores of clicks to perform simple tasks in their daily work, cutting and pasting text from multiple screens, or writing down notes on paper. All of these are examples of compensatory behaviors and workarounds for usability issues.

The most common reaction for developers after participating in a customer observation is dismay, often stating "how awful it was seeing the many ways we have been inflicting pain on our customers." These customer observations almost always result in significant learning and a fervent desire to improve the situation for the customer.

Our goal is to use this same technique to observe how our work affects our internal customers. Developers should follow their work downstream, so they can see how downstream work centers must interact with their product to get it running into production.[†]

---

† By following work downstream, we may uncover ways to help improve flow, such as automating complex, manual steps (e.g., pairing application server clusters that require six hours to successfully complete); performing packaging of code once instead of creating it multiple times at different stages of QA and Production deployment; working with testers to automate manual test suites, thus removing a common bottleneck for more frequent deployment; and creating more useful documentation instead of having someone decipher developer application notes to build packaged installers.

Developers want to follow their work downstream—by seeing customer difficulties firsthand, they make better and more informed decisions in their daily work.

By doing this, we create feedback on the non-functional aspects of our code—all the elements that are not related to the customer-facing feature—and identify ways that we can improve deployability, manageability, operability, and so on.

UX observation often has a powerful impact on the observers. When describing his first customer observation, Gene Kim, the founder and CTO at Tripwire for thirteen years and co-author of this book, said:

> One of the worst moments of my professional career was in 2006 when I spent an entire morning watching one of our customers use our product. I was watching him perform an operation that we expected customers to do weekly, and, to our extreme horror, we discovered that it required sixty-three clicks. This person kept apologizing, saying things like, "Sorry, there's probably a better way to do this."

> Unfortunately, there wasn't a better way to do that operation. Another customer described how initial product setup took 1,300 steps. Suddenly, I understood why the job of managing our product was always assigned to the newest engineer on the team—no one wanted the job of running our product. That was one of the reasons I helped create the UX practice at my company, to help atone for the pain we were inflicting on our customers.

UX observation enables the creation of quality at the source and results in far greater empathy for fellow team members in the value stream. Ideally, UX observation helps us as we create codified non-functional requirements to add to our shared backlog of work, eventually allowing us to proactively integrate them into every service we build, which is an important part of creating a DevOps work culture.[‡]

---

‡ More recently, Jeff Sussna attempted to further codify how to better achieve UX goals in what he calls "digital conversations," which are intended to help organizations understand the customer journey as a complex system, broadening the context of quality. The key concepts include designing for service, not software; minimizing latency and maximizing strength of feedback; designing for failure and operating to learn; using Operations as an input to design; and seeking empathy.

HAVE DEVELOPERS INITIALLY SELF-MANAGE THEIR PRODUCTION SERVICE

Even when Developers are writing and running their code in production-like environments in their daily work, Operations may still experience disastrous production releases because it is the first time we actually see how our code behaves during a release and under true production conditions. This result occurs because operational learnings often occur too late in the software life cycle.

Left unaddressed, the result is often production software that is difficult to operate. As an anonymous Ops engineer once said, "In our group, most system administrators lasted only six months. Things were always breaking in production, the hours were insane, and application deployments were painful beyond belief—the worst part was pairing the application server clusters, which would take us six hours. During each moment, we all felt like the developers personally hated us."

This can be an outcome of not having enough Ops engineers to support all the product teams and the services we already have in production, which can happen in both functionally- and market-oriented teams.

One potential countermeasure is to do what Google does, which is have Development groups self-manage their services in production before they become eligible for a centralized Ops group to manage. By having developers be responsible for deployment and production support, we are far more likely to have a smooth transition to Operations.[†]

To prevent the possibility of problematic, self-managed services going into production and creating organizational risk, we may define launch requirements that must be met in order for services to interact with real customers and be exposed to real production traffic. Furthermore, to help the product teams, Ops engineers should act as consultants to help them make their services production-ready.

By creating launch guidance, we help ensure that every product team benefits from the cumulative and collective experience of the entire organization, especially Operations. Launch guidance and requirements will likely include the following:

---

† We further increase the likelihood of production problems being fixed by ensuring that the Development teams remain intact, and not disbanded after the project is complete.

- **Defect counts and severity:** Does the application actually perform as designed?

- **Type/frequency of pager alerts:** Is the application generating an unsupportable number of alerts in production?

- **Monitoring coverage:** Is the coverage of monitoring sufficient to restore service when things go wrong?

- **System architecture:** Is the service loosely coupled enough to support a high rate of changes and deployments in production?

- **Deployment process:** Is there a predictable, deterministic, and sufficiently automated process to deploy code into production?

- **Production hygiene:** Is there evidence of enough good production habits that would allow production support to be managed by anyone else?

Superficially, these requirements may appear similar to traditional production checklists we have used in the past. However, the key differences are we require effective monitoring to be in place, deployments to be reliable and deterministic, and an architecture that supports fast and frequent deployments.

If any deficiencies are found during the review, the assigned Ops engineer should help the feature team resolve the issues or even help re-engineer the service if necessary, so that it can be easily deployed and managed in production.

At this time, we may also want to learn whether this service is subject to any regulatory compliance objectives or if it is likely to be in the future:

- Does the service generate a significant amount of revenue? (For example, if it is more than 5% of total revenue of a publicly-held US corporation, it is a "significant account" and in-scope for compliance with Section 404 of the Sarbanes-Oxley Act of 2002 [SOX].)

- Does the service have high user traffic or have high outage/impairment costs? (i.e., do operational issues risk creating availability or reputational risk?)

- Does the service store payment cardholder information, such as credit card numbers, or personally identifiable information, such as Social Security numbers or patient care records? Are there other security issues that could create regulatory, contractual obligation, privacy, or reputation risk?

- Does the service have any other regulatory or contractual compliance requirements associated with it, such as US export regulations, PCI-DSS, HIPAA, and so forth?

This information helps ensure that we effectively manage not only the technical risks associated with this service, but also any potential security and compliance risks. It also provides essential input into the design of the production control environment.

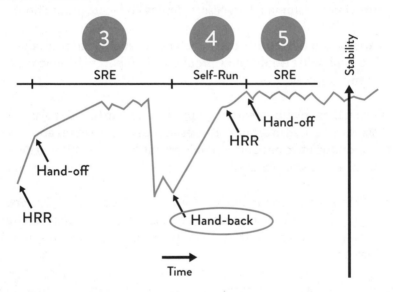

Figure 38: *The "Service Handback" at Google (Source: "SRE@Google: Thousands of DevOps Since 2004," YouTube video, 45:57, posted by USENIX, January 12, 2012, https://www.youtube.com/ watch?v=iIuTnhdTzK0.)*

By integrating operability requirements into the earliest stages of the development process and having Development initially self-manage their own applications and services, the process of transitioning new services into production becomes smoother, becoming far easier and more predictable to complete. However, for services already in production, we need a different mechanism to ensure that Operations is never stuck with an unsupportable service in production. This is especially relevant for functionally-oriented Operations organizations.

In this step, we may create a *service handback mechanism*—in other words, when a production service becomes sufficiently fragile, Operations has the ability to return production support responsibility back to Development.

When a service goes back into a developer-managed state, the role of Operations shifts from production support to consultation, helping the team make the service production-ready.

This mechanism serves as our pressure escape valve, ensuring that we never put Operations in a situation where they are trapped into managing a fragile service while an ever-increasing amount of technical debt buries them and amplifies a local problem into a global problem. This mechanism also helps ensure that Operations has enough capacity to work on improvement work and preventive projects.

The hand-back remains a long-standing practice at Google and is perhaps one of the best demonstrations of the mutual respect between Dev and Ops engineers. By doing this, Development is able to quickly generate new services, with Ops engineers joining the team when the services become strategically important to the company and, in rare cases, handing them back when they become too troublesome to manage in production.[†] The following case study of Site Reliability Engineering at Google describes how the Hand-off Readiness Review and Launch Readiness Review processes evolved, and the benefits that resulted.

Case Study
The Launch and Hand-off
Readiness Review at Google (2010)

One of the many surprising facts about Google is that they have a functional orientation for their Ops engineers, who are referred to as "Site Reliability Engineers" (SRE), a term coined by Ben Treynor Sloss in 2004.[‡] That year,

---

[†] In organizations with project-based funding, there may be no developers to hand the service back to, as the team has already been disbanded or may not have the budget or time to take on service responsibility. Potential countermeasures include holding an improvement blitz to improve the service, temporarily funding or staffing improvement efforts, or retiring the service.

[‡] In this book, we use the term "Ops engineer," but the two terms, "Ops Engineer" and "Site Reliability Engineer," are intended to be interchangeable.

Treynor Sloss started off with a staff of seven SREs that grew to over 1,200 SREs by 2014. As Treynor Sloss said, "If Google ever goes down, it's my fault." Treynor Sloss has resisted creating a single sentence definition of what SREs are, but, he once described SREs as "what happens when a software engineer is tasked with what used to be called operations."

Every SRE reports to Treynor Sloss's organization to help ensure consistency of quality of staffing and hiring, and they are embedded into product teams across Google (which also provide their funding). However, SREs are still so scarce they are assigned only to the product teams that have the highest importance to the company or those that must comply with regulatory requirements. Furthermore, those services must have low operational burden. Products that don't meet the necessary criteria remain in a developer-managed state.

Even when new products become important enough to the company to warrant being assigned an SRE, developers still must have self-managed their service in production for at least six months before it becomes eligible to have an SRE assigned to the team.

To help ensure that these self-managed product teams can still benefit from the collective experience of the SRE organization, Google created two sets of safety checks for two critical stages of releasing new services called the *Launch Readiness Review* and the *Hand-Off Readiness Review* (LRR and HRR, respectively).

The LRR must be performed and signed off on before any new Google service is made publicly available to customers and receives live production traffic, while the HRR is performed when the service is transitioned to an Ops-managed state, usually months after the LRR. The LRR and HRR checklists are similar, but the HRR is far more stringent and has higher acceptance standards, while the LRR is self-reported by the product teams.

Any product team going through an LRR or HRR has an SRE assigned to them to help them understand the requirements and to help them achieve those requirements. The LRR and HRR launch checklists have evolved over time so every team can benefit from the collective experiences of all previous launches, whether successful or unsuccessful. Tom Limoncelli noted during his "SRE@Google: Thousands of DevOps Since 2004" presentation in 2012, "Every time we do a launch, we learn something. There will always be some people who are less experienced than others doing releases and launches. The LRR and HRR checklists are a way to create that organizational memory."

Requiring product teams to self-manage their own services in production forces Development to walk in the shoes of Ops, but guided by the LRR and HRR, which not only makes service transition easier and more predictable, but also helps create empathy between upstream and downstream work centers.

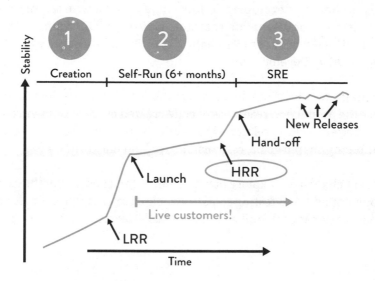

Figure 39: *The "Launch readiness review and hand-offs readiness review" at Google (Source: "SRE@Google: Thousands of DevOps Since 2004," YouTube video, 45:57, posted by USENIX, January 12, 2012, https://www.youtube.com/watch?v=iIuTnhdTzK0.)*

Limoncelli noted, "In the best case, product teams have been using the LRR checklist as a guideline, working on fulfilling it in parallel with developing their service, and reaching out to SREs to get help when they need it."

Furthermore, Limoncelli observed, "The teams that have the fastest HRR production approval are the ones that worked with SREs earliest, from the early design stages up until launch. And the great thing is, it's always easy to get an SRE to volunteer to help with your project. Every SRE sees value in giving advice to project teams early, and will likely volunteer a few hours or days to do just that."

The practice of SREs helping product teams early is an important cultural norm that is continually reinforced at Google. Limoncelli explained, "Helping product teams is a long-term investment that will pay off many months later when it comes time to launch. It is a form of 'good citizenship' and 'community service' that is valued, it is routinely considered when evaluating engineers for SRE promotions."

CONCLUSION

In this chapter, we discussed the feedback mechanisms that enable us to improve our service at every stage of our daily work, whether it is deploying changes into production, fixing code when things go wrong and engineers are paged, having developers follow their work downstream, creating non-functional requirements that help development teams write more production-ready code, or even handing problematic services back to be self-managed by Development.

By creating these feedback loops, we make production deployments safer, increase the production readiness of code created by Development, and help create a better working relationship between Development and Operations by reinforcing shared goals, responsibilities, and empathy.

In the next chapter, we explore how telemetry can enable hypothesis-driven development and A/B testing to perform experiments that help us achieve our organizational goals and win in the marketplace.

17 Integrate Hypothesis-Driven Development and A/B Testing into Our Daily Work

All too often in software projects, developers work on features for months or years, spanning multiple releases, without ever confirming whether the desired business outcomes are being met, such as whether a particular feature is achieving the desired results or even being used at all.

Worse, even when we discover that a given feature isn't achieving the desired results, making corrections to the feature may be out-prioritized by other new features, ensuring that the under-performing feature will never achieve its intended business goal. In general, Jez Humble observes, "the most inefficient way to test a business model or product idea is to build the complete product to see whether the predicted demand actually exists."

Before we build a feature, we should rigorously ask ourselves, "Should we build it, and why?" We should then perform the cheapest and fastest experiments possible to validate through user research whether the intended feature will actually achieve the desired outcomes. We can use techniques such as hypothesis-driven development, customer acquisition funnels, and A/B testing, concepts we explore throughout this chapter. Intuit, Inc. provides a dramatic example of how organizations use these techniques to create products that customers love, to promote organizational learning, and to win in the marketplace.

Intuit is focused on creating business and financial management solutions to simplify life for small businesses, consumers, and accounting professionals. In 2012, they had $4.5 billion in revenue and 8,500 employees, with flagship products that include QuickBooks, TurboTax, Mint, and, until recently, Quicken.[†]

---

† In 2016, Intuit sold the Quicken business to the private equity firm H.I.G. Capital.

Scott Cook, the founder of Intuit, has long advocated building a culture of innovation, encouraging teams to take an experimental approach to product development and exhorting leadership to support them. As he said, "Instead of focusing on the boss's vote...the emphasis is on getting real people to really behave in real experiments, and basing your decisions on that." This is the epitome of a scientific approach to product development.

Cook explained that what is needed is "a system where every employee can do rapid, high-velocity experiments....Dan Maurer runs our consumer division....[which] runs the TurboTax website. When he took over, we did about seven experiments a year."

He continued, "By installing a rampant innovation culture [in 2010], they now do 165 experiments in the three months of the [US] tax season. Business result? [The] conversion rate of the website is up 50 percent.... The folks [team members] just love it, because now their ideas can make it to market."

Aside from the effect on the website conversion rate, one of the most surprising elements of this story is that TurboTax performed production experiments during their peak traffic seasons. For decades, especially in retailing, the risk of revenue-impacting outages during the holiday season were so high that we would often put into place a change freeze from mid-October to mid-January.

However, by making software deployments and releases fast and safe, the TurboTax team made online user experimentation and any required production changes a low-risk activity that could be performed during the highest traffic and revenue generating periods.

This highlights the notion that the period when experimentation has the highest value is during peak traffic seasons. Had the TurboTax team waited until April 16th, the day after the US tax filing deadline, to implement these changes, the company could have lost many of its prospective customers, and even some of its existing customers, to the competition.

The faster we can experiment, iterate, and integrate feedback into our product or service, the faster we can learn and out-experiment the competition. And how quickly we can integrate our feedback depends on our ability to deploy and release software.

The Intuit example shows that the Intuit TurboTax team was able to make this situation work for them and won in the marketplace as a result.

A BRIEF HISTORY OF A/B TESTING

As the Intuit TurboTax story highlights, an extremely powerful user research technique is defining the customer acquisition funnel and performing A/B testing. A/B testing techniques were pioneered in *direct response marketing*, which is one of the two major categories of marketing strategies. The other is called *mass marketing* or *brand marketing* and often relies on placing as many ad impressions in front of people as possible to influence buying decisions.

In previous eras, before email and social media, direct response marketing meant sending thousands of postcards or flyers via postal mail, and asking prospects to accept an offer by calling a telephone number, returning a postcard, or placing an order.

In these campaigns, experiments were performed to determine which offer had the highest conversion rates. They experimented with modifying and adapting the offer, re-wording the offer, varying the copywriting styles, design and typography, packaging, and so forth, to determine which was most effective in generating the desired action (e.g., calling a phone number, ordering a product).

Each experiment often required doing another design and print run, mailing out thousands of offers, and waiting weeks for responses to come back. Each experiment typically cost tens of thousands of dollars per trial and required weeks or months to complete. However, despite the expense, iterative testing easily paid off if it significantly increased conversion rates (e.g., the percentage of respondents ordering a product going from 3%–12%).

Well-documented cases of A/B testing include campaign fundraising, Internet marketing, and the Lean Startup methodology. Interestingly, it has also been used by the British government to determine which letters were most effective in collecting overdue tax revenue from delinquent citizens.[†]

---

† There are many other ways to conduct user research before embarking on development. Among the most inexpensive methods include performing surveys, creating prototypes (either mockups using tools such as Balsamiq or interactive versions written in code), and performing usability testing. Alberto Savoia, Director of Engineering at Google, coined the term *pretotyping* for the practice of using prototypes to validate whether we are building the right thing. User research is so inexpensive and easy relative to the effort and cost of building a useless feature in code that, in almost every case, we shouldn't prioritize a feature without some form of validation.

INTEGRATING A/B TESTING INTO OUR FEATURE TESTING

The most commonly used A/B technique in modern UX practice involves a website where visitors are randomly selected to be shown one of two versions of a page, either a control (the "A") or a treatment (the "B"). Based on statistical analysis of the subsequent behavior of these two cohorts of users, we demonstrate whether there is a significant difference in the outcomes of the two, establishing a *causal* link between the treatment (e.g., a change in a feature, design element, background color) and the outcome (e.g., conversion rate, average order size).

For example, we may conduct an experiment to see whether modifying the text or color on a "buy" button increases revenue or whether slowing down the response time of a website (by introducing an artificial delay as the treatment) reduces revenue. This type of A/B testing allows us to establish a dollar value on performance improvements.

Sometimes, A/B tests are also known as online controlled experiments and split tests. It's also possible to run experiments with more than one variable. This allows us to see how the variables interact, a technique known as multivariate testing.

The outcomes of A/B tests are often startling. Ronny Kohavi, Distinguished Engineer and General Manager of the Analysis and Experimentation group at Microsoft, observed that after "evaluating well-designed and executed experiments that were designed to improve a key metric, only about one-third were successful at improving the key metric!" In other words, two-thirds of features either have a negligible impact or actually make things worse. Kohavi goes on to note that all these features were originally thought to be reasonable, good ideas, further elevating the need for user testing over intuition and expert opinions.

The implications of the Kohavi data are staggering. If we are not performing user research, the odds are that two-thirds of the features we are building deliver zero or *negative* value to our organization, even as they make our codebase ever more complex, thus increasing our maintenance costs over time and making our software more difficult to change. Furthermore, the effort to build these features is often made at the expense of delivering features that *would* deliver value (i.e., opportunity cost). Jez Humble joked, "Taken to an extreme, the organization and customers would have been better off giving the entire team a vacation, instead of building one of these non–value-adding features."

Our countermeasure is to integrate A/B testing into the way we design, implement, test, and deploy our features. Performing meaningful user research and experiments ensures that our efforts help achieve our customer and organizational goals, and help us win in the marketplace.

INTEGRATE A/B TESTING INTO OUR RELEASE

Fast and iterative A/B testing is made possible by being able to quickly and easily do production deployments on demand, using feature toggles and potentially delivering multiple versions of our code simultaneously to customer segments. Doing this requires useful production telemetry at all levels of the application stack.

By hooking into our feature toggles, we can control which percentage of users see the treatment version of an experiment. For example, we may have one-half of our customers be our treatment group and one-half get shown the following: "Similar items link on unavailable items in the cart." As part of our experiment, we compare the behavior of the control group (no offer made) against the treatment group (offer made), perhaps measuring number of purchases made in that session.

Etsy open-sourced their experimentation framework Feature API (formerly known as the Etsy A/B API), which not only supports A/B testing but also online ramp-ups, enabling throttling exposure to experiments. Other A/B testing products include Optimizely, Google Analytics, etc.

In a 2014 interview with Kendrick Wang of Apptimize, Lacy Rhoades at Etsy described their journey: "Experimentation at Etsy comes from a desire to make informed decisions, and ensure that when we launch features for our millions of members, they work. Too often, we had features that took a lot of time and had to be maintained without any proof of their success or any popularity among users. A/B testing allows us to...say a feature is worth working on as soon as it's underway."

INTEGRATING A/B TESTING INTO OUR FEATURE PLANNING

Once we have the infrastructure to support A/B feature release and testing, we must ensure that product owners think about each feature as a hypothesis and use our production releases as experiments with real users to prove or disprove that hypothesis. Constructing experiments should be designed in the context of the overall customer acquisition funnel. Barry O'Reilly, co-author of *Lean Enterprise: How High Performance Organizations Innovate at Scale*, described how we can frame hypotheses in feature development in the following form:

> **We Believe** That increasing the size of hotel images on the booking page
>
> **Will Result** In improved customer engagement and conversion
>
> **We Will Have Confidence To Proceed When** we see a 5% increase in customers who review hotel images who then proceed to book in forty-eight hours.

Adopting an experimental approach to product development requires us to not only break down work into small units (stories or requirements), but also validate whether each unit of work is delivering the expected outcomes. If it does not, we modify our road map of work with alternative paths that will actually achieve those outcomes.

Case Study
Doubling Revenue Growth through Fast Release Cycle Experimentation at Yahoo! Answers (2010)

The faster we can iterate and integrate feedback into the product or service we are delivering to customers, the faster we can learn and the bigger the impact we can create. How dramatically outcomes can be affected by faster cycle times was evident at Yahoo! Answers as they went from one release every six weeks to multiple releases every week.

In 2009, Jim Stoneham was General Manager of the Yahoo! Communities group that included Flickr and Answers. Previously, he had been primarily responsible for Yahoo! Answers, competing against other Q&A companies such as Quora, Aardvark, and Stack Exchange.

At that time, Answers had approximately 140 million monthly visitors, with over twenty million active users answering questions in over twenty different languages. However, user growth and revenue had flattened, and user engagement scores were declining.

Stoneham observes that "Yahoo Answers was and continues to be one of the biggest social games on the Internet; tens of millions of people are actively trying to 'level up' by providing quality answers to questions faster than the next member of the community. There were many opportunities to tweak the game mechanic, viral loops, and other community interactions. When you're dealing with these human behaviors, you've got to be able to do quick iterations and testing to see what clicks with people."

He continues, "These [experiments] are the things that Twitter, Facebook, and Zynga did so well. Those organizations were doing experiments at least twice per week—they were even reviewing the changes they made before their deployments, to make sure they were still on track. So here I am, running [the] largest Q&A site in the market, wanting to do rapid iterative feature testing, but we can't release any faster than once every 4 weeks. In contrast, the other people in the market had a feedback loop 10x faster than us."

Stoneham observed that as much as product owners and developers talk about being metrics-driven, if experiments are not performed frequently (daily or weekly), the focus of daily work is merely on the feature they're working on, as opposed to customer outcomes.

As the Yahoo! Answers team was able to move to weekly deployments, and later multiple deployments per week, their ability to experiment with new features increased dramatically. Their astounding achievements and learnings over the next twelve months of experimentation included increased monthly visits of 72%, increased user engagement of threefold, and the team doubled their revenue. To continue their success, the team focused on optimizing the following top metrics:

- Time to first answer: How quickly was an answer posted to a user question?

- Time to best answer: How quickly did the user community award a best answer?

- Upvotes per answer: How many times was an answer upvoted by the user community?

- Answers/week/person: How many answers were users creating?

- Second search rate: How often did visitors have to search again to get an answer? (Lower is better.)

Stoneham concluded, "This was exactly the learning that we needed to win in the marketplace—and it changed more than our feature velocity. We transformed from a team of employees to a team of owners. When you move at that speed, and are looking at the numbers and the results daily, your investment level radically changes."

CONCLUSION

Success requires us to not only deploy and release software quickly, but also to out-experiment our competition. Techniques such as hypothesis-driven development, defining and measuring out customer acquisition funnel, and A/B testing allow us to perform user-experiments safely and easily, enabling us to unleash creativity and innovation, and create organizational learning. And, while succeeding is important, the organizational learning that comes from experimentation also gives employees ownership of business objectives and customer satisfaction. In the next chapter, we examine and create review and coordination processes as a way to increase the quality of our current work.

18

Create Review and Coordination Processes to Increase Quality of Our Current Work

In the previous chapters, we created the telemetry necessary to see and solve problems in production and at all stages of our deployment pipeline, and created fast feedback loops from customers to help enhance organizational learning—learning that encourages ownership and responsibility for customer satisfaction and feature performance, which helps us succeed.

Our goal in this chapter is to enable Development and Operations to reduce the risk of production changes before they are made. Traditionally, when we review changes for deployment, we tend to rely heavily on reviews, inspections, and approvals just prior to deployment. Frequently those approvals are given by external teams who are often too far removed from the work to make informed decisions on whether a change is risky or not, and the time required to get all the necessary approvals also lengthens our change lead times.

The peer review process at GitHub is a striking example of how inspection can increase quality, make deployments safe, and be integrated into the flow of everyone's daily work. They pioneered the process called *pull request*, one of the most popular forms of peer review that span Dev and Ops.

Scott Chacon, CIO and co-founder of GitHub, wrote on his website that pull requests are the mechanism that lets engineers tell others about changes they have pushed to a repository on GitHub. Once a pull request is sent, interested parties can review the set of changes, discuss potential modifications, and even push follow-up commits if necessary. Engineers submitting a pull request will often request a "+1," "+2," or so forth, depending on how many reviews they need, or "@mention" engineers that they'd like to get reviews from.

At GitHub, pull requests are also the mechanism used to deploy code into production through a collective set of practices they call "GitHub Flow"—it's how engineers request code reviews, gather and integrate feedback, and announce that code will be deployed to production (i.e., "master" branch).

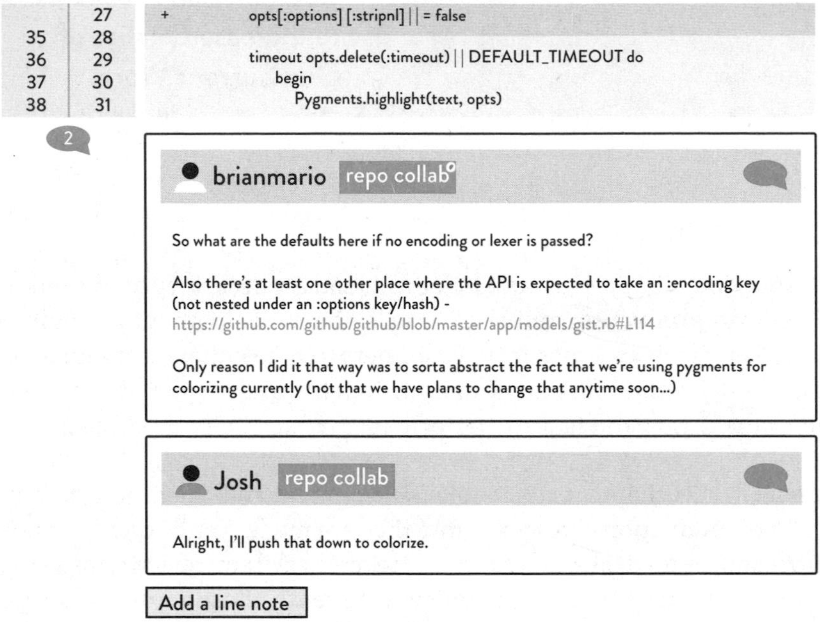

Figure 40: *Comments and suggestions on a GitHub pull request*
(Source: Scott Chacon, "GitHub Flow," ScottChacon.com, August 31, 2011, http://scottchacon. com/2011/08/31/github-flow.html.)

GitHub Flow is composed of five steps:

1. To work on something new, the engineer creates a descriptively named branch off of master (e.g., "new-oauth2-scopes").

2. The engineer commits to that branch locally, regularly pushing their work to the same named branch on the server.

3. When they need feedback or help, or when they think the branch is ready for merging, they open a pull request.

4. When they get their desired reviews and get any necessary approvals of the feature, the engineer can then merge it into master.

5. Once the code changes are merged and pushed to master, the engineer deploys them into production.

These practices, which integrate review and coordination into daliy work, have allowed GitHub to quickly and reliably deliver features to market with high quality and security. For example, in 2012 they performed an amazing 12,602 deployments. In particular, on August 23rd, after a company-wide summit where many exciting ideas were brainstormed and discussed, the company had their busiest deployment day of the year, with 563 builds and 175 successful deployments into production, all made possible through the pull request process.

Throughout this chapter we will integrate practices, such as those used at GitHub, to shift our reliance away from periodic inspections and approvals, and moving to integrated peer review performed continually as a part of our daily work. Our goal is to ensure that Development, Operations, and Infosec are continuously collaborating so that changes we make to our systems will operate reliably, securely, safely, and as designed.

THE DANGERS OF CHANGE APPROVAL PROCESSES

The Knight Capital failure is one of the most prominent software deployment errors in recent memory. A fifteen minute deployment error resulted in a $440 million trading loss, during which the engineering teams were unable to disable the production services. The financial losses jeopardized the firm's operations and forced the company to be sold over the weekend so they could continue operating without jeopardizing the entire financial system.

John Allspaw observed that when high-profile incidents occur, such as the Knight Capital deployment accident, there are typically two *counterfactual* narratives for why the accident occurred.[†]

The first narrative is that the accident was due to a change control failure, which seems valid because we can imagine a situation where better change control practices could have detected the risk earlier and prevented the change from going into production. And if we couldn't prevent it, we might have taken steps to enable faster detection and recovery.

---

† *Counterfactual thinking* is a term used in psychology that involves the human tendency to create possible alternatives to life events that have already occurred. In reliability engineering, it often involves narratives of the "system as imagined" as opposed to the "system in reality."

The second narrative is that the accident was due to a testing failure. This also seems valid, with better testing practices we could have identified the risk earlier and canceled the risky deployment, or we could have at least taken steps to enable faster detection and recovery.

The surprising reality is that in environments with low-trust, command-and-control cultures, the outcomes of these types of change control and testing countermeasures often result in an increased likelihood that problems will occur again, potentially with even worse outcomes.

Gene Kim (co-author of this book) describes his realization that change and testing controls can potentially have the opposite effect than intended as "one of the most important moments of my professional career. This 'aha' moment was the result of a conversation in 2013 with John Allspaw and Jez Humble about the Knight Capital accident, making me question some of my core beliefs that I've formed over the last ten years, especially having been trained as an auditor."

He continues, "However upsetting it was, it was also a very formative moment for me. Not only did they convince me that they were correct, we tested these beliefs in the 2014 *State of DevOps Report*, which led to some astonishing findings that reinforce that building high-trust cultures is likely the largest management challenge of this decade."

POTENTIAL DANGERS OF "OVERLY CONTROLLING CHANGES"

Traditional change controls can lead to unintended outcomes, such as contributing to long lead times, and reducing the strength and immediacy of feedback from the deployment process. In order to understand how this happens, let us examine the controls we often put in place when change control failures occur:

- Adding more questions that need to be answered to the change request form

- Requiring more authorizations, such as one more level of management approval (e.g., instead of merely the VP of Operations approving, we now require that the CIO also approve) or more stakeholders (e.g., network engineering, architecture review boards, etc.)

- Requiring more lead time for change approvals so that change requests can be properly evaluated

These controls often add more friction to the deployment process by multiplying the number of steps and approvals, and increasing batch sizes and deployment lead times, which we know reduces the likelihood of successful production outcomes for both Dev and Ops. These controls also reduce how quickly we get feedback from our work.

One of the core beliefs in the Toyota Production System is that "people closest to a problem typically know the most about it." This becomes more pronounced as the work being performed and the system the work occurs in become more complex and dynamic, as is typical in DevOps value streams. In these cases, creating approval steps from people who are located further and further away from the work may actually reduce the likelihood of success. As has been proven time and again, the further the distance between the person doing the work (i.e., the change implementer) and the person deciding to do the work (i.e., the change authorizer), the worse the outcome.

In Puppet Labs' 2014 *State of DevOps Report*, one of the key findings was that high-performing organizations relied more on peer review and less on external approval of changes. Figure 41 shows that the more organizations rely on change approvals, the worse their IT performance in terms of both stability (mean time to restore service and change fail rate) and throughput (deployment lead times, deployment frequency).

In many organizations, change advisory boards serve an important role in coordinating and governing the delivery process, but their job should not be to manually evaluate every change, nor does ITIL mandate such a practice.

To understand why this is the case, consider the predicament of being on a change advisory board, reviewing a complex change composed of hundreds of thousands of lines of code changes, and created by hundreds of engineers.

At one extreme, we cannot reliably predict whether a change will be successful either by reading a hundred-word description of the change or by merely validating that a checklist has been completed. At the other extreme, painfully scrutinizing thousands of lines of code changes is unlikely to reveal any new insights. Part of this is the nature of making changes inside of a complex system. Even the engineers who work inside the codebase as part of their daily work are often surprised by the side effects of what should be low-risk changes.

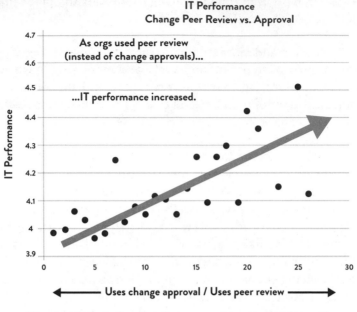

Figure 41: *Organizations that rely on peer review outperform those with change approvals (Source: Puppet Labs, DevOps Survey Of Practice 2014)*

For all these reasons, we need to create effective control practices that more closely resemble peer review, reducing our reliance on external bodies to authorize our changes. We also need to coordinate and schedule changes effectively. We explore both of these in the next two sections.

ENABLE COORDINATION AND SCHEDULING OF CHANGES

Whenever we have multiple groups working on systems that share dependencies, our changes will likely need to be coordinated to ensure that they don't interfere with each other (e.g., marshaling, batching, and sequencing the changes). In general, the more loosely coupled our architecture, the less we need to communicate and coordinate with other component teams—when the architecture is truly service-oriented, teams can make changes with a high degree of autonomy, where local changes are unlikely to create global disruptions.

However, even in a loosely coupled architecture, when many teams are doing hundreds of independent deployments per day, there may be a risk of changes interfering with each other (e.g., simultaneous A/B tests). To mitigate these risks, we may use chat rooms to announce changes and proactively find collisions that may exist.

For more complex organizations and organizations with more tightly coupled architectures, we may need to deliberately schedule our changes, where representatives from the teams get together, not to authorize changes, but to schedule and sequence their changes in order to minimize accidents.

However, certain areas, such as global infrastructure changes (e.g., core network switch changes) will always have a higher risk associated with them. These changes will always require technical countermeasures, such as redundancy, failover, comprehensive testing, and (ideally) simulation.

ENABLE PEER REVIEW OF CHANGES

Instead of requiring approval from an external body prior to deployment, we may require engineers to get peer reviews of their changes. In Development, this practice has been called *code review*, but it is equally applicable to any change we make to our applications or environments, including servers, networking, and databases.[†] The goal is to find errors by having fellow engineers close to the work scrutinize our changes. This review improves the quality of our changes, which also creates the benefits of cross-training, peer learning, and skill improvement.

A logical place to require reviews is prior to committing code to trunk in source control, where changes could potentially have a team-wide or global impact. At a minimum, fellow engineers should review our change, but for higher risk areas, such as database changes or business-critical components with poor automated test coverage, we may require further review from a subject matter expert (e.g., information security engineer, database engineer) or multiple reviews (e.g., "+2" instead of merely "+1").

The principle of small batch sizes also applies to code reviews. The larger the size of the change that needs to be reviewed, the longer it takes to understand and the larger the burden on the reviewing engineer. As Randy Shoup observed, "There is a non-linear relationship between the size of the change and the potential risk of integrating that change—when you go from a ten line code change to a one hundred line code, the risk of something going wrong is more than ten times higher, and so forth." This is why it's so essential for developers

---

† In this book, the terms *code review* and *change review* will be used interchangeably.

to work in small, incremental steps rather than on long-lived feature branches.

Furthermore, our ability to meaningfully critique code changes goes down as the change size goes up. As Giray Özil tweeted, "Ask a programmer to review ten lines of code, he'll find ten issues. Ask him to do five hundred lines, and he'll say it looks good."

Guidelines for code reviews include:

- Everyone must have someone to review their changes (e.g., to the code, environment, etc.) before committing to trunk.

- Everyone should monitor the commit stream of their fellow team members so that potential conflicts can be identified and reviewed.

- Define which changes qualify as high risk and may require review from a designated subject matter expert (e.g., database changes, security-sensitive modules such as authentication, etc.).[†]

- If someone submits a change that is too large to reason about easily—in other words, you can't understand its impact after reading through it a couple of times, or you need to ask the submitter for clarification—it should be split up into multiple, smaller changes that can be understood at a glance.

To ensure that we are not merely rubber stamping reviews, we may also want to inspect the code review statistics to determine the number of proposed changes approved versus not approved, and perhaps sample and inspect specific code reviews.

Code reviews come in various forms:

- **Pair programming:** programmers work in pairs (see section below)

- **"Over-the-shoulder:"** One developer looks over the author's shoulder as the latter walks through the code.

---

† Incidentally, a list of high-risk areas of code and environments has likely already been created by the change advisory board.

- **Email pass-around:** A source code management system emails code to reviewers automatically after the code is checked in.

- **Tool-assisted code review:** Authors and reviewers use specialized tools designed for peer code review (e.g., Gerrit, GitHub pull requests, etc.) or facilities provided by the source code repositories (e.g., GitHub, Mercurial, Subversion, as well as other platforms such as Gerrit, Atlassian Stash, and Atlassian Crucible).

Close scrutiny of changes in many forms is effective in locating errors previously overlooked. Code reviews can facilitate increased code commits and production deployments, and support trunk-based deployment and continuous delivery at scale, as we will see in the following case study.

Case Study
Code Reviews at Google (2010)

Google is an excellent example of a company that employees trunk-based development and continuous delivery at scale. As noted earlier in this book, Eran Messeri described that in 2013 the processes at Google enabled over thirteen thousand developers to work off of trunk on a single source code tree, performing over 5,500 code commits per week, resulting in hundreds of production deployments per week. In 2010, there were 20+ changes being checked in to trunk every minute, resulting in 50% of the codebase being changed every month.

This requires considerable discipline from Google team members and mandatory code reviews, which cover the following areas:

- Code readability for languages (enforces style guide)

- Ownership assignments for code sub-trees to maintain consistency and correctness

- Code transparency and code contributions across teams

Figure 42 shows how code review lead times are affected by the change size. On the x-axis is the size of the change, and on the y-axis is the lead time required for code review process. In general, the larger the change submitted for code reviews, the longer the lead time required to get the necessary sign offs. And the data points in the upper-left corner represent the more complex and potentially risky changes that required more deliberation and discussion.

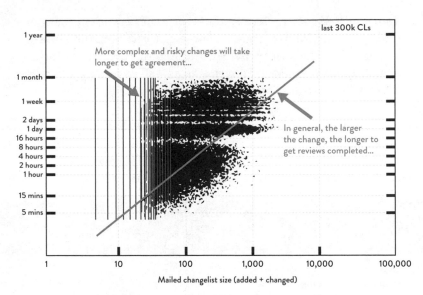

Figure 42: *Size of change vs. lead time for reviews at Google*
(Source: Ashish Kumar, "Development at the Speed and Scale of Google," presentation at QCon, San Francisco, CA, 2010, https://qconsf.com/sf2010/dl/qcon-sanfran-2010/slides/AshishKumar_Developing-ProductsattheSpeedandScaleofGoogle.pdf.)

While he was working as a Google engineering director, Randy Shoup started a personal project to solve a technical problem that the organization was facing. He said, "I worked on that project for weeks and finally got around to asking a subject matter expert to review my code. It was nearly three thousand lines of code, which took the reviewer days of work to go through. He told me, 'Please don't do that to me again.' I was grateful that this engineer took the time to do that. That was also when I learned how to make code reviews a part of my daily work."

POTENTIAL DANGERS OF DOING MORE MANUAL TESTING AND CHANGE FREEZES

Now that we have created peer reviews that reduce our risk, shorten lead times associated with change approval processes, and enable continuous delivery at scale, such as we saw in the Google case study, let us examine the effects of how testing countermeasure can sometimes backfire. When testing failures occur, our typical reaction is to do more testing. However, if we are merely performing more testing at the end of the project, we may worsen our outcomes.

This is especially true if we are doing manual testing, because manual testing is naturally slower and more tedious than automated testing and performing "additional testing" often has the consequence of taking significantly longer to test, which means we are deploying less frequently, thus increasing our deployment batch size. And we know from both theory and practice that when we increase our deployment batch size, our change success rates go down and our incident counts and MTTR go up—the opposite of the outcome we want.

Instead of performing testing on large batches of changes that are scheduled around change freeze periods, we want to fully integrate testing our daily work as part of the smooth and continual flow into production, and increase our deployment frequency. By doing this, we build in quality, which allows us to test, deploy, and release in ever smaller batch sizes.

ENABLE PAIR PROGRAMMING TO IMPROVE ALL OUR CHANGES

Pair programming is when two engineers work together at the same workstation, a method popularized by Extreme Programming and Agile in the early 2000s. As with code reviews, this practice started in Development but is equally applicable to the work that any engineer does in our value stream. In this book, we will use the term *pairing* and *pair programming* interchangeably, to indicate that the practice is not just for developers.

In one common pattern of pairing, one engineer fills the role of the *driver*, the person who actually writes the code, while the other engineer acts as the *navigator, observer,* or *pointer,* the person who reviews the work as it is being performed. While reviewing, the observer may also consider the strategic direction of the work, coming up with ideas for improvements and likely future problems to address. This frees the driver to focus all of his or her attention on the tactical aspects of completing the task, using the observer as a safety net and guide. When the two have differing specialties, skills are transferred as an automatic side effect, whether it's through ad-hoc training or by sharing techniques and workarounds.

Another pair programming pattern reinforces test-driven development (TDD) by having one engineer write the automated test and the other engineer implement the code. Jeff Atwood, one of the founders of Stack Exchange, wrote, "I can't help wondering if pair programming is nothing more than code review on steroids....The advantage of pair programming is its gripping immediacy: it is impossible to ignore the reviewer when he or she is sitting right next to you."

He continued, "Most people will passively opt out [of reviewing code] if given the choice. With pair programming, that's not possible. Each half of the pair *has* to understand the code, right then and there, as it's being written. Pairing may be invasive, but it can also force a level of communication that you'd otherwise never achieve."

Dr. Laurie Williams performed a study in 2001 that showed "paired programmers are 15% slower than two independent individual programmers, while 'error-free' code increased from 70% to 85%. Since testing and debugging are often many times more costly than initial programming, this is an impressive result. Pairs typically consider more design alternatives than programmers working alone and arrive at simpler, more maintainable designs; they also catch design defects early." Dr. Williams also reported that 96% of her respondents stated that they enjoyed their work more when they programmed in pairs than when they programmed alone.[†]

Pair programming has the additional benefit of spreading knowledge throughout the organization and increasing information flow within the team. Having more experienced engineers review while the less experienced engineer codes is also an effective way to teach and be taught.

Case Study
Pair Programming Replacing Broken
Code Review Processes at Pivotal Labs (2011)

Elisabeth Hendrickson, VP of Engineering at Pivotal Software, Inc. and author of *Explore It!: Reduce Risk and Increase Confidence with Exploratory Testing*, has spoken extensively about making every team responsible for their own quality, as opposed to making separate departments responsible. She argues that doing so not only increase quality, but significantly increases the flow of work into production.

---

† Some organizations may require pair programming, while in others, engineers find someone to pair program with when working in areas where they want more scrutiny (such as before checking in) or for challenging tasks. Another common practice is to set *pairing hours* for a subset of the working day, perhaps four hours from mid-morning to mid-afternoon.

In her 2015 DevOps Enterprise Summit presentation, she described how in 2011, there were two accepted methods of code review at Pivotal: pair programming (which ensured that every line of code was inspected by two people) or a code review process that was managed by Gerrit (which ensured that every code commit had two designated people "+1" the change before it was allowed into trunk).

The problem Hendrickson observed with the Gerrit code review process was that it would often take an entire week for developers to receive their required reviews. Worse, skilled developers were experiencing the "frustrating and soul crushing experience of not being able to get simple changes into the codebase, because we had inadvertently created intolerable bottlenecks."

Hendrickson lamented that "the only people who had the ability to '+1' the changes were senior engineers, who had many other responsibilities and often didn't care as much about the fixes the more junior developers were working on or their productivity. It created a terrible situation—while you were waiting for your changes to get reviewed, other developers were checking in their changes. So for a week, you would have to merge all their code changes onto your laptop, re-run all the tests to ensure that everything still worked, and (sometimes) you'd have to resubmit your changes for review again!"

To fix the problem and eliminate all of these delays, they ended up dismantling the entire Gerrit code review process, instead requiring pair programming to implement code changes into the system. By doing this, they reduced the amount of time required to get code reviewed from weeks to hours.

Hendrickson is quick to note that code reviews work fine in many organizations, but it requires a culture that values reviewing code as highly as it values writing the code in the first place. When that culture is not yet in place, pair programming can serve as a valuable interim practice.

EVALUATING THE EFFECTIVENESS OF PULL REQUEST PROCESSES
Because the peer review process is an important part of our control environment, we need to be able to determine whether it is working effectively or not. One method is to look at production outages and examine the peer review process for any relevant changes.

Another method comes from Ryan Tomayko, CIO and co-founder of GitHub and one of the inventors of the pull request process. When asked to describe the difference between a bad pull request and a good pull request, he said it has little to do with the production outcome. Instead, a bad pull request is one that doesn't have enough context for the reader, having little or no documentation of what the change is intended to do. For example, a pull request that merely has the following text: "Fixing issue #3616 and #3841."[†]

That was an actual internal GitHub pull request, which Tomayko critiqued, "This was probably written by a new engineer here. First off, no specific engineers were specifically @mentioned—at a minimum, the engineer should have mentioned their mentor or a subject matter expert in the area that they're modifying to ensure that someone appropriate reviews their change. Worse, there isn't any explanation of what the changes actually are, why it's important, or exposing any of the implementer's thinking."

On the other hand, when asked to describe a great pull request that indicates an effective review process, Tomayko quickly listed off the essential elements: there must be sufficient detail on why the change is being made, how the change was made, as well as any identified risks and resulting countermeasures.

Tomayko also looks for good discussion of the change, enabled by all the context that the pull request provided—often, there will be additional risks pointed out, ideas on better ways to implement the desired change, ideas on how to better mitigate the risk, and so forth. And if something bad or unexpected happens upon deployment, it is added to the pull request, with a link to the corresponding issue. All discussion happens without placing blame; instead, there is a candid conversation on how to prevent the problem from recurring in the future.

As an example, Tomayko produced another internal GitHub pull request for a database migration. It was many pages long, with lengthy discussions about the potential risks, leading up to the following statement by the pull request author: "I am pushing this now. Builds are now failing for the branch, because of a missing column in the CI servers. (Link to Post-Mortem: MySQL outage)"

The change submitter then apologized for the outage, describing what conditions and mistaken assumptions led to the accident, as well as a list of proposed countermeasures to prevent it from happening again. This was followed by pages and pages of discussion. Reading through the pull request, Tomayko smiled, "Now *that* is a great pull request."

---

† Gene Kim is grateful to Shawn Davenport, James Fryman, Will Farr, and Ryan Tomayko at GitHub for discussing the differences between good and bad pull requests.

As described above, we can evaluate the effectiveness of our peer review process by sampling and examining pull requests, either from the entire population of pull requests or those that are relevant to production incidents.

FEARLESSLY CUT BUREAUCRATIC PROCESSES

So far, we have discussed peer review and pair programming processes that enable us to increase the quality of our work without relying on external approvals for changes. However, many companies still have long-standing processes for approval that require months to navigate. These approval processes can significantly increase lead times, not only preventing us from delivering value quickly to customers, but potentially increasing the risk to our organizational objectives. When this happens, we must re-engineer our processes so that we can achieve our goals more quickly and safely.

As Adrian Cockcroft observed, "A great metric to publish widely is how many meetings and work tickets are mandatory to perform a release—the goal is to relentlessly reduce the effort required for engineers to perform work and deliver it to the customer."

Similarly, Dr. Tapabrata Pal, technical fellow at Capital One, described a program at Capital One called Got Goo?, which involves a dedicated team removing obstacles—including tools, processes, and approvals—that impede work completion. Jason Cox, Senior Director of Systems Engineering at Disney, described in his presentation at the DevOps Enterprise Summit in 2015 a program called Join The Rebellion that aimed to remove toil and obstacles from daily work.

At Target in 2012, a combination of the Technology Enterprise Adoption Process and Lead Architecture Review Board (TEAP-LARB process) resulted in complicated, long approval times for anyone attempting to bring in new technology. The TEAP form needed to be filled out by anyone wanting to propose new technologies to be adopted, such as a new database or monitoring technologies. These proposals were evaluated, and those deemed appropriate were put onto the monthly LARB meeting agenda.

Heather Mickman and Ross Clanton, Director of Development and Director of Operations at Target, Inc., respectively, were helping to lead the DevOps movement at Target. During their DevOps initiative, Mickman had identified a technology needed to enable an initiative from the lines of business (in this case, Tomcat and Cassandra). The decision from the LARB was that Operations could not support it at the time. However, because Mickman was so convinced that this technology was essential, she proposed that her Development team be responsible for service support as well as integration, availability, and security, instead of relying on the Operations team.

"As we went through the process, I wanted to better understand why the TEAP-LARB process took so long to get through, and I used the technique of 'the five why's'....Which eventually led to the question of why TEAP-LARB existed in the first place. The surprising thing was that no one knew, outside of a vague notion that we needed some sort of governance process. Many knew that there had been some sort of disaster that could never happen again years ago, but no one could remember exactly what that disaster was, either," Mickman observed.

Mickman concluded that this process was not necessary for her group if they were responsible for the operational responsibilities of the technology she was introducing. She added, "I let everyone know that any future technologies that we would support wouldn't have to go through the TEAP-LARB process, either."

The outcome was that Cassandra was successfully introduced inside Target and eventually widely adopted. Furthermore, the TEAP-LARB process was eventually dismantled. Out of appreciation, her team awarded Mickman the Lifetime Achievement Award for removing barriers to get technology work done within Target.

CONCLUSION

In this chapter, we discussed how to integrate practices into our daily work that increase the quality of our changes and reduce the risk of poor deployment outcomes, reducing our reliance on approval processes. Case studies from GitHub and Target show that these practices not only improve our outcomes, but also significantly reduce lead times and increase developer productivity. To do this kind of work requires a high-trust culture.

Consider a story that John Allspaw told about a newly hired junior engineer: The engineer asked if it was okay to deploy a small HTML change, and Allspaw responded, "I don't know, is it?" He then asked "Did you have someone review your change? Do you know who the best person to ask is for changes of this type? Did you do everything you absolutely could to assure yourself that this change operates in production as designed? If you did, then don't ask me—just make the change!"

By responding this way, Allspaw reminded the engineer that she was solely responsibility for the quality of her change—if she did everything she felt she could to give herself confidence that the change would work, then she didn't need to ask anyone for approval, she should make the change.

Creating the conditions that enable change implementers to fully own the quality of their changes is an essential part of the high-trust, generative culture we are striving to build. Furthermore, these conditions enable us to create an ever-safer system of work, where we are all helping each other achieve our goals, spanning whatever boundaries necessary to get there.

PART IV CONCLUSION

Part IV has shown us that by implementing feedback loops we can enable everyone to work together toward shared goals, see problems as they occur, and, with quick detection and recovery, ensure that features not only operate as designed in production, but also achieve organizational goals and organizational learning. We have also examined how to enable shared goals spanning Dev and Ops so that they can improve the health of the entire value stream.

We are now ready to enter Part V: The Third Way, The Technical Practices of Learning, so we can create opportunities for learning that happen earlier and ever more quickly and cheaply, and so that we can unleash a culture of innovation and experimentation that enables everyone to do meaningful work that helps our organization succeed.

PART Ⅴ

The Third Way
The Technical Practices of Continual Learning and Experimentation

Part V
Introduction

In Part III, The First Way: *The Technical Practices of Flow*, we discussed implementing the practices required to create fast flow in our value stream. In Part IV, The Second Way: *The Technical Practices of Feedback*, our goal was to create as much feedback as possible, from as many areas in our system as possible—sooner, faster, and cheaper.

In Part V, The Third Way: *The Technical Practices of Learning*, we present the practices that create opportunities for learning, as quickly, frequently, cheaply, and as soon as possible. This includes creating learnings from accidents and failures, which are inevitable when we work within complex systems, as well as organizing and designing our systems of work so that we are constantly experimenting and learning, continually making our systems safer. The results include higher resilience and an ever-growing collective knowledge of how our system actually works, so that we are better able to achieve our goals.

In the following chapters, we will institutionalize rituals that increase safety, continuous improvement, and learning by doing the following:

- Establish a just culture to make safety possible

- Inject production failures to create resilience

- Convert local discoveries into global improvements

- Reserve time to create organizational improvements and learning

We will also create mechanisms so that any new learnings generated in one area of the organization can be rapidly used across the entire organization, turning local improvements into global advancements. In this way, we not only learn faster than our competition, helping us win in the marketplace, but also create a safer, more resilient work culture that people are excited to be a part of and that helps them achieve their highest potential.

19 Enable and Inject Learning into Daily Work

When we work within a complex system, it is impossible for us to predict all the outcomes for the actions we take. This contributes to unexpected and sometimes catastrophic accidents, even when we use static precautionary tools, such as checklists and runbooks, which codify our current understanding of the system.

To enable us to safely work within complex systems, our organizations must become ever better at self-diagnostics and self-improvement and must be skilled at detecting problems, solving them, and multiplying the effects by making the solutions available throughout the organization. This creates a dynamic system of learning that allows us to understand our mistakes and translate that understanding into actions that prevent those mistakes from recurring in the future.

The result is what Dr. Steven Spear describes as resilient organizations, who are "skilled at detecting problems, solving them, and multiplying the effect by making the solutions available throughout the organization." These organizations can heal themselves. "For such an organization, responding to crises is not idiosyncratic work. It is something that is done all the time. It is this responsiveness that is their source of reliability."

A striking example of the incredible resilience that can result from these principles and practices was seen on April 21, 2011, when the entire Amazon AWS US-EAST availability zone went down, taking down virtually all of their customers who depended on it, including Reddit and Quora.[†] However, Netflix was a surprising exception, seemingly unaffected by this massive AWS outage.

---

† In January 2013 at re:Invent, James Hamilton, VP and Distinguished Engineer for Amazon Web Services said that the US East region had more than ten data centers all by itself, and added that a typical data center has between fifty thousand and eighty thousand servers. By this math, the 2011 EC2 outage affected customers on more than half a million servers.

Following the event, there was considerable speculation about how Netflix kept their services running. A popular theory was since Netflix was one of the largest customers of Amazon Web Services, it was given some special treatment that allowed them to keep running. However, a *Netflix Engineering* blog post explained that it was their architectural design decisions in 2009 enabled their exceptional resilience.

Back in 2008, Netflix's online video delivery service ran on a monolithic J2EE application hosted in one of their data centers. However, starting in 2009, they began re-architecting this system to be what they called *cloud native*—it was designed to run entirely in the Amazon public cloud and to be resilient enough to survive significant failures.

One of their specific design objectives was to ensure Netflix services kept running, even if an entire AWS availability zone went down, such as happened with US-EAST. To do this required that their system be loosely-coupled, with each component having aggressive timeouts to ensure that failing components didn't bring the entire system down.Instead, each feature and component was designed to gracefully degrade. For example, during traffic surges that created CPU-usage spikes, instead of showing a list of movies personalized to the user, they would show static content, such as cached or un-personalized results, which required less computation.

Furthermore, the blog post explained that, in addition to implementing these architectural patterns, they also built and had been running a surprising and audacious service called *Chaos Monkey*, which simulated AWS failures by constantly and randomly killing production servers. They did so because they wanted all "engineering teams to be used to a constant level of failure in the cloud" so that services could "automatically recover without any manual intervention."

In other words, the Netflix team ran Chaos Monkey to gain assurance that they had achieved their operational resilience objectives, constantly injecting failures into their pre-production and production environments.

As one might expect, when they first ran Chaos Monkey in their production environments, services failed in ways they never could have predicted or imagined—by constantly finding and fixing these issues during normal working hours, Netflix engineers quickly and iteratively created a more resilient service, while simultaneously creating organizational learnings (during normal working hours!) that enabled them to evolve their systems far beyond their competition.

Chaos Monkey is just one example of how learning can be integrated into daily work. The story also shows how learning organizations think about failures, accidents, and mistakes—as an opportunity for learning and not something to be punished. This chapter explores how to create a system of learning and how to establish a *just culture*, as well as how to routinely rehearse and deliberately create failures to accelerate learning.

ESTABLISH A JUST, LEARNING CULTURE

One of the prerequisites for a learning culture is that when accidents occur (which they undoubtedly will), the response to those accidents is seen as "just." Dr. Sidney Dekker, who helped codify some of the key elements of safety culture and coined the term *just culture*, writes, "When responses to incidents and accidents are seen as unjust, it can impede safety investigations, promoting fear rather than mindfulness in people who do safety-critical work, making organizations more bureaucratic rather than more careful, and cultivating professional secrecy, evasion, and self-protection."

This notion of punishment is present, either subtly or prominently, in the way many managers have operated during the last century. The thinking goes, in order to achieve the goals of the organization, leaders must command, control, establish procedures to eliminate errors, and enforce compliance of those procedures.

Dr. Dekker calls this notion of eliminating error by eliminating the people who caused the errors the *Bad Apple Theory*. He asserts that this is invalid, because "human error is not our cause of troubles; instead, human error is a consequence of the design of the tools that we gave them."

If accidents are not caused by "bad apples," but rather are due to inevitable design problems in the complex system that we created, then instead of "naming, blaming, and shaming" the person who caused the failure, our goal should always be to maximize opportunities for organizational learning, continually reinforcing that we value actions that expose and share more widely the problems in our daily work. This is what enables us to improve the quality and safety of the system we operate within and reinforce the relationships between everyone who operates within that system.

By turning information into knowledge and building the results of the learning into our systems, we start to achieve the goals of a just culture, balancing the needs for safety and accountability. As John Allspaw, CTO of Etsy, states, "Our goal at Etsy is to view mistakes, errors, slips, lapses, and so forth with a perspective of learning."

When engineers make mistakes and feel safe when giving details about it, they are not only willing to be held accountable, but they are also enthusiastic in helping the rest of the company avoid the same error in the future. This is what creates organizational learning. On the other hand, if we punish that engineer, everyone is dis-incentivized to provide the necessary details to get an understanding of the mechanism, pathology, and operation of the failure, which guarantees that the failure will occur again.

Two effective practices that help create a just, learning-based culture are blameless post-mortems and the controlled introduction of failures into production to create opportunities to practice for the inevitable problems that arise within complex systems. We will first look at blameless post-mortems and follow that with an exploration of why failure can be a good thing.

SCHEDULE BLAMELESS POST-MORTEM MEETINGS AFTER ACCIDENTS OCCUR

To help enable a just culture, when accidents and significant incidents occur (e.g., failed deployment, production issue that affected customers), we should conduct a *blameless post-mortem* after the incident has been resolved.[†] Blameless post-mortems, a term coined by John Allspaw, help us examine "mistakes in a way that focuses on the situational aspects of a failure's mechanism and the decision-making process of individuals proximate to the failure."

To do this, we schedule the post-mortem as soon as possible after the accident occurs and before memories and the links between cause and effect fade or circumstances change. (Of course, we wait until after the problem has been resolved so as not to distract the people who are still actively working on the issue.)

In the blameless post-mortem meeting, we will do the following:

- Construct a timeline and gather details from multiple perspectives on failures, ensuring we don't punish people for making mistakes

---

† This practice has also been called *blameless post-incident reviews* as well as *post-event retrospectives*. There is also a noteworthy similarity to the routine retrospectives that are a part of many iterative and agile development practices.

- Empower all engineers to improve safety by allowing them to give detailed accounts of their contributions to failures

- Enable and encourage people who do make mistakes to be the experts who educate the rest of the organization on how not to make them in the future

- Accept that there is always a discretionary space where humans can decide to take action or not, and that the judgment of those decisions lies in hindsight

- Propose countermeasures to prevent a similar accident from happening in the future and ensure these countermeasures are recorded with a target date and an owner for follow-up

To enable us to gain this understanding, the following stakeholders need to be present at the meeting:

- The people involved in decisions that may have contributed to the problem

- The people who identified the problem

- The people who responded to the problem

- The people who diagnosed the problem

- The people who were affected by the problem

- And anyone else who is interested in attending the meeting.

Our first task in the blameless post-mortem meeting is to record our best understanding of the timeline of relevant events as they occurred. This includes all actions we took and what time (ideally supported by chat logs, such as IRC or Slack), what effects we observed (ideally in the form of the specific metrics from our production telemetry, as opposed to merely subjective narratives), all investigation paths we followed, and what resolutions were considered.

To enable these outcomes, we must be rigorous about recording details and reinforcing a culture that information can be shared without fear of punishment or retribution. Because of this, especially for our first few post-mortems, it may be helpful to have the meeting led by a trained facilitator who wasn't involved in the accident.

During the meeting and the subsequent resolution, we should explicitly disallow the phrases "would have" or "could have," as they are *counterfactual* statements that result from our human tendency to create possible alternatives to events that have already occurred.

Counterfactual statements, such as "I could have..." or "If I had known about that, I should have...," frame the problem in terms of the *system as imagined* instead of in terms of the *system that actually exists*, which is the context we need to restrict ourselves to. (See Appendix 8.)

One of the potentially surprising outcomes of these meetings is that people will often blame themselves for things outside of their control or question their own abilities. Ian Malpass, an engineer at Etsy observes, "In that moment when we do something that causes the entire site to go down, we get this 'ice-water down the spine' feeling, and likely the first thought through our head is, 'I suck and I have no idea what I'm doing.' We need to stop ourselves from doing that, as it is route to madness, despair, and feelings of being an imposter, which is something that we can't let happen to good engineers. The better question to focus on is, 'Why did it make sense to me when I took that action?'"

In the meeting, we must reserve enough time for brainstorming and deciding which countermeasures to implement. Once the countermeasures have been identified, they must be prioritized and given an owner and timeline for implementation. Doing this further demonstrates that we value improvement of our daily work more than daily work itself.

Dan Milstein, one of the principal engineers at Hubspot, writes that he begins all blameless post-mortem meetings "by saying, 'We're trying to prepare for a future where we're as stupid as we are today.'" In other words, it is not acceptable to have a countermeasure to merely "be more careful" or "be less stupid"—instead, we must design real countermeasures to prevent these errors from happening again.

Examples of such countermeasures include new automated tests to detect dangerous conditions in our deployment pipeline, adding further production telemetry, identifying categories of changes that require additional peer review, and conducting rehearsals of this category of failure as part of regularly scheduled Game Day exercises.

PUBLISH OUR POST-MORTEMS AS WIDELY AS POSSIBLE

After we conduct a blameless post-mortem meeting, we should widely announce the availability of the meeting notes and any associated artifacts (e.g., timelines, IRC chat logs, external communications). This information should (ideally) be placed in a centralized location where our entire organization can access it and learn from the incident. Conducting post-mortems is so important that we may even prohibit production incidents from being closed until the post-mortem meeting has been completed.

Doing this helps us translate local learnings and improvements into global learnings and improvements. Randy Shoup, former engineering director for Google App Engine, describes how documentation of post-mortem meetings can have tremendous value to others in the organization, "As you can imagine at Google, everything is searchable. All the post-mortem documents are in places where other Googlers can see them. And trust me, when any group has an incident that sounds similar to something that happened before, these post-mortem documents are among the first documents being read and studied."[†]

Widely publishing post-mortems and encouraging others in the organization to read them increases organizational learning, and it also becoming increasingly commonplace for online service companies to publish post-mortems for customer-impacting outages. This often significantly increases the transparency we have with our internal and external customers, which in turn increases their trust in us.

This desire to conduct as many blameless post-mortem meetings as necessary at Etsy led to some problems—over the course of four years, Etsy accumulated a large number of post-mortem meeting notes in wiki pages, which became increasingly difficult to search, save, and collaborate from.

To help with this issue, they developed a tool called Morgue to easily record aspects of each accident, such as the incident MTTR and severity, better address

---

[†] We may also choose to extend the philosophies of Transparent Uptime to our post-mortem reports and, in addition to making a service dashboard available to the public, we may choose to publish (maybe sanitized) post-mortem meetings to the public. Some of the most widely admired public post-mortems include those posted by the Google App Engine team after a significant 2010 outage, as well as the post-mortem of the 2015 Amazon DynamoDB outage. Interestingly, Chef publishes their post-mortem meeting notes on their blog, as well as recorded videos of the actual post-mortem meetings.

time zones (which became relevant as more Etsy employees were working remotely), and include other data, such as rich text in Markdown format, embedded images, tags, and history.

Morgue was designed to make it easy for the team to record:

- Whether the problem was due to a scheduled or an unscheduled incident

- The post-mortem owner

- Relevant IRC chat logs (especially important for 3 a.m. issues when accurate note-taking may not happen)

- Relevant JIRA tickets for corrective actions and their due dates (information particularly important to management)

- Links to customer forum posts (where customers complain about issues)

After developing and using Morgue, the number of recorded post-mortems at Etsy increased significantly compared to when they used wiki pages, especially for P2, P3, and P4 incidents (i.e., lower severity problems). This result reinforced the hypothesis that if they made it easier to document post-mortems through tools such as Morgue, more people would record and detail the outcomes of their post-mortem meetings, enabling more organizational learning.

Dr. Amy C. Edmondson, Novartis Professor of Leadership and Management at Harvard Business School and co-author of *Building the Future: Big Teaming for Audacious Innovation,* writes:

> Again, the remedy—which does not necessarily involve much time and expense—is to reduce the stigma of failure. Eli Lilly has done this since the early 1990s by holding 'failure parties' to honor intelligent, high-quality scientific experiments that fail to achieve the desired results. The parties don't cost much, and redeploying valuable resources—particularly scientists—to new projects earlier rather than later can save hundreds of thousands of dollars, not to mention kickstart potential new discoveries.

DECREASE INCIDENT TOLERANCES TO FIND EVER-WEAKER FAILURE SIGNALS

Inevitably, as organizations learn how to see and solve problems efficiently, they need to decrease the threshold of what constitutes a problem in order to keep learning. To do this, we seek to amplify weak failure signals. For example, as described in chapter 4, when Alcoa was able to reduce the rate of workplace accidents so that they were no longer commonplace, Paul O'Neill, CEO of Alcoa, started to be notified of accident near-misses in addition to actual workplace accidents.

Dr. Spear summarizes O'Neill's accomplishments at Alcoa when he writes, "Though it started by focusing on problems related to workplace safety, it soon found that safety problems reflected process ignorance and that this ignorance would also manifest itself in other problems such as quality, timeliness, and yield versus scrap."

When we work within complex systems, this need to amplify weak failure signals is critical to averting catastrophic failures. The way NASA handled failure signals during the space shuttle era serves as an illustrative example: In 2003, sixteen days into the *Columbia* space shuttle mission, it exploded as it re-entered the earth's atmosphere. We now know that a piece of insulating foam had broken off the external fuel tank during takeoff.

However, prior to *Columbia's* re-entry, a handful of mid-level NASA engineers had reported this incident, but their voices had gone unheard. They observed the foam strike on video monitors during a post-launch review session and immediately notified NASA's managers, but they were told that the foam issue was nothing new. Foam dislodgement had damaged shuttles in previous launches, but had never resulted in an accident. It was considered a maintenance problem and not acted upon until it was too late.

Michael Roberto, Richard M.J. Bohmer, and Amy C. Edmondson wrote in a 2006 article for *Harvard Business Review* how NASA culture contributed to this problem. They describe how organizations are typically structured in one of two models: a *standardized model*, where routine and systems govern everything, including strict compliance with timelines and budgets, or an *experimental model*, where every day every exercise and every piece of new information is evaluated and debated in a culture that resembles a research and design (R&D) laboratory.

They observe, "Firms get into trouble when they apply the wrong mind-set to an organization [which dictates how they respond to *ambiguous threats* or, in the terminology of this book, *weak failure signals*]....By the 1970s, NASA had created a culture of rigid standardization, promoting to Congress the space shuttle as a cheap and reusable spacecraft." NASA favored strict process compliance instead of an experimental model where every piece of information needed to be evaluated as it occured without bias. The absence of continuous learning and experimentation had dire consequences. The authors conclude that it is culture and mind-set that matters, not just "being careful"—as they write, "vigilance alone will not prevent ambiguous threats [weak failure signals] from turning into costly (and sometimes tragic) failures."

Our work in the technology value stream, like space travel, should be approached as a fundamentally experimental endeavor and managed that way. All work we do is a potentially important hypothesis and a source of data, rather than a routine application and validation of past practice. Instead of treating technology work as entirely standardized, where we strive for process compliance, we must continually seek to find ever-weaker failure signals so that we can better understand and manage the system we operate in.

REDEFINE FAILURE AND ENCOURAGE CALCULATED RISK-TAKING

Leaders of an organization, whether deliberately or inadvertently, reinforce the organizational culture and values through their actions. Audit, accounting, and ethics experts have long observed that the "tone at the top" predicts the likelihood of fraud and other unethical practices. To reinforce our culture of learning and calculated risk-taking, we need leaders to continually reinforce that everyone should feel both comfortable with and responsible for surfacing and learning from failures.

On failures, Roy Rapoport from Netflix observes, "What the 2014 *State of DevOps Report* proved to me is that high performing DevOps organizations will fail and make mistakes more often. Not only is this okay, it's what organizations need! You can even see it in the data: if high performers are performing thirty times more frequently but with only half the change failure rate, they're obviously having more failures."

He continues, "I was talking with a co-worker about a massive outage we just had at Netflix—it was caused by, frankly, a dumb mistake. In fact, it was caused by an engineer who had taken down Netflix twice in the last eighteen months.

But, of course, this is a person we'd never fire. In that same eighteen months, this engineer moved the state of our operations and automation forward not by miles but by light-years. That work has enabled us to do deployments safely on a daily basis, and has personally performed huge numbers of production deployments."

He concludes, "DevOps must allow this sort of innovation and the resulting risks of people making mistakes. Yes, you'll have more failures in production. But that's a good thing, and should not be punished."

INJECT PRODUCTION FAILURES TO ENABLE RESILIENCE AND LEARNING

As we saw in the chapter introduction, injecting faults into the production environment (such as Chaos Monkey) is one way we can increase our resilience. In this section, we describe the processes involved in rehearsing and injecting failures into our system to confirm that we have designed and architected our systems properly, so that failures happen in specific and controlled ways. We do this by regularly (or even continuously) performing tests to make certain that our systems fail gracefully.

As Michael Nygard, author of *Release It! Design and Deploy Production-Ready Software,* comments, "Like building crumple zones into cars to absorb impacts and keep passengers safe, you can decide what features of the system are indispensable and build in failure modes that keep cracks away from those features. If you do not design your failure modes, then you will get whatever unpredictable—and usually dangerous—ones happen to emerge."

Resilience requires that we first define our failure modes and then perform testing to ensure that these failure modes operate as designed. One way we do this is by injecting faults into our production environment and rehearsing large-scale failures so we are confident we can recover from accidents when they occur, ideally without even impacting our customers.

The 2012 story about Netflix and the Amazon AWS-EAST outage presented in the introduction is just one example. An even more interesting example of resilience at Netflix was during the "Great Amazon Reboot of 2014," when nearly 10% of the entire Amazon EC2 server fleet had to be rebooted to apply an emergency Xen security patch. As Christos Kalantzis of Netflix Cloud Database Engineering recalled, "When we got the news about the emergency EC2 reboots, our jaws dropped. When we got the list of how many Cassandra nodes would be affected, I felt ill."But, Kalantzis continues, "Then I remembered all the Chaos Monkey exercises we've gone through. My reaction was, 'Bring it on!'"

Once again, the outcomes were astonishing. Of the 2,700+ Cassandra nodes used in production, 218 were rebooted, and twenty-two didn't reboot successfully. As Kalantzis and Bruce Wong from Netflix Chaos Engineering wrote, "Netflix experienced 0 downtime that weekend. Repeatedly and regularly exercising failure, even in the persistence [database] layer, should be part of every company's resilience planning. If it wasn't for Cassandra's participation in Chaos Monkey, this story would have ended much differently."

Even more surprising, not only was no one at Netflix working active incidents due to failed Cassandra nodes, no one was even in the office—they were in Hollywood at a party celebrating an acquisition milestone. This is another example demonstrating that proactively focusing on resilience often means that a firm can handle events that may cause crises for most organizations in a manner that is routine and mundane.† (See Appendix 9.)

INSTITUTE GAME DAYS TO REHEARSE FAILURES

In this section, we describe specific disaster recovery rehearsals called Game Days, a term popularized by Jesse Robbins, one of the founders of the Velocity Conference community and co-founder of Chef, for the work he did at Amazon, where he was responsible for programs to ensure site availability and was widely known internally as the "Master of Disaster."The concept of Game Days comes from the discipline of *resilience engineering*. Robbins defines resilience engineering as "an exercise designed to increase resilience through large-scale fault injection across critical systems."

---

† Specific architectural patterns that they implemented included fail fasts (setting aggressive timeouts such that failing components don't make the entire system crawl to a halt), fallbacks (designing each feature to degrade or fall back to a lower quality representation), and feature removal (removing non-critical features when they run slowly from any given page to prevent them from impacting the member experience). Another astonishing example of the resilience that the Netflix team created beyond preserving business continuity during the AWS outage, was that Netflix went over six hours into the AWS outage before declaring a Sev 1 incident, assuming that AWS service would eventually be restored (i.e., "AWS will come back... it usually does, right?"). Only after six hours into the outage did they activate any business continuity procedures.

Robbins observes that "whenever you set out to engineer a system at scale, the best you can hope for is to build a reliable software platform on top of components that are completely unreliable. That puts you in an environment where complex failures are both inevitable and unpredictable."

Consequently, we must ensure that services continue to operate when failures occur, potentially throughout our system, ideally without crisis or even manual intervention. As Robbins quips, "a service is not really tested until we break it in production."

Our goal for Game Day is to help teams simulate and rehearse accidents to give them the ability to practice. First, we schedule a catastrophic event, such as the simulated destruction of an entire data center, to happen at some point in the future. We then give teams time to prepare, to eliminate all the single points of failure, and to create the necessary monitoring procedures, failover procedures, etc.

Our Game Day team defines and executes drills, such as conducting database failovers (i.e., simulating a database failure and ensuring that the secondary database works) or turning off an important network connection to expose problems in the defined processes. Any problems or difficulties that are encountered are identified, addressed, and tested again.

At the scheduled time, we then execute the outage. As Robbins describes, at Amazon they "would literally power off a facility—without notice—and then let the systems fail naturally and [allow] the people to follow their processes wherever they led."

By doing this, we start to expose the *latent defects* in our system, which are the problems that appear only because of having injected faults into the system. Robbins explains, "You might discover that certain monitoring or management systems crucial to the recovery process end up getting turned off as part of the failure you've orchestrated. [Or] you would find some single points of failure you didn't know about that way." These exercises are then conducted in an increasingly intense and complex way with the goal of making them feel like just another part of an average day.

By executing Game Days, we progressively create a more resilient service and a higher degree of assurance that we can resume operations when inopportune events occur, as well create more learnings and a more resilient organization.

An excellent example of simulating disaster is Google's Disaster Recovery Program (DiRT). Kripa Krishnan is a technical program director at Google, and, at the time of this writing, has led the program for over seven years. During that time, they've simulated an earthquake in Silicon Valley, which resulted in the entire Mountain View campus being disconnected from Google; major data centers having complete loss of power; and even aliens attacking cities where engineers resided.

As Krishnan wrote, "An often-overlooked area of testing is business process and communications. Systems and processes are highly intertwined, and separating testing of systems from testing of business processes isn't realistic: a failure of a business system will affect the business process, and conversely a working system is not very useful without the right personnel."

Some of the learnings gained during these disasters included:

- When connectivity was lost, the failover to the engineer work-stations didn't work

- Engineers didn't know how to access a conference call bridge or the bridge only had capacity for fifty people or they needed a new conference call provider who would allow them to kick off engi-neers who had subjected the entire conference to hold music

- When the data centers ran out of diesel for the backup generators, no one knew the procedures for making emergency purchases through the supplier, resulting in someone using a personal credit card to purchase $50,000 worth of diesel.

By creating failure in a controlled situation, we can practice and create the playbooks we need. One of the other outputs of Game Days is that people actually know who to call and know who to talk to—by doing this, they develop relationships with people in other departments so they can work together during an incident, turning conscious actions into unconscious actions that are able to become routine.

CONCLUSION

To create a just culture that enables organizational learning, we have to re-contextualize so-called failures. When treated properly, errors that are inherent in complex systems can create a dynamic learning environment where all of the shareholders feel safe enough to come forward with ideas and observations, and where groups rebound more readily from projects that don't perform as expected.

Both blameless post-mortems and injecting production failures reinforce a culture that everyone should feel both comfortable with and responsible for surfacing and learning from failures. In fact, when we sufficiently reduce the number of accidents, we decrease our tolerance so that we can keep learning. As Peter Senge is known to say, "The only sustainable competitive advantage is an organization's ability to learn faster than the competition."

20 Convert Local Discoveries into Global Improvements

In the previous chapter, we discussed developing a safe learning culture by encouraging everyone to talk about mistakes and accidents through blameless post-mortems. We also explored finding and fixing ever-weaker failure signals, as well as reinforcing and rewarding experimentation and risk-taking. Furthermore, we helped make our system of work more resilient by proactively scheduling and testing failure scenarios, making our systems safer by finding latent defects and fixing them.

In this chapter, we will create mechanisms that make it possible for new learnings and improvements discovered locally to be captured and shared globally throughout the entire organization, multiplying the effect of global knowledge and improvement. By doing this, we elevate the state of the practice of the entire organization so that everyone doing work benefits from the cumulative experience of the organization.

USE CHAT ROOMS AND CHAT BOTS TO AUTOMATE AND CAPTURE ORGANIZATIONAL KNOWLEDGE

Many organizations have created chat rooms to facilitate fast communication within teams. However, chat rooms are also used to trigger automation.

This technique was pioneered in the ChatOps journey at GitHub. The goal was to put automation tools into the middle of the conversation in their chat rooms, helping create transparency and documentation of their work. As Jesse Newland, a systems engineer at GitHub, describes, "Even when you're new to the team, you can look in the chat logs and see how everything is done. It's as if you were pair-programming with them all the time."

They created *Hubot*, a software application that interacted with the Ops team in their chat rooms, where it could be instructed to perform actions merely by sending it a command (e.g., "@hubot deploy owl to production"). The results would also be sent back into the chat room.

Having this work performed by automation in the chat room (as opposed to running automated scripts via command line) had numerous benefits, including:

- Everyone saw everything that was happening.

- Engineers on their first day of work could see what daily work looked like and how it was performed.

- People were more apt to ask for help when they saw others helping each other.

- Rapid organizational learning was enabled and accumulated.

Furthermore, beyond the above tested benefits, chat rooms inherently record and make all communications public; in contrast, emails are private by default, and the information in them cannot easily be discovered or propagated within an organization.

Integrating our automation into chat rooms helps document and share our observations and problem solving as an inherent part of performing our work. This reinforces a culture of transparency and collaboration in everything we do.

This is also an extremely effective way of converting local learning to global knowledge. At Github, all the Operations staff worked remotely—in fact, no two engineers worked in the same city. As Mark Imbriaco, former VP of Operations at GitHub, recalls, "There was no physical water cooler at GitHub. The chat room was the water cooler."

Github enabled Hubot to trigger their automation technologies, including Puppet, Capistrano, Jenkins, resque (a Redis-backed library for creating background jobs), and graphme (which generates graphs from Graphite).

Actions performed through Hubot included checking the health of services, doing puppet pushes or code deployments into production, and muting alerts as services went into maintenance mode. Actions that were performed multiple times, such as pulling up the smoke test logs when a deployment failed, taking production servers out of rotation, reverting to master for production front-end services, or even apologizing to the engineers who were on call, also became Hubot actions.[†]

Similarly, commits to the source code repository and the commands that trigger production deployments both emit messages to the chat room. Additionally, as changes move through the deployment pipeline, their status is posted in the chat room.

A typical quick chat room exchange might look like:

> "@sr: @jnewland, how do you get that list of big repos? disk_hogs or something?"

> "@jnewland: /disk-hogs"

Newland observes that certain questions that were previously asked during the course of a project are rarely asked now. For example, engineers may ask each other, "How is that deploy going?" or "Are you deploying that, or should I?" or "How does the load look?"

Among all the benefits that Newland describes, which include faster onboarding of newer engineers and making all engineers more productive, the result that he felt was most important was that Ops work became more humane as Ops engineers were enabled to discover problems and help each other quickly and easily.

GitHub created an environment for collaborative local learning that could be transformed into learnings across the organization. Throughout the rest of this chapter we will explore ways to create and accelerate the spread of new organizational learnings.

AUTOMATE STANDARDIZED PROCESSES IN SOFTWARE FOR RE-USE

All too often, we codify our standards and processes for architecture, testing, deployment, and infrastructure management in prose, storing them in Word documents that are uploaded somewhere. The problem is that engineers who are building new applications or environments often don't know that these

---

† Hubot often performed tasks by calling shell scripts, which could then be executed from the chat room anywhere, including from an engineer's phone.

documents exist, or they don't have the time to implement the documented standards. The result is they create their own tools and processes, with all the disappointing outcomes we'd expect: fragile, insecure, and unmaintainable applications and environments that are expensive to run, maintain, and evolve.

Instead of putting our expertise into Word documents, we need to transform these documented standards and processes, which encompass the sum of our organizational learnings and knowledge, into an executable form that makes them easier to reuse. One of the best ways we can make this knowledge re-usable is by putting it into a centralized source code repository, making the tool available for everyone to search and use.

Justin Arbuckle was chief architect at GE Capital in 2013 when he said, "We needed to create a mechanism that would allow teams to easily comply with policy—national, regional, and industry regulations across dozens of regulatory frameworks, spanning thousands of applications running on tens of thousands of servers in tens of data centers."

The mechanism they created was called ArchOps, which "enabled our engineers to be builders, not bricklayers. By putting our design standards into automated blueprints that were able to be used easily by anyone, we achieved consistency as a byproduct."

By encoding our manual processes into code that is automated and executed, we enable the process to be widely adopted, providing value to anyone who uses them. Arbuckle concluded that "the actual compliance of an organization is in direct proportion to the degree to which its policies are expressed as code."

By making this automated process the easiest means to achieve the goal, we allow practices to be widely adopted—we may even consider turning them into shared services supported by the organization.

CREATE A SINGLE, SHARED SOURCE CODE REPOSITORY FOR OUR ENTIRE ORGANIZATION

A firm-wide, shared source code repository is one of the most powerful mechanisms used to integrate local discoveries across the entire organization. When we update anything in the source code repository (e.g., a shared library), it rapidly and automatically propagates to every other service that uses that library, and it is integrated through each team's deployment pipeline.

Google is one of the largest examples of using an organization-wide shared source code repository. By 2015, Google had a single shared source code repository with over one billion files and over two billion lines of code. This repository is used by every one of their twenty-five thousand engineers and spans every Google property, including Google Search, Google Maps, Google Docs, Google+, Google Calendar, Gmail, and YouTube.[†]

One of the valuable results of this is that engineers can leverage the diverse expertise of everyone in the organization. Rachel Potvin, a Google engineering manager overseeing the Developer Infrastructure group, told *Wired* that every Google engineer can access "a wealth of libraries" because "almost everything has already been done."

Furthermore, as Eran Messeri, an engineer in the Google Developer Infrastructure group, explains, one of the advantages of using a single repository is that it allows users to easily access all of the code in its most up-to-date form, without the need for coordination.

We put into our shared source code repository not only source code, but also other artifacts that encode knowledge and learning, including:

- Configuration standards for our libraries, infrastructure, and environments (Chef recipes, Puppet manifests, etc.)

- Deployment tools

- Testing standards and tools, including security

- Deployment pipeline tools

- Monitoring and analysis tools

- Tutorials and standards

Encoding knowledge and sharing it through this repository is one of the most powerful mechanisms we have for propagating knowledge. As Randy Shoup describes, "The most powerful mechanism for preventing failures at Google is the single code repository. Whenever someone checks in anything into the repo, it results in a new build, which always uses the latest version of every-

---

† The Chrome and Android projects reside in a separate source code repository, and certain algorithms that are kept secret, such as PageRank, are available only to certain teams.

thing. Everything is built from source rather than dynamically linked at runtime—there is always a single version of a library that is the current one in use, which is what gets statically linked during the build process."

Tom Limoncelli is the co-author of *The Practice of Cloud System Administration: Designing and Operating Large Distributed Systems* and a former Site Reliability Engineer at Google. In his book, he states that the value of having a single repository for an entire organization is so powerful it is difficult to even explain.

> You can write a tool exactly once and have it be usable for all projects. You have 100% accurate knowledge of who depends on a library; therefore, you can refactor it and be 100% sure of who will be affected and who needs to test for breakage. I could probably list one hundred more examples. I can't express in words how much of a competitive advantage this is for Google.

At Google, every library (e.g., libc, OpenSSL, as well internally developed libraries such as Java threading libraries) has an owner who is responsible for ensuring that the library not only compiles, but also successfully passes the tests for all projects that depend upon it, much like a real-world librarian. That owner is also responsible for migrating each project from one version to the next.

Consider the real-life example of an organization that runs eighty-one different versions of the Java Struts framework library in production—all but one of those versions have critical security vulnerabilities, and maintaining all those versions, each with its own quirks and idiosyncrasies, creates significant operational burden and stress. Furthermore, all this variance makes upgrading versions risky and unsafe, which in turn discourages developers from upgrading. And the cycle continues.

The single source repository solves much of this problem, as well as having automated tests that allow teams to migrate to new versions safely and confidently.

If we are not able to build everything off a single source tree, we must find another means to maintain known good versions of the libraries and their dependencies. For instance, we may have an organization-wide repository such as Nexus, Artifactory, or a Debian or RPM repository, which we must then update where there are known vulnerabilities, both in these repositories and in production systems.

SPREAD KNOWLEDGE BY USING AUTOMATED TESTS AS DOCUMENTATION AND COMMUNITIES OF PRACTICE

When we have shared libraries being used across the organization, we should enable rapid propagation of expertise and improvements. Ensuring that each of these libraries has significant amounts of automated testing included means these libraries become self-documenting and show other engineers how to use them.

This benefit will be nearly automatic if we have test-driven development (TDD) practices in place, where automated tests are written before we write the code. This discipline turns our test suites into a living, up-to-date specification of the system. Any engineer wishing to understand how to use the system can look at the test suite to find working examples of how to use the system's API.

Ideally, each library will have a single owner or a single team supporting it, representing where knowledge and expertise for the library resides. Furthermore, we should (ideally) only allow one version to be used in production, ensuring that whatever is in production leverages the best collective knowledge of the organization.

In this model, the library owner is also responsible for safely migrating each group using the repository from one version to the next. This in turn requires quick detection of regression errors through comprehensive automated testing and continuous integration for all systems that use the library.

In order to more rapidly propagate knowledge, we can also create discussion groups or chat rooms for each library or service, so anyone who has questions can get responses from other users, who are often faster to respond than the developers.

By using this type of communication tool instead of having isolated pockets of expertise spread throughout the organization, we facilitate an exchange of knowledge and experience, ensuring that workers are able to help each other with problems and new patterns.

DESIGN FOR OPERATIONS THROUGH CODIFIED NON-FUNCTIONAL REQUIREMENTS

When Development follows their work downstream and participates in production incident resolution activities, the application becomes increasingly better designed for Operations. Furthermore, as we start to deliberately design our code and application so that it can accommodate fast flow and deployability, we will likely identify a set of non-functional requirements that we will want to integrate into all of our production services.

Implementing these non-functional requirements will enable our services to be easy to deploy and keep running in production, where we can quickly detect and correct problems, and ensure it degrades gracefully when components fail. Examples of non-functional requirements include ensuring that we have:

- Sufficient production telemetry in our applications and environments

- The ability to accurately track dependencies

- Services that are resilient and degrade gracefully

- Forward and backward compatibility between versions

- The ability to archive data to manage the size of the production data set

- The ability to easily search and understand log messages across services

- The ability to trace requests from users through multiple services

- Simple, centralized runtime configuration using feature flags and so forth

By codifying these types of non-functional requirements, we make it easier for all our new and existing services to leverage the collective knowledge and experience of the organization. These are all responsibilities of the team building the service.

BUILD REUSABLE OPERATIONS USER STORIES INTO DEVELOPMENT

When there is Operations work that cannot be fully automated or made self-service, our goal is to make this recurring work as repeatable and deterministic as possible. We do this by standardizing the needed work, automating as much as possible, and documenting our work so that we can best enable product teams to better plan and resource this activity.

Instead of manually building servers and then putting them into production according to manual checklists, we should automate as much of this work as possible. Where certain steps cannot be automated (e.g., manually racking a server and having another team cable it), we should collectively define the handoffs as clearly as possible to reduce lead times and errors. This will also enable us to better plan and schedule these steps in the future. For instance, we can use tools such as Rundeck to automate and execute workflows, or work ticket systems such as JIRA or ServiceNow.

Ideally, for all our recurring Ops work we will know the following: what work is required, who is needed to perform it, what the steps to complete it are, and so forth. For instance, "We know a high-availability rollout takes fourteen steps, requiring work from four different teams, and the last five times we performed this, it took an average of three days."

Just as we create user stories in Development that we put into the backlog and then pull into work, we can create well-defined "Ops user stories" that represent work activities that can be reused across all our projects (e.g., deployment, capacity, security, etc.). By creating these well defined Ops user stories, we expose repeatable IT Operations work in a manner where it shows up alongside Development work, enabling better planning and more repeatable outcomes.

ENSURE TECHNOLOGY CHOICES HELP ACHIEVE ORGANIZATIONAL GOALS

When one of our goals is to maximize developer productivity and we have service-oriented architectures, small service teams can potentially build and run their service in whatever language or framework that best serves their specific needs. In some cases, this is what best enables us to achieve our organizational goals.

However, there are scenarios when the opposite occurs, such as when expertise for a critical service resides only in one team, and only that team can make changes or fix problems, creating a bottleneck. In other words, we may have optimized for team productivity but inadvertently impeded the achievement of organizational goals.

This often happens when we have a functionally-oriented Operations group that is responsible for any aspect of service support. In these scenarios, to ensure that we enable the deep skill sets in specific technologies, we want to make sure that Operations can influence which components are used in production, or give them the ability to not be responsible for unsupported platforms.

If we do not have a list of technologies that Operations will support, collectively generated by Development and Operations, we should systematically go through the production infrastructure and services, as well as all their dependencies that are currently supported, to find which ones are creating a disproportionate amount of failure demand and unplanned work. Our goal is to identify the technologies that:

- Impede or slow down the flow of work

- Disproportionately create high levels of unplanned work

- Disproportionately create large numbers of support requests

- Are most inconsistent with our desired architectural outcomes (e.g. throughput, stability, security, reliability, business continuity)

By removing these problematic infrastructures and platforms from the technologies supported by Ops, we enable them to focus on infrastructure that best helps achieve the global goals of the organization.

As Tom Limoncelli describes, "When I was at Google, we had one official compiled language, one official scripting language, and one official UI language. Yes, other languages were supported in some way or another, but sticking with 'the big three' meant support libraries, tools, and an easier way to find collaborators."[†] These standards were also reinforced by the code review process, as well as what languages were supported by their internal platforms.

In a presentation that he gave with Olivier Jacques and Rafael Garcia at the 2015 DevOps Enterprise Summit, Ralph Loura, CIO of HP, stated:

---

† Google used C++ as their official compiled language, Python (and later Go) as their official scripting language, and Java and JavaScript via Google Web Toolkit as their official UI languages.

Internally, we described our goal as creating "buoys, not boundaries." Instead of drawing hard boundaries that everyone has to stay within, we put buoys that indicate deep areas of the channel where you're safe and supported. You can go past the buoys as long as you follow the organizational principles. After all, how are we ever going to see the next innovation that helps us win if we're not exploring and testing at the edges? As leaders, we need to navigate the channel, mark the channel, and allow people to explore past it.

Case Study
Standardizing a New Technology
Stack at Etsy (2010)

In many organizations adopting DevOps, a common story developers tell is, "Ops wouldn't provide us what we needed, so we just built and supported it ourselves." However, in the early stages of the Etsy transformation, technology leadership took the opposite approach, significantly reducing the number of supported technologies in production.

In 2010, after a nearly disastrous peak holiday season, the Etsy team decided to massively reduce the number of technologies used in production, choosing a few that the entire organization could fully support and eradicating the rest.[‡]

Their goal was to standardize and very deliberately reduce the supported infrastructure and configurations. One of the early decisions was to migrate Etsy's entire platform to PHP and MySQL. This was primarily a philosophical decision rather than a technological decision—they wanted both Dev and Ops to be able to understand the full technology stack so that everyone could contribute to a single platform, as well as enable everyone to be able to read, rewrite, and fix each other's code. Over the next several years, as Michael Rembetsy, who was Etsy's Director of Operations at the time, recalls, "We retired some great technologies, taking them entirely out of production," including lighttpd, Postgres, MongoDB, Scala, CoffeeScript, Python, and many others.

Similarly, Dan McKinley, a developer on the feature team that introduced MongoDB into Etsy in 2010, writes on his blog that all the benefits of having a schema-less database were negated by all the operational problems the

---

‡ At that time, Etsy used PHP, lighttp, Postgres, MongoDB, Scala, CoffeeScript, Python, as well as many other platforms and languages.

team had to solve. These included problems concerning logging, graphing, monitoring, production telemetry, and backups and restoration, as well as numerous other issues that developers typically do not need to concern themselves with. The result was to abandon MongoDB, porting the new service to use the already supported MySQL database infrastructure.

CONCLUSION

The techniques described in this chapter enable every new learning to be incorporated into the collective knowledge of the organization, multiplying its effect. We do this by actively and widely communicating new knowledge, such as through chat rooms and through technology such as architecture as code, shared source code repositories, technology standardization, and so forth. By doing this, we elevate the state of the practice of not just Dev and Ops, but also the entire organization, so everyone who performs work does so with the cumulative experience of the entire organization.

21

Reserve Time to Create Organizational Learning and Improvement

One of the practices that forms part of the Toyota Production System is called the *improvement blitz* (or sometimes a *kaizen blitz*), defined as a dedicated and concentrated period of time to address a particular issue, often over the course of a several days. Dr. Spear explains, "...blitzes often take this form: A group is gathered to focus intently on a process with problems...The blitz lasts a few days, the objective is process improvement, and the means are the concentrated use of people from outside the process to advise those normally inside the process."

Spear observes that the output of the improvement blitz team will often be a new approach to solving a problem, such as new layouts of equipment, new means of conveying material and information, a more organized workspace, or standardized work. They may also leave behind a to-do list of changes to be made down the road.

An example of a DevOps improvement blitz is the Monthly Challenge program at the Target DevOps Dojo. Ross Clanton, Director of Operations at Target, is responsible for accelerating the adoption of DevOps. One of his primary mechanisms for this is the Technology Innovation Center, more popularly known as the DevOps Dojo.

The DevOps Dojo occupies about eighteen thousand square feet of open office space, where DevOps coaches help teams from across the Target technology organization elevate the state of their practice. The most intensive format is what they call "30-Day Challenges," where internal development teams come in for a month and work together with dedicated Dojo coaches and engineers. The team brings their work with them, with the goal of solving an internal problem they have been struggling with and to create a breakthrough in thirty days.

Throughout the thirty days, they work intensively with the Dojo coaches on the problem—planning, working, and doing demos in two-day sprints. When the 30-Day Challenge is complete, the internal teams return to their lines of business, not only having solved a significant problem, but bringing their new learnings back to their teams.

Clanton describes, "We currently have capacity to have eight teams doing 30-Day Challenges concurrently, so we are focused on the most strategic projects of the organization. So far, we've had some of our most critical capabilities come through the Dojo, including teams from Point Of Sale (POS), Inventory, Pricing, and Promotion."

By having full-time assigned Dojo staff and being focused on only one objective, teams going through a 30-Day Challenge make incredible improvements.

Ravi Pandey, a Target development manager who went through this program, explains, "In the old days, we would have to wait six weeks to get a test environment. Now, we get it in minutes, and we're working side by side with Ops engineers who are helping us increase our productivity and building tooling for us to help us achieve our goals." Clanton expands on this idea, "It is not uncommon for teams to achieve in days what would usually take them three to six months. So far, two hundred learners have come through the Dojo, having completed fourteen challenges."

The Dojo also supports less intensive engagement models, including Flash Builds, where teams come together for one- to three-day events, with the goal of shipping a minimal viable product (MVP) or a capability by the end of the event. They also host Open Labs every two weeks, where anyone can visit the Dojo to talk to the Dojo coaches, attend demos, or receive training.

In this chapter, we will describe this and other ways of reserving time for organizational learning and improvement, further institutionalizing the practice of dedicating time for improving daily work.

INSTITUTIONALIZE RITUALS TO PAY DOWN TECHNICAL DEBT

In this section, we schedule rituals that help enforce the practice of reserving Dev and Ops time for improvement work, such as nonfunctional requirements, automation, etc. One of the easiest ways to do this is to schedule and conduct day- or week-long improvement blitzes, where everyone on a team (or in the entire organization) self-organizes to fix problems they care about—no feature work is allowed. It could be a problematic area of the code, environment, architecture, tooling, and so forth. These teams span the entire value stream, often combining Development, Operations, and Infosec engineers. Teams that typically don't work together combine their skills and effort to improve a chosen area and then demonstrate their improvement to the rest of the company.

In addition to the Lean-oriented terms kaizen blitz and improvement blitz, the technique of dedicated rituals for improvement work has also been called *spring* or *fall cleanings* and *ticket queue inversion weeks*. Other terms have also been used, such as *hack days, hackathons,* and *20% innovation time*. Unfortunately, these specific rituals sometimes focus on product innovation and prototyping new market ideas, rather than on improvement work, and worse, they are often restricted to developers—which is considerably different than the goals of an improvement blitz.[†]

Our goal during these blitzes is not to simply experiment and innovate for the sake of testing out new technologies, but to improve our daily work, such as solving our daily workarounds. While experiments can also lead to improvements, improvement blitzes are very focused on solving specific problems we encounter in our daily work.

We may schedule week-long improvement blitzes that prioritize Dev and Ops working together toward improvement goals. These improvement blitzes are simple to administer: One week is selected where everyone in the technology organization works on an improvement activity at the same time. At the end of the period, each team makes a presentation to their peers that discusses the problem they were tackling and what they built. This practice reinforces a culture in which engineers work across the entire value stream to solve problems. Furthermore, it reinforces fixing problems as part of our daily work and demonstrates that we value paying down technical debt.

What makes improvement blitzes so powerful is that we are empowering those closest to the work to continually identify and solve their own problems. Consider for a moment that our complex system is like a spider web, with intertwining strands that are constantly weakening and breaking. If the right combination of strands breaks, the entire web collapses. There is no amount of command-and-control management that can direct workers to fix each strand one by one. Instead, we must create the organizational culture and norms that lead to everyone continually finding and fixing broken strands as

---

† From here on, the terms "hack week" and "hackathon" are used interchangeably with "improvement blitz," and not in the context of "you can work on whatever you want."

part of our daily work. As Dr. Spear observes, "No wonder then that spiders repair rips and tears in the web as they occur, not waiting for the failures to accumulate."

A great example of the success of the improvement blitz concept is described by Mark Zuckerberg, Facebook CEO. In an interview with Jessica Stillman of Inc.com, he says, "Every few months we have a hackathon, where everyone builds prototypes for new ideas they have. At the end, the whole team gets together and looks at everything that has been built. Many of our most successful products came out of hackathons, including Timeline, chat, video, our mobile development framework and some of our most important infrastructure like the HipHop compiler."

Of particular interest is the HipHop PHP compiler. In 2008, Facebook was facing significant capacity problems, with over one-hundred million active users and rapidly growing, creating tremendous problems for the entire engineering team. During a hack day, Haiping Zhao, Senior Server Engineer at Facebook, started experimenting with converting PHP code to compilable C++ code, with the hope of significantly increasing the capacity of their existing infrastructure. Over the next two years, a small team was assembled to build what became known as the HipHop compiler, converting all Facebook production services from interpreted PHP to compiled C++ binaries. HipHop enabled Facebook's platform to handle six times higher production loads than the native PHP.

In an interview with Cade Metz of *Wired*, Drew Paroski, one of the engineers who worked on the project, noted, "There was a moment where, if HipHop hadn't been there, we would have been in hot water. We would probably have needed more machines to serve the site than we could have gotten in time. It was a Hail Mary pass that worked out."

Later, Paroski and fellow engineers Keith Adams and Jason Evans decided that they could beat the performance of the HipHop compiler effort and reduce some of its limitations that reduced developer productivity. The resulting project was the HipHop virtual machine project ("HHVM"), taking a just-in-time compilation approach. By 2012, HHVM had completely replaced the HipHop compiler in production, with nearly twenty engineers contributing to the project.

By performing regularly scheduled improvement blitzes and hack weeks, we enable everyone in the value stream to take pride and ownership in the innovations they create, and we continually integrate improvements into our system, further enabling safety, reliability, and learning.

ENABLE EVERYONE TO TEACH AND LEARN

A dynamic culture of learning creates conditions so that everyone can not only learn, but also teach, whether through traditional didactic methods (e.g., people taking classes, attending training) or more experiential or open methods (e.g., conferences, workshops, mentoring). One way that we can foster this teaching and learning is to dedicate organizational time to it.

Steve Farley, VP of Information Technology at Nationwide Insurance, said, "We have five thousand technology professionals, who we call 'associates.' Since 2011, we have been committed to create a culture of learning—part of that is something we call Teaching Thursday, where each week we create time for our associates to learn. For two hours, each associate is expected to teach or learn. The topics are whatever our associates want to learn about—some of them are on technology, on new software development or process improvement techniques, or even on how to better manage their career. The most valuable thing any associate can do is mentor or learn from other associates."

As has been made evident throughout this book, certain skills are becoming increasingly needed by all engineers, not just by developers. For instance, it is becoming more important for all Operations and Test engineers to be familiar with Development techniques, rituals, and skills, such as version control, automated testing, deployment pipelines, configuration management, and creating automation. Familiarity with Development techniques helps Operations engineers remain relevant as more technology value streams adopt DevOps principles and patterns.

Although the prospect of learning something new may be intimidating or cause a sense of embarrassment or shame, it shouldn't. After all, we are all lifelong learners, and one of the best ways to learn is from our peers. Karthik Gaekwad, who was part of the National Instruments DevOps transformation, said, "For Operations people who are trying to learn automation, it shouldn't be scary—just ask a friendly developer, because they would love to help."

We can help further help teach skills through our daily work by jointly performing code reviews that include both parties so that we learn by doing, as well as by having Development and Operations work together to solve small problems. For instance, we might have Development show Operations how to authenticate an application, and login and run automated tests against various parts of the application to ensure that critical components are working correctly (e.g., key application functionality, database transactions, message queues). We would then integrate this new automated test into our deployment pipeline and run it periodically, sending the results to our monitoring and alerting systems so that we get earlier detection when critical components fail.

As Glenn O'Donnell from Forrester Research quipped in his 2014 DevOps Enterprise Summit presentation, "For all technology professionals who love innovating, love change, there is a wonderful and vibrant future ahead of us."

SHARE YOUR EXPERIENCES FROM DEVOPS CONFERENCES

In many cost-focused organizations, engineers are often discouraged from attending conferences and learning from their peers. To help build a learning organization, we should encourage our engineers (both from Development and Operations) to attend conferences, give talks at them, and, when necessary, create and organize internal or external conferences themselves.

DevOpsDays remains one of the most vibrant self-organized conference series today. Many DevOps practices have been shared and promulgated at these events. It has remained free or nearly free, supported by a vibrant community of practitioner communities and vendors.

The DevOps Enterprise Summit was created in 2014 for technology leaders to share their experiences adopting DevOps principles and practices in large, complex organizations. The program is organized primarily around experience reports from technology leaders on the DevOps journey, as well as subject matter experts on topics selected by the community.

Case Study
Internal Technology Conferences at Nationwide Insurance, Capital One, and Target (2014)

Along with attending external conferences, many companies, including those described in this section, have internal conferences for their technology employees.

Nationwide Insurance is a leading provider of insurance and financial services, and operates in heavily regulated industries. Their many offerings include auto and homeowners insurance, and they are the top provider of public-sector retirement plans and pet insurance. As of 2014, $195 billion in assets, with $24 billion in revenue. Since 2005, Nationwide has been adopting Agile and Lean principles to elevate the state of practice for their five thousand technology professionals, enabling grassroots innovation.

Steve Farley, VP of Information Technology, remembers, "Exciting technology conferences were starting to appear around that time, such as the Agile national conference. In 2011, the technology leadership at Nationwide agreed that we should create a technology conference, called TechCon. By holding this event, we wanted to create a better way to teach ourselves, as well as ensure that everything had a Nationwide context, as opposed to sending everyone to an external conference."

Capital One, one of the largest banks in the US with over $298 billion in assets and $24 billion in revenue in 2015, held their first internal software engineering conference in 2015 as part of their goal to create a world-class technology organization. The mission was to promote a culture of sharing and collaboration, and to build relationships between the technology professionals and enable learning. The conference had thirteen learning tracks and fifty-two sessions, and over 1,200 internal employees attended.

Dr. Tapabrata Pal, a technical fellow at Capital One and one of the organizers of the event, describes, "We even had an expo hall, where we had twenty-eight booths, where internal Capital One teams were showing off all the amazing capabilities they were working on. We even decided very deliberately that there would be no vendors there, because we wanted to keep the focus on Capital One goals."

Target is the sixth largest retailer in the US, with $72 billion in revenue in 2014 and 1,799 retail stores and 347,000 employees worldwide. Heather Mickman, a director of Development, and Ross Clanton have held six internal DevOpsDays events since 2014 and have over 975 followers inside their internal technology community, modeled after the DevOpsDays held at ING in Amsterdam in 2013.[†]

After Mickman and Clanton attended the DevOps Enterprise Summit in 2014, they held their own internal conference, inviting many of the speakers

---

† Incidentally, the first Target internal DevOpsDays event was modeled after the first ING DevOpsDays that was organized by Ingrid Algra, Jan-Joost Bouwman, Evelijn Van Leeuwen, and Kris Buytaert in 2013, after some of the ING team attended the 2013 Paris DevOpsDays.

from outside firms so that they could re-create their experience for their senior leadership. Clanton describes, "2015 was the year when we got executive attention and when we built up momentum. After that event, tons of people came up to us, asking how they could get involved and how they could help."

CREATE INTERNAL CONSULTING AND COACHES TO SPREAD PRACTICES

Creating an internal coaching and consulting organization is a method commonly used to spread expertise across an organization. This can come in many different forms. At Capital One, designated subject matter experts hold office hours where anyone can consult with them, ask questions, etc.

Earlier in the book, we began the story of how the Testing Grouplet built a world-class automated testing culture at Google starting in 2005. Their story continues here, as they try to improve the state of automated testing across all of Google by using dedicated improvement blitzes, internal coaches, and even an internal certification program.

Bland said, at that time, there was a 20% innovation time policy at Google, enabling developers to spend roughly one day per week on a Google-related project outside of their primary area of responsibility. Some engineers chose to form *grouplets*, ad hoc teams of like-minded engineers who wanted to pool their 20% time, allowing them to do focused improvement blitzes.

A testing grouplet was formed by Bharat Mediratta and Nick Lesiecki, with the mission of driving the adoption of automated testing across Google. Even though they had no budget or formal authority, as Mike Bland described, "There were no explicit constraints put upon us, either. And we took advantage of that."

They used several mechanisms to drive adoption, but one of the most famous was *Testing on the Toilet* (or TotT), their weekly testing periodical. Each week, they published a newsletter in nearly every bathroom in nearly every Google office worldwide. Bland said, "The goal was to raise the degree of testing knowledge and sophistication throughout the company. It's doubtful an online-only publication would've involved people to the same degree."

Bland continues, "One of the most significant TotT episodes was the one titled, 'Test Certified: Lousy Name, Great Results,' because it outlined two initiatives that had significant success in advancing the use of automated testing."

Test Certified (TC) provided a road map to improve the state of automated testing. As Bland describes, "It was intended to hack the measurement-focused priorities of Google culture…and to overcome the first, scary obstacle of not knowing where or how to start. Level 1 was to quickly establish a baseline metric, Level 2 was setting a policy and reaching an automated test coverage goal, and Level 3 was striving towards a long-term coverage goal."

The second capability was providing Test Certified mentors to any team who wanted advice or help, and Test Mercenaries (i.e., a full-time team of internal coaches and consultants) to work hands-on with teams to improve their testing practices and code quality. The Mercenaries did so by applying the Testing Grouplet's knowledge, tools, and techniques to a team's own code, using TC as both a guide and a goal. Bland was eventually a leader of the Testing Grouplet from 2006 to 2007, and a member of the Test Mercenaries from 2007 to 2009.

Bland continues, "It was our goal to get every team to TC Level 3, whether they were enrolled in our program our not. We also collaborated closely with the internal testing tools teams, providing feedback as we tackled testing challenges with the product teams. We were boots on the ground, applying the tools we built, and eventually, we were able to remove 'I don't have time to test' as a legitimate excuse."

He continues, "The TC levels exploited the Google metrics-driven culture—the three levels of testing were something that people could discuss and brag about at performance review time. The Testing Grouplet eventually got funding for the Test Mercenaries, a staffed team of full-time internal consultants. This was an important step, because now management was fully onboard, not with edicts, but by actual funding."

Another important construct was leveraging company-wide "Fixit" improvement blitzes. Bland describes Fixits as "when ordinary engineers with an idea and a sense of mission recruit all of Google engineering for one-day, intensive sprints of code reform and tool adoption." He organized four company-wide Fixits, two pure Testing Fixits and two that were more tools-related, the last involving more than one hundred volunteers in over twenty offices in thirteen countries. He also led the Fixit Grouplet from 2007 to 2008.

These Fixits, as Bland describes means that we should provide focused missions at critical points in time to generate excitement and energy, which helps advance the state-of-the-art. This will help the long-term culture change mission reach a new plateau with every big, visible effort.

The results of the testing culture are self-evident in the amazing results Google has achieved, presented throughout the book.

CONCLUSION

This chapter described how we can institute rituals that help reinforce the culture that we are all lifelong learners and that we value the improvement of daily work over daily work itself. We do this by reserving time to pay down technical debt, create forums that allow everyone to learn from and teach each other, both inside our organization and outside it. And we make experts available to help internal teams, either by coaching or consulting or even just holding office hours to answer questions.

By having everyone help each other learn in our daily work, we out-learn the competition, helping us win in the marketplace. But also we help each other achieve our full potential as human beings.

CONCLUSION TO PART V

Throughout Part V, we explored the practices that help create a culture of learning and experimentation in your organization. Learning from incidents, creating shared repositories, and sharing learnings is essential when we work in complex systems, helping to make our work culture more just and our systems safer and more resilient.

In Part VI, we'll explore how to extend flow, feedback, and learning and experimentation by using them to simultaneously help us achieve our Information Security goals.

PART VI

The Technological Practices
of Integrating Information
Security, Change Management,
and Compliance

Part VI
Introduction

In the previous chapters, we discussed enabling the fast flow of work from check-in to release, as well as creating the reciprocal fast flow of feedback. We explored the cultural rituals that reinforce the acceleration of organizational learning and amplification of weak failure signals that help us create an ever safer system of work.

In Part VI, we further extend these activities so that we not only achieve Development and Operations goals, but also simultaneously achieve Information Security goals, helping us create a high degree of assurance around the confidentiality, integrity, and availability of our services and data.

Instead of inspecting security into our product at the end of the process, we will create and integrate security controls into the daily work of Development and Operations, so that security is part of everyone's job, every day. Ideally, this work will be automated and put into our deployment pipeline. Furthermore, we will augment our manual practices, acceptances, and approval processes with automated controls, relying less on controls such as separation of duties and change approval processes.

By automating these activities, we can generate evidence on demand to demonstrate that our controls are operating effectively, whether to auditors, assessors, or anyone else working in our value stream.

In the end, we will not only improve security, but also create processes that are easier to audit and that attest to the effectiveness of controls, in support of compliance with regulatory and contractual obligations. We do this by:

- Making security a part of everyone's job

- Integrating preventative controls into our shared source code repository

- Integrating security with our deployment pipeline

- Integrating security with our telemetry to better enable detection and recovery

- Protecting our deployment pipeline

- Integrating our deployment activities with our change approval processes

- Reducing reliance on separation of duty

When we integrate security work into everyone's daily work, making it everyone's responsibility, we help the organization have better security. Better security means that we are defensible and sensible with our data. It means that we are reliable and have business continuity by being more available and more capable of easily recovering from issues. We are also able to overcome security problems before they cause catastrophic results, and we can increase the predictability of our systems. And, perhaps most importantly, we can secure our systems and data better than ever.

22

Information Security as
Everyone's Job, Every Day

One of the top objections to implementing DevOps principles and patterns has been, "Information security and compliance won't let us." And yet, DevOps may be one of the best ways to better integrate information security into the daily work of everyone in the technology value stream.

When Infosec is organized as a silo outside of Development and Operations, many problems arise. James Wickett, one of the creators of the Gauntlt security tool and organizer of DevOpsDays Austin and the Lonestar Application Security conference, observed:

> One interpretation of DevOps is that it came from the need to enable developers productivity, because as the number of developers grew, there weren't enough Ops people to handle all the resulting deployment work. This shortage is even worse in Infosec—the ratio of engineers in Development, Operations, and Infosec in a typical technology organization is 100:10:1. When Infosec is that outnumbered, without automation and integrating information security into the daily work of Dev and Ops, Infosec can only do compliance checking, which is the opposite of security engineering—and besides, it also makes everyone hate us.

James Wickett and Josh Corman, former CTO of Sonatype and respected information security researcher, have written about incorporating information security objectives into DevOps, a set of practices and principles termed *Rugged DevOps*. Similar ideas were created by Dr. Tapabrata Pal, Director and Platform Engineering Technical Fellow at Capital One, and the Capital One team, who describe their processes as *DevOpsSec*, where Infosec is integrated into all stages of the SDLC. Rugged DevOps traces some of its history to *Visible Ops Security*, written by Gene Kim, Paul Love, and George Spafford.

Throughout *The DevOps Handbook*, we have explored how to fully integrate the QA and Operations objectives throughout our entire technology value stream. In this chapter, we describe how to similarly integrate Infosec objectives into our daily work, where we can increase developer and operational productivity, increase safety, and increase our security.

INTEGRATE SECURITY INTO DEVELOPMENT ITERATION DEMONSTRATIONS

One of our goals is to have feature teams engaged with Infosec as early as possible, as opposed to primarily engaging at the end of the project. One way we can do this is by inviting Infosec to the product demonstrations at the end of each development interval so that they can better understand the team goals in the context of organizational goals, observe their implementations as they are being built, and provide guidance and feedback at the earliest stages of the project, when there is the most amount of time and freedom to make corrections.

Justin Arbuckle, former chief architect at GE Capital, observes, "When it came to information security and compliance, we found that blockages at the end of the project were much more expensive than at the beginning—and Infosec blockages were among the worst. 'Compliance by demonstration' became one of the rituals we used to shift all this complexity earlier in the process."

He continues, "By having Infosec involved throughout the creation of any new capability, we were able to reduce our use of static checklists dramatically and rely more on using their expertise throughout the entire software development process."

This helped the organization achieve its goals. Snehal Antani, former CIO of Enterprise Architecture at GE Capital Americas, described their top three key business measurements were "development velocity (i.e., speed of delivering features to market), failed customer interactions (i.e., outages, errors), and compliance response time (i.e., lead time from audit request to delivery of all quantitative and qualitative information required to fulfill the request)."

When Infosec is an assigned part of the team, even if they are only being kept informed and observing the process, they gain the business context they need to make better risk-based decisions. Furthermore, Infosec is able to help feature teams learn what is required to meet security and compliance objectives.

INTEGRATE SECURITY INTO DEFECT TRACKING AND POST-MORTEMS

When possible, we want to track all open security issues in the same work tracking system that Development and Operations are using, ensuring the work is visible and can be prioritized against all other work. This is very different from how Infosec has traditionally worked, where all security vulnerabilities are stored in a GRC (governance, risk, and compliance) tool that only Infosec has access to. Instead, we will put any needed work in the systems that Dev and Ops use.

In a presentation at the 2012 Austin DevOpsDays, Nick Galbreath, who headed up Information Security at Etsy for many years, describes how they treated security issues, "We put all security issues into JIRA, which all engineers use in their daily work, and they were either 'P1' or 'P2,' meaning that they had to be fixed immediately or by the end of the week, even if the issue is only an internally-facing application."

Furthermore, he states, "Any time we had a security issue, we would conduct a post-mortem, because it would result in better educating our engineers on how to prevent it from happening again in the future, as well as a fantastic mechanism for transferring security knowledge to our engineering teams."

INTEGRATE PREVENTIVE SECURITY CONTROLS INTO SHARED SOURCE CODE REPOSITORIES AND SHARED SERVICES

In chapter 20, we created a shared source code repository that makes it easy for anyone to discover and reuse the collective knowledge of our organization—not only for our code, but also for our toolchains, deployment pipeline, standards, etc. By doing this, anyone can benefit from the cumulative experience of everyone in the organization.

Now we will add to our shared source code repository any mechanisms or tools that help enable us to ensure our applications and environments are secure. We will add libraries that are pre-blessed by security to fulfill specific Infosec objectives, such as authentication and encryption libraries and services. Because everyone in the DevOps value stream uses version control for anything they build or support, putting our information security artifacts there makes it much easier to influence the daily work of Dev and Ops, because anything we create is available, searchable, and reusable. Version control also serves as a omni-directional communication mechanism to keep all parties aware of changes being made.

If we have a centralized shared services organization, we may also collaborate with them to create and operate shared security-relevant platforms, such as authentication, authorization, logging, and other security and auditing services that Dev and Ops require. When engineers use one of these predefined libraries or services, they won't need to schedule a separate security design review for that module; they'll be using the guidance we've created concerning configuration hardening, database security settings, key lengths, and so forth.

To further increase the likelihood that the services and libraries we provide will be used correctly, we can provide security training to Dev and Ops, as well as review what they've created to help ensure that security objectives are being implemented correctly, especially for teams using these tools for the first time.

Ultimately, our goal is to provide the security libraries or services that every modern application or environment requires, such as enabling user authentication, authorization, password management, data encryption, and so forth. Furthermore, we can provide Dev and Ops with effective security-specific configuration settings for the components they use in their application stacks, such as for logging, authentication, and encryption. We may include items such as:

- Code libraries and their recommended configurations (e.g., 2FA [two-factor authentication library], bcrypt password hashing, logging)

- Secret management (e.g., connection settings, encryption keys) using tools such as Vault, sneaker, Keywhiz, credstash, Trousseau, Red October, etc.

- OS packages and builds (e.g., NTP for time syncing, secure versions of OpenSSL with correct configurations, OSSEC or Tripwire for file integrity monitoring, syslog configuration to ensure logging of critical security into our centralized ELK stack)

By putting all these into our shared source code repository, we make it easy for any engineer to correctly create and use logging and encryption standards in their applications and environments, with no further work from us.

We should also collaborate with Ops teams to create a base cookbook or build image of our OS, databases, and other infrastructure (e.g., NGINX, Apache, Tomcat), showing they are in a known, secure, and risk-reduced state. Our shared repository not only becomes the place where we can get the latest versions, but also becomes a place where we can collaborate with other engineers and monitor and alert on changes made to security-sensitive modules.

INTEGRATE SECURITY INTO OUR DEPLOYMENT PIPELINE

In previous eras, in order to harden and secure our application, we would start our security review after development was completed. Often, the output of this review would be hundreds of pages of vulnerabilities in a PDF, which we'd give to Development and Operations, which would be completely un-addressed due to project due date pressure or problems being found too late in the software life cycle to be easily corrected.

In this step, we will automate as many of our information security tests as possible, so that they run alongside all our other automated tests in our deployment pipeline, being performed (ideally) upon every code commit by Dev or Ops, and even in the earliest stages of a software project.

Our goal is to provide both Dev and Ops with fast feedback on their work so that they are notified whenever they commit changes that are potentially insecure. By doing this, we enable them to quickly detect and correct security problems as part of their daily work, which enables learning and prevents future errors.

Ideally, these automated security tests will be run in our deployment pipeline alongside the other static code analysis tools.

Tools such as Gauntlt have been designed to integrate into the deployment pipelines, which run automated security tests on our applications, our application dependencies, our environment, etc. Remarkably, Gauntlt even puts all its security tests in Gherkin syntax test scripts, which is widely used by developers for unit and functional testing. Doing this puts security testing in a framework they are likely already familiar with. This also allows security tests to easily run in a deployment pipeline on every committed change, such as static code analysis, checking for vulnerable dependencies, or dynamic testing.

Jenkins					
S	W	Name	Last Success	Last Failure	Last Duration
●	☀	Static analysis scan	7 days 1 hr - #2	N/A	6.3 sec
●	☁	Check known vulnerabilities in dependencies	N/A	7 days 1 hr - #2	1.6 sec
●	☀	Download and unit test	7 days 1 hr - #2	N/A	32 sec
●	☀	Scan with OWASP ZAP	7 days 1 hr - #2	N/A	4 min 43 sec
●	☀	Start	7 days 1 hr - #2	N/A	5 min 46 sec
●	☀	Virus scanning	7 days 1 hr - #2	N/A	4.7 sec

Figure 43: *Jenkins running automated security testing (Source: James Wicket and Gareth Rushgrove, "Battle-tested code without the battle," Velocity 2014 conference presentation, posted to Speakerdeck.com, June 24, 2014, https://speakerdeck.com/garethr/battle-tested-code-without-the-battle.)*

By doing this, we provide everyone in the value stream with the fastest possible feedback about the security of what they are creating, enabling Dev and Ops engineers to find and fix issues quickly.

ENSURE SECURITY OF THE APPLICATION

Often, Development testing focuses on the correctness of functionality, looking at positive logic flows. This type of testing is often referred to as the *happy path*, which validates user journeys (and sometimes alternative paths) where everything goes as expected, with no exceptions or error conditions.

On the other hand, effective QA, Infosec, and Fraud practitioners will often focus on the *sad paths*, which happen when things go wrong, especially in relation to security-related error conditions. (These types of security-specific conditions are often jokingly referred to as the *bad paths*.)

For instance, suppose we have an e-commerce site with a customer input form that accepts credit card numbers as part of generating a customer order. We want to define all the sad and bath paths required to ensure that invalid credit cards are properly rejected to prevent fraud and security exploits, such as SQL injections, buffer overruns, and other undesirable outcomes.

Instead of performing these tests manually, we would ideally generate them as part of our automated unit or functional tests so that they can be run continuously in our deployment pipeline. As part of our testing, we will want to include the following:

- **Static analysis:** This is testing that we perform in a non-runtime environment, ideally in the deployment pipeline. Typically, a static analysis tool will inspect program code for all possible run-time behaviors and seek out coding flaws, back doors, and potentially malicious code (this is sometimes known as "testing from the inside-out"). Examples of tools include Brakeman, Code Climate, and searching for banned code functions (e.g., "exec()").

- **Dynamic analysis:** As opposed to static testing, dynamic analysis consists of tests executed while a program is in operation. Dynamic tests monitor items such as system memory, functional behavior, response time, and overall performance of the system. This method (sometimes known as "testing from the outside-in") is similar to the manner in which a malicious third party might interact with an application. Examples include Arachni and OWASP ZAP (Zed Attack Proxy).[†] Some types of penetration testing can also be performed in an automated fashion and should be included as part of dynamic analysis using tools such as Nmap and Metasploit. Ideally, we should perform automated dynamic testing during the automated functional testing phase of our deployment pipeline, or even against our services while they are in production. To ensure correct security handling, tools like OWASP ZAP can be configured to attack our services through a web browser proxy and inspect the network traffic within our test harness.

- **Dependency scanning:** Another type of static testing we would normally perform at build time inside of our deployment pipeline involves inventorying all our dependencies for binaries and executables, and ensuring that these dependencies, which we often don't have control over, are free of vulnerabilities or malicious binaries. Examples include Gemnasium and bundler audit for Ruby, Maven for Java, and the OWASP Dependency-Check.

- **Source code integrity and code signing:** All developers should have their own PGP key, perhaps created and managed in a system such as keybase.io. All commits to version control should be signed—that is straightforward to configure using the open source tools gpg and git. Furthermore, all packages created by the CI

---

† The Open Web Application Security Project (OWASP) is a non-profit organization focused on improving the security of software.

process should be signed, and their hash recorded in the centralized logging service for audit purposes.

Furthermore, we should define design patterns to help developers write code
to prevent abuse, such as putting in rate limits for our services and graying
out submit buttons after they have being pressed. OWASP publishes a great
deal of useful guidance such as the Cheat Sheet series, which includes:

- How to store passwords

- How to handle forgotten passwords

- How to handle logging

- How to prevent cross-site scripting (XSS) vulnerabilities

Case Study
Static Security Testing at Twitter (2009)

The "10 Deploys per Day: Dev and Ops Cooperation at Flickr" presentation
by John Allspaw and Paul Hammond is famous for catalyzing the Dev and
Ops community in 2009. The equivalent for the information security community is likely the presentation that Justin Collins, Alex Smolen, and Neil
Matatall gave on their information security transformation work at Twitter
at the AppSecUSA conference in 2012.

Twitter had many challenges due to hyper-growth. For years, the famous
Fail Whale error page would be displayed when Twitter did not have sufficient
capacity to keep up with user demand, showing a graphic of a whale being
lifted by eight birds. The scale of user growth was breathtaking—between
January and March 2009, the number of active Twitter users went from 2.5
million to 10 million.

Twitter also had security problems during this period. In early 2009, two
serious security breaches occurred. First, in January the @BarackObama
Twitter account was hacked. Then in April, the Twitter administrative accounts
were compromised through a brute-force dictionary attack. These events
led the Federal Trade Commission to judge that Twitter was misleading its
users into believing that their accounts were secure and issued an FTC
consent order.

The consent order required that Twitter comply within sixty days by instituting a set of processes that were to be enforced for the following twenty years and would do the following:

- Designate an employee or employees to be responsible for Twitter's information security plan

- Identify reasonably foreseeable risks, both internal and external, that could lead to an intrusion incident and create and implement a plan to address these risks[†]

- Maintain the privacy of user information, not just from outside sources but also internally, with an outline of possible sources of verification and testing of the security and correctness of these implementations

The group of engineers assigned to solve this problem had to integrate security into the daily work of Dev and Ops and close the security holes that allowed the breaches to happen in the first place.

In their previously mentioned presentation, Collins, Smolen, and Matatall identified several problems they needed to address:

- **Prevent security mistakes from being repeated:** They found that they were fixing the same defects and vulnerabilities over and over again. They needed to modify the system of work and automation tools to prevent the issues from happening again.

- **Integrate security objectives into existing developer tools:** They identified early on that the major source of vulnerabilities were code issues. They couldn't run a tool that generated a huge PDF report and then email it to someone in Development or Operations. Instead, they needed to provide the developer who had created the vulnerability with the exact information needed to fix it.

- **Preserve trust of Development:** They needed to earn and maintain the trust of Development. That meant they needed to know when they sent Development false positives, so they could fix the error

---

† Strategies for managing these risks include providing employee training and management; rethinking the design of information systems, including network and software; and instituting processes designed to prevent, detect, and respond to attacks.

that prompted the false positive and avoid wasting Development's time.

- **Maintain fast flow through Infosec through automation:** Even when code vulnerability scanning was automated, Infosec still had to do lots of manual work and waiting. They had to wait for the scan to complete, get back the big stack of reports, interpret the reports, and then find the person responsible for fixing it. And when the code changed, it had to be done all over again. By automating the manual work, they did fewer dumb "button-pushing" tasks, enabling them to use more creativity and judgment.

- **Make everything security related self-service, if possible:** They trusted that most people wanted to do the right thing, so it was necessary to provide them with all the context and information they needed to fix any issues.

- **Take a holistic approach to achieving Infosec objectives:** Their goal was to do analysis from all the angles: source code, the production environment, and even what their customers were seeing.

The first big breakthrough for the Infosec team occured during a company-wide hack week when they integrated static code analysis into the Twitter build process. The team used Brakeman, which scans Ruby on Rails applications for vulnerabilities. The goal was to integrate security scanning into the earliest stages of the Development process, not just when the code was committed into the source code repo.

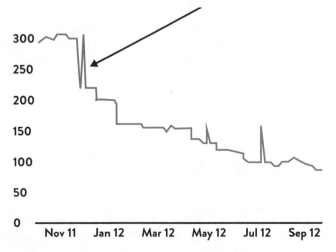

Figure 44: *Number of Brakeman security vulnerabilities detected*

The results of integrating security testing into the development process were breathtaking. Over the years, by creating fast feedback for developers when they write insecure code and showing them how to fix the vulnerabilities, Brakeman has reduced the rate of vulnerabilities found by 60%, as shown in figure 44. (The spikes are usually associated with new releases of Brakeman.)

This cases study illustrates just how necessary it is to integrate security into the daily work and tools of DevOps and how effectively it can work. Doing so mitigates security risk, reduces the probability of vulnerabilities in the system, and helps teach developers to write more secure code.

ENSURE SECURITY OF OUR SOFTWARE SUPPLY CHAIN

Josh Corman observed that as developers "we are no longer writing customized software—instead, we assemble what we need from open source parts, which has become the software supply chain that we are very much reliant upon." In other words, when we use components or libraries—either commercial or open source—in our software, we not only inherit their functionality, but also any security vulnerabilities they contain.

When selecting software, we detect when our software projects are relying on components or libraries that have known vulnerabilities, and help developers choose the components they use deliberately and with due care, selecting those components (e.g., open source projects) that have a demonstrated history of quickly fixing software vulnerabilities. We also look for multiple versions of the same library being used across our production landscape, particularly the presence of older versions of libraries which contain known vulnerabilities.

Examining cardholder data breaches shows how important the security of open source components we choose can be. Since 2008, the annual Verizon PCI Data Breach Investigation Report (DBIR) has been the most authoritative voice on data breaches where cardholder data was lost or stolen. In the 2014 report, they studied over eighty-five thousand breaches to better understand where attacks were coming from, how cardholder data was stolen, and factors leading to the breach.

The DBIR found that ten vulnerabilities (i.e., CVEs) accounted for almost 97% of the exploits used in studied cardholder data breaches in 2014. Of these ten vulnerabilities, eight of them were over ten years old.

The 2015 *Sonatype State of the Software Supply Chain Report* further analyzed the vulnerability data from the Nexus Central Repository. In 2015, this repository provided the build artifacts for over 605,000 open source projects, servicing over seventeen billion download requests of artifacts and dependencies primarily for the Java platform, originating from 106,000 organizations.

The report included these startling findings:

- The typical organization relied upon 7,601 build artifacts (i.e., software suppliers or components) and used 18,614 different versions (i.e., software parts).

- Of those components being used, 7.5% had known vulnerabilities, with over 66% of those vulnerabilities being over two years old without having been resolved.

The last statistic confirms another information security study by Dr. Dan Geer and Josh Corman, which showed that of the open source projects with known vulnerabilities registered in the National Vulnerability Database, only 41% were ever fixed and required, on average, 390 days to publish a fix. For those vulnerabilities that were labeled at the highest severity (i.e., those scored as CVSS level 10), fixes required 224 days.[†]

ENSURE SECURITY OF THE ENVIRONMENT

In this step, we should do whatever is required to help ensure that the environments are in a hardened, risk-reduced state. Although we may have created known, good configurations already, we must put in monitoring controls to ensure that all production instances match these known good states.

We do this by generating automated tests to ensure that all appropriate settings have been correctly applied for configuration hardening, database security settings, key lengths, and so forth. Furthermore, we will use tests to scan our environments for known vulnerabilities.[‡]

[†] Tools that can help ensure the integrity of our software dependencies include OWASP Dependency Check and Sonatype Nexus Lifecycle.

[‡] Examples of tools that can help with security correctness testing (i.e., "as it should be") include automated configuration management systems (e.g., Puppet, Chef, Ansible, Salt), as well as tools such as ServerSpec and the Netflix Simian Army (e.g., Conformity Monkey, Security Monkey, etc.).

Another category of security verification is understanding actual environments (i.e., "as they actually are"). Examples of tools for this include Nmap to ensure that only expected ports are open and Metasploit to ensure that we've adequately hardened our environments against known vulnerabilities, such as scanning with SQL injection attacks. The output of these tools should be put into our artifact repository and compared with the previous version as part of our functional testing process. Doing this will help us detect any undesirable changes as soon as they occur.

Case Study
18F Automating Compliance for the Federal Government with Compliance Masonry

US Federal Government agencies were projected to spend nearly $80 billion on IT in 2016, supporting the mission of all the executive branch agencies. Regardless of agency, to take any system from "dev complete" to "live in production" requires obtaining an Authority to Operate (ATO) from a Designated Approving Authority (DAA). The laws and policies that govern complience in government are comprised of tens of documents that together number over four thousand pages, littered with acronyms such as FISMA, FedRAMP, and FITARA. Even for systems that only require low levels of confidentiality, integrity, and availability, over one hundred controls must be implemented, documented, and tested. It typically takes between eight and fourteen months for an ATO to be granted following "dev complete."

The 18F team in the federal government's General Services Administration has taken a multi-pronged approach to solving this problem. Mike Bland explains, "18F was created within the General Services Administration to capitalize on the momentum generated by the Healthcare.gov recovery to reform how the government builds and buys software."

One 18F effort is a platform as a service called Cloud.gov, created from open source components. Cloud.gov runs on AWS GovCloud at present. Not only does the platform handle many of the operational concerns delivery teams might otherwise have to take care of, such as logging, monitoring, alerting, and service lifecycle management, it also handles the bulk of compliance concerns. By running on this platform, a large majority of the controls that government systems must implement can be taken care of at the infrastructure and platform level. Then, only the remaining controls that are in scope at the application layer have to be documented and tested, significantly reducing the compliance burden and the time it takes to receive an ATO.

AWS GovCloud has already been approved for use for federal government systems of all types, including those which require high levels of confidentiality, integrity, and availability. By the time you read this book, it is expected that Cloud.gov will be approved for all systems that require moderate levels of confidentiality, integrity, and availability.[†]

Furthermore, the Cloud.gov team is building a framework to automate the creation of system security plans (SSPs), which are "comprehensive descriptions of the system's architecture, implemented controls, and general security posture...[which are] often incredibly complex, running several hundred pages in length." They developed a prototype tool called compliance masonry so that SSP data is stored in machine-readable YAML and then turned into GitBooks and PDFs automatically.

18F is dedicated to working in the open and publishes its work open source in the public domain. You can find compliance masonry and the components that make up Cloud.gov in 18F's GitHub repositories—you can even stand up your own instance of Cloud.gov. The work on open documentation for SSPs is being done in close partnership with the OpenControl community.

INTEGRATE INFORMATION SECURITY INTO PRODUCTION TELEMETRY

Marcus Sachs, one of the Verizon Data Breach researchers, observed in 2010, "Year after year, in the vast majority of cardholder data breaches, the organization detected the security breach months or quarters after the breach occurred. Worse, the way the breach was detected was not an internal monitoring control, but was far more likely someone outside of the organization, usually a business partner or the customer who notices fraudulent transactions. One of the primary reasons for this is that no one in the organization was regularly reviewing the log files."

In other words, internal security controls are often ineffective in successfully detecting breaches in a timely manner, either because of blind spots in our monitoring or because no one in our organization is examining the relevant telemetry in their daily work.

In chapter 14, we discussed creating a culture in Dev and Ops where everyone in the value stream is creating production telemetry and metrics, making

---

† These approvals are known as FedRAMP JAB P-ATOs.

them visible in prominent public places so that everyone can see how our services are performing in production. Furthermore, we explored the necessity of relentlessly seeking ever-weaker failure signals so that we can find and fix problems before they result in a catastrophic failure.

Here, we deploy the monitoring, logging, and alerting required to fulfill our information security objectives throughout our applications and environments, as well as ensure that it is adequately centralized to facilitate easy and meaningful analysis and response.

We do this by integrating our security telemetry into the same tools that Development, QA, and Operations are using, giving everyone in the value stream visibility into how their application and environments are performing in a hostile threat environment where attackers are constantly attempting to exploit vulnerabilities, gain unauthorized access, plant backdoors, commit fraud, perform denials-of-service, and so forth.

By radiating how our services are being attacked in the production environment, we reinforce that everyone needs to be thinking about security risks and designing countermeasures in their daily work.

CREATING SECURITY TELEMETRY IN OUR APPLICATIONS

In order to detect problematic user behavior that could be an indicator or enabler of fraud and unauthorized access, we must create the relevant telemetry in our applications.

Examples may include:

- Successful and unsuccessful user logins

- User password resets

- User email address resets

- User credit card changes

For instance, as an early indicator of brute-force login attempts to gain unauthorized access, we might display the ratio of unsuccessful login attempts to successful logins. And, of course, we should create alerting around important events to ensure we can detect and correct issues quickly.

CREATING SECURITY TELEMETRY IN OUR ENVIRONMENT

In addition to instrumenting our application, we also need to create sufficient telemetry in our environments so that we can detect early indicators of unauthorized access, especially in the components that are running on infrastructure that we do not control (e.g., hosting environments, in the cloud).

We need to monitor and potentially alert on items, including the following:

- OS changes (e.g., in production, in our build infrastructure)

- Security group changes

- Changes to configurations (e.g., OSSEC, Puppet, Chef, Tripwire)

- Cloud infrastructure changes (e.g., VPC, security groups, users and privileges)

- XSS attempts (i.e., "cross-site scripting attacks")

- SQLi attempts (i.e., "SQL injection attacks")

- Web server errors (e.g., 4XX and 5XX errors)

We also want to confirm that we've correctly configured our logging so that all telemetry is being sent to the right place. When we detect attacks, in addition to logging that it happened, we may also choose to block access and store information about the source to aid us in choosing the best mitigation actions.

Case Study
Instrumenting the Environment at Etsy (2010)

In 2010, Nick Galbreath was director of engineering at Etsy and responsible for information security, fraud control, and privacy. Galbreath defined *fraud* as when "the system works incorrectly, allowing invalid or un-inspected input into the system, causing financial loss, data loss/theft, system downtime, vandalism, or an attack on another system."

To achieve these goals, Galbreath did not create a separate fraud control or information security department; instead, he embedded those responsibilities throughout the DevOps value stream.

Galbreath created security-related telemetry that were displayed alongside all the other more Dev and Ops oriented metrics, which every Etsy engineer routinely saw:

- **Abnormal production program terminations (e.g., segmentation faults, core dumps, etc.):** "Of particular concern was why certain processes kept dumping core across our entire production environment, triggered from traffic coming from the one IP address, over and over again. Of equal concern were those HTTP '500 Internal Server Errors.' These are indicators that a vulnerability was being exploited to gain unauthorized access to our systems, and that a patch needs to be urgently applied."

- **Database syntax error:** "We were always looking for database syntax errors inside our code—these either enabled SQL Injection attacks or were actual attacks in progress. For this reason, we had zero-tolerance for database syntax errors in our code, because it remains one of the leading attack vectors used to compromise systems."

- **Indications of SQL injection attacks:** "This was a ridiculously simple test—we'd merely alert whenever 'UNION ALL' showed up in user-input fields, since it almost always indicates a SQL injection attack. We also added unit tests to make sure that this type of uncontrolled user input could never be allowed into our database queries."

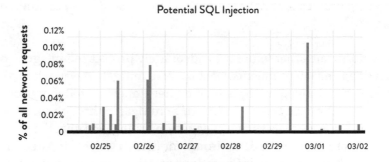

Figure 45: *Developers would see SQL injection attempts in Graphite at Etsy*
(Source: "DevOpsSec: Appling DevOps Priciples to Security, DevOpsDays Austin 2012," SlideShare.net, posted by Nick Galbreath, April 12, 2012, http://www.slideshare.net/nickgsuperstar/ devopssec-apply-devops-principles-to-security.)

Figure 45 is an example of a graph that every developer would see, which shows the number of potential SQL injection attacks that were attempted in the production environment. As Galbreath observed, "Nothing helps developers understand how hostile the operating environment is than seeing their code being attacked in real-time."

Galbreath observed, "One of the results of showing this graph was that developers realized that they were being attacked all the time! And that was awesome, because it changed how developers thought about the security of their code as they were writing the code."

PROTECT OUR DEPLOYMENT PIPELINE

The infrastructure that supports our continuous integration and continuous deployment processes also presents a new surface area vulnerable to attack. For instance, if someone compromises the servers running deployment pipeline that has the credentials for our version control system, it could enable someone to steal source code. Worse, if the deployment pipeline has write access, an attacker could also inject malicious changes into our version control repository, and, therefore, inject malicious changes into our application and services.

As Jonathan Claudius, former Senior Security Tester at TrustWave SpiderLabs, observed, "Continuous build and test servers are awesome, and I use them myself. But I started thinking about ways to use CI/CD as a way to inject malicious code. Which led to the question of where would be a good place to hide malicious code? The answer was obvious: in the unit tests. No one actually looks at the unit tests, and they're run every time someone commits code to the repo."

This demonstrates that in order to adequately protect the integrity of our applications and environments, we must also mitigate the attack vectors on our deployment pipeline. Risks include developers introducing code that enables unauthorized access (which we've mitigated through controls such as code testing, code reviews, and penetration testing) and unauthorized users gaining access to our code or environment (which we've mitigated through controls such as ensuring configurations match known, good states, and effective patching).

However, in order to protect our continuous build, integration, or deployment pipeline, our mitigation strategies may include:

- Hardening continuous build and integration servers and ensuring we can reproduce them in an automated manner, just as we would for infrastructure that supports customer-facing production services, to prevent our continuous build and integration servers from being compromised

- Reviewing all changes introduced into version control, either through pair programming at commit time or by a code review process between commit and merge into trunk, to prevent continuous integration servers from running uncontrolled code (e.g., unit tests may contain malicious code that allows or enables unauthorized access)

- Instrumenting our repository to detect when test code contains suspicious API calls (e.g., unit tests accessing the filesystem or network) is checked in to the repository, perhaps quarantining it and triggering an immediate code review

- Ensuring every CI process runs on its own isolated container or VM

- Ensuring the version control credentials used by the CI system are read-only

CONCLUSION

Throughout this chapter we have described ways to integrate information security objectives into all stages of our daily work. We do this by integrating security controls into the mechanisms we've already created, ensuring that all on-demand environments are also in a hardened, risk-reduced state—by integrating security testing into the deployment pipeline and ensuring the creation of security telemetry in pre-production and production environments. By doing so, we enable developer and operational productivity to increase while simultaneously increasing our overall safety. Our next step is to protect the deployment pipeline.

23 Protecting the Deployment Pipeline

Throughout this chapter we will look at how to protect our deployment pipeline, as well as how to acheive security and compliance objectives in our control environment, including change management and separation of duty.

INTEGRATE SECURITY AND COMPLIANCE INTO CHANGE APPROVAL PROCESSES

Almost any IT organization of any significant size will have existing change management processes, which are the primary controls to reduce operations and security risks. Compliance manager and security managers place reliance on change management processes for compliance requirements, and they typically require evidence that all changes have been appropriately authorized.

If we have constructed our deployment pipeline correctly so that deployments are low-risk, the majority of our changes won't need to go through a manual change approval process, because we will have placed our reliance on controls such as automated testing and proactive production monitoring.

In this step, we will do what is required to ensure that we can successfully integrate security and compliance into any existing change management process. Effective change management policies will recognize that there are different risks associated with different types of changes and that those changes are all handled differently. These processes are defined in ITIL, which breaks changes down into three categories:

- **Standard changes:** These are lower-risk changes that follow an established and approved process, but can also be pre-approved. They include monthly updates of application tax tables or country codes, website content and styling changes, and certain types of application or operating system patches that have a well-understood impact. The change proposer does not require approval before deploying the change, and change deployments can be completely automated and should be logged so there is traceability.

- **Normal changes:** These are higher-risk changes that require review or approval from the agreed upon change authority. In many organizations, this responsibility is inappropriately placed on the change advisory board (CAB) or emergency change advisory board (ECAB), which may lack the required expertise to understand the full impact of the change, often leading to unacceptably long lead times. This problem is especially relevant for large code deployments, which may contain hundreds of thousands (or even millions) of lines of new code, submitted by hundreds of developers over the course of several months. In order for normal changes to be authorized, the CAB will almost certainly have a well-defined request for change (RFC) form that defines what information is required for the go/no-go decision. The RFC form usually includes the desired business outcomes, planned utility and warranty,[†] a business case with risks and alternatives, and a proposed schedule.[‡]

- **Urgent changes:** These are emergency, and, consequently, potentially high risk, changes that must be put into production immediately (e.g., urgent security patch, restore service). These

---

† ITIL defines utility as "what the service does," while warranty is defined as "how the service is delivered and can be used to determine whether a service is 'fit for use.'"

‡ To further manage risk changes, we may also have defined rules, such as certain changes can only be implemented by a certain group or individual (e.g., only DBAs can deploy database schema changes). Traditionally, the CAB meetings have been held weekly, where the change requests are approved and scheduled. From ITIL version 3 onward, it is acceptable for changes to be approved electronically in a just-in-time fashion through a change management tool. It also specifically recommends that "standard changes should be identified early on when building the Change Management process to promote efficiency. Otherwise, a Change Management implementation can create unnecessarily high levels of administration and resistance to the Change Management process."

changes often require senior management approval, but allow documentation to be performed after the fact. A key goal of DevOps practices is to streamline our normal change process such that it is also suitable for emergency changes.

RE-CATEGORIZE THE MAJORITY OF OUR LOWER RISK CHANGES AS STANDARD CHANGES

Ideally, by having a reliable deployment pipeline in place, we will have already earned a reputation for fast, reliable, and non-dramatic deployments. At this point, we should seek to gain agreement from Operations and the relevant change authorities that our changes have been demonstrated to be low risk enough to be defined as standard changes, pre-approved by the CAB. This enables us to deploy into production without need for further approval, although the changes should still be properly recorded.

One way to support an assertion that our changes are low risk is to show a history of changes over a significant time period (e.g., months or quarters) and provide a complete list of production issues during that same period. If we can show high change success rates and low MTTR, we can assert that we have a control environment that is effectively preventing deployment errors, as well as prove that we can effectively and quickly detect and correct any resulting problems.

Even when our changes are categorized as standard changes, they still need to be visual and recorded in our change management systems (e.g., Remedy or ServiceNow). Ideally, deployments will be performed automatically by our configuration management and deployment pipeline tools (e.g., Puppet, Chef, Jenkins) and the results will be automatically recorded. By doing this, everyone in our organization (DevOps or not) will have visibility into our changes in addition to all the other changes happening in the organization.

We may automatically link these change request records to specific items in our work planning tools (e.g., JIRA, Rally, LeanKit, ThoughtWorks Mingle), allowing us to create more context for our changes, such as linking to feature defects, production incidents, or user stories. This can be accomplished in a lightweight way by including ticket numbers from planning tools in the comments associated with version control check ins.[§] By doing this, we can

---

§ The term *ticket* is used generically to indicate any uniquely identifiable work item.

trace a production deployment to the changes in version control and, from there, trace them further back to the planning tool tickets.

Creating this traceability and context should be easy and should not create an overly onerous or time-consuming burden for engineers. Linking to user stories, requirements, or defects is almost certainly sufficient—any further detail, such as opening a ticket for each commit to version control, is likely not useful, and thus unnecessary and undesired, as it will impose a significant level of friction on their daily work.

WHAT TO DO WHEN CHANGES ARE CATEGORIZED AS NORMAL CHANGES

For those changes that we cannot get classified as standard changes, they will be considered *normal changes* and will require approval from at least a subset of the CAB before deployment. In this case, our goal is still to ensure that we can deploy quickly, even if it is not fully automated.

In this case, we must ensure that any submitted change requests are as complete and accurate as possible, giving the CAB everything they need to properly evaluate our change—after all, if our change request is malformed or incomplete, it will be bounced back to us, increasing the time required for us to get into production and casting doubt on whether we actually understand the goals of the change management process.

We can almost certainly automate the creation of complete and accurate RFCs, populating the ticket with details of exactly what is to be changed. For instance, we could automatically create a ServiceNow change ticket with a link to the JIRA user story, along with the build manifests and test output from our deployment pipeline tool and links to the Puppet/Chef scripts that will be run.

Because our submitted changes will be manually evaluated by people, it is even more important that we describe the context of the change. This includes identifying why we are making the change (e.g., providing a link to the features, defects, or incidents), who is affected by the change, and what is going to be changed.

Our goal is to share the evidence and artifacts that give us confidence that the change will operate in production as designed. Although RFCs typically have free-form text fields, we should provide links to machine-readable data to enable others to integrate and process our data (e.g., links to JSON files).

In many toolchains, this can be done in a compliant and fully automated way. For example, ThoughtWorks' Mingle and Go can automatically link this information together, such as a list of defects fixed and new features completed that are associated with the change, and put it into an RFC.

Upon submission of our RFC, the relevant members of the CAB will review, process, and approve these changes as they would any other submitted change request. If all goes well, the change authorities will appreciate the thoroughness and detail of our submitted changes, because we have allowed them to quickly validate the correctness of the information we've provided (e.g., viewing the links to artifacts from our deployment pipeline tools). However, our goal should be to continually show an exemplary track record of successful changes, so we can eventually gain their agreement that our automated changes can be safely classified as standard changes.

Case Study
Automated Infrastructure Changes as Standard Changes at Salesforce.com (2012)

Salesforce was founded in 2000 with the aim of making customer relationship management easily available and deliverable as a service. Salesforce's offerings were widely adopted by the marketplace, leading to a successful IPO in 2004. By 2007, the company had over fifty-nine thousand enterprise customers, processing hundreds of millions of transactions per day, with annual revenue of $497 million.

However, around that same time, their ability to develop and release new functionality to their customers seemed to grind to a halt. In 2006, they had four major customer releases, but in 2007 they were only able to do one customer release despite having hired more engineers. The result was that the number of features delivered per team kept decreasing and the days between major releases kept increasing.

And because the batch size of each release kept getting larger, the deployment outcomes also kept getting worse. Karthik Rajan, then VP of Infrastructure Engineering, reports in a 2013 presentation that 2007 marked "the last year when software was created and shipped using a waterfall process and when we made our shift to a more incremental delivery process."

At the 2014 DevOps Enterprise Summit, Dave Mangot and Reena Mathew described the resulting multi-year DevOps transformation that started in

2009. According to Mangot and Mathew, by implementing DevOps principles and practices, the company reduced their deployment lead times from six days to five minutes by 2013. As a result, they were able to scale capacity more easily, allowing them to process over one billion transactions per day.

One of the main themes of the Salesforce transformation was to make quality engineering everyone's job, regardless of whether they were part of Development, Operations, or Infosec. To do this, they integrated automated testing into all stages of the application and environment creation, as well as into the continuous integration and deployment process, and created the open source tool Rouster to conduct functional testing of their Puppet modules.

They also started to routinely perform *destructive testing*, a term used in manufacturing to refer to performing prolonged endurance testing under the most severe operating conditions until the component being tested is destroyed. The Salesforce team started routinely testing their services under increasingly higher loads until the service broke, which helped them understand their failure modes and make appropriate corrections. Unsurprisingly, the result was significantly higher service quality with normal production loads.

Information Security also worked with Quality Engineering at the earliest stages of their project, continually collaborating in critical phases such as architecture and test design, as well as properly integrating security tools into the automated testing process.

For Mangot and Mathew, one of the key successes from all the repeatability and rigor they designed into the process was being told by their change management group that "infrastructure changes made through Puppet would now be treated as 'standard changes,' requiring far less or even no further approvals from the CAB." Furthermore, they noted that "manual changes to infrastructure would still require approvals."

By doing this, they had not only integrated their DevOps processes with the change management process, but also created further motivation to automate the change process for more of their infrastructure.

REDUCE RELIANCE ON SEPARATION OF DUTY

For decades, we have used separation of duty as one of our primary controls to reduce the risk of fraud or mistakes in the software development process. It has been the accepted practice in most SDLCs to require developer changes to be submitted to a code librarian, who would review and approve the change before IT Operations promoted the change into production.

There are plenty of other less contentious examples of separation of duty in Ops work, such as server administrators ideally being able to view logs but not delete or modify them, in order to prevent someone with privileged access from deleting evidence of fraud or other issues.

When we did production deployments less frequently (e.g., annually) and when our work was less complex, compartmentalizing our work and doing hand-offs were tenable ways of conducting business. However, as complexity and deployment frequency increase, performing production deployments successfully increasingly requires everyone in the value stream to quickly see the outcomes of their actions.

Separation of duty often can impede this by slowing down and reducing the feedback engineers receive on their work. This prevents engineers from taking full responsibility for the quality of their work and reduces a firm's ability to create organizational learning.

Consequently, wherever possible, we should avoid using separation of duties as a control. Instead, we should choose controls such as pair programming, continuous inspection of code check-ins, and code review. These controls can give us the necessary reassurance about the quality of our work. Furthermore, by putting these controls in place, if separation of duties is required, we can show that we achieve equivalent outcomes with the controls we have created.

Case Study
PCI Compliance and a Cautionary Tale of Separating Duties at Etsy (2014)

Bill Massie is a development manager at Etsy and is responsible for the payment application called ICHT (an abbreviation for "I Can Haz Tokens"). ICHT takes customer credit orders through a set of internally-developed payment processing applications that handle online order entry by taking customer-entered cardholder data, tokenizing it, communicating with the payment processor, and completing the order transaction.[†]

---

† The authors thank Bill Massie and John Allspaw for spending an entire day with Gene Kim sharing their compliance experience.

Because the scope of the Payment Card Industry Data Security Standards (PCI DSS) cardholder data environment (CDE) is "the people, processes and technology that store, process or transmit cardholder data or sensitive authentication data," including any connected system components, the ICHT application has in scope for the PCI DSS.

To contain the PCI DSS scope, the ICHT application is physically and logically separated from the rest of the Etsy organization and is managed by a completely separate application team of developers, database engineers, networking engineers, and ops engineers. Each team member is issued two laptops: one for ICHT (which are configured differently to meet the DSS requirements, as well as being locked in a safe when not in use) and one for the rest of Etsy.

By doing this, they were able to decouple the CDE environment from the rest of the Etsy organization, limiting the scope of the PCI DSS regulations to one segregated area. The systems that form the CDE are separated (and managed differently) from the rest of Etsy's environments at the physical, network, source code, and logical infrastructure levels. Furthermore, the CDE is built and operated by a cross-functional team that is solely responsible for the CDE.

The ICHT team had to modify their continuous delivery practices in order to accommodate the need for code approvals. According to Section 6.3.2 of the PCI DSS v3.1, teams should review:

All custom code prior to release to production or customers in order to identify any potential coding vulnerability (using either manual or automated processes) as follows:

- Are code changes reviewed by individuals other than the originating code author, and by individuals knowledgeable about code-review techniques and secure coding practices?

- Do code reviews ensure code is developed according to secure coding guidelines?

- Are appropriate corrections implemented prior to release?

- Are code review results reviewed and approved by management prior to release?

To fulfill this requirement, the team initially decided to designate Massie as the change approver responsible for deploying any changes into production. Desired deployments would be flagged in JIRA, and Massie would mark them as reviewed and approved, and manually deploy them into the ICHT production.

This has enabled Etsy to meet their PCI DSS requirements and get their signed Report of Compliance from their assessors. However, with regard to the team, significant problems have resulted.

Massie observes that one troubling side-effect "is a level of 'compartmentalization' that is happening in the ICHT team that no other group is having at Etsy. Ever since we implemented separation of duty and other controls required by the PCI DSS compliance, no one can be a full-stack engineer in this environment."

As a result, while the rest of the Development and Operations teams at Etsy work together closely and deploy changes smoothly and with confidence, Massie notes that "within our PCI environment, there is fear and reluctance around deployment and maintenance because no one has visibility outside their portion of the software stack. The seemingly minor changes we made to the way we work seem to have created an impenetrable wall between developers and ops, and creates an undeniable tension that no one at Etsy has had since 2008. Even if you have confidence in your portion, it's impossible to get confidence that someone else's change isn't going to break your part of the stack."

This case study shows that compliance is possible in organizations using DevOps. However, the potentially cautionary tale here is that all the virtues that we associate with high-performing DevOps teams are fragile— even a team that has shared experiences with high trust and shared goals can begin to struggle when low trust control mechanisms are put into place.

ENSURE DOCUMENTATION AND PROOF FOR AUDITORS AND COMPLIANCE OFFICERS

As technology organizations increasingly adopt DevOps patterns, there is more tension than ever between IT and audit. These new DevOps patterns challenge traditional thinking about auditing, controls, and risk mitigation.

As Bill Shinn, a principal security solutions architect at Amazon Web Services, observes, "DevOps is all about bridging the gap between Dev and Ops. In some ways, the challenge of bridging the gap between DevOps and auditors and compliance officers is even larger. For instance, how many auditors can read code and how many developers have read NIST 800-37 or the Gramm-Leach-Bliley Act? That creates a gap of knowledge, and the DevOps community needs to help bridge that gap."

Case Study
Proving Compliance in
Regulated Environments (2015)

Helping large enterprise customers show that they can still comply with all relevant laws and regulations is among Bill Shinn's responsibilities as a principal security solutions architect at Amazon Web Services. Over the years, he has spent time with over one thousand enterprise customers, including Hearst Media, GE, Phillips, and Pacific Life, who have publicly referenced their use of public clouds in highly regulated environments.

Shinn notes, "One of the problems is that auditors have been trained in methods that aren't very suitable for DevOps work patterns. For example, if an auditor saw an environment with ten thousand productions servers, they have been traditionally trained to ask for a sample of one thousand servers, along with screenshot evidence of asset management, access control settings, agent installations, server logs, and so forth."

"That was fine with physical environments," Shinn continues. "But when infrastructure is code, and when auto-scaling makes servers appear and disappear all the time, how do you sample that? You run into the same problems when you have a deployment pipeline, which is very different than the traditional software development process, where one group writes the code and another group deploys that code into production."

He explains, "In audit fieldwork, the most commonplace methods of gathering evidence are still screenshots and CSV files filled with configuration settings and logs. Our goal is to create alternative methods of presenting the data that clearly show auditors that our controls are operating and effective."

To help bridge that gap, he has teams work with auditors in the control design process. They use an iterative approach, assigning a single control for each sprint to determine what is needed in terms of audit evidence. This has helped ensure that auditors get the information they need when the service is in production, entirely on demand.

Shinn states that the best way to accomplish this is to "send all data into our telemetry systems, such as Splunk or Kibana. This way auditors can get what they need, completely self-serviced. They don't need to request a data sample—instead, they log into Kibana, and then search for audit evidence they need for a given time range. Ideally, they'll see very quickly that there's evidence to support that our controls are working."

Shinn continues, "With modern audit logging, chat rooms, and deployment pipelines, there's unprecedented visibility and transparency into what's happening in production, especially compared to how Operations used to be done, with far lower probability of errors and security flaws being introduced. So, the challenge is to turn all that evidence into something an auditor recognizes."

That requires deriving the engineering requirements from the actual regulations. Shinn explains, "To discover what HIPAA requires from an information security perspective, you have to look into the forty-five CFR Part 160 legislation, go into Subparts A and C of Part 164. Even then, you need to keep reading until you get into 'technical safeguards and audit controls.' Only there will you see that what is required is that we need to determine activities that will be tracked and audited relevant to Patient Healthcare Information, document and implement those controls, select tools, and then finally review and capture the appropriate information."

Shinn continues, "How to fulfill that requirement is the discussion that needs to be happening between compliance and regulatory officers, and the security and DevOps teams, specifically around how to prevent, detect, and correct problems. Sometimes they can be fulfilled in a configuration setting in version control. Other times, it's a monitoring control."

Shinn gives an example: "We may choose to implement one of those controls using AWS CloudWatch, and we can test that the control is operating with one command line. Furthermore, we need to show where the logs are going—in the ideal, we push all this into our logging framework, where we can link the audit evidence with the actual control requirement."

To help solve this problem, the *DevOps Audit Defense Toolkit* describes the end-to-end narrative of the compliance and audit process for a fictitious organization (Parts Unlimited from *The Phoenix Project*). It starts by describing the entity's organizational goals, business processes, top risks, and resulting control environment, as well as how management could successfully prove that controls exist and are effective. A set of audit objections is also presented, as well as how to overcome them.

The document describes how controls could be designed in a deployment pipeline to mitigate the stated risks, and provides examples of control attestations and control artifacts to demonstrate control effectiveness. It was intended to be general to all control objectives, including in support of accurate financial reporting, regulatory compliance (e.g., SEC SOX-404, HIPAA, FedRAMP, EU Model Contracts, and the proposed SEC Reg-SCI regulations), contractual obligations (e.g., PCI DSS, DOD DISA), and effective and efficient operations.

Case Study
Relying on Production Telemetry for ATM Systems

Mary Smith (a pseudonym) heads up the DevOps initiative for the consumer banking property of a large US financial services organization. She made the observation that information security, auditors, and regulators often put too much reliance on code reviews to detect fraud. Instead, they should be relying on production monitoring controls in addition to using automated testing, code reviews, and approvals, to effectively mitigate the risks associated with errors and fraud.

She observed:

> Many years ago, we had a developer who planted a backdoor in the code that we deploy to our ATM cash machines. They were able to put the ATMs into maintenance mode at certain times, allowing them to take cash out of the machines. We were able to detect the fraud very quickly, and it wasn't through a code review. These types of backdoors are difficult, or even impossible, to detect when the perpetrators have sufficient means, motive, and opportunity.

> However, we quickly detected the fraud during our regularly operations review meeting when someone noticed that ATMs in a city were being put into maintenance mode at unscheduled times. We found the fraud even before the scheduled

cash audit process, when they reconcile the amount of cash in the ATMs with authorized transactions.

In this case study, the fraud occurred despite separation of duties between Development and Operations and a change approval process, but was quickly detected and corrected through effective production telemetry.

CONCLUSION

Throughout this chapter, we have discussed practices that make information security everyone's job, where all of our information security objectives are integrated into the daily work of everyone in the value stream. By doing this, we significantly improve the effectiveness of our controls, so that we can better prevent security breaches, as well as detect and recover from them faster. And we significantly reduce the work associated with preparing and passing compliance audits.

PART VI CONCLUSION

Throughout the previous chapters, we explored how to take DevOps principles and apply them to Information Security, helping us achieve our goals, and making sure security is a part of everyone's job, every day. Better security ensures that we are defensible and sensible with our data, that we can recover from security problems before they become catastrophic, and, most importantly, that we can make the security of our systems and data better than ever.

We have come to the end of a detailed exploration of both the principles and technical practices of DevOps. At a time when every technology leader is challenged with enabling security, reliability, and agility, and at a time when security breaches, time to market, and massive technology transformation is taking place, DevOps offers a solution. Hopefully, this book has provided an in-depth understanding of the problem and a road map to creating relevant solutions.

As we have explored throughout *The DevOps Handbook*, we know that, left unmanaged, an inherent conflict can exist between Development and Operations that creates ever-worsening problems,which results in slower time to market for new products and features, poor quality, increased outages and technical debt, reduced engineering productivity, as well as increased employee dissatisfaction and burnout.

DevOps principles and patterns enable us to break this core, chronic conflict. After reading this book, we hope you see how a DevOps transformation can enable the creation of dynamic learning organizations, achieving the amazing outcomes of fast flow and world-class reliability and security, as well as increased competitiveness and employee satisfaction.

DevOps requires potentially new cultural and management norms, and changes in our technical practices and architecture. This requires a coalition that spans business leadership, Product Management, Development, QA, IT Operations, Information Security, and even Marketing, where many technology initiatives originate. When all these teams work together, we can create a safe system of work, enabling small teams to quickly and independently develop and validate code that can be safely deployed to customers. This results in maximizing developer productivity, organizational learning, high employee satisfaction, and the ability to win in the marketplace.

Our goal in writing this book was to sufficiently codify DevOps principles and practices so that the amazing outcomes achieved within the DevOps community could be replicated by others. We hope to accelerate the adoption of DevOps initiatives and support their successful implementations while lowering the activation energy required for them to be completed.

We know the dangers of postponing improvements and settling for daily work-arounds, as well as the difficulties of changing how we prioritize and perform our daily work. Furthermore, we understand the risks and effort required to get organizations to embrace a different way of working, as well as the perception that DevOps is another passing fad, soon to replaced by the next buzzword.

We assert that DevOps is transformational to how we perform technology work, just as Lean forever transformed how manufacturing work was performed in the 1980s. Those that adopt DevOps will win in the marketplace, at the expense of those that do not. They will create energized and continually learning organizations that out-perform and out-innovate their competitors.

Because of this, DevOps is not just a technology imperative, but also an organizational imperative. The bottom line is, DevOps is applicable and relevant to any and all organizations that must increase flow of planned work through the technology organization, while maintaining quality, reliability, and security for our customers.

Our call to action is this: no matter what role you play in your organization, start finding people around you who want to change how work is performed. Show this book to others and create a coalition of like-minded thinkers to break out of the downward spiral. Ask organizational leaders to support these efforts, or, better yet, sponsor and lead these efforts yourself.

Finally, since you've made it this far, we have a dirty secret to reveal. In many of our case studies, following the achievement of the breakthrough results presented, many of the change agents were promoted—but, in some cases, there was later a change of leadership which resulted in many of the people involved leaving, accompanied by a rolling back of the organizational changes they had created.

We believe it's important not to be cynical about this possibility. The people involved in these transformations knew up front that what they were doing had a high chance of failure, and they did it anyway. In doing so, perhaps most importantly, they inspired the rest of us by showing us what can be done. Innovation is impossible without risk taking, and if you haven't managed to upset at least some people in management, you're probably not trying hard enough. Don't let your organization's immune system deter or distract you from your vision. As Jesse Robbins, previously "master of disaster" at Amazon, likes to say, "Don't fight stupid, make more awesome."

DevOps benefits all of us in the technology value stream, whether we are Dev, Ops, QA, Infosec, Product Owners, or customers. It brings joy back to developing great products, with fewer death marches. It enables humane work conditions with fewer weekends and missed holidays with our loved ones. It enables teams to work together to survive, learn, thrive, delight our customers, and help our organization succeed.

We sincerely hope *The DevOps Handbook* helps you achieve these goals.

ADDITIONAL MATERIAL

APPENDIX 1   THE CONVERGENCE OF DEVOPS

We believe that DevOps is benefiting from an incredible convergence of management movements, which are all mutually reinforcing and can help create a powerful coalition to transform how organizations develop and deliver IT products and services.

John Willis named this "the Convergence of DevOps." The various elements of this convergence are described below in approximate chronological order. (Note that these descriptions are not intended to be an exhaustive description, but merely enough to show the progression of thinking and the rather improbable connections that led to DevOps.)

THE LEAN MOVEMENT

The Lean Movement started in the 1980s as an attempt to codify the Toyota Production System with the popularization of techniques such as Value Stream Mapping, kanban boards, and Total Productive Maintenance.

Two major tenets of Lean were the deeply held belief that lead time (i.e., the time required to convert raw materials into finished goods) was the best predictor of quality, customer satisfaction, and employee happiness; and that one of the best predictors of short lead times was small batch sizes, with the theoretical ideal being "single piece flow" (i.e., "1x1" flow: inventory of 1, batch size of 1).

Lean principles focus on creating value for the customer—thinking systematically, creating constancy of purpose, embracing scientific thinking, creating flow and pull (versus push), assuring quality at the source, leading with humility, and respecting every individual.

THE AGILE MOVEMENT
Started in 2001, the Agile Manifesto was created by seventeen of the leading thinkers in software development, with the goal of turning lightweight methods such as DP and DSDM into a wider movement that could take on heavyweight software development processes such as waterfall development and methodologies such as the Rational Unified Process.

A key principle was to "deliver working software frequently, from a couple of weeks to a couple of months, with a preference to the shorter timescale." Two other principles focus on the need for small, self-motivated teams, working in a high-trust management model and an emphasis on small batch sizes. Agile is also associated with a set of tools and practices such as Scrum, Standups, and so on.

THE VELOCITY CONFERENCE MOVEMENT
Started in 2007, the Velocity Conference was created by Steve Souders, John Allspaw, and Jesse Robbins to provide a home for the IT Operations and Web Performance tribe. At the Velocity 2009 conference, John Allspaw and Paul Hammond gave the seminal "10 Deploys per Day: Dev and Ops Cooperation at Flickr."

THE AGILE INFRASTRUCTURE MOVEMENT
At the 2008 Agile Toronto conference, Patrick Dubois and Andrew Schafer held a "birds of a feather" session on applying Agile principles to infrastructure as opposed to application code. They rapidly gained a following of like-minded thinkers, including John Willis. Later, Dubois was so excited by Allspaw and Hammond's "10 Deploys per Day: Dev and Ops Cooperation at Flickr" presentation that he created the first DevOpsDays in Ghent, Belgium, in 2009, coining the word "DevOps."

THE CONTINUOUS DELIVERY MOVEMENT
Building upon the Development discipline of continuous build, test, and integration, Jez Humble and David Farley extended the concept of continuous delivery, which included a "deployment pipeline" to ensure that code and infrastructure are always in a deployable state and that all code checked in to truck is deployed into production.

This idea was first presented at Agile 2006 and was also independently developed by Tim Fitz in a blog post titled "Continuous Deployment."

THE TOYOTA KATA MOVEMENT

In 2009, Mike Rother wrote *Toyota Kata: Managing People for Improvement, Adaptiveness and Superior Results*, which described learnings over his twenty-year journey to understand and codify the causal mechanisms of the Toyota Production System. *Toyota Kata* describes the "unseen managerial routines and thinking that lie behind Toyota's success with continuous improvement and adaptation... and how other companies develop similar routines and thinking in their organizations."

His conclusion was that the Lean community missed the most important practice of all, which he described as the Improvement Kata. He explains that every organization has work routines, and the critical factor in Toyota was making improvement work habitual, and building it into the daily work of everyone in the organization. The Toyota Kata institutes an iterative, incremental, scientific approach to problem-solving in the pursuit of a shared organizational true north.

THE LEAN STARTUP MOVEMENT

In 2011, Eric Ries wrote *The Lean Startup: How Today's Entrepreneurs Use Continuous Innovation to Create Radically Successful Businesses*, codifying his lessons learned at IMVU, a Silicon Valley startup, which built upon the work of Steve Blank in *The Four Steps to the Epiphany* as well as continuous deployment techniques. Eric Ries also codified related practices and terms including Minimum Viable Product, the build-measure-learn cycle, and many continuous deployment technical patterns.

THE LEAN UX MOVEMENT

In 2013, Jeff Gothelf wrote *Lean UX: Applying Lean Principles to Improve User Experience*, which codified how to improve the "fuzzy front end" and explained how product owners can frame business hypotheses, experiment, and gain confidence in those business hypotheses before investing time and resources in the resulting features. By adding Lean UX, we now have the tools to fully optimize the flow between business hypotheses, feature development, testing, deployment, and service delivery to the customer.

THE RUGGED COMPUTING MOVEMENT

In 2011, Joshua Corman, David Rice, and Jeff Williams examined the apparent futility of securing applications and environments late in the life cycle. In response, they created a philosophy called "Rugged Computing," which attempts to frame the non-functional requirements of stability, scalability, availability, survivability, sustainability, security, supportability, manageability, and defensibility.

Because of the potential for high release rates, DevOps can put incredible pressure on QA and Infosec, because when deploy rates go from monthly or quarterly to hundreds or thousands daily, no longer are two week turnaround times from Infosec or QA tenable. The Rugged Computing movement posited that the current approach to fighting the vulnerable industrial complex being employed by most information security programs is hopeless.

APPENDIX 2 THEORY OF CONSTRAINTS AND CORE, CHRONIC CONFLICTS

The Theory of Constraints body of knowledge extensively discusses the use of creating core conflict clouds (often referred to as "C³"). Here is the conflict cloud for IT:

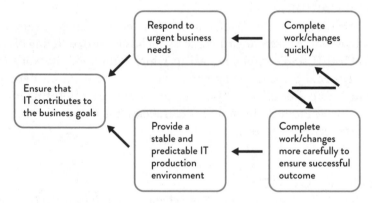

Figure 46: *The core, chronic conflict facing every IT organization*

During the 1980s, there was a very well-known core, chronic conflict in manufacturing. Every plant manager had two valid business goals: protect sales and reduce costs. The problem was that in order to protect sales, sales management was incentivized to increase inventory to ensure that it was always possible to fulfill customer demand.

On the other hand, in order to reduce cost, production management was incentivized to decrease inventory to ensure that money was not tied up in work in progress that wasn't immediately shippable to the customer in the form of fulfilled sales.

They were able to break the conflict by adopting Lean principles, such as reducing batch sizes, reducing work in process, and shortening and amplifying feedback loops. This resulted in dramatic increases in plant productivity, product quality, and customer satisfaction.

The principles behind DevOps work patterns are the same as those that transformed manufacturing, allowing us to optimize the IT value stream, converting business needs into capabilities and services that provide value for our customers.

APPENDIX 3   TABULAR FORM OF DOWNWARD SPIRAL

The columnar form of the downward spiral depicted in *The Phoenix Project* is shown below:

Table 4: *The Downward Spiral*

IT Operations sees...	Development sees...
Fragile applications are prone to failure	Fragile applications are prone to failure
Long time required to figure out which bit got flipped	More urgent, date-driven projects put into the queue
Detective control is a salesperson	Even more fragile code (less secure) put into production
Too much time required to restore service	More releases have increasingly turbulent installs
Too much firefighting and unplanned work	Release cycles lengthen to amortize cost of deployments
Urgent security rework and remediation	Failing bigger deployments more difficult to diagnose
Planned project work cannot be completed	Most senior and constrained IT Operations resources have less time to fix underlying process problems
Frustrated customers leave	Ever increasing backlog of work that could help the business win
Market share goes down	Ever increasing amount of tension between IT Operations, Development, Design
Business misses Wall Street commitments	
Business makes even larger promises to Wall Street	

The problem with high amounts of queue time is exacerbated when there are many handoffs, because that is where queues are created. Figure 47 shows wait time as a function of how busy a resource at a work center is. The asymptotic curve shows why a "simple 30 minute change" often takes weeks to complete—specific engineers and work centers often become problematic bottlenecks when they operate at high utilization. As a work center approaches 100% utilization, any work required from it will languish in queues and won't be worked on without someone expediting/escalating.

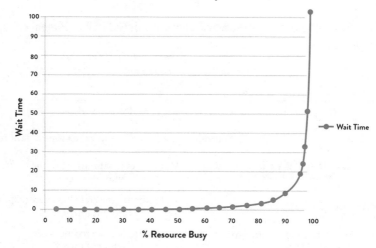

Figure 47: *Queue size and wait times as function of percent utilization (Source: Kim, Behr, and Spafford,* The Phoenix Project, *ePub edition, 557.)*

In figure 47, the x-axis is the percent busy for a given resource at a work center, and the y-axis is the approximate wait time (or, more precisely stated, the queue length). What the shape of the line shows is that as resource utilization goes past 80%, wait time goes through the roof.

In *The Phoenix Project*, here's how Bill and his team realized the devastating consequences of this property on lead times for the commitments they were making to the project management office:

> I tell them about what Erik told me at MRP-8, about how wait times depend upon resource utilization. "The wait time is the 'percentage of time busy' divided by the 'percentage of time idle.' In other words, if a resource is fifty percent busy, then it's fifty percent idle. The wait

time is fifty percent divided by fifty percent, so one unit of time. Let's call it one hour.

So, on average, our task would wait in the queue for one hour before it gets worked.

"On the other hand, if a resource is ninety percent busy, the wait time is "ninety percent divided by ten percent", or nine hours. In other words, our task would wait in queue nine times longer than if the resource were fifty percent idle."

I conclude, "So... For the Phoenix task, assuming we have seven handoffs, and that each of those resources is busy ninety percent of the time, the tasks would spend in queue a total of nine hours times the seven steps..."

"What? Sixty-three hours, just in queue time?" Wes says, incredulously. "That's impossible!"

Patty says with a smirk, "Oh, of course. Because it's only thirty seconds of typing, right?"

Bill and team realize that their "simple 30 minute task" actually requires seven handoffs (e.g., server team, networking team, database team, virtualization team, and, of course, Brent, the 'rockstar' engineer).

Assuming that all work centers were 90% busy, the figure shows us that the average wait time at each work center is nine hours—and because the work had to go through seven work centers, the total wait time is seven times that: sixty-three hours.

In other words, the total % of *value added time* (sometimes known as process time) was only 0.16% of the total lead time (thirty minutes divided by sixty-three hours). That means that for 99.8% of our total lead time, the work was simply sitting in queue, waiting to be worked on.

APPENDIX 5 MYTHS OF INDUSTRIAL SAFETY

Decades of research into complex systems shows that countermeasures are based on several myths. In "Some Myths about Industrial Safety," by Denis Besnard and Erik Hollnagel, they are summarized as such:

- **Myth 1:** "Human error is the largest single cause of accidents and incidents."

- **Myth 2:** "Systems will be safe if people comply with the procedures they have been given."

- **Myth 3:** "Safety can be improved by barriers and protection; more layers of protection results in higher safety."

- **Myth 4:** "Accident analysis can identify the root cause (the 'truth') of why the accident happened."

- **Myth 5:** "Accident investigation is the logical and rational identification of causes based on facts."

- **Myth 6:** "Safety always has the highest priority and will never be compromised."

The differences between what is myth and what is true are shown below:

Table 5: *Two Stories*

Myth	Reality
Human error is seen as the cause of failure.	Human error is seen as the effect of systemic vulnerabilities deeper inside the organization.
Saying what people should have done is a satisfying way to describe failure.	Saying what people should have done doesn't explain why it made sense for them to do what they did.
Telling people to be more careful will make the problem go away.	Only by constantly seeking out their vulnerabilities can organizations enhance safety.

APPENDIX 6   THE TOYOTA ANDON CORD

Many ask how can any work be completed if the Andon cord is being pulled over five thousand times per day? To be precise, not every Andon cord pull results in stopping the entire assembly line. Rather, when the Andon cord is pulled, the team leader overseeing the specified work center has fifty seconds to resolve the problem. If the problem has not been resolved by the time the fifty seconds is up, the partially assembled vehicle will cross a physically drawn line on the floor, and the assembly line will be stopped.

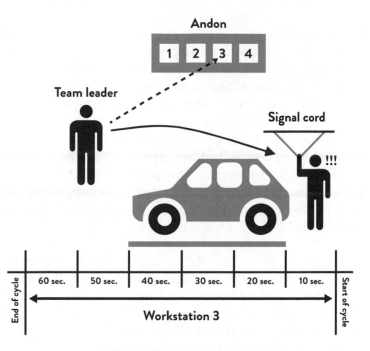

Figure 48: *The Toyota Andon cord*

APPENDIX 7   COTS SOFTWARE

Currently, in order to get complex COTS (commercial off-the-shelf) software (e.g., SAP, IBM WebSphere, Oracle WebLogic) into version control, we may have to eliminate the use of graphical point-and-click vendor installer tools. To do that, we need to discover what the vendor installer is doing, and we may need to do an install on a clean server image, diff the file system, and put those added files into version control. Files that don't vary by environment are put into one place ("base install"), while environment-specific files are put into their own directory ("test" or "production"). By doing this, software install operations become merely a version control operation, enabling better visibility, repeatability, and speed.

We may also have to transform any application configuration settings so that they are in version control. For instance, we may transform application configurations that are stored in a database into XML files and vice versa.

A sample agenda of the post-mortem meeting is shown below:

- An initial statement will be made by the meeting leader or facilitator to reinforce that this meeting is a blameless post-mortem and that we will not focus on past events or speculate on "would haves" or "could haves." Facilitators might read the "Retrospective Prime Directive" from the website Retrospective.com.

  Furthermore, the facilitator will remind everyone that any countermeasures must be assigned to someone, and if the corrective action does not warrant being a top priority when the meeting is over, then it is not a corrective action. (This is to prevent the meeting from generating a list of good ideas that are never implemented.)

- Those at the meeting will reach an agreement on the complete timeline of the incident, including when and who detected the issue, how it was discovered (e.g., automated monitoring, manual detection, customer notified us), when service was satisfactorily restored, and so forth. We will also integrate into the timeline all external communications during the incident.

  When we use the word "timeline," it may evoke the image of a linear set of steps of how we gained an understanding of the problem and eventually fixed it. In reality, especially in complex systems, there will likely be many events that contributed to the accident, and many troubleshooting paths and actions will have been taken in an effort to fix it. In this activity, we seek to chronicle all of these events and the perspectives of the actors and establish hypotheses concerning cause and effect where possible.

- The team will create a list of all the factors which contributed to the incident, both human and technical. They may then sort them into categories, such as 'design decision,' 'remediation,' 'discovering there was a problem,' and so forth. The team will use techniques such as brainstorming and the 'infinite hows' to drill down on contributing factors they deem particularly important to discover deeper levels of contributing factors. All perspectives should be included and respected—nobody shod be permitted to argue with or deny the reality of a contributing factor somebody else has identified. It's important for the post-mortem facilitator to ensure that sufficient time is spent on this activity, and that the team doesn't try and engage in convergent behavior such as trying to identify one or more 'root causes.'

- Those at the meeting will reach an agreement on the list of corrective actions that will be made top priorities after the meeting. Assembling this list will require brainstorming and choosing the best potential actions to either prevent the issue from occurring or enable faster detection or recovery. Other ways to improve the systems may also be included.

  Our goal is to identify the smallest number of incremental steps to achieve the desired outcomes, as opposed to "big bang" changes, which not only take longer to implement, but delay the improvements we need.

  We will also generate a separate list of lower priority ideas and assign an owner. If similar problems occur in the future, these ideas may serve as the foundation for crafting future countermeasures.

- Those at the meeting will reach an agreement on the incident metrics and their organizational impact. For example, we may choose to measure our incidents by the following metrics:

  ▷ **Event severity:** How severe was this issue? This directly relates to the impact on the service and our customers.

  ▷ **Total downtime:** How long were customers unable to use the service to any degree?

  ▷ **Time to detect:** How long did it take for us or our systems to know there was a problem?

  ▷ **Time to resolve:** How long after we knew there was a problem did it take for us to restore service?

Bethany Macri from Etsy observed, "Blamelessness in a post-mortem does not mean that no one takes responsibility. It means that we want to find out what the circumstances were that allowed the person making the change or who introduced the problem to do this. What was the larger environment....

The idea is that by removing blame, you remove fear, and by removing fear, you get honesty."

APPENDIX 9   THE SIMIAN ARMY

After the 2011 AWS EAST Outage, Netflix had numerous discussions about engineering their systems to automatically deal with failure. These discussions have evolved into a service called "Chaos Monkey."

Since then, Chaos Monkey has evolved into a whole family of tools, known internally as the "Netflix Simian Army," to simulate increasingly catastrophic levels of failures:

- **Chaos Gorilla:** simulates the failure of an entire AWS availability zone

- **Chaos Kong:** simulates failure of entire AWS regions, such as North America or Europe

Other member of the Simian Army now include:

- **Latency Monkey:** induces artificial delays or downtime in their RESTful client-server communication layer to simulate service degradation and ensure that dependent services respond appropriately

- **Conformity Monkey:** finds and shuts down AWS instances that don't adhere to best-practices (e.g., when instances don't belong to an auto-scaling group or when there is no escalation engineer email address listed in the service catalog)

- **Doctor Monkey:** taps into health checks that run on each instance and finds unhealthy instances and proactively shuts them down if owners don't fix the root cause in time

- **Janitor Monkey:** ensures that their cloud environment is running free of clutter and waste; searches for unused resources and disposes of them

- **Security Monkey:** an extension of Conformity Monkey; finds and terminates instances with security violations or vulnerabilities, such as improperly configured AWS security groups

APPENDIX 10   TRANSPARENT UPTIME

Lenny Rachitsky wrote about the benefits of what he called "transparent uptime:"

1. Your support costs go down as your users are able to self-identify system wide problems without calling or emailing your support department. Users will no longer have to guess whether their issues are local or global, and can more quickly get to the root of the problem before complaining to you.

2. You are better able to communicate with your users during downtime events, taking advantage of the broadcast nature of the Internet versus the one-to-one nature of email and the phone. You spend less time communicating the same thing over and over and more time resolving the issue.

3. You create a single and obvious place for your users to come to when they are experiencing downtime. You save your users' time currently spent searching forums, Twitter, or your blog.

4. Trust is the cornerstone of any successful SaaS adoption. Your customers are betting their business and their livelihoods on your service or platform. Both current and prospective customers require confidence in your service. Both need to know they won't be left in the dark, alone and uninformed, when you run into trouble. Real time insight into unexpected events is the best way to build this trust. Keeping them in the dark and alone is no longer an option.

5. It's only a matter of time before every serious SaaS provider will be offering a public health dashboard. Your users will demand it.

- Many of the common problems faced by IT organizations are discussed in the first half of the book *The Phoenix Project: A Novel about IT, DevOps, and Helping Your Business Win* by Gene Kim, Kevin Behr, and George Spafford.

- This video shows a speech Paul O'Neill gave on his tenure as CEO of Alcoa, including the investigation he took part in after a teenage worker was killed at one of Alcoa's plants: https://www.youtube.com/watch?v=tC2ucDs_XJY.

- For more on value stream mapping, see *Value Stream Mapping: How to Visualize Work and Align Leadership for Organizational Transformation* by Karen Martin and Mike Osterling.

- For more on ORMs, visit Stack Overflow: http://stackoverflow.com/questions/1279613/what-is-an-orm-and-where-can-i-learn-more-about-it.

- An excellent primer on many agile development rituals and how to use them in IT Operations work can be found in a series of posts written on the Agile Admin blog: http://theagileadmin.com/2011/02/21/scrum-for-operations-what-is-scrum/.

- For more information on architecting for fast builds, see Daniel Worthington-Bodart's blog post "Crazy Fast Build Times (or When 10 Seconds Starts to Make You Nervous):" http://dan.bodar.com/2012/02/28/crazy-fast-build-times-or-when-10-seconds-starts-to-make-you-nervous/.

- For more details on performance testing at Facebook, along with some detailed information on Facebook's release process, check out Chuck Rossi's presentation "The Facebook Release Process:" http://www.infoq.com/presentations/Facebook-Release-Process.

- Many more variants of dark launching can be found in chapter 8 of *The Practice of Cloud System Administration: Designing and Operating Large Distributed Systems, Volume 2* by Thomas A. Limoncelli, Strata R. Chalup, and Christina J. Hogan.

- There is an excellent technical discussion of feature toggles here: http://martinfowler.com/articles/feature-toggles.html.

- Releases are discussed in more detail in *The Practice of Cloud System Administration: Designing and Operating Large Distributed Systems, Volume 2* by Thomas A. Limoncelli, Strata R. Chalup, and Christina J. Hogan; *Continuous Delivery: Reliable Software Releases Through Build, Test, and Deployment Automation* by Jez Humble and David Farley; and *Release It! Design and Deploy Production-Ready Software* by Michael T. Nygard.

- A description of the circuit breaker pattern can be found here: http://martinfowler.com/bliki/CircuitBreaker.html.

- For more on the cost of delay see *The Principles of Product Development Flow: Second Generation Lean Product Development* by Donald G. Reinertsen.

- A further discussion on staying ahead of failures for the Amazon S3 service can be found here: https://qconsf.com/sf2010/dl/qcon-sanfran-2009/slides/JasonMcHugh_AmazonS3ArchitectingForResiliencyInTheFaceOfFailures.pdf.

- For an excellent guide on conducting user research, see *Lean UX: Applying Lean Principles to Improve User Experience* by Jeff Gothelf and Josh Seiden.

- Which Test Won? is a site that displays hundreds of real-life A/B tests and asks the viewer to guess which variant performed better, reinforcing the key that unless we actually test, we're merely guessing. Visit it here: http://whichtestwon.com/.

- A list of architectural patterns can be found in *Release It! Design and Deploy Production-Ready Software* by Michael T. Nygard.

- An example of published Chef post-mortem meeting notes can be found here: https://www.chef.io/blog/2014/08/14/cookbook -dependency-api-postmortem/. A video of the meeting can be found here: https://www.youtube.com/watch?v=Rmi1Tn50WfI.

- A current schedule of upcoming DevOpsDays can be found on the DevOpsDays website: http://www.devopsdays.org/. Instructions on organizing a new DevOpsDays can be found on the DevOpsDay Organizing Guide page: http://www.devopsdays.org /pages/organizing/.

- More on using tools to manage secrets can be found in Noah Kantrowitz's post "Secrets Management and Chef" on his blog: https://coderanger.net/chef-secrets/.

- James Wickett and Gareth Rushgrove have put all their examples of secure pipelines on the GitHub website: https://github.com /secure-pipeline.

- The National Vulnerability Database website and XML data feeds can be found at: https://nvd.nist.gov/.

- A concrete scenario involving integration between Puppet and ThoughtWorks' Go and Mingle (a project management application) can be found in a Puppet Labs blog post by Andrew Cunningham and Andrew Myers and edited by Jez Humble: https:// puppetlabs.com/blog/a-deployment-pipeline-for-infrastructure.

- Preparing and passing compliance audits is further explored in Jason Chan's 2015 presentation "SEC310: Splitting the Check on Compliance and Security: Keeping Developers and Auditors Happy in the Cloud:" https://www.youtube.com/watch?v=Ioo0_K4v12Y& feature=youtu.be.

- The story of how application configuration settings were transformed by Jez Humble and David Farley for Oracle WebLogic was described in the book *Continuous Delivery: Reliable Software Releases Through Build, Test, and Deployment Automation*. Mirco Hering described a more generic approach to this process here: http:// notafactoryanymore.com/2015/10/19/devops-for-systems-of -record-a-new-hope-preview-of-does-talk/.

- A sample list of DevOps operational requirements can be found here: http://blog.devopsguys.com/2013/12/19/the-top-ten -devops-operational-requirements/.

Endnotes

INTRODUCTION

xxii   *Before the revolution...* Eliyahu M. Goldratt, *Beyond the Goal: Eliyahu Goldratt Speaks on the Theory of Constraints (Your Coach in a Box)* (Prince Frederick, Maryland: Gildan Media, 2005), Audiobook.

xxiv   *Put even more...* Jeff Immelt, "GE CEO Jeff Immelt: Let's Finally End the Debate over Whether We Are in a Tech Bubble," *Business Insider*, December 9, 2015, http://www.businessinsider.com /ceo-of-ge-lets-finally-end-the-debate-over-whether-we-are-in -a-tech-bubble-2015-12.

        Or as Jeffrey... "Weekly Top 10: Your DevOps Flavor," *Electric Cloud*, April 1, 2016, http://electric-cloud.com/blog/2016/04/weekly-top -10-devops-flavor/.

xxv   *Dr. Eliyahu M. Goldratt...* Goldratt, *Beyond the Goal*.

xvi   *As Christopher Little...* Christopher Little, personal correspondence with Gene Kim, 2010.

xxvii   *As Steven J. Spear...* Steven J. Spear, *The High-Velocity Edge: How Market Leaders Leverage Operational Excellence to Beat the Competition* (New York, NY: McGraw Hill Education), Kindle edition, chap. 3.

        In 2013, the... Chris Skinner, "Banks have bigger development shops than Microsoft," Chris Skinner's Blog, accessed July 28, 2016, http:// thefinanser.com/2011/09/banks-have-bigger-development-shops -than-microsoft.html/.

xxviii *Projects are typically...* Nico Stehr and Reiner Grundmann, *Knowledge: Critical Concepts, Volume 3* (London: Routledge, 2005), 139.

        Dr. Vernon Richardson... A. Masli, V. Richardson, M. Widenmier, and R. Zmud, "Senior Executive's IT Management Responsibilities: Serious IT Deficiencies and CEO-CFO Turnover," *MIS Quaterly* (published electronically June 21, 2016).

xxix   *Consider the following...* "IDC Forecasts Worldwide IT Spending to Grow 6% in 2012, Despite Economic Uncertainty," *Business Wire*, September 10, 2012, http://www.businesswire.com/news/home /20120910005280/en/IDC-Forecasts-Worldwide-Spending-Grow -6-2012.

xxxii   *The first surprise...* Nigel Kersten, IT Revolution, and PwC, *2015 State of DevOps Report* (Portland, OR: Puppet Labs, 2015), https://puppet .com/resources/white-paper/2015-state-of-devops-report?_ga=1.66 12658.168869.1464412647&link=blog.

xxxiii   *This is highlighted...* Frederick P. Brooks, Jr., *The Mythical Man-Month: Essays on Software Engineering, Anniversary Edition* (Upper Saddle River, NJ: Addison-Wesley, 1995).

xxxiv   *As Randy Shoup...* Gene Kim, Gary Gruver, Randy Shoup, and Andrew Phillips, "Exploring the Uncharted Territory of Microservices," XebiaLabs.com, webinar, February 20, 2015, https:// xebialabs.com/community/webinars/exploring-the-uncharted -territory-of-microservices/.

The 2015 State... Kersten, IT Revolution, and PwC, *2015 State of DevOps Report*.

Another more extreme... "Velocity 2011: Jon Jenkins, 'Velocity Culture'," YouTube video, 15:13, posted by O'Reilly, June 20, 2011, https://www.youtube.com/watch?v=dxk8b9rSKOo; "Transforming Software Development," YouTube video, 40:57, posted by Amazon Web Service, April 10, 2015, https://www .youtube.com/watch?v=YCrhemssYuI&feature=youtu.be.

xxxv   *Later in his...* Eliyahu M. Goldratt, *Beyond the Goal*.

As with The... JGFLL, review of *The Phoenix Project: A Novel About IT, DevOps, and Helping Your Business Win*, by Gene Kim, Kevin Behr, and George Spafford, Amazon.com review, March 4, 2013, http:// www.amazon.com/review/R1KSSPTEGLWJ23; Mark L Townsend, review of *The Phoenix Project: A Novel About IT, DevOps, and Helping Your Business Win*, by Gene Kim, Kevin Behr, and George Spafford, Amazon.com review, March 2, 2013, http://uedata.amazon.com/gp /customer-reviews/R1097DFODM12VD/ref=cm_cr_getr_d_rvw _ttl?ie=UTF8&ASIN=B00VATFAMI; Scott Van Den Elzen, review of *The Phoenix Project: A Novel About IT, DevOps, and Helping Your Business Win*, by Gene Kim, Kevin Behr, and George Spafford, Amazon.com review, March 13, 2013, http://uedata.amazon.com /gp/customer-reviews/R2K95XEH5OL3Q5/ref=cm_cr_getr_d_rvw_ ttl?ie=UTF8&ASIN=B00VATFAMI.

PART I INTRODUCTION

5   *One key principle...* Kent Beck, et al., "Twelve Principles of Agile Software," AgileManifesto.org, 2001, http://agilemanifesto.org/principles.html.

6   *He concluded that...* Mike Rother, *Toyota Kata: Managing People for Improvement, Adaptiveness and Superior Results* (New York: McGraw Hill, 2010), Kindle edition, Part III.

CHAPTER 1

7   *Karen Martin and...* Karen Martin and Mike Osterling, *Value Stream Mapping: How to Visualize Work and Align Leadership for Organizational Transformation* (New York: McGraw Hill, 2013), Kindle edition, chap 1.

9   *In this book...* Ibid., chap. 3.

11   *Karen Martin and...* Ibid.

CHAPTER 2

17   *Studies have shown...* Joshua S. Rubinstein, David E. Meyer, and Jeffrey E. Evans, "Executive Control of Cognitive Processes in Task Switching," *Journal of Experimental Psychology: Human Perception and Performance* 27, no. 4 (2001): 763-797, doi: 10.1037//0096-1523.27.4.763, http://www.umich.edu/~bcalab/documents/RubinsteinMeyerEvans2001.pdf.

18   *Dominica DeGrandis, one...* "DOES15—Dominica DeGrandis—The Shape of Uncertainty," YouTube video, 22:54, posted by DevOps Enterprise Summit, November 5, 2015, https://www.youtube.com/watch?v=Gpo5iod34gg.

     Taiichi Ohno compared... Sami Bahri, "Few Patients-In-Process and Less Safety Scheduling; Incoming Supplies are Secondary," The Deming Institute Blog, August 22, 2013, https://blog.deming.org/2013/08/fewer-patients-in-process-and-less-safety-scheduling-incoming-supplies-are-secondary/.

     In other words... Meeting between David J. Andersen and team at Motorola with Daniel S. Vacanti, February 24, 2004; story retold at USC CSSE Research Review with Barry Boehm in March 2004.

19   *The dramatic differences...* James P. Womack and Daniel T. Jones, *Lean Thinking: Banish Waste and Create Wealth in Your Corporation* (New York: Free Press, 2010), Kindle edition, chap. 1.

20   *There are many...* Eric Ries, "Work in small batches," StartupLessonsLearned.com, February 20, 2009, http://www.startuplessonslearned.com/2009/02/work-in-small-batches.html.

21   *In Beyond the…* Goldratt, *Beyond the Goal.*

22   *As a solution…* Eliyahu M. Goldratt, *The Goal: A Process of Ongoing Improvement* (Great Barrington, MA: North River Press, 2014), Kindle edition, "Five Focusing Steps."

23   *Shigeo Shingo, one…* Shigeo Shingo, *A Study of the Toyota Production System: From an Industrial Engineering Viewpoint* (London: Productivity Press, 1989); "The 7 Wastes (Seven forms of Muda)," BeyondLean.com, accessed July 28, 2016, http://www.beyondlean.com/7-wastes.html.

24   *In the book…* Mary Poppendieck and Tom Poppendieck, *Implementing Lean Software: From Concept to Cash*, (Upper Saddle River, NJ: Addison-Wesley, 2007), 74.

        The following categories… Adapted from Damon Edwards, "DevOps Kaizen: Find and Fix What Is Really Behind Your Problems," Slideshare.net, posted by dev2ops, May 4, 2015, http://www.slideshare.net/dev2ops/dev-ops-kaizen-damon-edwards.

CHAPTER 3

28   *Dr. Charles Perrow…* Charles Perrow, *Normal Accidents: Living with High Risk Technologies* (Princeton, NJ: Princeton University Press, 1999).

        Dr. Sidney Dekker… Dr. Sidney Dekker, *The Field Guide to Understanding Human Error* (Lund University, Sweden: Ashgate, 2006).

        After he decoded… Spear, *The High-Velocity Edge*, chap. 8.

        Dr. Spear extended… Ibid.

29   *Dr. Peter Senge…* Peter M. Senge, *The Fifth Discipline: The Art & Practice of the Learning Organization* (New York: Doubleday, 2006), Kindle edition, chap. 5.

        In one well-documented… "NUMMI," *This American Life*, March 26, 2010, http://www.thisamericanlife.org/radio-archives/episode/403/transcript.

30   *As Elisabeth Hendrickson…* "DOES15 - Elisabeth Hendrickson - Its All About Feedback," YouTube video, 34:47, posted by DevOps Enterprise Summit, November 5, 2015, https://www.youtube.com/watch?v=r2BFTXBundQ.

        "In doings so… Spear, *The High-Velocity Edge*, chap. 1.

31   *As Dr. Spear…* Ibid., chap. 4.

33   *Examples of ineffective…* Jez Humble, Joanne Molesky, and Barry O'Reilly, *Lean Enterprise: How High Performance Organizations*

Innovate at Scale (Sebastopol, CA: O'Reilly Media, 2015), Kindle edition, Part IV.

In the 1700s... Dr. Thomas Sowell, *Knowledge and Decisions* (New York: Basic Books, 1980), 222.

34 *As Gary Gruver...* Gary Gruver, personal correspondence with Gene Kim, 2014.

CHAPTER 4

37 *For instance, in...* Paul Adler, "Time-and-Motion Regained," *Harvard Business Review*, January-February 1993, https://hbr.org/1993/01/time-and-motion-regained.

38 *The "name, blame...* Dekker, *The Field Guide to Understanding Human Error*, chap. 1.

Dr. Sidney Dekker... "Just Culture: Balancing Safety and Accountability," Lund University, Human Factors & System Safety website, November 6, 2015, http://www.humanfactors.lth.se/sidney-dekker/books/just-culture/.

39 *He observed that...* Ron Westrum, "The study of information flow: A personal journey," *Proceedings of Safety Science* 67 (August 2014): 58-63, https://www.researchgate.net/publication/261186680_The_study_of_information_flow_A_personal_journey.

40 *Just as Dr. Westrum...* Nicole Forsgren Velasquez, Gene Kim, Nigel Kersten, and Jez Humble, *2014 State of DevOps Report* (Portland, OR: Puppet Labs, IT Revolution Press, and ThoughtWorks, 2014), http://puppetlabs.com/2014-devops-report.

As Bethany Macri... Bethany Macri, "Morgue: Helping Better Understand Events by Building a Post Mortem Tool - Bethany Macri," Vimeo video, 33:34, posted by info@devopsdays.org, October 18, 2013, http://vimeo.com/77206751.

Dr. Spear observes... Spear, *The High-Velocity Edge*, chap. 1.

In The Fifth... Senge, *The Fifth Discipline*, chap. 1.

Mike Rother observed... Mike Rother, *Toyota Kata*, 12.

This is why... Mike Orzen, personal correspondence with Gene Kim, 2012.

41 *Consider the following...* "Paul O'Neill," *Forbes*, October 11, 2001, http://www.forbes.com/2001/10/16/poneill.html.

In 1987, Alcoa... Spear, *The High-Velocity Edge*, chap. 4.

As Dr. Spear... Ibid.

42 *A remarkable example...* Ibid., chap. 5.

44   *This process of...* Nassim Nicholas Taleb, *Antifragile: Things That Gain from Disorder* (Incerto), (New York: Random House, 2012).

According to Womack... Jim Womack, *Gemba Walks* (Cambridge, MA: Lean Enterprise Institute, 2011), Kindle edition, location 4113.

45   *Mike Rother formalized...* Rother, *Toyota Kata*, Part IV.

Mike Rother observes... Ibid., Conclusion.

CHAPTER 5

51   *Therefore, we must...* Michael Rembetsy and Patrick McDonnell, "Continuously Deploying Culture [at Etsy]," Slideshare.net, October 4, 2012, posted by Patrick McDonnel.bl, http://www.slideshare.net/mcdonnps/continuously-deploying-culture-scaling-culture-at-etsy-14588485.

In 2015, Nordstrom... "Nordstrom, Inc.," company profile on Vault.com, http://www.vault.com/company-profiles/retail/nordstrom,-inc/company-overview.aspx.

The stage for... Courtney Kissler, "DOES14 - Courtney Kissler - Nordstrom - Transforming to a Culture of Continuous Improvement," YouTube video, 29:59, posted by DevOps Enterprise Summit 2014, October 29, 2014, https://www.youtube.com/watch?v=0ZAcsrZBSlo.

These organizations were... Tom Gardner, "Barnes & Noble, Blockbuster, Borders: The Killer B's Are Dying," *The Motley Fool*, July 21, 2010, http://www.fool.com/investing/general/2010/07/21/barnes-noble-blockbuster-borders-the-killer-bs-are.aspx.

52   *As Kissler described...* Kissler, "DOES14 - Courtney Kissler - Nordstrom."

As Kissler said... Ibid; Alterations to quote made by Courtney Kissler via personal correspondence with Gene Kim, 2016.

53   *As Kissler stated...* Ibid; Alterations to quote made by Courtney Kissler via personal correspondence with Gene Kim, 2016.

In 2015, Kissler... Ibid.

She continued, "This... Ibid.

54   *Kissler concluded, "From...* Ibid.

An example of... Ernest Mueller, "Business model driven cloud adoption: what NI Is doing in the cloud," Slideshare.net, June 28, 2011, posted by Ernest Mueller, http://www.slideshare.net/mxyzplk/business-model-driven-cloud-adoption-what-ni-is-doing-in-the-cloud.

55   *Although many believe...* Unpublished calculation by Gene Kim after the 2014 DevOps Enterprise Summit.

        Indeed, one of... Kersten, IT Revolution, and PwC, *2015 State of DevOps Report.*

56   *CSG (2013): In...* Prugh, "DOES14: Scott Prugh, CSG - DevOps and Lean in Legacy Environments," Slideshare.net, November 14, 2014, posted by DevOps Enterprise Summit, http://www.slideshare.net /DevOpsEnterpriseSummit/scott-prugh.

        Etsy (2009): In... Rembetsy and McDonnell, "Continuously Deploying Culture [at Etsy]."

56   *The Gartner research...* Bernard Golden, "What Gartner's Bimodal IT Model Means to Enterprise CIOs," *CIO Magazine*, January 27, 2015, http://www.cio.com/article/2875803/cio-role/what-gartner -s-bimodal-it-model-means-to-enterprise-cios.html.

        Systems of record... Ibid.

        Systems of engagement... Ibid.

57   *The data from...* Kersten, IT Revolution, and PwC, *2015 State of DevOps Report.*

        Scott Prugh, VP... Scott Prugh, personal correspondence with Gene Kim, 2014.

        Geoffrey A. Moore... Geoffrey A. Moore and Regis McKenna, *Crossing the Chasm: Marketing and Selling High-Tech Products to Mainstream Customers* (New York: HarperCollins, 2009), 11.

58   *Big bang, top-down...* Linda Tucci, "Four Pillars of PayPal's 'Big Bang' Agile Transformation," *TechTarget*, August 2014, http://searchcio .techtarget.com/feature/Four-pillars-of-PayPals-big-bang-Agile -transformation.

59   *The following list...* "Creating High Velocity Organizations," description of course by Roberto Fernandez and Steve Spear, MIT Sloan Executive Education website, accessed May 30, 2016, http:// executive.mit.edu/openenrollment/program/organizational -development-high-velocity-organizations.

        But as Ron van Kemenade... Ron Van Kemande, "Nothing Beats Engineering Talent: The Agile Transformation at ING," presentation at the DevOps Enterprise Summit, London, UK, June 30-July 1, 2016.

60   *Peter Drucker, a...* Leigh Buchanan, "The Wisdom of Peter Drucker from A to Z," *Inc.*, November 19, 2009, http://www.inc.com/articles /2009/11/drucker.html.

CHAPTER 6

61   *Over the years...* Kissler, "DOES14 - Courtney Kissler - Nordstrom."

        Kissler explained:... Ross Clanton and Michael Ducy, interview of Courtney Kissler and Jason Josephy, "Continuous Improvement at Nordstrom," *The Goat Farm*, podcast audio, June 25, 2015, http://goatcan.do/2015/06/25/the-goat-farm-episode-7-continuous-improvement-at-nordstrom/.

62   *She said proudly...* Ibid.

63   *Technology executives or...* Brian Maskell, "What Does This Guy Do? Role of Value Stream Manager," *Maskell*, July 3, 2015, http://blog.maskell.com/?p=2106http://www.lean.org/common/display/?o=221.

64   *Damon Edwards observed...* Damon Edwards, "DevOps Kaizen: Find and Fix What Is Really Behind Your Problems," Slideshare.net, posted by dev2ops, May 4, 2015, http://www.slideshare.net/dev2ops/dev-ops-kaizen-damon-edwards.

66   *In their book ...* Vijay Govindarajan and Chris Trimble, *The Other Side of Innovation: Solving the Execution Challenge* (Boston, MA: Harvard Business Review, 2010) Kindle edition.

67   *Based on their...* Ibid., Part I.

70   *After the near-death...* Marty Cagan, *Inspired: How to Create Products Customers Love* (Saratoga, CA: SVPG Press, 2008), 12.

        Cagan notes that... Ibid.

71   *Six months after...* Ashlee Vance, "LinkedIn: A Story About Silicon Valley's Possibly Unhealthy Need for Speed," *Bloomberg*, April 30, 2013, http://www.bloomberg.com/bw/articles/2013-04-29/linkedin-a-story-about-silicon-valleys-possibly-unhealthy-need-for-speed.

        LinkedIn was created... "LinkedIn started back in 2003 — Scaling LinkedIn - A Brief History," Slideshare.net, posted by Josh Clemm, November 9, 2015, http://www.slideshare.net/joshclemm/how-linkedin-scaled-a-brief-history/3-LinkedIn_started_back_in_2003.

        One year later... Jonas Klit Nielsen, "8 Years with LinkedIn – Looking at the Growth [Infographic]," MindJumpers.com, May 10, 2011, http://www.mindjumpers.com/blog/2011/05/linkedin-growth-infographic/.

        By November 2015... "LinkedIn started back in 2003," Slideshare.net.

        The problem was... "From a Monolith to Microservices + REST: The Evolution of LinkedIn's Architecture," Slideshare.net, posted by Karan Parikh, November 6, 2014, http://www.slideshare.net/parikhk/restli-and-deco.

Josh Clemm, a... "LinkedIn started back in 2003," Slideshare.net.

72   *In 2013, journalist...* Vance, "LinkedIn: A Story About," *Bloomberg*.

Scott launched Operation... "How I Structured Engineering Teams at LinkedIn and AdMob for Success," *First Round Review*, 2015, http:// firstround.com/review/how-i-structured-engineering-teams-at -linkedin-and-admob-for-success/.

Scott described one... Ashlee Vance, "Inside Operation InVersion, the Code Freeze that Saved LinkedIn," *Bloomberg*, April 11, 2013, http://www.bloomberg.com/news/articles/2013-04-10/inside -operation-inversion-the-code-freeze-that-saved-linkedin.

However, Vance described... Vance, "LinkedIn: A Story About," *Bloomberg*.

As Josh Clemm... "LinkedIn started back in 2003," Slideshare.net.

Kevin Scott stated... "How I Structured Engineering Teams," *First Round Review*.

73   *As Christopher Little...* Christopher Little, personal correspondence with Gene Kim, 2011.

74   *As Ryan Martens...* Ryan Martens, personal correspondence with Gene Kim, 2013.

CHAPTER 7

77   *He observed, "After...*Dr. Melvin E. Conway, "How Do Committees Invent?" MelConway.com, http://www.melconway.com/research /committees.html, previously published in *Datamation*, April 1968.

These observations led... Ibid.

77   *Eric S. Raymond, author...* Eric S. Raymond, "Conway's Law," catb. org, accessed May 31, 2016, http://catb.org/~esr/jargon/.

78   *Etsy's DevOps journey...* Sarah Buhr, "Etsy Closes Up 86 Percent on First Day of Trading," *Tech Crunch*, April 16, 2015, http://techcrunch .com/2015/04/16/etsy-stock-surges-86-percent-at-close-of-first -day-of-trading-to-30-per-share/.

As Ross Snyder... "Scaling Etsy: What Went Wrong, What Went Right," Slideshare.net, posted by Ross Snyder, October 5, 2011, http://www.slideshare.net/beamrider9/scaling-etsy-what-went -wrong-what-went-right.

As Snyder observed... Ibid.

In other words... Sean Gallagher, "When 'Clever' Goes Wrong: How Etsy Overcame Poor Architectural Choices," *Arstechnica*, October 3, 2011, http://arstechnica.com/business/2011/10/when-clever-goes -wrong-how-etsy-overcame-poor-architectural-choices/.

Snyder explained that... "Scaling Etsy" Slideshare.net.

79   *Etsy initially had...* Ibid.

In the spring... Ibid.

As Snyder described... Ross Snyder, "Surge 2011—Scaling Etsy: What Went Wrong, What Went Right," YouTube video, posted by Surge Conference, December 23, 2011, https://www.youtube.com/watch?v=eenrfm50mXw.

80   *As Snyder said...* Ibid.

Sprouter was one... "Continuously Deploying Culture: Scaling Culture at Etsy - Velocity Europe 2012," Slideshare.net, posted by Patrick McDonnell, October 4, 2012, http://www.slideshare.net/mcdonnps/continuously-deploying-culture-scaling-culture-at-etsy-14588485.

They are defined... "Creating High Velocity Organizations," description of course by Roberto Fernandez and Steven Spear.

82   *Adrian Cockcroft remarked...* Adrian Cockcroft, personal correspondence with Gene Kim, 2014.

84   *In the Lean...* Spear, *The High-Velocity Edge*, chap. 8.

As Mike Rother... Rother, *Toyota Kata*, 250.

Reflecting on shared... "DOES15 - Jody Mulkey - DevOps in the Enterprise: A Transformation Journey," YouTube video, 28:22, posted by DevOps Enterprise Summit, November 5, 2015, https://www.youtube.com/watch?v=USYrDaPEFtM.

85   *He continued, "The...* Ibid.

Pedro Canahuati, their... Pedro Canahuati, "Growing from the Few to the Many: Scaling the Operations Organization at Facebook," *InfoQ*, December 16, 2013, http://www.infoq.com/presentations/scaling-operations-facebook.

When departments over-specialize... Spear, *The High-Velocity Edge*, chap. 1.

86   *Scott Prugh writes...* Scott Prugh, "Continuous Delivery," Scaled Agile Framework, updated February 14, 2013, http://www.scaledagileframework.com/continuous-delivery/.

"By cross-training... Ibid.

"Traditional managers will... Ibid.

87   *Furthermore, as Prugh...* Ibid.

When we value... Dr. Carol Dweck, "Carol Dweck Revisits the 'Growth Mindset,'" *Education Week*, September 22, 2015, http://www.edweek.org/ew

/articles/2015/09/23/carol-dweck-revisits-the-growth-mindset
.html.

As Jason Cox... Jason Cox, "Disney DevOps: To Infinity and Beyond,"
presentation at DevOps Enterprise Summit 2014, San Francisco,
CA, October 2014.

88   *As John Lauderbach...* John Lauderbach, personal conversation with
Gene Kim, 2001.

89   *These properties are...* Tony Mauro, "Adopting Microservices at
Netflix: Lessons for Architectural Design," *NGINX*, February 19,
2015, https://www.nginx.com/blog/microservices-at-netflix
-architectural-best-practices/.; Adam Wiggins, "The Twelve-Factor
App," 12Factor.net, January 30, 2012, http://12factor.net/.

90   *Randy Shoup, former...* "Exploring the Uncharted Territory of
Microservices," YouTube video, 56:50, posted by XebiaLabs, Inc.,
February 20, 2015, https://www.youtube.com/watch?v
=MRa21icSIQk.

As part of... Humble, O'Reilly, and Molesky, *Lean Enterprise*, Part III.

In the Netflix... Reed Hastings, "Netflix Culture: Freedom and
Responsibility," Slideshare.net, August 1, 2009, http://www
.slideshare.net/reed2001/culture-1798664.

91   *Amazon CTO Werner...* Larry Dignan, "Little Things Add Up,"
Baseline, October 19, 2005, http://www.baselinemag.com/c/a
/Projects-Management/Profiles-Lessons-From-the-Leaders-in-the
-iBaselinei500/3.

Target is the... Heather Mickman and Ross Clanton, "DOES15
- Heather Mickman & Ross Clanton - (Re)building an Engineering
Culture: DevOps at Target," YouTube video, 33:39, posted by DevOps
Enterprise Summit, November 5, 2015, https://www.youtube.com
/watch?v=7s-VbB1fG5o.

As Mickman described... Ibid.

92   *In an attempt...* Ibid.

Because our team... Ibid.

In the following... Ibid.

93   *These changes have...* Ibid.

The API Enablement... Ibid.

CHAPTER 8

95   *At Big Fish...* "Big Fish Celebrates 11th Consecutive Year of Record
Growth," BigFishGames.com, January 28, 2014, http://pressroom

.bigfishgames.com/2014-01-28-Big-Fish-Celebrates-11th
-Consecutive-Year-of-Record-Growth.

96   *He observed that*...Paul Farrall, personal correspondence with Gene Kim, January 2015.

      Farrall defined two... Ibid., 2014.

      He concludes, "The... Ibid.

97   *Ernest Mueller observed*... Ernest Mueller, personal correspondence with Gene Kim, 2014.

      As Damon Edwards... Edwards, "DevOps Kaizen."

98   *Dianne Marsh, Director*... "Dianne Marsh 'Introducing Change while Preserving Engineering Velocity," YouTube video, 17:37, posted by Flowcon, November 11, 2014, https://www.youtube.com/watch?v=eW3ZxY67fnc.

99   *Jason Cox said*... Jason Cox, "Disney DevOps."

100   *At Etsy, this*... "devopsdays Minneapolis 2015 - Katherine Daniels - DevOps: The Missing Pieces," YouTube video, 33:26, posted by DevOps Minneapolis, July 13, 2015, https://www.youtube.com/watch?v=LNJkVw93yTU.

102   *As Ernest Mueller*... Ernest Mueller, personal correspondence with Gene Kim, 2015.

      Scrum is an agile... Hirotaka Takeuchi and Ikujiro Nonaka, "New Product Development Game," *Harvard Business Review* (January 1986): 137-146.

CHAPTER 9

111   *In her presentation*... Em Campbell-Pretty, "DOES14 - Em Campbell-Pretty - How a Business Exec Led Agile, Lead, CI/CD," YouTube video, 29:47, posted by DevOps Enterprise Summit, April 20, 2014, https://www.youtube.com/watch?v=-4pIMMTbtwE.

      Campbell-Pretty became... Ibid.

112   *They created a*... Ibid.

      Campbell-Pretty observed... Ibid.

      Camplbell-Pretty described... Ibid.

115   *The first version*... "Version Control History," PlasticSCM.com, accessed May 31, 2016, https://www.plasticscm.com/version-control-history.html.

      A version control... Jennifer Davis and Katherine Daniels, Effective DevOps: Building a Culture of Collaboration, Affinity, and Tooling at Scale (Sebastopol, CA: O'Reilly Media, 2016), 37.

118   *Bill Baker, a...* Simon Sharwood, "Are Your Servers PETS or CATTLE?," *The Register*, March 18 2013, http://www.theregister.co.uk/2013/03/18/servers_pets_or_cattle_cern/.

118   *At Netflix, the...* Jason Chan, "OWASP AppSecUSA 2012: Real World Cloud Application Security," YouTube video, 37:45, posted by Christiaan008, December 10, 2012, https://www.youtube.com/watch?v=daNAojXDvYk.

119   *The latter pattern...* Chad Fowler, "Trash Your Servers and Burn Your Code: Immutable Infrastructure and Disposable Components," ChadFowler.com, June 23, 2013, http://chadfowler.com/2013/06/23/immutable-deployments.html.

        The entire application... John Willis, "Docker and the Three Ways of DevOps Part 1: The First Way—Systems Thinking," *Docker*, May 26, 2015, https://blog.docker.com/2015/05/docker-three-ways-devops/.

CHAPTER 10

123   *Gary Gruver, former...* Gary Gruver, personal correspondence with Gene Kim, 2014.

        They had problems... "DOES15 - Mike Bland - Pain Is Over, If You Want It," Slideshare.net, posted by Gene Kim, November 18, 2015, http://www.slideshare.net/ITRevolution/does15-mike-bland-pain-is-over-if-you-want-it-55236521.

124   *Bland describes how...* Ibid.

        Bland described that... Ibid.

        As Bland describes... Ibid.

        As Bland notes... Ibid.

125   *Over the next...* Ibid.

        Eran Messeri, an... Eran Messeri, "What Goes Wrong When Thousands of Engineers Share the Same Continuous Build?," presentation at the GOTO Conference, Aarhus, Denmark, October 2, 2013.

        Messeri explains, "There... Ibid.

        All their code... Ibid.

126   *Some of the...* Ibid.

        In Development, continuous... Jez Humble and David Farley, personal correspondence with Gene Kim, 2012.

        The deployment pipeline... Jez Humble and David Farley, *Continuous Delivery: Reliable Software Releases through Build, Test, and Deployment Automation* (Upper Saddle River, NJ: Addison-Wesly, 2011), 3.

131　　*Humble and Farley*... Ibid., 188.

　　　　As Humble and... Ibid., 258.

132　　*Martin Fowler observes*... Martin Fowler, "Continuous Integration," MartinFowler.com, May 1, 2006, http://www.martinfowler.com /articles/continuousIntegration.html.

132　　*Martin Fowler described*... Martin Fowler, "TestPyramid," MartinFowler.com, May 1, 2012, http://martinfowler.com/bliki /TestPyramid.html.

134　　*This technique was*.. Martin Fowler, "Test Driven Development," MartinFowler.com, March 5, 2005, http://martinfowler.com/bliki /TestDrivenDevelopment.html.

135　　*Nachi Nagappan, E. Michael*... Nachiappan Nagappan, E. Michael Maximilien, Thirumalesh Bhat, and Laurie Williams, "Realizing quality improvement through test driven development: results and experiences of four industrial teams," *Empir Software Engineering*, 13, (2008): 289-302, http://research.microsoft.com/en-us/groups /ese/nagappan_tdd.pdf.

　　　　In her 2013... Elisabeth Hendrickson, "On the Care and Feeding of Feedback Cycles," Slideshare.net, posted by Elisabeth Hendrickson, November 1, 2013, http://www.slideshare.net/ehendrickson/care -and-feeding-of-feedback-cycles.

　　　　However, merely automating... "Decreasing false positives in automated testing," Slideshare.net, posted by Sauce Labs, March 24, 2015, http://www.slideshare.net/saucelabs/decreasing-false -positives-in-automated-testing.; Martin Fowler, "Eradicating Non-determinism in Tests," MartinFowler.com, April 14, 2011, http://martinfowler.com/articles/nonDeterminism.html.

136　　*As Gary Gruver*... Gary Gruver, "DOES14 - Gary Gruver - Macy's - Transforming Traditional Enterprise Software Development Processes," YouTube video, 27:24, posted by DevOps Enterprise Summit 2014, October 29, 2014, https://www.youtube.com/watch?v =-HSSGiYXA7U.

139　　*Randy Shoup, former*... Randy Shoup, "The Virtuous Cycle of Velocity: What I Learned About Going Fast at eBay and Google by Randy Shoup," YouTube video, 30:05, posted by Flowcon, December 26, 2013, https://www.youtube.com/watch?v=EwLBoRyXTOI.

　　　　This is sometimes... David West, "Water scrum-fall is-reality_of_ agile_for_most," Slideshare.net, posted by harsoft, April 22, 2013, http://www.slideshare.net/harsoft/water-scrumfall -isrealityofagileformost.

CHAPTER 11

144   *The surprising breadth...* Gene Kim, "The Amazing DevOps
       Transformation of the HP LaserJet Firmware Team (Gary Gruver),"
       ITRevolution.com, 2013, http://itrevolution.com/the-amazing
       -devops-transformation-of-the-hp-laserjet-firmware-team-gary
       -gruver/.

       Gruvery described this... Ibid.

145   *Compile flags (#define...* Ibid.

       *Gruver admits trunk-based...*Gary Gruver and Tommy Mouser,
       *Leading the Transformation: Applying Agile and DevOps Principles at
       Scale* (Portland, OR: IT Revolution Press), 60.

       Gruver observed, "Without... Kim, "The Amazing DevOps
       Transformation " ITRevolution.com.

147   *Jeff Atwood, founder...*Jeff Atwood, "Software Branching and Parallel
       Universes," CodingHorror.com, October 2, 2007, http://blog
       .codinghorror.com/software-branching-and-parallel-universes/.

148   *This is how...* Ward Cunningham, "Ward Explains Debt Metaphor,"
       c2.com, 2011, http://c2.com/cgi/wiki?WardExplainsDebtMetaphor.

149   *Ernest Mueller, who...* Ernest Mueller, "2012: A Release Odyssey,"
       Slideshare.net, posted by Ernest Mueller, March 12, 2014, http://
       www.slideshare.net/mxyzplk/2012-a-release-odyssey.

       At that time... "Bazaarvoice, Inc. Announces Its Financial Results
       for the Fourth Fiscal Quarter and Fiscal Year Ended April 30, 2012,"
       BasaarVoice.com, June 6, 2012, http://investors.bazaarvoice.com
       /releasedetail.cfm?ReleaseID=680964.

150   *Mueller observed, "It...* Ernest Mueller, "DOES15 - Ernest Mueller
       - DevOps Transformations At National Instruments and...,"
       YouTube video, 34:14, posted by DevOps Enterprise Summit,
       November 5, 2015, https://www.youtube.com/watch?v
       =6Ry4oh1UAyE.

       "By running these... Ibid.

151   *Mueller further described...* Ibid.

       *However, the data...*Kersten, IT Revolution, and PwC, *2015 State of
       DevOps Report.*

CHAPTER 12

153   *In 2012, Rossi...* Chuck Rossi, "Release engineering and push karma:
       Chuck Rossi," post on Chuck Rossi's Facebook page, April 5, 2012,
       https://www.facebook.com

/notes/facebook-engineering/release-engineering-and-push
-karma-chuck-rossi/10150660826788920.

Just prior to... Ryan Paul, "Exclusive: a behind-the-scenes look at
Facebook release engineering," *Ars Technica*, April 5, 2012, http://
arstechnica.com/business/2012/04/exclusive-a-behind-the-scenes
-look-at-facebook-release-engineering/1/.

Rossi continued, "If... Chuck Rossi, "Release engineering and push
karma."

The Facebook frontend... Paul, "Exclusive: a behind-the-scenes look
at Facebook release engineering," *Ars Technica*.

He explained that... Chuck Rossi, "Ship early and ship twice as
often," post on Chuck Rossi's Facebook page, August 3, 2012,
https://www.facebook.com/notes/facebook-engineering/ship
-early-and-ship-twice-as-often/10150985860363920.

154   *Kent Beck, the..* Kent Beck, "Slow Deployment Causes Meetings,"
post on Kent Beck's Facebook page, November 19, 2015), https://
www.facebook.com/notes/kent-beck/slow-deployment-causes
-meetings/1055427371156793?_rdr=p.

157   *Scott Prugh, their...* Prugh, "DOES14: Scott Prugh, CSG - DevOps and
Lean in Legacy Environments."

Prugh observed, "It... Ibid.

158   *Prugh writes, "We...* Ibid.

Prugh also observes:... Ibid.

In their experiments... Puppet Labs and IT Revolution Press, *2013
State of DevOps Report* (Portland, OR: Puppet Labs, 2013), http://
www.exin-library.com/Player/eKnowledge/2013-state-of-devops
-report.pdf.

Prugh reported that... Scott Prugh and Erica Morrison, "DOES15
- Scott Prugh & Erica Morrison - Conway & Taylor Meet the
Strangler (v2.0)," YouTube video, 29:39, posted by DevOps
Enterprise Summit, November 5, 2015, https://www.youtube.com
/watch?v=tKdIHCLoDUg.

159   *Consider the following...* Tim Tischler, personal conversation with
Gene Kim, FlowCon 2013.

In practice, the... Puppet Labs and IT Revolution Press, *2013 State of
DevOps Report*.

161   *In Puppet Lab's...* Velasquez, Kim, Kersten, and Humble, *2014 State
of DevOps Report*.

162   *The deployment process...* Chad Dickerson, "Optimizing for developer happiness," CodeAsCraft.com, June 6, 2011, https://codeascraft.com/2011/06/06/optimizing-for-developer-happiness/.

As Noah Sussman... Noah Sussman and Laura Beth Denker, "Divide and Conquer," CodeAsCraft.com, April 20, 2011, https://codeascraft.com/2011/04/20/divide-and-concur/.

Sussman writes, "Through... Ibid.

163   *If all the tests...* Ibid.

Once it is an.. Erik Kastner, "Quantum of Deployment," CodeAsCraft.com, May 20, 2010, https://codeascraft.com/2010/05/20/quantum-of-deployment/.

168   *This technique was...* Timothy Fitz, "Continuous Deployment at IMVU: Doing the impossible fifty times a day," TimothyFitz.com, February 10, 2009, http://timothyfitz.com/2009/02/10/continuous-deployment-at-imvu-doing-the-impossible-fifty-times-a-day/.

This pattern is... Fitz, "Continuous Deployment," TimothyFitz.com.; Michael Hrenko, "DOES15 - Michael Hrenko - DevOps Insured By Blue Shield of California," YouTube video, 42:24, posted by DevOps Enterprise Summit, November 5, 2015, https://www.youtube.com/watch?v=NlgrOT24UDw.

Dan North and Dave... Humble and Farley, *Continuous Delivery*, 265.

171   *The cluster immune...* Eric Ries, *The Lean Startup: How Today's Entrepreneurs Use Continuous Innovation to Create Radically Successful Businesses* (New York: Random House, 2011), Audiobook.

172   *One sophisticated example...* Andrew 'Boz' Bosworth, "Building and testing at Facebook," post on Boz Facebook page, August 8, 2012, https://www.facebook.com/notes/facebook-engineering/building-and-testing-at-facebook/10151004157328920; "Etsy's Feature flagging API used for operational rampups and A/B testing," GitHub.com, https://github.com/etsy/feature; "Library for configuration management API," GitHub.com, https://github.com/Netflix/archaius.

173   *In 2009, when...* John Allspaw, "Convincing management that cooperation and collaboration was worth it," KitchenSoap.com, January 5, 2012, http://www.kitchensoap.com/2012/01/05/convincing-management-that-cooperation-and-collaboration-was-worth-it/.

174   *Similarly, as Chuck...* Rossi, "Release engineering and push karma."

For nearly a decade... Emil Protalinski, "Facebook passes 1.55B monthly active users and 1.01B daily active users," *Venture Beat*, November 4, 2015, http://venturebeat.com/2015/11/04/facebook -passes-1-55b-monthly-active-users-and-1-01-billion-daily-active -users/.

174 *By 2015, Facebook...* Ibid.

*Eugene Letuchy, an...*Eugene Letuchy, "Facebook Chat," post on Eugene Letuchy's Facebook page, May 3, 2008, http://www .facebook.com/note.php?note_id=14218138919&id=944554719.

Implementing this computationally-intensive... Ibid.

175 *As Letuchy wrote...* Ibid.

*However, in 2015...*Jez Humble, personal correspondence with Gene Kim, 2014.

176 *His updated definitions...*Ibid.

*At Amazon and...*Ibid.

CHAPTER 13

179 *This is the...*Jez Humble, "What is Continuous Delivery," ContinuousDelivery.com, accessed May 28, 2016, https:// continuousdelivery.com/.

He observes that... Kim, Gruver, Shoup, and Phillips, "Exploring the Uncharted Territory of Microservices."

He reflects, "Looking... Ibid.

eBay's architecture went... Shoup, "From Monolith to Micro-services."

180 *Charles Betz, author...* Charles Betz, *Architecture and Patterns for IT Service Management, Resource Planning, and Governance: Making Shoes for the Cobbler's Children* (Witham, MA: Morgan Kaufmann, 2011), 300.

182 *As Randy Shoup...* Randy Shoup, "From the Monolith to Micro-services," Slideshare.net, posted by Randy Shoup, October 8, 2014, http://www.slideshare.net/RandyShoup/goto-aarhus2014 -enterprisearchitecturemicroservices.

Shoup notes, "Organizations... Ibid.

As Randy Shoup observes... Ibid.

184 *One of the most...* Werner Vogels, "A Conversation with Werner Vogels," *acmqueue* 4, no. 4 (2006): 14-22, http://queue.acm.org /detail.cfm?id=1142065.

Vogel tells Gray... Ibid.

Describing the thought... Ibid.

Vogel notes, "The... Ibid.

185   *In 2011, Amazon...* John Jenkins, "Velocity 2011: Jon Jenkins, "Velocity Culture,"" YouTube video, 15:13, posted by O'Reilly, June 20, 2011, {https://www.youtube.com/watch?v=dxk8b9rSKOo.

185   *By 2015, they...* Ken Exner, "Transforming Software Development," YouTube video, 40:57, posted by Amazon Web Services, April 10, 2015, https://www.youtube.com/watch?v=YCrhemssYuI&feature =youtu.be.

The term strangler... Martin Fowler, "StranglerApplication," MartinFowler.com, June 29, 2004, http://www.martinfowler.com /bliki/StranglerApplication.html.

When we implement... Boris Lublinsky, "Versioning in SOA," *The Architecture Journal,* April 2007, https://msdn.microsoft.com/en-us /library/bb491124.aspx.

186   *The strangler application...* Paul Hammant, "Introducing Branch by Abstraction," PaulHammant.com, April 26, 2007, http://paulhammant .com/blog/branch_by_abstraction.html.

An observation from... Martin Fowler, "StranglerApplication," MartinFowler.com, June 29, 2004, http://www.martinfowler.com /bliki/StranglerApplication.html.

Blackboard Inc., is... Gregory T. Huang, "Blackboard CEO Jay Bhatt on the Global Future of Edtech," *Xconomy,* June 2, 2014, http://www .xconomy.com/boston/2014/06/02/blackboard-ceo-jay-bhatt-on -the-global-future-of-edtech/.

187   *As David Ashman...* David Ashman, "DOES14 - David Ashman - Blackboard Learn - Keep Your Head in the Clouds," YouTube video, 30:43, posted by DevOps Enterprise Summit 2014, October 28, 2014, https://www.youtube.com/watch?v=SSmixnMpsI4.

In 2010, Ashman... Ibid.

How this started... David Ashman, personal correspondence with Gene Kim, 2014.

Ashman noted. "To... Ibid.

188   *"In fact," Ashman...* Ibid.

189   *Ashman concluded, "Having...* Ibid.

CHAPTER 14

195   *In Operations, we...* Kim, Behr, and Spafford, *The Visible Ops Handbook: Implementing ITIL in 4 Practical and Auditable Steps*

(Eugene, OR: IT Process Institute, 2004), Kindle edition, Introduction.

In contrast, the... Ibid.

*In other words...*Ibid.

196   *To enable this...* "Telemetry," *Wikipedia*, last modified May 5, 2016, https://en.wikipedia.org/wiki/Telemetry.

McDonnell described how... Michael Rembetsy and Patrick McDonnell, "Continuously Deploying Culture: Scaling Culture at Etsy - Velocity Europe 2012," Slideshare.net, posted by Patrick McDonnell, October 4, 2012, http://www.slideshare.net/mcdonnps /continuously-deploying-culture-scaling-culture-at-etsy-14588485.

McDonnell explained further... Ibid.

By 2011, Etsy... John Allspaw, personal conversation with Gene Kim, 2014.

197   *As Ian Malpass...* Ian Malpass, "Measure Anything, Measure Everything," CodeAsCraft.com, February 15, 2011, http://codeascraft .com/2011/02/15/measure-anything-measure-everything/.

197   *One of the findings...* Kersten, IT Revolution, and PwC, *2015 State of DevOps Report*.

The top two... "2014 State Of DevOps Findings! Velocity Conference," Slideshare.net, posted by Gene Kim, June 30, 2014, http://www .slideshare.net/realgenekim/2014-state-of-devops-findings -velocity-conference.

198   *In The Art...* James Turnbull, *The Art of Monitoring* (Seattle, WA: Amazon Digital Services, 2016), Kindle edition, Introduction.

200   *The resulting capability...* "Monitorama - Please, no more Minutes, Milliseconds, Monoliths or Monitoring Tools," Slideshare.net, posted by Adrian Cockcroft, May 5, 2014, http://www.slideshare .net/adriancockcroft/monitorama-please-no-more.

201   *Scott Prugh, Chief...* Prugh, "DOES14: Scott Prugh, CSG - DevOps and Lean in Legacy Environments."

To support these... Brice Figureau, "The 10 Commandments of Logging," Mastersen's Blog, January 13, 2013, http://www .masterzen.fr/2013/01/13/the-10-commandments-of-logging/.

202   *Choosing the right...* Dan North, personal correspondence with Gene Kim, 2016.

To help ensure... Anton Chuvakin, "LogLogic/Chuvakin Log Checklist," republished with permission, 2008, http://juliusdavies .ca/logging/llclc.html.

203   *In 2004, Kim...* Kim, Behr, and Spafford, *The Visible Ops Handbook*, Introduction.

204   *This was the...* Dan North, "Ops and Operability," SpeakerDeck.com, February 25, 2016, https://speakerdeck.com/tastapod/ops-and-operability.

        As John Allspaw... John Allspaw, personal correspondence with Gene Kim, 2011.

206   *This is often...* "Information Radiators," AgileAlliance.com, accessed May 31, 2016, https://www.agilealliance.org/glossary/incremental-radiators/.

207   *Although there may..* Ernest Mueller, personal correspondence with Gene Kim, 2014.

        Prachi Gupta, Director... Prachi Gupta, "Visualizing LinkedIn's Site Performance," LinkedIn Engineering blog, June 13, 2011, https://engineering.linkedin.com/25/visualizing-linkedins-site-performance.

208   *Thus began Eric...* Eric Wong, "Eric the Intern: the Origin of InGraphs," LinkedIn, June 30, 2011, http://engineering.linkedin.com/32/eric-intern-origin-ingraphs.

        Wong wrote, "To... Ibid.

        At the time... Ibid.

        In writing about... Gupta, "Visualizing LinkedIn's Site Performance."

210   *Ed Blankenship, Senior...* Ed Blankenship, personal correspondence with Gene Kim, 2016.

212   *However, increasingly these...* Mike Burrows, "The Chubby lock service for loosely-coupled distributed systems," *OSDI'06: Seventh Symposium on Operating System Design and Implementation*, November 2006, http://static.googleusercontent.com/media/research.google.com/en//archive/chubby-osdi06.pdf.

212   *Consul may be...* Jeff Lindsay, "Consul Service Discovery with Docker," Progrium.com, August 20, 2014, http://progrium.com/blog/2014/08/20/consul-service-discovery-with-docker.

213   *As Jody Mulkey...* Jody Mulkey, "DOES15 - Jody Mulkey - DevOps in the Enterprise: A Transformation Journey," YouTube video, 28:22, posted by DevOps Enterprise Summit, November 5, 2015, https://www.youtube.com/watch?v=USYrDaPEFtM.

CHAPTER 15

215   *In 2015, Netflix...* Netflix Letter to Shareholders, January 19, 2016, http://files.shareholder.com/downloads/NFLX/2432188684

x0x870685/C6213FF9-5498-4084-A0FF-74363CEE35A1/Q4_15 _Letter_to_Shareholders_-_COMBINED.pdf.

Roy Rapoport describes... Roy Rapoport, personal correspondence with Gene Kim, 2014.

One of the statistical... Victoria Hodge and Jim Austin, "A Survey of Outlier Detection Methodologies," *Artificial Intelligence Review* 22, no. 2 (October 2004): 85-126, http://www.geo.upm.es/postgrado/ CarlosLopez/papers/Hodge+Austin_OutlierDetection_AIRE381 .pdf.

Rapoport explains that.. Roy Rapoport, personal correspondence with Gene Kim, 2014.

216   *Rapoport continues, "We...* Ibid.

       Rapoport states that... Ibid.

       As John Vincent... Toufic Boubez, "Simple math for anomaly detection toufic boubez - metafor software - monitorama pdx 2014-05-05," Slideshare.net, posted by tboubez, May 6, 2014, http:// www.slideshare.net/tboubez/simple-math-for-anomaly -detection-toufic-boubez-metafor-software-monitorama-pdx -20140505.

218   *Tom Limoncelli, co-author...* Tom Limoncelli, "Stop monitoring whether or not your service is up!," EverythingSysAdmin.com, November 27, 2013, http://everythingsysadmin.com/2013/11/stop -monitoring-if-service-is-up.html.

219   *As Dr. Toufic...* Toufic Boubez, "Simple math for anomaly detection toufic boubez - metafor software - monitorama pdx 2014-05-05," Slideshare.net, posted by tboubez, May 6, 2014, http://www. slideshare.net/tboubez/simple-math-for-anomaly-detection -toufic-boubez-metafor-software-monitorama-pdx -20140505.

220   *Dr. Nicole Forsgren...* Dr. Nicole Forsgren, personal correspondence with Gene Kim, 2015.

221   *Scryer works by...* Daniel Jacobson, Danny Yuan, and Neeraj Joshi, "Scryer: Netflix's Predictive Auto Scaling Engine," *The Netflix Tech Blog*, November 5, 2013, http://techblog.netflix.com/2013/11 /scryer-netflixs-predictive-auto-scaling.html.

222   *These techniques are...* Varun Chandola, Arindam Banerjee, and Vipin Kumar, "Anomaly detection: A survey," *ACM Computing Surveys* 41, no. 3 (July 2009): article no. 15, http://doi.acm.org/10 .1145/1541880.1541882.

Tarun Reddy, VP... Tarun Reddy, personal interview with Gene Kim, Rally headquarters, Boulder, CO, 2014.

224 *At Monitorama in 2014...* "Kolmogorov-Smirnov Test," *Wikipedia*, last modified May 19, 2016, http://en.wikipedia.org/wiki /Kolmogorov%E2%80%93Smirnov_test.

225 *Even saying Kilmogorov-Smirnov...*"Simple math for anomaly detection toufic boubez - metafor software - monitorama pdx 2014-05-05," Slideshare.net, posted by tboubez, May 6, 2014, http:// www.slideshare.net/tboubez/simple-math-for-anomaly-detection -toufic-boubez-metafor-software-monitorama-pdx-20140505.

CHAPTER 16

227 *In 2006, Nick...* Mark Walsh, "Ad Firms Right Media, AdInterax Sell To Yahoo," *MediaPost,* October 18, 2006, http://www.mediapost.com /publications/article/49779/ad-firms-right-media-adinterax-sell -to-yahoo.html?edition=.

Galbreath described the... Nick Galbreath, personal conversation with Gene, 2013.

However, Galbreath observed... Nick Galbreath, "Continuous Deployment - The New #1 Security Feature, from BSildesLA 2012," Slideshare.net, posted by Nick Galbreath, Aug 16, 2012, http://www. slideshare.net/nickgsuperstar/continuous-deployment-the-new-1 -security-feature.

After observing many... Ibid.

228 *Galbreath observes that...* Ibid.

231 *As Patrick Lightbody...* "Volocity 2011: Patrick Lightbody, 'From Inception to Acquisition,'" YouTube video, 15:28, posted by O'Reilly, June 17, 2011, https://www.youtube.com/watch?v=ShmPod8JecQ.

232 *As Arup Chakrabarti...* Arup Chakrabarti, "Common Ops Mistakes," presentation at Heavy Bit Industries, June 3, 2014, http://www .heavybit.com/library/video/common-ops-mistakes/

233 *More recently, Jeff...* "From Design Thinking to DevOps and Back Again: Unifying Design & Operations," Vimeo video, 21:19, posted by William Evans, June 5, 2015, https://vimeo.com/129939230.

234 *As an anonymous...* Anonymous, personal conversation with Gene Kim, 2005.

Launch guidance and.. Tom Limoncelli, "SRE@Google: Thousands Of DevOps Since 2004," YouTube video of USENIX Association Talk, NYC, posted by USENIX, 45:57, posted January 12, 2012, http:// www.youtube.com/watch?v=iIuTnhdTzK0.

238   *As Treynor Sloss has…* Ben Treynor, "Keys to SRE" (presentation, Usenix SREcon14, Santa Clara, CA, May 30, 2014), https://www .usenix.org/conference/srecon14/technical-sessions/presentation /keys-sre.

Treynor Sloss has resisted… Ibid.

Even when new… Limoncelli, "SRE@Google."

Tom Limoncelli noted… Ibid.

239   *Limoncelli noted, "In…* Ibid.

Furthemore, Limoncelli observed… Tom Limoncelli, personal correspondence with Gene Kim, 2016.

239   *Limoncelli explained, "Helping…*Ibid., 2015.

CHAPTER 17

241   *In general, Jez…* Humble, O'Reilly and Molesky, *Lean Enterprise*, Part II.

In 2012, they… Intuit, Inc., "2012 Annual Report: Form 10-K," July 31, 2012, http://s1.q4cdn.com/018592547/files/doc_financials/2012 /INTU_2012_7_31_10K_r230_at_09_13_12_FINAL_and_Camera _Ready.pdf.

242   *Cook explained that…* Scott Cook, "Leadership in an Agile Age: An Interview with Scott Cook," Intuit.com, April 20, 2011, https://web .archive.org/web/20160205050418/http://network.intuit.com/2011 /04/20/leadership-in-the-agile-age/

He continued, "By… Ibid.

243   *In previous eras…* "Direct Marketing," Wikipedia, last modified May 28, 2016, https://en.wikipedia.org/wiki/Direct_marketing.

Interestingly, it has… Freakonomics, "Fighting Poverty With Actual Evidence: Full Transcript," Freakonomics.com, November 27, 2013, http://freakonomics.com/2013/11/27/fighting-poverty-with-actual -evidence-full-transcript/.

244   *Ronny Kohavi, Distinguished…* Ron Kohavi, Thomas Crook, and Roger Longbotham, "Online Experimentation at Microsoft," (paper presented at the Fifteenth ACM SIGKDD International Conference on Knowledge Discovery and Data Mining, Paris, France, 2009), http://www.exp-platform.com/documents/exp_dmcasestudies .pdf.

*Kohavi goes on…*Ibid.

Jez Humble joked… Jez Humble, personal correspondence with Gene Kim, 2015.

245   *In a 2014...* Wang, Kendrick, "Etsy's Culture Of Continuous Experimentation and A/B Testing Spurs Mobile Innovation," Apptimize.com, January 30, 2014, http://apptimize.com/blog/2014/01/etsy-continuous-innovation-ab-testing/.

246   *Barry O'Reilly, co-author...* Barry O'Reilly, "How to Implement Hypothesis-Driven Development," BarryOReilly.com, October 21, 2013, http://barryoreilly.com/2013/10/21/how-to-implement-hypothesis-driven-development/.

       In 2009, Jim... Gene Kim, "Organizational Learning and Competitiveness: Revisiting the "Allspaw/Hammond 10 Deploys Per Day at Flickr" Story," ITRevolution.com, 2015, http://itrevolution.com/organizational-learning-and-competitiveness-a-different-view-of-the-allspawhammond-10-deploys-per-day-at-flickr-story/.

247   *Stoneham observes that...* Ibid.

       *He continues, "These...*Ibid.

       Their astounding achievements... Ibid.

248   *Stoneham concluded, "This...* Ibid.

CHAPTER 18

249   *Once a pull...* Scott Chacon, "Github Flow," ScottChacon.com, August 31, 2011, http://scottchacon.com/2011/08/31/github-flow.html.

251   *For example, in...* Jake Douglas, "Deploying at Github," GitHub.com, August 29, 2012, https://github.com/blog/1241-deploying-at-github.

       A fifteen minute... John Allspaw, "Counterfactual Thinking, Rules, and the Knight Capital Accident," KitchenSoap.com, October 29, 2013, http://www.kitchensoap.com/2013/10/29/counterfactuals-knight-capital/.

253   *One of the core...* Bradley Staats and David M. Upton, "Lean Knowledge Work," *Harvard Business Review*, October 2011, https://hbr.org/2011/10/lean-knowledge-work.

       In the 2014... Velasquez, Kim, Kersten, and Humble, *2014 State of DevOps Report*.

255   *As Randy Shoup...* Randy Shoup, personal interview with Gene Kim, 2015.

256   *As Giary Özil...* Giray Özil, Twitter post, February 27, 2013, 10:42 a.m., https://twitter.com/girayozil/status/306836785739210752.

257   *As noted earlier...* Eran Messeri, "What Goes Wrong When Thousands of Engineers Share the Same Continuous Build?," (2013), http://scribes.tweetscriber.com/realgenekim/206.

      In 2010, there... John Thomas and Ashish Kumar, "Welcome to the Google Engineering Tools Blog," Google Engineering Tools blog, posted May 3, 2011, http://google-engtools.blogspot.com/2011/05/welcome-to-google-engineering-tools.html.

      This requires considerable... Ashish Kumar, "Development at the Speed and Scale of Google," (presentation at QCon, San Francisco, CA, 2010), https://qconsf.com/sf2010/dl/qcon-sanfran-2010/slides/AshishKumar_DevelopingProductsattheSpeedandScaleofGoogle.pdf.

258   *He said, "I...* Randy Shoup, personal correspondence with Gene Kim, 2014.

259   *Jeff Atwood, one...* Jeff Atwood, "Pair Programming vs. Code Reviews," CodingHorror.com, November 18, 2013, http://blog.codinghorror.com/pair-programming-vs-code-reviews/.

260   *He continued, "Most...* Ibid.

      Dr. Laurie Williams performed... "Pair Programming," ALICE Wiki page, last modified April 4, 2014, http://euler.math.uga.edu/wiki/index.php?title=Pair_programming.

      She argues that... Elisabeth Hendrickson, "DOES15 - Elisabeth Hendrickson - Its All About Feedback," YouTube video, 34:47, posted by DevOps Enterprise Summit, November 5, 2015, https://www.youtube.com/watch?v=r2BFTXBundQ.

261   *In her 2015...* Ibid.

      The problem Hendrickson... Ibid.

      Worse, skilled developers... Ibid.

      Hendrickson lamented that... Ibid.

262   *That was an actual...* Ryan Tomayko and Shawn Davenport, personal interview with Gene Kim, 2013.

      It is many... Ibid.

      Reading through the... Ibid.

263   *Adrian Cockcroft observed...* Adrian Cockcroft, interview by Michael Ducy and Ross Clanton, "Adrian Cockcroft of Battery Ventures – the Goat Farm – Episode 8," *The Goat Farm*, podcast audio, July 31, 2015, http://goatcan.do/2015/07/31/adrian-cockcroft-of-battery-ventures-the-goat-farm-episode-8/.

Similarly, Dr. Tapabrata Pal... Tapabrata Pal, "DOES15 - Tapabrata Pal - Banking on Innovation & DevOps," YouTube video, 32:57, posted by DevOps Enterprise Summit, January 4, 2016, https://www.youtube.com/watch?v=bbWFCKGhxOs.

Jason Cox, Senior... Jason Cox, "Disney DevOps."

At Target in... Ross Clanton and Heather Mickman, 'DOES14 - Ross Clanton and Heather Mickman - DevOps at Target," YouTube video, 29:20, posted by DevOps Enterprise Summit 2014, October 29, 2014, https://www.youtube.com/watch?v=exrjV9V9vhY.

264 *"As we went...* Ibid.

She added, "I... Ibid.

Consider a story... John Allspaw and Jez Humble, personal correspondence with Gene Kim, 2014.

CHAPTER 19

271 *The result is...* Spear, *The High-Velocity Edge*, chap. 1.

"For such an... Ibid., chap. 10.

A striking example... Julianne Pepitone, "Amazon EC2 Outage Downs Reddit, Quora," *CNN Money*, April 22, 2011, http://money.cnn.com/2011/04/21/technology/amazon_server_outage.

In January 2013... Timothy Prickett Morgan, "A Rare Peek Into The Massive Scale of AWS," *Enterprise Tech*, November 14, 2014, http://www.enterprisetech.com/2014/11/14/rare-peek-massive-scale-aws/.

272 *However, a Netflix...* Adrian Cockcroft, Cory Hicks, and Greg Orzell, "Lessons Netflix Learned from the AWS Outage," *The Netflix Tech Blog*, April 29, 2011, http://techblog.netflix.com/2011/04/lessons-netflix-learned-from-aws-outage.html.

They did so... Ibid.

273 *Dr. Sidney Dekker...* Sidney Dekker, *Just Culture: Balancing Safety and Accountability* (Lund University, Sweden: Ashgate Publishing Company, 2007), 152.

He asserts that... "DevOpsDays Brisbane 2014 - Sidney Decker - System Failure, Human Error: Who's to Blame?" Vimeo video, 1:07:38, posted by info@devopsdays.org, 2014, https://vimeo.com/102167635.

273 *As John Allspaw...* Jenn Webb, interview with John Allspaw, "Post-Mortems, Sans Finger-Pointing," *The O'Reilly Radar Postcast*, podcast audio, August 21, 2014, http://radar.oreilly.com/2014/08

/postmortems-sans-finger-pointing-the-oreilly-radar-podcast
.html.

274   *Blameless post-mortems, a...* John Allspaw, "Blameless PostMortems
and a Just Culture," CodeAsCraft.com, May 22, 2012, http://
codeascraft.com/2012/05/22/blameless-postmortems/.

276   *Ian Malpass, an...* Ian Malpass, "DevOpsDays Minneapolis 2014
-- Ian Malpass, Fallible humans," YouTube video, 35:48, posted by
DevOps Minneapolis, July 20, 2014, https://www.youtube.com
/watch?v=5NY-SrQFrBU.

      Dan Milstein, one... Dan Milstein, "Post-Mortems at HubSpot: What
I Learned from 250 Whys," *HubSpot*, June 1, 2011, http://product
.hubspot.com/blog/bid/64771/Post-Mortems-at-HubSpot-What-I
-Learned-From-250-Whys.

277   *Randy Shoup, former...* Randy Shoup, personal correspondence with
Gene Kim, 2014.

      We may also... "Post-Mortem for February 24, 2010 Outage," Google
App Engine website, March 4, 2010, https://groups.google.com
/forum/#!topic/google-appengine/p2QKJoOSLc8; "Summary of the
Amazon DynamoDB Service Disruption and Related Impacts in the
US-East Region," Amazon Web Services website, accessed May 28,
2016, https://aws.amazon.com/message/5467D2/.

      This desire to... Bethany Macri, "Morgue: Helping Better Understand
Events by Building a Post Mortem Tool - Bethany Macri," Vimeo
video, 33:34, posted by info@devopsdays.org, October 18, 2013,
http://vimeo.com/77206751.

      For example, as... Spear, *The High-Velocity Edge*, chap. 4.

278   *Dr. Amy C. Edmondson...* Amy C. Edmondson, "Strategies for
Learning from Failure," *Harvard Business Review*, April 2011, https://
hbr.org/2011/04/strategies-for-learning-from-failure.

279   *Dr. Spear summarizes...* Ibid.

      We now know... Ibid., chap. 3.

      However, prior to... Michael Roberto, Richard M.J. Bohmer, and
Amy C. Edmondson, "Facing Ambiguous Threats," *Harvard
Business Review*, November 2006, https://hbr.org/2006/11/facing
-ambiguous-threats/ar/1.

      They describe how... Ibid.

280   *They observe, "Firms...* Ibid.

      The authors conclude... Ibid.

On failures, Roy... Roy Rapoport, personal correspondence with Gene Kim, 2012.

He continues, "I... Ibid.

281   *He concludes, "DevOps...* Ibid.

As Michael Nygard... Michael T. Nygard, *Release It!: Design and Deploy Production-Ready Software* (Pragmatic Bookshelf: Raleigh, NC, 2007), Kindle edition, Part I.

281   *An even more...* Jeff Barr, "EC2 Maintenance Update," *AWS Blog*, September 25, 2014, https://aws.amazon.com/blogs/aws/ec2 -maintenance-update/.

As Christos Kalantzis... Bruce Wong and Christos Kalantzis, "A State of Xen - Chaos Monkey & Cassandra," *The Netflix Tech Blog*, October 2, 2014, http://techblog.netflix.com/2014/10/a-state-of-xen-chaos -monkey-cassandra.html.

282   *But, Kalantzis continues...* Ibid.

As Kalantzis and... Ibid.

Even more surprising... Roy Rapoport, personal correspondence with Gene Kim, 2015.

Specific architectural patterns... Adrian Cockcroft, personal correspondence with Gene Kim, 2012.

In this section... Jesse Robbins, "GameDay: Creating Resiliency Through Destruction - LISA11," Slideshare.net, posted by Jesse Robbins, December 7, 2011, http://www.slideshare.net/jesserobbins /ameday-creating-resiliency-through-destruction.

Robbins defines resilience... Ibid.

283   *Jesse Robbins observes...* Jesse Robbins, Kripa Krishnan, John Allspaw, and Tom Limoncelli, "Resilience Engineering: Learning to Embrace Failure," *amcqueue* 10, no. 9 (September 13, 2012): https:// queue.acm.org/detail.cfm?id=2371297.

As Robbins quips... Ibid.

As Robbins describes... Ibid.

Robbins explains, "You... Ibid.

284   *During that time...* "Kripa Krishnan: 'Learning Continuously From Failures' at Google," YouTube video, 21:35, posted by Flowcon, November 11, 2014, https://www.youtube.com/watch?v =KqqS3wgQum0.

Krishnan wrote, "An... Kripa Krishnan, "Weathering the Unexpected," *Communications of the ACM* 55, no. 11 (November

2012): 48-52, http://cacm.acm.org/magazines/2012/11/156583
-weathering-the-unexpected/abstract.

Some of the learnings... Ibid.

285   *As Peter Senge...* Widely attributed to Peter Senge.

CHAPTER 20

287   *As Jesse Newland...* Jesse Newland, "ChatOps at GitHub,"
SpeakerDeck.com, February 7, 2013, https://speakerdeck.com
/jnewland/chatops-at-github.

288   *As Mark Imbriaco...* Mark Imbriaco, personal correspondence with
Gene Kim, 2015.

They enabled Hubot... Newland, "ChatOps at GitHub."

289   *Hubot often performed...* Ibid.

289   *Newland observes that...*Ibid.

290   *Instead of putting...* Leon Osterweil, "Software processes are
software too," paper presented at International Conference on
Software Engineering, Monterey, CA, 1987, http://www.cs.unibo.it
/cianca/wwwpages/ids/letture/Osterweil.pdf.

Justin Arbuckle was... Justin Arbuckle, "What Is ArchOps: Chef
Executive Roundtable" (2013).

What resulted was... Ibid.

Arbuckle's conclusion was... Ibid.

291   *By 2015, Google...* Cade Metz, "Google Is 2 Billion Lines of Code—
and It's All in One Place," *Wired*, September 16, 2015, http://www
.wired.com/2015/09/google-2-billion
-lines-codeand-one-place/.

The Chrome and... Ibid.

Rachel Potvin, a... Ibid.

Furthermore, as Eran... Eran Messeri, "What Goes Wrong When
Thousands of Engineers Share the Same Continuous Build?" (2013),
http://scribes.tweetscriber.com/realgenekim/206.

As Randy Shoup... Randy Shoup, personal correspondence with
Gene Kim, 2014.

292   *Tom Limoncelli, co-author...* Tom Limoncelli, "Yes, you can really
work from HEAD," EverythingSysAdmin.com, March 15, 2014,
http://everythingsysadmin.com/2014/03/yes-you-really-can-work
-from-head.html.

296   *Tom Limoncelli describes...* Tom Limoncelli, "Python is better than
Perl6," EverythingSysAdmin.com, January 10, 2011, http://

everythingsysadmin.com/2011/01/python-is-better-than-perl6
.html.

297   *Google used C++...* "Which programming languages does Google use internally?," Quora.com forum, accessed May 29, 2016, https://www.quora.com/Which
-programming-languages-does-Google-use-internally.; "When will Google permit languages other than Python, C++, Java and Go to be used for internal projects?," Quora.com forum, accessed May 29, 2016, https://www.quora.com/When-will-Google-permit
-languages-other-than-Python-C-Java-and-Go-to-be-used-for
-internal-projects/answer/Neil-Kandalgaonkar.

In a presentation... Ralph Loura, Olivier Jacques, and Rafael Garcia, "DOES15 - Ralph Loura, Olivier Jacques, & Rafael Garcia - Breaking Traditional IT Paradigms to...," YouTube video, 31:07, posted by DevOps Enterprise Summit, November 16, 2015, https://www
.youtube.com/watch?v=q9nNqqie_sM.

In many organizations... Michael Rembetsy and Patrick McDonnell, "Continuously Deploying Culture: Scaling Culture at Etsy - Velocity Europe 2012," Slideshare.net, posted by Patrick McDonnell, October 4, 2012, http://www.slideshare.net/mcdonnps/continuously
-deploying-culture-scaling-culture-at-etsy-14588485.

At that time, Etsy... Ibid.

298   *Over the next...* Ibid.

Similarly, Dan McKinley... Dan McKinley, "Why MongoDB Never Worked Out at Etsy," McFunley.com, December 26, 2012, http://mcfunley.com/why-mongodb-never-worked-out-at-etsy.

CHAPTER 21

299   *One of the...* "Kaizen," *Wikipedia*, last modified May 12, 2016, https://en.wikipedia.org/wiki/Kaizen.

Dr. Spear explains... Spear, *The High-Velocity Edge*, chap. 8.

Spear observes that... Ibid.

300   *Clanton describes, "We...* Mickman and Clanton, "(Re)building an Engineering Culture."

Ravi Pandey, a... Ravi Pandey, personal correspondence with Gene Kim, 2015.

Clanton expands on... Mickman and Clanton, "(Re)building an Engineering Culture."

301 *In addition to...* Hal Pomeranz, "Queue Inversion Week," *Righteous IT*, February 12, 2009, https://righteousit.wordpress.com/2009/02/12/queue-inversion-week/.

302 *As Dr. Spear...* Spear, *The High-Velocity Edge*, chap. 3.

In an interview with Jessica... Jessica Stillman, "Hack Days: Not Just for Facebookers," *Inc.*, February 3, 2012, http://www.inc.com/jessica-stillman/hack-days-not-just-for-facebookers.html.

In 2008, Facebook... AP, "Number of active users at Facebook over the years," *Yahoo! News*, May 1, 2013, https://www.yahoo.com/news/number-active-users-facebook-over-230449748.html?ref=gs.

During a hack... Haiping Zhao, "HipHop for PHP: Move Fast," post on Haiping Zhao's Facebook page, February 2, 2010, https://www.facebook.com/notes/facebook-engineering/hiphop-for-php-move-fast/280583813919.

In an interview with Cade... Cade Metz, "How Three Guys Rebuilt the Foundation of Facebook," *Wired*, June 10, 2013, http://www.wired.com/wiredenterprise/2013/06/facebook-hhvm-saga/all/.

303 *Steve Farley, VP...* Steve Farley, personal correspondence with Gene Kim, January 5, 2016.

Karthik Gaekwad, who... "Agile 2013 Talk: How DevOps Change Everything," Slideshare.net, posted by Karthik Gaekwad, August 7, 2013, http://www.slideshare.net/karthequian/howdevops changeseverythingagile2013karthikgaekwad/.

304 *As Glenn O'Donnell...* Glenn O'Donnell, "DOES14 - Glenn O'Donnell - Forrester - Modern Services Demand a DevOps Culture Beyond Apps," YouTube video, 12:20, posted by DevOps Enterprise Summit 2014, November 5, 2014, https://www.youtube.com/watch?v=pvPWKuO4_48.

305 *As of 2014...* Nationwide, *2014 Annual Report*, https://www.nationwide.com/about-us/nationwide-annual-report-2014.jsp.

Steve Farley, VP... Steve Farley, personal correspondence with Gene Kim, 2016.

305 *Capital One, one...* "DOES15 - Tapabrata Pal - Banking on Innovation & DevOps," YouTube video, 32:57, posted by DevOps Enterprise Summit, January 4, 2016, https://www.youtube.com/watch?v=bbWFCKGhxOs.

Dr. Tapabrata Pal... Tapabrata Pal, personal correspondence with Gene Kim, 2015.

Target is the... "Corporate Fact Sheet," Target company website, accessed June 9, 2016, https://corporate.target.com/press/corporate.

Incidentally, the first... Evelijn Van Leeuwen and Kris Buytaert, "DOES15 - Evelijn Van Leeuwen and Kris Buytaert - Turning Around the Containership," YouTube video, 30:28, posted by DevOps Enterprise Summit, December 21, 2015, https://www.youtube.com/watch?v=0GId4AMKvPc.

306 Clanton describes, "2015... Mickman and Clanton, "(Re)building an Engineering Culture."

At Capital One... "DOES15 - Tapabrata Pal - Banking on Innovation & DevOps," YouTube video, 32:57, posted by DevOps Enterprise Summit, January 4, 2016, https://www.youtube.com/watch?v=bbWFCKGhxOs.

Bland explains that...Bland, "DOES15 - Mike Bland - Pain Is Over, If You Want It."

Even though they... Ibid.

They used several... Ibid.

Bland described, "The... Ibid.

Bland continues, "One ... Ibid.

307 As Bland describes ... Ibid.

Bland continues, "It ... Ibid.

He continues, "The ... Ibid.

Bland describes fixits... Mike Bland, "Fixits, or I Am the Walrus," Mike-Bland.com, October 4, 2011, https://mike-bland.com/2011/10/04/fixits.html.

This Fixits, as... Ibid.

CHAPTER 22

313 One of the top... James Wickett, "Attacking Pipelines--Security meets Continuous Delivery," Slideshare.net, posted by James Wickett, June 11, 2014, http://www.slideshare.net/wickett/attacking-pipelinessecurity-meets-continuous-delivery.

James Wickett, one... Ibid.

Similar ideas were... Tapabrata Pal, "DOES15 - Tapabrata Pal - Banking on Innovation & DevOps," YouTube video, 32:57, posted by DevOps Enterprise Summit, January 4, 2016, https://www.youtube.com/watch?v=bbWFCKGhxOs.

314   *Justin Arbuckle, former...* Justin Arbuckle, personal interview with
        Gene Kim, 2015.

        He continues, "By... Ibid.

314   *This helped the...* Snehal Antani, "IBM Innovate DevOps Keynote,"
        YouTube video, 47:57, posted by IBM DevOps, June 12, 2014, https://
        www.youtube.com/watch?v=s0M1P05-6I0.

315   *In a presentation...* Nick Galbreath, "DevOpsSec: Appling DevOps
        Principles to Security, DevOpsDays Austin 2012," Slideshare, posted
        by Nick Galbreath, April 12, 2012, http://www.slideshare.net/
        nickgsuperstar/devopssec-apply-devops-principles-to-security.

        Furthermore, he states... Ibid.

320   *Furthermore, we should...* "OWASP Cheat Sheet Series," OWASP.org,
        last modified March 2, 2016, https://www.owasp.org/index.php
        /OWASP_Cheat_Sheet_Series.

        The scale of... Justin Collins, Alex Smolen, and Neil Matatall,
        "Putting to your Robots to Work V1.1," Slideshare.net, posted by
        Neil Matatall, April 24, 2012, http://www.slideshare.net/xplodersuv
        /sf-2013-robots/.

        In early 2009... "What Happens to Companies That Get Hacked?
        FTC Cases," Giant Bomb forum, posted by SuicidalSnowman, July
        2012, http://www.giantbomb.com/forums/off-topic-31/what
        -happens-to-companies-that-get-hacked-ftc-case-540466/.

321   *In their previously...* Collins, Smolen, and Matatall, "Putting to your
        Robots to Work V1.1."

322   *The first big...* Twitter Engineering, "Hack Week @ Twitter," Twitter
        blog, January 25, 2012, https://blog.twitter.com/2012/hack-week
        -twitter.

323   *Josh Corman observed...* Josh Corman and John Willis, "Immutable
        Awesomeness - Josh Corman and John Willis at DevOps Enterprise
        Summit 2015," YouTube video, 34:25, posted by Sonatype, October
        21, 2015, https://www.youtube.com/watch?v=-S8-lrm3iV4.

        In the 2014... Verizon, "2014 Data Breach Investigations Report,"
        (Verizon Enterprise Solutions, 2014), https://dti.delaware.gov/pdfs
        /rp_Verizon-DBIR-2014_en_xg.pdf.

324   *In 2015, this...* "2015 State of the Software Supply Chain Report:
        Hidden Speed Bumps on the Way to 'Continuous,'" (Fulton, MD:
        Sonatype, Inc, 2015), http://cdn2.hubspot.net/hubfs/1958393
        /White_Papers/2015_State_of_the_Software_Supply_Chain
        _Report-.pdf?t=1466775053631.

The last statistic... Dan Geer and Joshua Corman, "Almost Too Big to Fail," ;login:: The Usenix Magazine, 39, no. 4 (August 2014): 66-68, https://www.usenix.org/system/files/login/articles/15_geer_0.pdf.

325   US Federal Government... Wyatt Kash, "New details released on proposed 2016 IT spending," FedScoop, February 4, 2015, http://fedscoop.com/what-top-agencies-would-spend-on-it-projects-in-2016.

As Mike Bland... Bland, "DOES15 - Mike Bland - Pain Is Over, If You Want It."

326   Furthermore, the Cloud.gov... Mossadeq Zia, Gabriel Ramírez, Noah Kunin, "Compliance Masonry: Bulding a risk management platform, brick by brick," 18F, April 15, 2016, https://18f.gsa.gov/2016/04/15/compliance-masonry-buildling-a-risk-management-platform/.

Marcus Sachs, one... Marcus Sachs, personal correspondence with Gene Kim, 2010.

328   We need to... "VPC Best Configuration Practices," Flux7 blog, January 23, 2014, http://blog.flux7.com/blogs/aws/vpc-best-configuration-practices.

In 2010, Nick... Nick Galbreath, "Fraud Engineering, from Merchant Risk Council Annual Meeting 2012," Slideshare.net, posted by Nick Galbreath, May 3, 2012, http://www.slideshare.net/nickgsuperstar/fraud-engineering.

329   Of particular concern... Nick Galbreath, "DevOpsSec: Appling DevOps Principles to Security, DevOpsDays Austin 2012," Slideshare.net, posted by Nick Galbreath, April 12, 2013, http://www.slideshare.net/nickgsuperstar/devopssec-apply-devops-principles-to-security.

We were always... Ibid.

This was a ridiculously... Ibid.

As Galbreath observed... Ibid.

330   Galbreath observed, "One... Ibid.

As Jonathan Claudius... Jonathan Claudius, "Attacking Cloud Services with Source Code," Speakerdeck.com, posted by Jonathan Claudius, April 16, 2013, https://speakerdeck.com/claudijd/attacking-cloud-services-with-source-code.

CHAPTER 23

334   ITIL defines utility... Axelos, ITIL Service Transition (ITIL Lifecycle Suite) (Belfast, Ireland: TSO, 2011), 48.

337 *Salesforce was founded...* Reena Matthew and Dave Mangot, "DOES14 - Reena Mathew and Dave Mangot - Salesforce," Slideshare.net, posted by ITRevolution, October 29, 2014, http://www.slideshare.net/ITRevolution/does14-reena-matthew-and-dave-mangot-salesforce.

 By 2007, the... Dave Mangot and Karthik Rajan, "Agile.2013. effecting.a.dev ops.transformation.at.salesforce," Slideshare.net, posted by Dave Mangot, August 12, 2013, http://www.slideshare.net/dmangot/agile2013effectingadev-opstransformationat salesforce.

 Karthik Rajan, then... Ibid.

 At the 2014... Matthew and Mangot, "DOES14 - Salesforce."

338 *For Mangot and ...* Ibid.

 Furthermore, they noted ... Ibid.

339 *Bill Massie is...* Bill Massie, personal correspondence with Gene Kim, 2014.

340 *Because the scope...* "Glossary," PCI Security Standards Council website, accessed May 30, 2016, https://www.pcisecuritystandards.org/pci_security/glossary.

 Are code review... PCI Security Standards Council, *Payment Card Industry (PCI) Data Security Stands: Requirements and Security Assessment Procedures, Version 3.1* (PCI Security Standards Council, 2015), Section 6.3.2. https://webcache.googleusercontent.com/search?q=cache:hpRe2COzzdAJ:https://www.cisecuritystandards.org/documents/PCI_DSS_v3-1_SAQ_D_Merchant_rev1-1.docx+&cd=2&hl=en&ct=clnk&gl=us.

341 *To fulfill this...* Bill Massie, personal correspondence with Gene Kim, 2014.

 Massie observes that... Ibid.

 As a result... Ibid.

342 *As Bill Shinn...* Bill Shinn, "DOES15 - Bill Shinn - Prove it! The Last Mile for DevOps in Regulated Organizations," Slideshare.net, posted by ITRevolution, November 20, 2015, http://www.slideshare.net/ITRevolution/does15-bill-shinn-prove-it-the-last-mile-for-devops-in-regulated-organizations.

 Helping large enterprise... Ibid.

 Shinn notes, "One ... Ibid.

 "That was fine ... Ibid.

 He explains, "In ... Ibid.

343   *Shinn states that* ... Ibid.

    Shinn continues, "With... Ibid.

    That requires deriving ... Ibid.

    Shinn continues, "How ... Ibid.

    Shinn gives an... Ibid.

    To helps solve... James DeLuccia, Jeff Gallimore, Gene Kim, and Byron Miller, *DevOps Audit Defense Toolkit* (Portland, OR: IT Revolution, 2015), http://itrevolution.com/devops-and-auditors -the-devops-audit-defense-toolkit.

344   *She made the*... Mary Smith (a pseudonym), personal correspondence with Gene Kim, 2013

    She observed: ... Ibid., 2014.

CONCLUSION

349   *As Jesse Robbins*... "Hacking Culture at VelocityConf," Slideshare. net, posted by Jesse Robbins, June 28, 2012, http://www.slideshare .net/jesserobbins/hacking-culture-at-velocityconf.

APPENDIX

353   *The Lean movement started*... Ries, *The Lean Startup.*

354   *A key principal*... Kent Beck et al., "Twelve Principles of Agile Software," AgileManifesto.org, 2001, http://agilemanifesto.org /principles.html.

    Building upon the... Humble and Farley, *Continuous Delivery.*

    This idea was... Fitz, "Continuous Deployment at IMVU."

355   *Toyota Kata describes*... Rother, *Toyota Kata,* Introduction.

    His conclusion was... Ibid..

355   *In 2011, Eric*... Ries, *The Lean Startup.*

358   *In the Phoenix*... Kim, Behr, and Spafford, *The Phoenix Project,* 365.

360   *Myth 1: "Human*... Denis Besnard and Erik Hollnagel, *Some Myths about Industrial Safety*(Paris, Centre De Recherche Sur Les Risques Et Les Crises Mines, 2012), 3, http://gswong.com/?wpfb_dl=31.

    Myth 2: "Systems... Ibid., 4.

    Myth 3: "Safety... Ibid., 6.

    Myth 4: "Accident... Ibid., 8.

    Myth 5: "Accident... Ibid., 9.

    Myth 6: Safety... Ibid., 11.

Rather, when the... John Shook, "Five Missing Pieces in Your Standardized Work (Part 3 of 3)," Lean.org, October 27, 2009, http://www.lean.org/shook/DisplayObject.cfm?o=1321.

363   *Time to resolve...* "Post Event Retrospective - Part 1," Rally Blogs, accessed May 31, 2016, https://www.rallydev.com/blog/engineering/post-event-retrospective-part-i.

Bethany Macri, from... "Morgue: Helping Better Understand events by Building a Post Mortem Tool - Bethany Macri," Vimeo video, 33:34, posted by info@devopsdays.org, October 18, 2013, http://vimeo.com/77206751.

364   *These discussions have...* Cockcroft, Hicks, and Orzell, "Lessons Netflix Learned."

*Since then, Chaos...*Ibid.

365   *Lenny Rachitsky wrote...* Lenny Rachitsky, "7 Keys to a Successful Public Health Dashboard," *Transparent Uptime*, December 1, 2008, http://www.transparentuptime.com/2008/11/rules-for-successful-public-health.html.

Index

Note: Figures are indicated with *f*; footnotes are indicated with *n*

application-based release patterns, 171–175

Arbuckle, Justin, 290, 314

architecture, evolutionary
Amazon case study, 184–185
architectural archetypes, 183f
Blackboard Learn case study, 186–189, 187f, 188f
code repository, 187f, 188f
decoupling functionality, 186
description of, 179–180
immutable services, 185
loosely-coupled architecture, 181–182
monoliths vs microservices, 182–185
Second Law of Architectural Thermodynamics, 180–181
service-oriented architecture, 182
strangler application pattern, 180, 185–189
tightly-coupled architecture, 180–181, 185
versioned APIs, 185
versioned services, 185

architecture, loosely-coupled, 89–93, 181–182, 254–255

architecture, monitoring, 198–199

architecture, service-oriented, 89, 90–91, 182

Ashman, David, 187

ATDD. *See* development, acceptance test-driven

Atwood, Jeff, 147, 259–260

Austin, Jim, 215–216

automated environment build process
assets to check into version control repository, 116
automated configuration systems, 118
benefits of automation, 114–115

common build mechanisms, 113
critical role of version control, 117
environment consistency, 118
environment development on demand, 113–115
environment re-build vs repair, 118
environments stored in version control, 115–116
immutable infrastructure, 119
metadata, 115
new definition of finished development, 119–121
quick environment development, 112
shared version control repository, 115–118
sprints, 119–120
standardization, 114
testing, 113
testing environments, 113
uses of automation, 114
version control as predictor of organizational performance, 117
version control systems, 115–118

automated validation test suite
acceptance test-driven development, 134–135
acceptance tests, 131, 132
analysis tools, 138
automating manual tests, 135–136
code configuration management tools, 138
environment validation, 137–138
error detection, 132–133
fast testing, 132, 133–134
feedback, 130
green builds, 129–130
ideal vs non-ideal testing, 133f
integration tests, 131, 132
non-functional requirements testing, 137–138

CSG International
  brownfield services, 56
  cross-training, 86–87
  daily deployments, 157–159
Cunningham, Ward, 148

D
dark launches, 173–175
dashboards, 207n
data sets. *See* telemetry
Debois, Patrick, 5
dedicated release engineer, 96
DeGrandis, Dominica, 18
Dekker, Sidney
  just culture, 273
  safety culture, 28, 38
dependency scanning
  Java, 319
  Ruby on Rails, 319
Deployinator, 163–164, 163f
deployment
  automated self-service, 159–160
  blue-green pattern, 166–169, 166f,
    167n
  change, 124
  code, 22, 154, 160–162
  consistency, 156
  continuous, 20, 175–177
  daily, 157–159
  decoupling from releases, 164–175
  defined, 164
  on demand, 165
  fast, 161, 161f
  flow, 156
  issues, 78
  lead time, 8–11, 9f, 165
  making safer, 229–230
  overlay of production deployment
  activities, 213
  pace, 154
  pipeline requirements, 156–157
  process automation, 155–164, 159f

self-service developer, 162–164
  speed and success, 79
  tool, 163–164, 163f
deployment lead time
  design and development, 8
  lead time vs processing time,
    9–10, 9f
  Lean Manufacturing, 9
  Lean Product Development, 8
  long, 10, 10f, 165
  short, 10–11, 11f
  testing and operations, 9
  workflow, 9
deployment pipeline
  breakdown, 138–140
  containers in, 128n
  continuous delivery, 127–129, 127f
  and information security, 330–331
deployment pipeline protection
  Amazon AWS case study, 342–344
  audit and compliance documen-
    tation and proof, 341–345
  categories of changes, 334–335,
    334n
  compliance in regulated environ-
    ments, 341–345
  destructive testing, 338
  Etsy case study, 339–341
  normal changes, 334, 336–338
  production telemetry for ATM
  systems, 344–345
  Salesforce case study, 337–338
  security and compliance and
  change approval processes,
    333–335
  separation of duties, 338–341
  standard changes, 334, 335–336
  urgent changes, 334–335
deployment process automation
  automated self-service deploy-
    ments, 159–160
  automating manual steps, 155–156

Spear, Steven, 299
    Toyota Production System, 299
improvement goal examples, 68
improvement kata, 6, 355
industrial safety, 359–360
information radiator, 206–208
information security
    18F team, 325–326
    application security, 318–323
    automated security testing, 318f
    bad paths, 318
    Brakeman, 322, 322f
    build images, 317
    Cloud.gov, 325–326
    code signing, 319–320
    creating security telemetry, 327–330
    data breaches, 323–324
    and defect tracking and post-mortems, 315
    dependency scanning, 319
    and the deployment pipeline, 317–318, 330–331
    dynamic analysis, 319
    environment security, 324–326
    Etsy case study, 328–330
    Federal Government case study, 325–326
    Gauntlt, 313, 317
    Graphite, 329f
    happy paths, 318
    integrating into production telemetry, 326–327
    inviting InfoSec to product demonstrations, 314
    Java, 324
    Metasploit, 325
    Nmap, 325
    preventive security controls, 315–317
    Ruby on Rails, 322
    rugged DevOps, 313

sad paths, 318
    security libraries, 316
    shared code repositories and services, 315–317
    software supply chain security, 323–324
    source code integrity, 319–320
    SQL injection attempts, 329, 329f
    static analysis, 319, 320–323
    Twitter case study, 320–323
    value stream, 63
Infosec. See information security
infrastructure as code, 6n
infrastructure metrics, 213n
InGraphs, 208
integrated development environment, 128n
integration, 120n
Intuit, 241–248
iteration length, 68
ITIL, 116n, 231n, 253, 333, 334n
ITIL CMDB, 212, 212n

J

Jacob, Adam, 6n
Jacques, Olivier, 297
Java
    automation, 127
    Bazaarvoice, 149
    dependency scanning, 319
    eBay, 179n
    Google, 296n
    information security, 324
    LinkedIn, 71
    logging infrastructure, 201n
    ORM, 79n
    production metrics, 204
    threading libraries, 292
JavaScript
    Facebook, 175
    Google, 296n
    production telemetry, 209

Z

Zenoss, 198, 208
Zhao, Haiping, 302
Zuckerberg, Mark, 302

Acknowledgments

Jez Humble

Creating this book has been a labor of love for Gene in particular. It's an immense privilege and pleasure to have worked with Gene and my other co-authors, John and Pat, along with Todd, Anna, Robyn and the editorial and production team at IT Revolution preparing this work—thank you. I also want to thank Nicole Forsgren whose work with Gene, Alanna Brown, Nigel Kersten and I on the PuppetLabs/DORA *State of DevOps Report* over the last three years has been instrumental in developing, testing and refining many of the ideas in this book. My wife, Rani, and my two daughters, Amrita and Reshmi, have given me boundless love and support during my work on this book, as in every part of my life. Thank you. I love you. Finally, I feel incredibly lucky to be part of the DevOps community, which almost without exception walks the talk of practicing empathy and growing a culture of respect and learning. Thanks to each and every one of you.

John Willis

First and foremost, I need to acknowledge my saint of a wife for putting up with my crazy career. It would take another book to express how much I learned from my co-authors Patrick, Gene and Jez. Other very important influencers and advisers in my journey are Mark Hinkle, Mark Burgess, Andrew Clay Shafer, and Michael Cote. I also want to give a shout out to Adam Jacob for hiring me at Chef and giving me the freedom to explore, in the early days, this thing we call Devops. Last but definitely not least is my partner in crime, my *Devops Cafe* cohost, Damon Edwards.

Patrick Debois

I would like to thank those who were on this ride, much gratitude to you all.

Gene Kim

I cannot thank Margueritte, my loving wife of nearly eleven amazing years, enough for putting up with me being in deadline mode for over five years, as well as my sons, Reid, Parker, and Grant. And of course, my parents, Ben and Gail Kim, for helping me become a nerd early in life. I also want to thank my fellow co-authors for everything that I learned from them, as well as Anna Noak, Aly Hoffman, Robyn Crummer-Olsen, Todd Sattersten, and the rest of the IT Revolution team for shepherding this book to its completion.

I am so grateful for all the people who taught me so many things, which form the foundation of this book: John Allspaw (Etsy), Alanna Brown (Puppet), Adrian Cockcroft (Battery Ventures), Justin Collins (Brakeman Pro), Josh Corman (Atlantic Council), Jason Cox (The Walt Disney Company), Dominica DeGrandis (LeanKit), Damon Edwards (DTO Solutions), Dr. Nicole Forsgren (Chef), Gary Gruver, Sam Guckenheimer (Microsoft), Elisabeth Hendrickson (Pivotal Software), Nick Galbreath (Signal Sciences), Tom Limoncelli (Stack Exchange), Chris Little, Ryan Martens, Ernest Mueller (AlienVault), Mike Orzen, Scott Prugh (CSG International), Roy Rapoport (Netflix), Tarun Reddy (CA/Rally), Jesse Robbins (Orion Labs), Ben Rockwood (Chef), Andrew Shafer (Pivotal), Randy Shoup (Stitch Fix), James Turnbull (Kickstarter), and James Wickett (Signal Sciences).

I also want to thank the many people whose incredible DevOps journeys we studied, including Justin Arbuckle, David Ashman, Charlie Betz, Mike Bland, Dr. Toufic Boubez, Em Campbell-Pretty, Jason Chan, Pete Cheslock, Ross Clanton, Jonathan Claudius, Shawn Davenport, James DeLuccia, Rob England, John Esser, James Fryman, Paul Farrall, Nathen Harvey, Mirco Hering, Adam Jacob, Luke Kanies, Kaimar Karu, Nigel Kersten, Courtney Kissler, Bethany Macri, Simon Morris, Ian Malpass, Dianne Marsh, Norman Marks, Bill Massie, Neil Matatall, Michael Nygard, Patrick McDonnell, Eran Messeri, Heather Mickman, Jody Mulkey, Paul Muller, Jesse Newland, Dan North, Dr. Tapabrata Pal, Michael Rembetsy, Mike Rother, Paul Stack, Gareth Rushgrove, Mark Schwartz, Nathan Shimek, Bill Shinn, JP Schneider, Dr. Steven Spear, Laurence Sweeney, Jim Stoneham, and Ryan Tomayko.

And I am so profoundly grateful for the many reviewers who gave us fantastic feedback that shaped this book: Will Albenzi, JT Armstrong, Paul Auclair, Ed Bellis, Daniel Blander, Matt Brender, Alanna Brown, Branden Burton, Ross Clanton, Adrian Cockcroft, Jennifer Davis, Jessica DeVita, Stephen Feldman, Martin Fisher, Stephen Fishman, Jeff Gallimore, Becky Hartman, Matt Hatch, William Hertling, Rob Hirschfeld, Tim Hunter, Stein Inge Morisbak, Mark Klein, Alan Kraft, Bridget Kromhaut, Chris Leavory, Chris Leavoy, Jenny Madorsky, Dave Mangot, Chris McDevitt, Chris McEniry, Mike McGarr, Thomas McGonagle, Sam McLeod, Byron Miller, David Mortman, Chivas Nambiar, Charles Nelles, John Osborne, Matt O'Keefe, Manuel Pais, Gary Pedretti, Dan Piessens, Brian Prince, Dennis Ravenelle, Pete Reid, Markos Rendell, Trevor Roberts, Jr., Frederick Scholl, Matthew Selheimer, David Severski, Samir Shah, Paul Stack, Scott Stockton, Dave Tempero, Todd Varland, Jeremy Voorhis, and Branden Williams.

And several people gave me an amazing glimpse of what the future of authoring with modern toolchains looks like, including Andrew Odewahn (O'Reilly Media) who let us use the fantastic Chimera reviewing platform, James Turnbull (Kickstarter) for his help creating my first publishing rendering toolchain, and Scott Chacon (GitHub) for his work on GitHub Flow for authors.

Author Biographies

GENE KIM

Gene Kim is a multiple award-winning CTO, researcher, and author of *The Phoenix Project: A Novel About IT, DevOps, and Helping Your Business Win* and *The Visible Ops Handbook*. He is founder of IT Revolution and hosts the DevOps Enteprise Summit conferences.

JEZ HUMBLE

Jez Humble is co-author of the Jolt Award–winning *Continuous Delivery* and the groundbreaking *Lean Enterprise*. His focus is on helping organizations deliver valuable, high-quality software frequently and reliably through implementing effective engineering practices.

PATRICK DEBOIS

Patrick Debois is an independent IT consultant who is bridging the gap between projects and operations by using Agile techniques, in development, project management, and system administration.

JOHN WILLIS

John Willis has worked in the IT management industry for more than thirty-five years. He has authored six IBM Redbooks and was the founder and chief architect at Chain Bridge Systems. Currently he is an Evangelist at Docker, Inc.